BEYOND BLOOD LUST

In the dark pit of their twisted souls, there is a place where lust and evil come together. The pain and fear of their doomed victims provide the obscene thrills that they crave. Any man, woman, or child who crosses their path risks agonizing torment and the final violation: death.

TRUE DETECTIVE's top crime reporters document the most frightening psychosexual pathology of our time, with raw, hard-hitting inside stories that expose the sadistic sex slayers who lurk among us:

—JASON ERIC MASSEY, a 21-year-old double murderer whose secret diaries detail his urges to kill girls and have sex with their dead bodies.

—MICHAEL CHARLES SATCHER, who held Washington, D.C., in a five-month nightmare grip as he beat, raped, and murdered defenseless female joggers and bicyclists.

—RONALD ELLIOT PORTER, a suave silver-haired man who cruised the freeway picking up female hitchhikers, choking them into unconsciousness and raping them, then leaving them to die.

<u>BOOK YOUR PLACE ON OUR WEBSITE</u> <u>AND MAKE THE</u> <u>READING CONNECTION!</u>

We've created a customized website just for our very special readers, where you can get the inside scoop on everything that's going on with Zebra, Pinnacle and Kensington books.

When you come online, you'll have the exciting opportunity to:

- View covers of upcoming books
- Read sample chapters
- Learn about our future publishing schedule (listed by publication month *and author*)
- Find out when your favorite authors will be visiting a city near you
- Search for and order backlist books from our online catalog
- Check out author bios and background information
- Send e-mail to your favorite authors
- Meet the Kensington staff online
- Join us in weekly chats with authors, readers and other guests
- Get writing guidelines
- AND MUCH MORE!

Visit our website at
http://www.pinnaclebooks.com

FROM THE FILES OF
TRUE DETECTIVE
MAGAZINE

SEX SADISTS

Edited by
David Jacobs

Pinnacle Books
Kensington Publishing Corp.
http://www.pinnaclebooks.com

CONTENTS

"DIARIES OF A HOMICIDAL SOCIOPATH"

by Bill G. Cox

The summer day was blazing hot, and the workman operating a road grader along Cutoff Road near the small rural community of Telico, Texas, was sweating rivers. The woods surrounding that area appeared hazy through the blurriness caused by the sweat in his eyes. But as the worker made another run, he suddenly braked the grader. Through an opening in the canopy of trees he had spotted something, a glare of white that seemed to be disturbingly out of place. He backed up twice before being sure of what he was seeing.

It looked like a human body. The worker got off the grader and walked toward the object. About the same moment when he was visually sure that what he was looking at was a body, a smell reached him that he would never forget—the nauseating scent of death and decay. And now he could see that the body had no head or hands.

It was shortly after 2:45 P.M. on Thursday, July 29, 1993, when the Ellis County Sheriff's Department in Waxahachie, Texas, received the shocked workman's call. Sheriff John Gage's investigative force lost no time in responding to the alert.

The officers who arrived at the scene included sheriff's lieutenant Royce Gothard, head of the Criminal Investigation Division, patrol captain Ray Stewart, and Deputies Johnny Cruz, O.D. "Butch" Smith, John Goss, Brian Thompson, and Clint Tims.

The investigators immediately saw that the body was a young woman, lying about 100 feet from the gravel road. Her head and hands had been cut off. The grim-faced lawmen noted numerous cuts and slashes on the torso and legs, along with what appeared to be a bullet wound in the victim's back.

The probers could see nothing on or near the body to help identify the victim. They spread out over the area of brush and woods in search of the young woman's missing body parts. The location was about three miles east of Telico, in the vicinity of Cutoff Road and Route 2.

A short time later, as Deputy Tims was walking onto a nearby bridge, he took a look over the side. He didn't find the dead woman's missing head and hands, but he found himself staring at another startling discovery. It was the fully clothed body of a young man sprawled facedown in the dry creek bed. Tims yelled to the other searchers.

The 100-degree-plus temperatures of recent days had taken their toll on both corpses. Because of the advanced decomposition, the cause of the body's death could not be determined immediately at the scene.

Even before they pulled a wallet from the boy's jeans—his billfold contained a library card and other identifying membership cards—the deputies had a shared gut feeling that they might already know the victims' names. Two days earlier, 14-year-old James Brian King and his stepsister, 13-year-old Christina Ann Benjamin, had been reported missing from their home in nearby Garrett, Texas.

The officers' speculation proved to be at least half right when they saw that the name on the cards was James Brian King.

James and Christina had not been seen or heard from since

early Tuesday, July 27. Just after midnight on that date, James's father told the police, he heard a car horn honking outside his home, where the youngsters lived with James's father and Christina's mother. When he looked out the window, the father saw the pair talking to someone in a light-colored, older-model automobile he thought was a Ford. But he didn't see who was inside the car.

The family waited a few hours before notifying the authorities that the two teens were missing because, a relative explained, "They'd never run off before. We figured we'd give them a chance to come back first."

When the missing-person report was filed, investigators checked out information that indicated the pair had said something about going to a local convenience store to get a soft drink. But a check with employees of the store established that James and Christina had not been there on the night they vanished.

Now, with one body tentatively identified and the other thought to be the missing girl, the sheriff's probers were unsure how the pair had been killed or where. While the bodies were being photographed, the officers continued to search for the girl's head and hands and any clues that might throw some light on the ghastly murders.

Lieutenant Gothard and his colleagues quickly concluded that the murders must have been committed elsewhere. They found no signs of a struggle or any other evidence that the boy and girl had met their deaths at the location where their bodies were found. It was likely that the victims were slain at another location, and the killer had then hauled the bodies to this isolated site in a vehicle. The investigators surmised that the boy's body had been tossed off the bridge.

Since the girl's body was nude, it was possible that she had been sexually assaulted. But neither this possibility, nor the cause of their deaths, would be determined until the autopsies were performed. In fact, any motive for the brutal murders—

other than the possible sexual assault on the girl—was completely up in the air, at this point.

The sheriff's officers called in a team of special investigators with trained search dogs to scour the dense foliage in the swampy area for the girl's head and hands. But the dogs failed to find the missing body parts. In fact, they never were found.

Meanwhile, the autopsy performed by a pathologist of the Dallas County Medical Examiner's Office in nearby Dallas, where the bodies were sent, did confirm that the headless body was what remained of Christina Benjamin. The positive identification was made when X rays previously taken of Christina's ankle after she'd been injured on a trampoline were compared with X rays of the body, and they matched.

The pathologist also reported that James King had died from two gunshot wounds in the head. The girl had received a gunshot wound in her back, but that was described as a "flesh wound."

The autopsy could not establish the cause of the girl's death, but it was believed to be either from a wound in the missing head or the result of the decapitation itself.

The autopsy report indicated that the teens might have died sometime between midnight of July 26 and 10 A.M. the next day. The advanced state of decomposition made it impossible to confirm if the girl had been sexually attacked.

As for the cuts and slashes on Christina's body, it could not be determined whether she had been tortured or the wounds were inflicted after death. Whichever the case, those wounds indicated a killer who had a strange twist of mind.

The M.E.'s report declared that the girl died as the result of "homicidal violence" that included "sharp force injuries and a gunshot wound of the back."

One thing that puzzled the sheriff's investigators was the female victim's decapitation and partial dismemberment. The boy's fully clothed body was left intact and in plain view, with his identification cards left in his pocket. If the purpose of the mutilation had been to thwart identification, why had the identification been left on the male victim?

"What I keep going over in my mind is, why do something like that to one body and not the other?" Lieutenant Gothard said later. "There are just so many questions that are left unanswered at this point."

One of the bigger questions was, where had the killings occurred? After searching the body site thoroughly, the probers came to believe that the corpses had been transported and dumped there by the killer or killers—the boy's body lying about 185 feet from the girl's.

The nature of these bizarre double murders cast a shadow of fear over the small rural communities near where the bodies were discovered. Because of the girl's decapitation, some residents speculated that the teens' violent deaths might be linked to satanic rituals. In past weeks, rumors were circulated about animals having been sacrificed in rituals that hinted of a satanic cult.

Lieutenant Gothard issued a request to the general public for any information that might help solve the macabre case.

"We need all the help we can get on this one," he said, adding that it was one of the worst homicides he had investigated in his years of police work.

Meanwhile, Gothard and his investigators were concentrating on the nearest thing they had to a lead: the light-colored vehicle seen by James's father outside the house before the two teenagers disappeared.

The probers also started checking on the youngsters' friends and acquaintances, especially any persons the two had been with in the last day or two before they disappeared. The sleuths were especially interested in anyone who owned a car similar to the vehicle described by James's father.

This phase of the probe proved to be tedious and time-consuming because both of the slain kids had been active in their school and social circles. The sleuths would therefore have a considerable number of individuals to interview.

Christina was described by relatives and friends as a good student who participated in sports and played the flute in the junior-high school band. Her mother said Christina was looking forward to her freshman year at Ennis High School. Ennis was another town close to Garrett—it was a town large enough to have its own high school. The fall term was scheduled to begin in August.

James, too, had a host of school buddies and had been busy in school activities. He was known by his family and friends as a comedian.

The investigators were not entirely without physical clues, to be sure, since the autopsies had recovered three .22-caliber bullets from the victims' bodies. Those slugs could be compared with the gun that was used to snuff out the boy's life, if or when the weapon was ever found.

First, however, the sleuths needed a break to get them on the killer's trail—a lead that might well turn up in the two teenagers' recent relationships with their peers.

As the detectives interviewed various young people who had known the victims, one youth recalled an incident that had occurred on July 16, 1993, little more than a week before Christina and James disappeared.

Charles Butler, an unsavory type himself who had been arrested on a robbery charge, told the investigators that one of his buddies, 20-year-old Jason Eric Massey, had accompanied him to visit with Christina. Charles recalled that while they were at her home, Jason flirted with the 13-year-old Christina, told her that she was pretty and looked older than her age.

During that visit, Charles and Jason made arrangements with the young girl to meet her later, about midnight. Charles said that the plan was that they would honk the horn of their car twice and the girl would sneak out to meet them.

That clandestine meeting never took place because something unforeseen came up, Charles told the investigators. What aroused the probers' interests, though, was that Charles remembered some strange comments Massey made to him as they drove home following their visit with Christina.

Charles Butler said that Jason Massey told him he wanted to have sex with Christina, kill her, sexually mutilate her, and then eat her sexually mutilated body parts.

Moreover, the detectives learned from Butler that Massey owned a tan-colored 1982 Subaru that was similar in appearance to the one observed and described by James's father on the night he'd seen Christina and James talking to an unseen driver. In the poor lighting, the tan Subaru could have been mistaken for gray, the deputies realized.

Other weird stories about Massey, who formerly lived in Ennis, Texas, but now made his home in Canton, Texas—both towns in the general area of Garrett—continued to reach the ears of the investigators as they questioned teenage boys and girls who knew Massey.

One witness told Deputy Cruz that Massey was known to kill and decapitate dogs and cats. Sometimes he carried the heads around in his vehicle, or stored them in a rusty metal cooler that he kept buried in the woods.

"He collected the heads as trophies," the witness said.

Those who knew Massey said that he frequently talked about murder and his ambitions to become a "serial killer." Even so, his pals said they had shrugged off Massey's bizarrre conversations as instances of his "just blowing a lot of air" at times when the youths were drinking together.

"You known how some guys are—they talk about all kinds of stuff just to make you think they're big shots," one boy commented.

Lieutenant Gothard and Deputy Cruz, who was the lead investigator in the case, knew one thing for sure—they wanted to find out everything they could about Jason Massey, and to do so as quickly as possible. Of all the boys Christina and James knew, Massey looked like the hottest suspect, based on the comments he had made and his oddball activities.

When the Ellis County sheriff's investigators started checking in Ennis on Massey's background, Ennis police chief Dale Holt disclosed that he was already familiar with Massey. The chief remembered him as a strange boy indeed.

Back in 1987, when Massey was about 15 years old and living in northeast Dallas, Holt's department had received a complaint from the father of a 13-year-old Ennis girl.

"He said this weird kid had been harassing his daughter with letters and making threatening phone calls," the chief recalled about the complaint. Unbelievably, the written and verbal terrorism of the girl had covered a period of five years.

In his letters and calls, the apparently depraved writer told the girl that he wanted to slash her throat and drink her blood—and, almost as an afterthought, take her to a movie! It sounded like some kid who'd seen one too many horror movies.

Since Massey was living in Dallas at that time, Chief Holt contacted that city's juvenile authorities, and they visited Massey's relatives to talk about the boy's *Twilight Zone* activities and put a stop to them.

"When you're dealing with a fifteen-year-old, unfortunately, that's about all you can do," the chief said. "The harassment stopped for a while, but then it started back up."

The girl's father came to Chief Holt again after the family's pet poodle was found hanging dead from the windshield wiper of their car, and written across the windshield in blood were the words, "Suzy is dead." Suzy happened to be the first name of the girl being terrorized by Massey.

Although the Ennis PD investigated the report, the chief said, they could not find evidence to tie Massey to the dog's killing.

"The family said they were sure of it," Holt told the Ellis County sleuths, "but in our business, if you can't prove it, you have to leave it alone. We could not put it on him."

What the investigation did indicate was that the girl hadn't been chosen at random. The campaign of terror started after Massey and Suzy graduated from an Ennis junior-high school. From where he lived in Dallas, Massey mailed Suzy pictures of disemboweled women. One time, the victim told the authorities, he sent her a photo that appeared to be covered in blood.

Suzy said that Massey's warped letters were always about killing. One letter even included lyrics he had written specifically about killing and mutilating Suzy. Incredibly, in that same letter, he asked her to go to a movie.

Another of Massey's letters described one of his fantasies to Suzy. In it, he visualized waiting for her as she took out the family garbage, coming up behind her, putting a knife to her throat, and trying to slash her. The knife was too dull, as he envisioned the scene, so he stabbed it into her skull instead.

Chief Holt said that the police warned Massey to stop sending those twisted letters, but there was little else they could do.

In the meantime, other pals of Massey's who were grilled by Deputy Cruz and the sheriff's investigative team revealed still more about the dark side of Massey's character.

One of his buddies recalled that Massey once carried a dead cat wrapped in a plastic bag in his car and talked to it as though the cat were alive. Echoing another boy questioned by the sleuths, the witness said that Massey talked of becoming a serial killer with an unsurpassed total of victims.

Once, while driving through some woods, Massey pointed out to his friend various places "that would be good for hiding a dead body."

"He told me the next day that if I ever heard about a serial killer around the Ennis area, it would be him, Jason Massey," the youth said to the probers. He also repeated the tale the detectives had already heard from another teen: how Massey would like to kill Christina Benjamin, cut up her body, and eat the sexual parts.

The sheriff's investigators noted that some of the slashes found on the girl's body were consistent with those described by Massey in his alleged conversations.

Massey's name continued to surface in the murder probe. On July 31, two days after the bodies were found, the Ennis

Police Department received an anonymous phone call from a male who said Massey had told him that he was going to kill Christina and gave some details on how it would be done.

At this point, the Ellis County sheriff's team agreed that all the leads were pointing to Jason Massey, but the crimefighters were not discarding the possibility that more than one person might be involved.

Nonetheless, on the basis of the information the sleuths had put together so far, they obtained an arrest warrant for Massey and a search warrant for his home in Canton.

Late on Tuesday, August 3, following an intense six-day investigation, Lieutenant Gothard and Deputies Cruz, Tims, Smith, and Thompson drove to Canton to execute the warrants. They worked in conjunction with sheriff's officers of Van Zandt County, the jurisdiction in which Canton is located.

The handsome suspect was arrested without any resistance. He denied knowing anything about the slayings of the two teenagers. While he was taken to the sheriff's office for questioning, other officers began the authorized search of his residence. They also impounded Massey's tan 1982 Subaru, which generally fit the description of the car seen outside the King home when the two young victims were last seen alive and talking to someone in the vehicle. The car was later turned over to the physical evidence division of the Dallas County Sheriff's Department to be processed thoroughly for possible evidence.

When the deputies searched Massey's dwelling, which was in general disarray and badly kept, they found newspaper clippings about the disappearance and murders of Christina Benjamin and James King. The clipped reports were underneath the mattress of Massey's bed.

"And look what we have here!" one deputy exclaimed, gesturing toward some books stacked haphazardly. Among them was material on satanic cult activities and serial murders. One book, described as a satanic bible, contained a list of girls' names.

Another odd item discovered in Massey's dwelling was a pair of bloodstained handcuffs.

When the officers inspected the suspect's Subaru before having it taken to Dallas for evidential scrutiny, they found it to be clean and neat—a condition that was not typical of Massey, according to the people who knew him. Those people said that Massey's vehicle was usually littered with papers and junk.

From what the investigators could see, the car appeared to have undergone a thorough cleaning recently. Even so, what looked like bloodstains were visible in the interior.

While inspecting the trunk, the deputies found a claw hammer, a small ax, a folding knife with a four-inch blade, and a roll of duct tape. The items appeared to be stained with blood, as well. There also was a paper sack that contained a leaf which appeared to have blood on it.

The following day, at a jam-packed press conference, Lieutenant Gothard announced the arrest of Jason Massey, who was arraigned on two counts of capital murder and ordered held in the county jail under a half-million-dollar bond. The lawman said that it had not yet been determined whether the murders were committed by one person or by a group.

Following a remark by Massey's lawyer in which he declared his belief that his client was innocent, a response of sorts came from Sheriff Gage, who told reporters, "We've got a good case—a very good case. If it wasn't a good case, we wouldn't have filed a capital murder charge against him. All the evidence we've got right now points to this individual."

Nevertheless, the sheriff said, his detectives had not ruled out the possible involvement of others. "We're not going to preclude anything," he declared. "We're going to be looking at everything."

Lieutenant Gothard echoed his boss's statement: "A lot of people think you make an arrest, and that's it. But that's really when you just get started. You have to keep beating the bushes—that's what it amounts to."

And that, in effect, was what the sheriff's officers were doing as they continued to hunt for the missing head and hands of the slain girl. They searched many abandoned buildings in the Telico area, fields surrounding Massey's former home in Ennis, and numerous other locales—all without success.

Three days after Massey's arrest, Lieutenant Gothard was stricken by a heart attack and had to be rushed to a hospital. The long hours he had spent with little sleep during the intensive murder probe had taken their toll on the 57-year-old law-enforcement veteran. The dedicated lawman had to undergo quadruple-bypass heart surgery, and he was back at work again after an appropriate period of recuperation.

In the meantime, his colleagues on the sheriff's team continued to glean information on the case, including what they learned from a girlfriend of Massey's. She reportedly said that when she had last seen Massey in Ennis on the night of July 26, a few hours before the murders, he'd had a gun tucked in his belt. One other girl confirmed that Massey had been in Ennis as late as 10 P.M. on July 26, just a short time before the teen siblings vanished from their residence in nearby Garrett.

In their investigative efforts, the crimefighters turned up other witnesses who told them that Massey had stolen a .22-caliber pistol from a relative on July 19, a week before the murders. Moreover, the probers learned that he had purchased bullets and handcuffs at a large discount store several days before the slayings. And they interviewed another witness who had been with Massey when he engaged in target practice in the woods after buying the gun.

On Wednesday, August 11, 1993, an Ellis County grand jury returned two capital-murder indictments against Jason Eric Massey in the deaths of Christina Ann Benjamin and James Brian King. The indictments alleged that the suspect used a knife, a machete, an ax, and a firearm to kill them.

Testimony in Massey's trial began in Waxahachie, Texas, on Wednesday, September 28, 1994, before a jury of seven women and five men, with District Judge Gene Knize presiding.

In his opening statement, Chief Prosecutor Clay Strange warned the jury that they would "encounter an evil you've never seen before and will hopefully never see again." He declared that Jason Massey was the only person "who could've, would've, and did kill" the young victims. He said that trace evidence and DNA blood tests would link the defendant to the slayings, and witnesses would testify that Massey had expressed a burning desire to sexually attack, mutilate, kill, and cannibalize Christina Benjamin.

After the main part of the trial got under way, the sheriff's investigators described the discovery of the bodies and pertinent details of the subsequent investigation that led to the arrest of Massey. Then a forensic serologist told the jury that a large quantity of blood residue had been found in Massey's 1982 Subaru—on the front seat, the floorboard, the dash, and elsewhere. Other officers testified about several items found at a car wash shortly after Massey cleaned out his car and had it washed following the murders—items which included a bandanna and a paycheck stub with his name on it from an Ennis fast-food restaurant where Massey had worked as a cook.

One of the testifying investigators told of how an employee of a discount store picked Massey from a police lineup, identifying him as the man who bought ammunition and handcuffs in that store just a few days before the killings.

Next, a forensic expert told the jury that, in all likelihood, the blood found in Massey's car belonged to Christina Benjamin. He explained that the victim's blood had been compared to blood samples taken from the front seat and from a hammer, some duct tape, and a leaf found in the car.

The prosecution also called to the stand Charles Butler, Massey's buddy, who testified about the statements made by Massey shortly before the murders, indicating that he wanted to kill Christina and have sex with her. The district attorney requested that the witness repeat the actual language used by Massey. As a result, the witness's testimony about Massey's declared desires was shockingly explicit, filled with vulgar and obscene words.

During Butler's cross-examination, the defense attorney suggested that "talking tough" was part of the young men's lifestyle, meaning that the defendant's declarations had been no more than talk designed to impress his chums.

Butler responded to the defense attorney: "But Jason was the only one who always talked about killing girls."

The next prosecution move was to introduce as evidence some letters that Massey had written to a 16-year-old girl who was a patient in a state mental hospital. The letters had been written while Massey was in jail awaiting trial, an investigator for the D.A.'s office testified.

In those letters, Massey told the teenager that once he knew her better, he would tell her "things you cannot imagine in all your wildest dreams." He specified "July 27, 1993" as the day "it all began." Massey wrote of having seen six angels take a girl's spirit to heaven while he was on a road in the woods at night.

Then the prosecutor called Suzy McMillan of Ennis to the stand. She testified about being terrorized by Massey for five years in a twisted campaign that included a series of letters and phone calls in which he threatened to slash her throat and drink her blood.

The incriminating evidence piled up against Massey as the prosecutor presented it before the jury. It included hair from Christina Benjamin's hairbrush that had the same microscopic characteristics as hair recovered from a barbed-wire fence in the woods where the bodies were found, hair retrieved from the floorboard of Massey's car, and hair collected from the bandanna found at the car wash.

Expert witnesses testified that a fiber found on the sole of James King's shoe matched the fibers of the carpeting in Massey's car, and that the .22 slugs taken from the bodies were the same kind that Massey had bought at the discount store five days before the murder (no gun was recovered in the probe, which precluded any ballistic comparison of the fatal slugs with a weapon). Other evidence included the newspapers with stories about the murders found under Massey's bed.

In summing up, the assistant D.A. told the jury he knew of nothing worse than the "brutal, horrifying butchering" of two children. The teenagers made a mistake in leaving their home without permission and a second mistake in that they did "not see the evil that lies within that man," the prosecutor declared, pointing to Massey.

While no one knew for certain what happened that night, Prosecutor Strange said, he believed that James King was the one who was slain first—shot twice, then removed from the car and tossed off the bridge.

"From that moment on, Christina Benjamin began a time of terror that none of us want to think about," the prosecutor went on. "She knew she was going to die. The only question was, what was going to happen to her before her death? Was she on her knees?"

As the prosecutor described the girl's ghastly slaying, the members of the victims' family who were attending the trial began to weep.

Continuing his summation, Strange told the jury that Massey was not driven by any usual motive, but was "driven by lust, a desire to commit a sexual homicide."

"What would make a person do that? Evil—evil that lies within that man, and evil waiting to get out again!" the prosecutor declared.

The defense tried to explain away some of the state's evidence, asserting that Massey was carrying a gun because he was afraid of former friends who wanted to punish him for trying to date their girlfriends.

As for the date ("July 27, 1993—the day it all began") mentioned by Massey in his letter to the pen pal in the state hospital, the defense lawyer pointed out that it was the date when Massey was converted to Christianity, as one of his relatives had testified. Then the attorney accused the investigators of not following up on other suspects after the probe pointed to Massey.

The prosecutor slammed back, declaring that there was no conspiracy by the investigators and forensic experts who testified in the case. "Who in all the world—who had blood in his car?" the prosecutor demanded. "My God, what was he doing with human blood in the trunk of his car?"

Prosecutor Strange concluded, "We tell our children there are no such things as monsters. . . . But there are monsters. That man is a monster. He doesn't look like one now, but he did that night in Telico."

The jury deliberated three hours before returning with their verdict. They found Jason Massey guilty of capital murder in the two grisly slayings.

Whether he would be executed or given a life sentence would be decided by the same jury the next day. As if by a bizarre decree of fate, the most dramatic testimony of the trial would burst upon the courtroom during the penalty phase. For even as the state's final arguments on guilt or innocence were being heard, a scene was unfolding in the woods not far from where the bodies of Christina Benjamin and James King had been found.

Edward Denning, a local resident, was walking in the woods about half a mile behind his house when he came upon a red-colored cooler lying in the weeds. Curious, he opened it. He was startled by what he saw inside—a bunch of cat skulls.

"It was in thick bushes," Denning later told investigators. "It was like something drew me right to it. I smelled it and knew something was dead inside. That's when I opened the bags up and found the books in there wrapped in plastic. You have to be pretty sick to write stuff like that. Right off, I knew it had to do with Jason Massey."

And if the man needed anything else to make him sure that the cooler belonged to Massey, who'd once been his neighbor, it was those volumes inside the cooler—several diaries, volumes one through four, which were collectively titled, "Slayer's Book of Death, by Jason Massey."

Before the contents of these diabolical diaries were entered into evidence in the penalty phase of the trial, the prosecution called a witness whose testimony left no doubts about Massey's reputation of killing and mutilating cats, dogs, and livestock. The witness identified himself as a friend of Massey's from 1989 through 1991.

The witness testified that he saw, took part in, and heard directly from Massey about numerous animal slayings by Massey. He said Massey told him of pouring gasoline on a dog, igniting it, and watching as the flaming dog ran howling in its death agonies through a field. He told also of once seeing Massey beat a calf over the head and slice it open with a machete.

Asked why he thought Massey did that, the witness said, "The adrenaline rush. He loved to mutilate."

Then the prosecution began the reading into evidence of the appalling entries in the convicted killer's diaries of depravity. They were the vile fantasies of a sex ghoul obsessed by a veritable "vampire" lust, a thirst and hunger for the blood and sexual body parts of young girls, a goal of "murdering countless young women." These were the ramblings of a mind of what psychiatrists would describe as a "sociopathic killer," laid bare by the killer himself.

An FBI behavioral expert testified that Massey's writings represented the most detailed collection of murderous fantasies and plans he had ever seen.

The journals, in which the name Jason Massey was used in the first person and was on the cover of each volume, outlined the writer's plans to become "one of the best-known serial killers in history." Those recorded plans projected the murders of a half-dozen girls, as well as Ennis Police Chief Holt.

"And my campaign has only begun," Massey had written.

In the sinister passages, he mentioned "tripping on acid" and being depressed because he had not carried out his murderous plans. If he got caught, he'd written, he "would become a Christian," but he added that the changes of being caught the first time "are too slim."

The grim diaries went on with his declaration that he would never give up his plot to murder young girls, especially those who had rejected him. He wrote of how much he loved his prey and went into detail about how he would kill and mutilate them and eat their body parts.

There was a passage that declared that one woman who had given him herpes "would pay for what she did," but the sections about butchering and cannibalizing girls focused on those who had turned him down at various times. Pretty women made him want to abduct and kill them, he wrote.

"Somehow, the thought of killing a lot of young girls makes me happy," the convicted killer had written. He expressed his plans to seek out "girls who were drunk," because their intoxication would make them "easy prey."

It was determined that most of the diaries were written when Massey was 19 and 20, for he had penned his dreams of turning 21, when he would be able to murder more freely because the "bar scene" would be open to him.

In one terrifying passage, he recalled that he'd tried his first murder when he was only 13 by putting poison into a girl's drink, but she had not drunk it.

In another section, he even planned a physical-conditioning program so that he would be fit to become the successful serial killer he wanted to be. He figured on fulfilling his grisly ambition by laying off drugs and alcohol, building his body, and "eating right."

Massey also repeatedly noted the need for a driver's license, which would enable him "to seek whom I may devour."

The fearsome journals included a declaration that he knew right from wrong, but also expressed the belief that it was his "destiny to kill many, many beautiful girls." Massey wrote that every young girl he immediately saw he wanted to hurt.

"It makes me happy to think of all the hurt I can cause,"

he declared. Moreover, his ambition was that, during the course of his entire life, he wanted to kill 700 victims. However, he added, he had to kill only 86 to break the record of murders by one person. He also told of killing his first cat at age nine and then committing five sexual murders of cows. Dozens of animal killings and mutilations were listed in these horrifying passages.

As the convicted killer's perverted sexual fantasies were read into evidence, they left everyone in court—jurors, officials, and spectators—stunned. And the evidential reading wasn't over yet.

Massey wrote that he was preparing for the "greatest slaughter and carnage wrought upon the earth by one man." After he killed, mutilated, and buried girls, he wanted "to hear their bones cry to me from the earth." He wanted to preserve some of their bodies so he "could play with them" later.

In one frightening passage, he wrote of once having lain with a pregnant woman while harboring desires to kill her and her unborn baby. His campaign of endless murder included plans to stalk girls at junior-high schools, beauty salons, the movies, and ballet classes.

Another horrifying passage related his attempt to rape a 12-year-old girl in Dallas while holding a knife to her throat, and his delight in "tasting her tears" as she cried for him to stop. Before he could finish, however, the girl's mother walked in, thwarting him.

In a 1992 entry, Massey wrote that he would murder two people in 1993 and accomplish this by perfecting "a nice-guy act just like Ted Bundy."

With the revolting readings completed for the court record, Prosecutor Strange called a psychiatrist to the stand and asked him a "hypothetical" question, which he set up as follows: "Let's assume you have a twenty-one-year-old Caucasian male who began having fantasies as early as the fourth grade about murdering girls, spoke to a ninth-grade teacher daily about his desire to kill, committed an armed robbery, attempted to rape a twelve-year-old girl while he was dating her mother, kept animal skulls in a cooler, had a fascination with fire, wrote letters to a fellow former student he had a crush on about ramming a knife through her skull and sent her pictures of disemboweled women, and was convicted of decapitating and mutilating a thirteen-year-old girl . . .

"Would that person be a future menace to society?"

The psychiatrist replied that such a person would always be a risk for murdering again and would not be a candidate for rehabilitation. He said that the profile as characterized by the prosecutor resembled that of a "lust murderer." The doctor went on to explain that the term refers to "sexually sadistic killers who show signs of vampirism or necrophilia."

The psychiatrist further testified that a member of Massey's family had brought the young man to his office in 1991 after she found some writings about his wishes to kill and butcher young women. What was the most alarming thing the doctor saw in those journals was a shift from fantasizing about killing girls to making actual plans for murders.

In cross-examining the psychiatrist, the defense attorney also posed a hypothetical question about a young man who never had affection from his mother, was rejected by his father, was beaten and "sexually touched" by a baby-sitter, and was constantly moved from place to place.

"Wouldn't that permanently affect that person?" the defense lawyer asked.

The doctor replied that he had treated many persons such as the one described by the attorney, then pointed out, "But none of them went on to become lust murderers."

In his final arguments to the jury, Prosecutor Strange asserted that as long as Massey had the breath of life, he would be a danger to society. Therefore, he should be put to death.

Quoting from Massey's journals the statement, "I'll carry on until I'm dead or until I'm finished," the prosecutor added, "He's not finished. You must finish him. He's worse than any nightmare you can imagine. This is as bad as it gets. He is a butcher of human beings."

The defense attorney portrayed Massey as a neglected and abused youth and asked that his life be spared because of this disturbed background.

"Jason Massey was not born a capital murderer," the lawyer declared. "He was a baby. He wanted a dad. He wanted love. Instead, he got rejection. He got hit." The attorney also maintained that Massey "was crying out for help" in his death journals.

It took the jury only 15 minutes to complete their penalty-phase deliberations. They returned with a verdict that mandated the death penalty for Jason Massey.

Massey showed no emotion as he heard the recommendation that he be put to death by lethal injection.

When Massey was brought before Judge Knize for formal sentencing, the judge told the convicted killer, "Mr. Massey, I suppose the only injustice in this case is that you will be permitted a more humane method of death than you gave your victims."

Later, when Massey was being taken in cuffs and leg chains from the courthouse, a young woman suddenly jumped on him, pinned him against a patrol car, and began pummeling him before she was pulled away by deputies. Massey received minor injuries in the attack.

It was later learned that the woman had been a friend of Christina Benjamin and her family. She was charged with simple assault and assessed a $200 fine.

Massey was transferred to death row at the state prison in Huntsville, Texas. At the same time this report was filed, he was awaiting the outcome of an automatic appeal of the death sentence.

"RAPE AND MURDER ALL NIGHT LONG!"

by Steven Barry

Sondra Bray's telephone rang at 6:48 A.M. on the mild winter's day of Sunday, February 10, 1991.

"I can't come to work today," the female caller said. "I'm sick and I'm in pain."

Sondra recognized the voice at once. Sondra's husband Robert owned a motor lodge just north of Wilmington, Delaware. The voice belonged to 52-year-old Joanna Stuart, a long-time employee and friend.

"Do you want Robert to come over?" Sondra asked, trying to help.

"No, I'm sick and I can't come to work today," Joanna replied. To Sondra, Joanna's voice had an alarming ring.

"Do you need an ambulance?"

"No," Joanna replied, then repeated, "I'm sick and I can't come to work today."

Although Sondra had no way of knowing that Joanna Stuart had been held hostage all night and had been repeatedly raped and sodomized, she knew something was wrong. If nothing else, Sondra knew Joanna wasn't scheduled to work that day.

"Do you want me to call the police?"

"Yes," Joanna replied. "Thank you very much."

As soon as the call ended, Sondra Bray immediately dialed 911.

Her call went to the Delaware State Police dispatcher. Within minutes, Troopers Mark Hawk and Blaine Quickel arrived at Joanna Stuart's home in the 300 block of Marsh Road in Penny Hill. It was a nice neighborhood on the eastern edge of Wilmington.

Robert Bray was waiting for them out front.

Room by room, the troopers searched the first floor but saw nothing out of order. But upstairs, in one of the bedrooms, they found lengths of rope that had been tied to all four of Joanna's bedposts. In addition, the closet door was open, and, on the closet floor, they found a pajama top and a rolled-up throw rug, both stained with blood. There were no signs of Joanna Stuart, but one area of the home remained to be searched: the basement.

The troopers went back downstairs, flicked on the light switch, and slowly creaked down the old wooden stairway toward the cellar. At the bottom, they proceeded through a long, narrow laundry area. On top of the washing machine, they saw a pair of bloodstained rubber gloves, a roll of duct tape, and a pair of bloodstained socks. They continued cautiously. Around the corner, on the floor beside a workbench, they found a body.

It was not Joanna Stuart.

The body was that of a 30-year-old white male who was wearing nothing but a pair of pajama bottoms. Lying face up, the victim's eyes were open and his lips were parted. His hands had been bound behind his back, and his wrists had been encircled 11 times with gray duct tape. His feet had been hog-tied with electrical cord, wrapped nine times around his ankles, and his throat had been slashed from ear to ear, nearly decapitating him.

Virtually every drop of the man's blood had emptied onto the floor and sought its level along a 10-foot stretch of concrete. Some of the blood was now dry and blackish-brown in color, some of it was congealing, but most of it was still in a red liquid state.

Robert Bray identified the victim as Hugh Pennington, a relative of Joanna Stuart's, who shared the home with her and worked at the motor lodge as a night auditor. He said Hugh was well liked and always did a good job. Neighbors called him quiet and friendly. Relatives described him as a poet and artist, an environmentalist and pacifist, a film connoisseur, inventor, and electronics wizard. Just one day earlier, Pennington had been celebrating the acceptance of his patent application for a method turning aluminum cans into a building material.

"Hugh was a very noble person," a close relative would say later. "He's the only person I can think of who's never hurt anyone, and he had a keen intellect.

"That workshop was his sanctuary. Everything creative from him came from there. Now I think of Hugh and the fear and pain he experienced, and it really bothers me a lot. I visualize him in the basement, and I think it must've been cold and he must've been scared."

Cold, scared, and dead. But why?

While one of the troopers called the Criminal Investigation Unit, the other sealed off the crime scene with yellow tape. Sergeant Mark Daniels arrived shortly thereafter to take charge of the investigation.

Daniels concluded that nothing had been taken from the home. So if it wasn't a robbery, and drugs weren't involved, and if there was no history of domestic disputes, what was the motive for Hugh Pennington's brutal slaying? And what had happened to Joanna Stuart? Had she, too, been butchered?

Twenty minutes later, Sergeant Daniels was standing on the front sidewalk awaiting the arrival of a search warrant. A woman approached him. She said she was Joanna Stuart's best friend and had spent the previous night with Joanna.

She said Joanna had invited her to dinner. She, Joanna, and Hugh ate, then Hugh went to bed around 7:30. She and Joanna started watching a movie, then she remembered she'd forgotten to engage her call-forwarding. Since she was expecting a call from her husband, she suggested going to her house to watch the rest of the movie, which they did.

Around midnight, her husband, Jim Red Dog, came home. At 37, Red Dog was a full-blooded Sioux Indian, a member of the Lakota tribe. He was a ruggedly attractive man, 190 muscular pounds spread over a 6-foot 3-inch frame, with straight, long, dark hair and thick glasses. Red Dog drummed and performed traditional dances at regional Indian ceremonies.

"Jim is a very charismatic person," one friend later described him. "You can't help but like him."

But that particular night, when he walked in, Jim Red Dog was carrying a whiskey bottle—and he was drunk. He told the women he had to go back out to help a friend whose truck had gotten stuck in a ditch, and he asked Joanna if she'd give him a ride. When he said it was just up the street, Joanna agreed. On the front porch, Red Dog picked up a clothesline, saying he needed it to pull his friend's truck out of the ditch.

And that was the last time the woman saw her husband or Joanna.

"By the way," she said to Daniels, "I better tell you something. . . . My husband's a convicted murderer."

That hit Daniels like a ton of bricks.

"Where do you think he might go?" he asked her.

"Yesterday, he went to Millsboro to sell some jewelry at the Indian museum. He has a lot of friends down there." But, she told the investigator, her husband also had friends in New Jersey and Washington, D.C.

Sergeant Daniels accompanied the woman home to obtain a list of her husband's friends. At the same time, he asked if she'd consent to a search of her home. She agreed. Daniels found several pairs of surgical gloves similar to the pair found on Joanna Stuart's washing machine. Afterward, Daniels detailed a trooper to remain with the woman while he returned to the crime scene.

The warrant arrived at 8:30 A.M., and a retinue of homicide investigators began going over every inch of the house. They were lucky; the killer had been careless. Despite having worn the rubber gloves, he'd left a bloody fingerprint from the middle finger of his left hand on a piece of cardboard, a few strands of waist-long hair, and a pack of cigarettes. And he'd left so many bloody prints from his shoeless feet on the cellar floor, it looked as if he'd performed a dance over the slain body.

In examining the body, the medical examiner noticed a blister on the victim's right thumb. He theorized that Hugh Pennington must have struggled to free himself for some time prior to having his throat slashed. In addition, the victim's back and arms were characterized by a purplish lividity.

"He was helpless," the medical examiner explained. "There was no way he could run—or even move. He lost consciousness almost immediately after his throat was cut, and death came quickly."

By noon, Daniels had called half the names on Jim Red Dog's list of friends, but no one had seen him. Daniels was beginning to think that, just maybe, Joanna Stuart had met the same fate as Hugh Pennington. But, unbeknown to him, at least for the moment, she was still alive.

When they had left Jim Red Dog's home the night before, Red Dog told Joanna he had something very important to discuss with her. He told her to take him to her house. Once inside, he pushed Joanna onto a living-room chair, straddled her, and pulled out a bone-handled hunting knife.

"This is it," he told Joanna. "You have to do what I want. No one can help you."

Earlier that evening, Red Dog explained, he'd stopped to visit a friend in Millsboro. They drank beer for a few hours, picked up two women, and went bowling. In the men's room at the bowling alley, Red Dog snorted cocaine. Earlier in the evening, he'd been charming and lighthearted; now he suddenly grew belligerent. He started kissing and fondling one of the women present. When she resisted his advances, he threatened her. But she refused to be bullied. So Red Dog stormed out and bought a bottle of whiskey for the ride home. By the time he was alone with Joanna Stuart, his libido was not to be denied.

"I want you," Red Dog told Joanna.

"No, you don't," she pleaded. "Go back home to your wife."

"I can't," Red Dog said. He owed $30,000 to Mafia hit men, he explained. He said the hit men had kidnapped Hugh and were holding him hostage until Red Dog paid them the $30,000. At that very moment, he told Joanna, the hit men were on their way to her house to collect. Once they were paid, they would release Hugh.

"Is Hugh hurt?" Joanna asked.

"Oh, he's hurt," Red Dog answered, and he laughed maniacally. Frightened, Joanna burst into a fit of tears. At the same time, she began struggling, trying to get up.

"He's okay now," Red Dog assured her. "He's okay now."

Hugh Pennington, in fact, was not okay. He was dead. And there were no Mafia hit men.

Jim Red Dog's fable was confusing to Joanna Stuart, but Hugh's well-being was all that mattered to her. She agreed to do whatever Red Dog suggested. He led her upstairs to her bedroom and said he wanted to make it look good for the hit men. He was going to tie her to the bed and tell them he'd raped her.

Red Dog then tied one of Joanna's wrists to the headboard and began removing her clothes. Joanna resisted. When she began to put her clothing back on, Red Dog's mood turned nasty. He ripped off everything Joanna was wearing and tied her hands and feet tightly to the bed.

"Now, I might as well rape you," he said—and he did.

The rape seemed to last an hour and a half. When Red Dog

finally finished, he rolled off Joanna and passed out on the bed next to her.

In the middle of the night, Joanna woke up Red Dog and said she had to go to the bathroom. He cut her ropes and escorted her. Then, just as soon as she'd finished, he sodomized her. And before morning, Jim Red Dog sodomized Joanna twice more and raped her once again. Then he ordered her to get dressed.

After Joanna finished dressing, Red Dog told her to phone Robert Bray to say she wouldn't be coming to work. As soon as she hung up—just moments before the state troopers arrived—Red Dog led Joanna out of the house.

Telling Joanna that they had to help Hugh, he instructed her to drive to Oak Orchard, a seasonal resort community near Millsboro on an inlet of the Atlantic Ocean, about 75 miles south of Wilmington. At that time of the year, most of the homes were unoccupied.

In Oak Orchard, Jim Red Dog had no problem breaking into and entering a vacant farmhouse. There, he forced Joanna into one of the bedrooms and raped her once more. Afterward, Joanna thought she might have an opportunity to escape, but fear of her captor paralyzed her—and rightly so.

Jim Red Dog was born and raised on the Fort Peck Indian Reservation in Poplar, Montana, the second child in a family with eight sisters and two half brothers. His parents were good people, despite their poverty. He dropped out of school after the 11th grade to get married. He lied about his age and joined the Marines. After three years, he attained the rank of corporal, but a series of AWOLs and a fight in an officers' club resulted in a general discharge.

By then, Red Dog's wife had borne him three children. Also by then, he'd become an alcoholic and a drug addict, and his troubles with the law were about to begin.

On October 13, 1973, Jim Red Dog, only 19 years old, went

hunting with an Indian friend on the Wolf Point Reservation in Montana. Afterward, the two friends went to a party. They started drinking and met another friend. The conversation got around to the then-recent killings of two FBI agents at Wounded Knee by members of the American Indian Movement and three centuries of the white man's oppression of their red brothers. With each beer, their oaths of vengeance and bravado grew more outlandish. But sometime after midnight, the men ran out of beer and money.

The drunken trio grabbed a pistol and two rifles and knocked on the back door of Bill's Pizza Parlor, which had just closed.

Inside, owner William Veseth was sitting at the bar with two waitresses, unwinding after a long day. He was talking about retiring soon, selling the shop, and buying a boat. When he heard the knocking, he answered the door.

The three Indians demanded beer.

"No," Veseth told them, "we're closed."

A struggle ensued. Shots were fired and a bullet hit Veseth in the chest, sending him tumbling down the steps into the basement.

With rifle in hand, Jim Red Dog ran into the pizza shop. He emptied the cash register, stole a case of beer, and fled.

William Veseth died a few hours later.

Heading for Canada, the fugitives drove for 18 hours before they were captured.

Jim Red Dog was tried and convicted of robbery and manslaughter, but the verdict created a problem: Since Veseth was killed during the commission of a robbery, technically, Veseth's death mandated a murder conviction or an acquittal. Unwittingly, the jury had opened a legal loophole which negated the manslaughter conviction and made it impossible to retry Jim Red Dog.

Since the robbery was committed on an Indian reservation, which is a federal preserve, Red Dog was sentenced to 15

years in the federal prison in Lompoc, California. Soon thereafter, his wife divorced him.

Three years later, on August 6, 1977, prison guards escorted
Jim Red Dog and Raymond Tapaha, another American Indian,
to a powwow in Santa Barbara, where they were scheduled to
perform ceremonial dances. En route, Red Dog and Tapaha
escaped and headed toward Los Angeles.

Three nights later, at a bar in Hollywood, the escapees met
a trio of Indians—Stanley Large, John Moses, and Vincent
Castille. Shooting pool and drinking beer, they became
friendly. At closing time, Large invited them to his home on
the outskirts of L.A. There, they continued drinking, smoked
marijuana, and dropped LSD. Later, Red Dog and Tapaha
passed out in a rear bedroom.

The following morning, Vincent Castille entered the bedroom in search of his car keys. Castille was Large's cousin.
An 18-year-old from Wyoming, Castille had graduated from
high school just two months earlier and had come out to visit
his cousin in hopes of pursuing his lifelong dream of breaking
into the movie business. Castille had driven to California in a
red Monte Carlo, which his parents had given him as a graduation present.

Tapaha pulled out a butcher knife. He ordered the teenager
to strip, then raped him—orally and anally.

After the sex acts, Red Dog asked Castille for the car keys.

"I don't have them," Castille replied, "because I didn't drive
home."

Red Dog dragged the teenager into the living room, where
Large and Moses were asleep on two couches. Red Dog and
Tapaha tied up the sleeping men. Then Red Dog raised the
butcher knife.

"I'll ask you one more time," he told the teenager. "Where
are your keys?"

"I don't have them," Castille repeated.

Without another word, Jim Red Dog plunged the knife into
the chest of Stanley Large five times. When he was done, he

stabbed John Moses 17 times in the chest. Red Dog removed the dead men's wristwatches, searched their pockets, and eventually found the car keys.

Red Dog took the Monte Carlo's wheel, and Tapaha forced the teenager into the back. Destination: Las Vegas, Nevada.

During the seven-hour drive, Tapaha forced Castille to submit to a half-dozen oral and anal sex acts in the backseat of the Monte Carlo. Soon after their arrival in Las Vegas, Red Dog and Tapaha fell asleep, and the teenager was able to escape.

Two days later, the fugitives were arrested at a gas station outside Las Vegas. But California, where the murders were committed, wanted no part of Jim Red Dog. He was a federal prisoner and the state wanted him to remain within the federal domain.

On May 5, 1978, Jim Red Dog was allowed to plead guilty to two counts of second-degree homicide in exchange for a nine-year sentence, which was scheduled to run concurrently with the balance of his prior conviction.

"He got no additional time for a double homicide and sodomy and kidnapping," Delaware Deputy Attorney General Peggy Jo Hageman said later. "What did that tell Red Dog? 'You are free to kill again.' "

Once back behind bars, Red Dog met a woman who was visiting another prisoner, and they were married soon afterward. Then followed two years at the federal penitentiary in Leavenworth, Kansas, then a transfer to Marion, Illinois. There he joined two prison gangs, the Mexican Mafia and the Aryan Brotherhood.

Wherever Red Dog went, his new wife followed. On prison visits, she would smuggled drugs into him, packaging the contraband inside balloons, then hiding the balloons in her bra. In this fashion, Red Dog became the prison pipeline for marijuana, cocaine, methamphetamine, and heroin. He also established a gambling ring. And he killed again.

Red Dog's next victim was Joe Ortega, an inmate known throughout the prison as a locker thief. He'd once stolen some of Red Dog's possessions, and Red Dog had sworn to get even. As a member of the Mexican Mafia, Joe Ortega's actions were an embarrassment to the gang. Its leaders wanted him dead.

Ortega was also a heroin addict.

In February 1983, Red Dog suggested that Ortega be given a "hot-shot" of heroin. The gang leaders agreed.

On February 22, Red Dog's wife smuggled 16 marijuana-filled balloons, along with a 17th balloon, into Marion Prison. To differentiate it from the others, the 17th balloon was the only lime-colored one. It contained the overdose of heroin targeted for Ortega.

"I went ahead and swallowed the marijuana balloons," Red Dog admitted later. He regurgitated them after returning to his cell and he "keistered" the other one, meaning he inserted it in his rectum. Later, he put the heroin in a sock and gave it to three members of the Mexican Mafia.

Joe Ortega was found dead the next morning.

Less than a year later, Red Dog found himself in deep trouble. Because he couldn't cover his gambling debts, inmates were threatening to kill him.

Early in 1984, Red Dog contacted the FBI and confessed to his involvement in the killing of Joe Ortega. He also told FBI agents that he could supply information about prison vice rings—drugs, gambling, and prostitution—and provide intelligence about the inner sanctum of the American Indian Movement. He said he belonged to a secret society of warriors who robbed and killed to promote the Indians' cause.

A deal was struck.

For the next four years, Jim Red Dog supplied information to the government. In addition, he and his wife both testified before a grand jury. As his reward, Jim Red Dog was paroled on February 2, 1988.

Although he refused to enter the Witness Protection Program, Red Dog and his wife were relocated to Delaware for their own protection. Upon their arrival in Delaware, they were housed temporarily at the motel where Hugh Pennington and

Joanna Stuart worked. The women became friends, the families became neighbors—and Hugh Pennington and Joanna Stuart ultimately became Red Dog's next victims.

As he tormented her in the abandoned farmhouse, Jim Red Dog kept telling Joanna that all he had to do was make a phone call, and he could save Hugh's life. But there was no phone in the farmhouse, so he waited until after dark. Then, around 5:30 P.M., he told Joanna to drive him to a friend's mobile home just outside Oak Orchard so he could use the phone. By then, it was cold outside, in the upper teens, and Joanna had trouble starting her car.

A few minutes later, they arrived at the mobile home.

Red Dog went inside, and Joanna waited in the car by herself. As fate would have it, Red Dog had neglected to remove the keys from the ignition, which brought Joanna Stuart face-to-face with the most-terrifying dilemma of her life.

Should she chance an escape? Or should she not?

Joanna struggled with the decision. Every moment she delayed, she knew her chances of escaping were growing slimmer. Her heart was pounding and her throat kept constricting, tighter and tighter. When the tension reached the point where Joanna thought she was going to throw up, she reached down with her right hand and turned the key.

The engine groaned. It didn't start.

Joanna looked over her shoulder at the front door. Had Red Dog heard her attempt to start the car? Would he come racing out and hurt her? Would he kill her?

The trailer door remained closed.

Joanna turned the key once more.

This time, the engine roared. She eased the accelerator toward the floor. As the car inched forward, Joanna glanced at the trailer once more. To her horror, the door burst open and Red Dog raced outside. He began chasing her, waving his arms and yelling as he ran.

Joanna Stuart floored the accelerator and prayed.

At 5:43 P.M., the phone range at Jim Red Dog's house. With state trooper Ed Mayfield listening, Red Dog's wife picked up the phone.

"Hi, babes," a man's voice said. She nodded at the trooper, indicating it was her husband. "It's me. Are they listening?"

"No," she lied. "Where are you?"

"They probably have it tapped," Red Dog said. "Do you know what happened?"

"Yes," she said. "Hugh's dead. I just have to ask you, did you do it?"

"No," Red Dog said, "but I know who did."

"Who?"

"A guy named Bill."

"Who's that?"

"I'm coming home," Red Dog said. "I'll tell you when I get home."

"Do you know what happened to Joanna?"

"She's fine, but she's no longer with me."

After the call ended, believing Red Dog to be headed home, several teams of state troopers set a trap, positioning themselves inside and outside his house.

At that moment, Joanna Stuart was speeding down the highway, certain Red Dog would get another car and try to catch her. She flashed her headlights at the two or three cars she passed.

A mile or so down the road, she came to a tavern and pulled into the parking lot. As she was getting out, another car screeched to a stop in front of her and a man got out. Joanna's heart skipped a beat. But the driver was not Jim Red Dog. He was someone who'd seen Joanna's flashing headlights and stopped to see if she needed help. Together, they ran into the tavern and called the state police.

When the troopers arrived at the tavern a short while later, they found a rifle and a bone-handled hunting knife in Joanna's car. They impounded the car and whisked Joanna via helicopter to a Wilmington hospital.

Based on Joanna Stuart's statements, the state police Mobile Crime Unit was dispatched to the Oak Orchard/Millsboro area and an APB was teletyped to every police force along the eastern seaboard. Using helicopters, K-9 units, and every available trooper, an air-and-ground search for Jim Red Dog began within the hour. In the bitter cold, it lasted all night, but no trace of the five-time killer turned up.

The next morning, the manhunt intensified. Troopers went door-to-door checking occupied and vacant homes. By mid-morning, they had identified the farmhouse that Red Dog had used the previous day. Inside, they found his black leather jacket and a pair of notes, one apologizing for breaking into the home, the other a confession to his wife.

"Babes," the note read, "I went crazy last night and killed Hugh. I'm sitting here now wishing you were here to talk to me at least. I know this is it for me so I'll make one last request. Say a prayer for me every day and know that if it wasn't for my mind being so whacked out that we would've lived the life we dreamed of. I love you my sweet precious lady! I just wish things could've turned out better for us. My last thoughts will be of you and me. God! I love you so much and I'm so sorry for what I've done. Hold me baby always don't let me go never!!!"

But the manhunt failed to make contact with Red Dog.

Early the next morning, Tuesday, an area resident spotted Jim Red Dog getting into a newer-model pickup truck, possibly a Ford. It was dark in color and had a sliding chrome-and-glass rear window. The pickup was last seen heading toward Georgetown, a small town a few miles to the west. The search moved westward, but hours passed without another sighting.

Around eight o'clock that night, Red Dog knocked on a friend's front door in Oak Orchard, but the friend refused to open the door. Red Dog took off running, into the woods, and his friend called the police.

Within 10 minutes, troopers and dogs swarmed the area and helicopters hovered overhead. But Red Dog had vanished once again.

The rest of Tuesday night and most of Wednesday passed without a sign of the dangerous fugitive. Then, around 5 P.M. on Wednesday, another resident spotted him in the woods near Millsboro. Once again, the manhunt switched venues. But once again, Red Dog gave his posse the slip.

Early the next morning, Thursday, troopers found long, dark hairs and a blanket in an abandoned car in Oak Orchard, and the search switched back to that locale. But Red Dog was 75 miles away. In the middle of the previous night, he'd stolen a pickup truck and driven to Wilmington.

Around 8:30 A.M., Red Dog ditched the pickup on the shoulder of I-495 near the 12th Street exit and continued on foot. At 8:44, the dispatcher's phone rang at the Wilmington Police Department.

"We received an anonymous call from someone who said he knew Red Dog," an officer recalled, "and that the suspect was crossing the Winchester Bridge at Fourth and Chestnut Streets on foot."

Less than a minute later, two Wilmington police officers arrived at the bridge and observed a lone figure, walking halfway across. They approached the suspect cautiously. He appeared to be tired, cold, and possibly strung out on drugs.

"What's your name?" one of the officers asked.

"Jim Red Dog."

The officers arrested Red Dog, who was transferred to state police custody at the Troop 2 Barracks. There, Mark Daniels advised him of his rights. Red Dog refused a lawyer and said he was willing to speak. But he didn't say much.

At 5 P.M., Daniels and Ed Mayfield transported the suspect to Magistrate Court 18. Two hours later, Red Dog was arraigned and charged with kidnapping, unlawful sexual intercourse, two counts of possessing a deadly weapon during the commission of a felony, and murder in the first degree. His bail was set at $2.5 million for the sex attacks on Joanna Stuart, but he was denied bail on the murder charges.

Thirteen months later, on March 12, 1992, Jim Red Dog pleaded "no contest" to all of his charges. But one drama remained to be played out: Would he get the death penalty? Co-prosecutors Steven Wood and Peggy Jo Hageman were determined that he would.

"As soon as Peggy Jo and I learned about his twenty-year history of eluding justice," explained Wood, "we decided to spare no expense and to do everything we could to make sure it wouldn't happen again.

"Red Dog is a brutal, merciless, and remorseless killer, and the evidence suggests he will kill again if we allow him to continue."

Hageman expressed outrage that Red Dog "never served a day for four killings—even though he admitted involvement in all of them. If the justice system had not failed in the past, Hugh Pennington would not have been his fifth victim.

"I value human life, yet this man needs to be killed," Hageman argued. "If he is not executed, he will kill again."

In Delaware, before a person can be condemned to death, the state must prove "aggravating circumstances." Ironically, as grisly as Hugh Pennington's murder had been, it alone did not meet the requirements for aggravating circumstances—not even when parlayed with the kidnapping and sexual abuse inflicted upon Joanna Stuart. Therefore, the prosecution's strategy was to portray the string of violence in Red Dog's past as the aggravating circumstances.

In mid-November 1992, the prosecutors presented their case to Judge Norman Barron. The trial lasted a little better than two weeks and the moment of truth came on December 3.

For the crimes against Joanna Stuart, Judge Barron sentenced Red Dog to four life terms, plus 80 years, plus an additional six months of work release. For murdering Hugh Pennington, the judge said, "A sentence of death, perhaps, is too kind. But death it shall be."

As Jim Red Dog was led out of the courtroom, his hands and feet manacled, he paused as he passed Sergeant Mark Daniels, just long enough to make an obscene gesture at the trooper.

"Same to you," Daniels retorted with a laugh.

A year later, his automatic appeals exhausted, Jim Red Dog ate a hearty meal of lobster tail, steamed and fried shrimp, steamed and fried clams, cocktail sauce, rolls, seedless grapes, apple pie, and coffee. The date was March 2, 1993.

At nine o'clock the next morning, in the 14-by-70-foot execution chamber at Gander Hill Prison, a medicine man performed a prayer ceremony to prepare Red Dog for his journey into death. He laid a white sheet beneath the condemned man, placed a string of beads around his neck, and painted a red stripe on his head.

The witnesses began arriving at 9:30. There were 21 in all, including Red Dog's wife and Sergeant Daniels. The witnesses stood in two rows in an adjacent room on the opposite side of two picture windows.

Red Dog, strapped to a T-shaped table, with his arms extended, was wearing prison blues, white socks, and no shoes. Intravenous tubes protruded from the veins in his arms.

"I remember you!" Red Dog said to his wife in a Sioux dialect. "I remember you! Saying this, I dance toward you. I love you, my wife."

In English, he spoke to the witnesses. "I'd like to thank my family and friends and [my lawyer], and all the others who treated me with kindness."

Then he paused.

"And for the rest of you, you can all kiss my ass."

Another pause.

"I'm going home, babes."

"I know," his wife replied through the glass. "I know. I love you. I'll be there soon."

"I love you, too," were Jim Red Dog's last words.

At 10:24, the warden tapped Red Dog's shoulder. It was the

signal to release a sequence of sodium pentathol, pancuronium bromide, and potassium chloride into the intravenous tubes.

Red Dog's eyes closed and his chest heaved.

Two minutes later, his face turned bright red. Then his lips turned blue. Another two minutes passed. By then, all of the color had drained from Red Dog's face.

The curtains were drawn shut.

"James Allen Red Dog," the warden announced over the public address system, "was pronounced dead at 10:28 A.M."

"MOM AND TWO DAUGHTERS DEFILED— AND DUMPED AT SEA!"

by Patty Shipp

The breeze that blew over Tampa Bay on Sunday, June 4, 1989, proved to be an ill wind indeed. And with good reason. What pleasure boaters found floating in the bay that day would probably haunt them for years to come.

About 18 miles out in the bay, southeast of the St. Petersburg Pier, three decomposing female floaters surfaced. The U.S. Coast Guard team that retrieved the bodies could not believe what they saw. All three victims were bound hand and foot, duct tape was strapped over their mouths, and their bodies were stripped from the waist down. The ropes tied around their necks had apparently been anchored by concrete blocks. One of the victims had managed to get a hand free before she died.

Dr. Edward Corcoran, the associate medical examiner who performed all three autopsies, determined that the victims died of asphyxiation, either by strangulation or drowning, or both. For four days, however, the police didn't have a clue as to the identity of the victims.

On Thursday, June 8, motel employees at the Rocky Point Days Inn on the Tampa end of the Courtney Campbell Parkway, a causeway that connects Hillsborough and Pinellas counties, called the Tampa Police Department to report that a room rented to Joan Rogers and her daughters, Michelle and Christe, on June 1 had not been slept in. A cursory check of the room revealed the presence of brushes, combs, toothpaste, and several articles of new clothing, including new swimsuits still containing the price tags from the Mass Brothers department store. Also found were a high-school class ring, ladies' sandals, sneakers, and new bikini panties with the price tags still on.

From the wet towels and swimsuits lying on a vanity in the bathroom, it appeared that the trio had recently been to the swimming pool.

"We haven't seen them since the first day they checked in," one of the motel employees reported. "The last time anybody here saw the woman and her girls was at the motel restaurant about five-thirty in the evening."

On Saturday, June 10, Detectives Dan McLaughlin and Steve Corbet, of the St. Petersburg Police Department, joined other St. Petersburg and Tampa police officers at the Courtney Campbell causeway boat ramp, located just off the Courtney Campbell Parkway, where a 1986 blue Oldsmobile Cutlass registered to 36-year-old Joan Rogers was found. Inside, the officers found a note, written on motel stationery, bearing directions from the motel to the ramp. The contents of the note included the words "blue and white." This bit of information led the detectives to believe that the Rogers women, still missing from the motel, had been looking for a blue and white boat.

The car registration showed that Joan Rogers lived in Ohio. In checking the registration, the police learned that on Tuesday, June 6, a family member had notified the Ohio and Florida Highway Patrols that Joan Rogers and her two daughters, 17-year-old Michelle and 14-year-old Christe, were missing. They had been due to return home on June 5, but nobody had heard from them.

A check of dental records showed that the floaters were indeed Joan, Michelle, and Christe Rogers. As hard as it was to imagine, somebody had bound the mother and daughters, stripped them from the waist down, put duct tape over their mouths, weighted them by the neck with concrete blocks, then tossed them over the side of a boat into the bay.

As the news of the horrible homicide hit the bay area and spread, some witnesses began to surface. One couple came forward to report seeing an Oldsmobile at the causeway boat ramp about 2 P.M. Thursday, June 1. That was just 90 minutes after Joan Rogers and her daughters checked into the motel.

Meanwhile, the investigation was expanded to Ohio, where investigators interviewed friends and family of the three mercilessly slain victims.

Their kin said that Joan, Michelle, and Christe had left Ohio for what they thought would be a fun and relaxing time in Florida. Equipped with a Nikon camera and five rolls of film, the trio drove from their dairy farm in Willshire, Ohio, and headed for Florida. That was on Friday, May 26. Once in Florida, they visited Walt Disney World, Silver Springs, and other Florida amusement attractions. They had one last stop to make, Busch Gardens in Tampa, before their vacation was complete. Then they would head for home.

The Rogers women arrived in Tampa on June 1, and checked into the Rocky Point Days Inn Motel, located at the east end of the Courtney Campbell Parkway.

As news of the horrible slayings spread across the Tampa Bay area, phone calls poured in to the police from people who claimed they might have information that would lead to a suspect. In one instance, police learned that an individual who had been serving time on a rape charge had been released at 9:30 A.M. on June 1. An inmate told a corrections officer that the freed convict was picked up by someone driving a dark-colored Bronco. Detectives immediately set up a tight surveillance on the suspect.

On Friday, June 16, St. Petersburg detective Don Rivers went to Orlando, about 125 miles northeast of St. Petersburg, to check other places where Joan Rogers and her daughters had stayed. Perhaps someone had been traveling with them and had decided to do them in. But Rivers soon established that the three women had been alone the whole time they were in Orlando.

As the investigation continued, more people who wanted to help detectives solve the case were heard from. Numerous phone calls from individuals who thought they had leads flooded the St. Petersburg and Tampa Police Departments.

Detective Robert Schock, of the St. Petersburg PD's Major Crime Unit, sought out everyone who had stayed at the Rocky Point motel on June 1, to see if anyone knew anything or had seen something unusual in connection with the victims, or if they had seen a blue-and-white boat parked at the motel pier.

Upon checking the guest register, Detective Schock discovered that Clancy Jennings, a local man who owned a boat, had signed into that motel using a false name. Jennings was not really a suspect at this point, but Schock obtained his address and went to interview him.

The investigation continued for a year, with about 40 detectives spending more than 10,000 hours working on the still-unsolved crime. The case was even featured on the national television shows *Unsolved Mysteries* and *Hard Copy*. St. Petersburg detectives went over the facts again and again. They kept coming up empty.

The only real evidence the homicide cops had to work with were two handwritten notes. One note, the experts concluded, was written by Joan Rogers herself. On motel stationery she had noted directions from the Rocky Point Days Inn motel on the Courtney Campbell Parkway to the boat ramp, located about a mile west, on a side road that ran alongside the parkway (causeway).

But the second sample of handwriting, which was found on a tourist brochure giving directions to the Rocky Point Days Inn, was a mystery. Handwriting experts determined that it was not written by Joan, Michelle, or Christe Rogers.

Meanwhile, Tampa PD Detective Kevin Dunkin determined that Clancy Jennings, who had given a phony name on the motel registration on June 1, could not possibly be a suspect. Jennings, who had a boat, had used an alias at the motel because he was having an extramarital affair. Upon checking his story, Detective Kevin Dunkin found that Jennings's boat was being painted on June 1.

Two years after the bodies were found, the investigation led back to the victims' home state. Investigators took a closer look at people who knew the victims, at relatives, and at an individual who had molested Michelle Rogers several times while she was growing up. The probers considered that the killer might be someone who knew the three victims well.

On Sunday, January 27, 1991, St. Petersburg Detectives Cindra Cummings and John Geoghehan went to Van Wert County, Ohio, where they conducted interviews through Tuesday, February 5. While there, Cummings and Geoghehan reinterviewed friends and relatives who had been questioned shortly after the murders. The sleuths also interviewed mental health counselors who had connections with the Rogers family. Altogether, 70 people were interviewed during the detectives' 10-day stay.

Leaving no stones unturned, Detectives Cummings and Geoghehan also obtained a videotape taken by a television news crew from Fort Wayne, Indiana, at the victims' funeral. The tape was impounded and viewed numerous times by investigators, who made it their business to study the faces of people who attended.

While carrying on their investigation in Ohio, Detectives Cummings and Geoghehan learned that one member of the family went to the bank on June 6, 1989, and withdrew $6,000. When they questioned him, the family member said he had withdrawn the money just in case he needed to travel to Florida to look for Joan and the girls.

In April 1991, Cummings and Geoghehan, along with St. Petersburg sergeant Glen Moore, who had been placed in charge of the investigation, met with FBI specialists in Quantico, Virginia, to go over the available clues and to assist the FBI in developing a profile of the triple killer.

An analysis done at the University of South Florida showed that the victims actually died in the waters near where their bodies were found. This led the sleuths to believe that whoever dumped the bodies had spent many hours on the bay, because it would be difficult for someone inexperienced with boats and unfamiliar with the area to maneuver that far out at night.

This case continued to baffle Sergeant Moore and the other detectives. Moore repeatedly issued public alerts via television and newspapers, saying that the police were looking for somebody who had a blue-and-white boat that had left the causeway on June 1 with the woman and her daughters aboard. During the investigation, 17 witnesses told the police they had noticed a dark-colored Bronco or Blazer truck and a blue-and-white boat parked behind the Rocky Point Days Inn within the time frame of the killings.

By May 1991, Sergeant Moore dismissed any suspicions that any of the victims' kin might have been involved in the case. The probers were focusing on two possible suspects, both of whom had been identified to the authorities by persons who knew them. One of these individuals wintered in Florida. The second one lived in the area the year round. Still, the crimefighters had no evidence connecting either man to the Rogers slayings.

That same month, Sergeant Moore called a press conference and released the FBI profile of the killer to the media. The description was run over and over again on television, on the radio, and in the newspapers. The person being sought was believed to have the following characteristics: a man of social skills who could present a nonthreatening manner; a neat and meticulous individual who exhibits compulsive-type behavior; people who know him would describe him as being controlled, rigid, and confident; one who derives pleasure and satisfaction from controlling and dominating his victims, and enjoys their suffering; he is white, possibly in his early 30s, with above-average intelligence; he has a fantasy life and is interested in bondage. When the victims' bodies were found, the killer must have been edgy, tense, and perhaps withdrawn while assessing the possibility of discovery. Afterward, he must have displayed an avid interest in the case, possibly clipping articles about it from newspapers.

"The police believe the man has killed before and will kill again," said Sergeant Moore. "Police believe he has probably killed since the bodies of Joan, Michelle, and Christe were found.

"The killer charmed the woman and her daughters into an evening trip on his tidy boat," Sergeant Moore went on. "He remorselessly planned and carried out their killings. It is believed the killer raped and killed the women because he enjoyed the suffering of others.

"There are people out there who know something about this case. It just hasn't rung any bells yet," Moore continued.

"There are significant indications that anyone who knows the killer's identity is in danger because of their knowledge," Moore said. "Anybody with information should call the St. Petersburg police as soon as possible.

"This is a very heinous crime, particularly when you have family members probably seeing each other being violated sexually and then seeing the mother, sister, or daughter thrown into the water to die a horrible death.

"I would say the honeymoon is over for this killer. We're going to hunt him down until we find him," Moore said.

After numerous phone tips and interviews, Moore obtained a better description of the vehicle that was seen parked at the motel on June 1. It was described as a dark-colored Bronco or Blazer, with dark-tinted windows, pulling an 18- to 24-foot blue-and-white boat.

Detective Ralph Pflieger was one of the many investigators trying to solve the Rogers murder case. One day, as he was reading a Florida Department of Law Enforcement (FDLE) flier, an item caught his eye about a rape case that had occurred off the shore of Madeira Beach, just north of St. Petersburg Beach. That crime had occurred in May 1989, just two weeks before the Rogers murders.

The victim, a Canadian tourist, said that a stranger had noticed her taking pictures and started talking with her. Then he invited her and her female traveling companion for a sunset cruise on the Gulf of Mexico to take pictures. The tourist accepted the boat ride, but her friend refused to go, which seemed to disappoint the stranger, according to the police report. While out on the Gulf, the man raped the tourist in his boat. Afterward, he ripped the film from her camera and threw it overboard, then wiped her camera clean, as if trying to remove fingerprints from its surface.

When the Canadian tourist began to scream, her assailant threatened to put duct tape over her mouth. "Don't scream. Is sex worth losing your life over?" he demanded. The woman later described her attacker's boat as a blue-and-white craft. Although the tourist was traumatized and upset, she was going to return to Canada without reporting the rape, but her traveling companion talked her into going to the police. As the victim tourist described her attacker, a composite of the suspect was developed.

The rape and the murders could have been committed by the same person, but who was he? Sergeant Moore and his team of detectives were frustrated. It was already 1992, and they had yet to arrest a single suspect in the Rogers slayings. So far, all during the investigation, whenever the police had asked for help from the public in obtaining information, witnesses had come forth, even though nothing solid had turned up. Now, the sleuths had another idea. They had one piece of physical evidence that might lead to the killer: the brochure with the unidentified handwriting giving directions to the Rocky Point motel.

Sergeant Moore released pictures of the brochure to the press. He followed up with a long shot: he posted copies of the note with the unidentified handwriting on billboards in the Tampa Bay area.

Then, in May 1992, a Tampa woman called the police with a lead. She said that her former neighbor, a man named Oba Chandler, might be the killer in the Rogers case. She noticed that when Chandler, an aluminum contractor she had hired to do some work at her house, signed their contract, his handwriting appeared to be the same as the handwriting on the billboard. On top of that, she said, the composite of the rapist looked like Chandler. The investigators wasted no time in interviewing the woman.

Handwriting experts analyzed the writing on the contract, comparing it to what was on the travel brochure, and determined that the samples had been written by the same person.

Though Oba Chandler no longer lived at the Tampa address near that woman caller's home, the police learned that he was an avid boater and had owned a blue-and-white boat until he sold it in August 1989. Upon checking whether Chandler had a record, the detectives discovered that he had a long history of criminal activity.

Detective Katherine Connor-Dubina flew to Canada to show a photo lineup to the Canadian rape victim. The victim immediately picked Oba Chandler's photo from it.

In September 1992, Special FDLE Agent John Halliday arrested Oba Chandler at his home in Port Orange, Florida, and charged him with the May 15, 1989, rape of the Canadian tourist. A search of Chandler's home turned up a mint-green short-sleeved shirt with a mesh bottom half, like the one the woman had told the police her attacker had worn.

A description of the boat the woman said she was raped on, matched the description of the boat owned by Chandler, which he sold in the fall of 1989. Investigators were able to find the boat through the original for-sale advertisement Chandler had placed in a boating magazine. They had it hauled to the sheriff's impound lot in Pinellas County as evidence in the probe.

After Chandler's arrest on the rape charge, Sergeant Moore figured there was a strong possibility that Chandler was the person who had killed Joan Rogers and her daughters, Michelle and Christe, just two weeks after the rape of the Canadian tourist. While the detectives continued working to gather enough evidence to charge Chandler with the murders, Chandler was held in jail in lieu of a $1 million bond on the rape charge.

While he was in custody, the authorities slapped another charge on Chandler for an unrelated $750,000 armed robbery, which had occurred September 11, 1992, outside a motel in Pinellas Park, near St. Petersburg. Chandler was alleged to have robbed, at gunpoint, two employees of a wholesale jewelry manufacturer with headquarters in California. According to Assistant State Attorney Bob Lewis, the property was recovered from Chandler's car, home, and from his relatives and friends he had sold items to in the states of Ohio and Kentucky.

By this time, St. Petersburg Chief of Police Terry Upman was ready to charge Oba Chandler with the murders of Joan, Michelle, and Christe Rogers. The similarities between the rape and the slayings were too many to ignore. In addition, the police had now lifted Chandler's palm print from the tourist brochure found in Joan Rogers's car.

The local grand jury decided that Oba Chandler should stand trial for the slayings of Joan, Michelle, and Christe Rogers. On Tuesday, November 10, 1992, he was indicted on three counts of first-degree murder.

At his murder trial during the last week of September 1994, five years after the bodies of the Rogers women had turned up in Tampa Bay, Chandler waived his right to remain silent and testified in his own behalf. Executive Assistant State Attorney Doug Crow asked him several times about the Madeira

Beach rape for which he had been accused and which had similarities to the murder.

"I will answer no questions, sir, that relates to that case," Chandler said, citing the Fifth Amendment.

"Did you meet the Rogers women in Tampa?" Crow asked.

"I don't remember," Chandler answered, noting that he drove 40,000 to 50,000 miles a year while working in the Tampa area and he could not recall everybody he met.

Chandler later admitted that he had given Michelle Rogers directions to the Rocky Point Days Inn motel when he'd stopped at a convenience store, just off Interstate 275, in Tampa. "Michelle pulled herself from the car window. I could see her pulling herself up over the roof of the car," he said, noting that the teenage girl handed him a brochure and he wrote down directions to the motel.

When the three female floaters appeared in the bay three days later, Chandler told the court he didn't realize they were the same people he had directed to the motel. He said he finally recognized Michelle Rogers's photograph in the newspaper when an article appeared linking the Madeira Beach rape with the Rogers murders. Once he saw authorities were checking the handwriting samples, he said, "I panicked—it freaked me right out."

Chandler declared that he did not remember where he was on the evening of June 1 and morning of June 2, when the women were murdered, until he saw his own phone records, which showed that he had used his cellular phone to call home from his boat. He had been out fishing on Tampa Bay, he said, and his boat had broken down, so he ended up staying out all night. Chandler explained that his gas line had sprung a leak. He tried to flag down a Coast Guard vessel, but the crew did not respond to his call. Later that morning, two men and a woman came by in a boat and helped him tape up his gas line so he could return to shore.

In November 1989, Chandler knew he was a suspect in the

homicide, he testified, but his reason for fleeing the state was the Madeira Beach rape.

When Prosecutor Crow asked Chandler if it worried him that he was suspected of the Roger murders, Chandler replied, "Well, it worried me, but I figured you people were smart enough to find out who did it."

"Perhaps we have, Mr. Chandler," Crow shot back. Chandler said that in November 1989, he went to Ohio to "make some money" to hire an attorney in case he got arrested on the beach rape case. He used pay phones to call his home in Florida to inquire if police had been to his house looking for him, in case his own telephone was tapped.

In June 1989, Chandler moved to California, but stayed there less than a month because he found the cost of living was too high. Then he moved to Ormond Beach, a city on Florida's east coast, where he stayed for a year.

The day after Chandler testified, rebuttal witnesses for the state contradicted his testimony. The prosecutors obtained an expert boat mechanic who had designed fuel systems for several kinds of vessels to go to the police impound and check Chandler's boat to see if there could be any truth to his fuel-leak alibi.

The expert testified that it would have been impossible for the gas tank to have gone dry, as Chandler had said. The boat had an anti-siphon valve, which has been standard equipment on boats for more than a decade, to prevent fuel from draining due to a leak in the line. Even if the fuel line were to rupture, the gas would not leak out because, as the mechanic explained, "The fuel line and all the connections are above the top of the tank." Gravity would therefore prevent the fuel from running out of the tank.

Chandler's defense attorneys asked the judge for permission to bring in their own boat expert from Tarpon Springs, since the prosecution had called a surprise witness after Chandler's testimony. Circuit Judge Susan Schaeffer allowed the defense to contact their own expert, but after the attorneys conferred with that expert, they decided not to call him as a witness.

Normally, under Florida law, a surprise witness cannot be called to the witness stand. In this case, however, since the prosecutors didn't know in advance what Chandler would say on the witness stand, they were allowed to bring in the boat expert following Chandler's testimony.

After closing statements were presented, it took the jury one and a half hours to return a verdict. They found Oba Chandler guilty as charged. One juror was later quoted as saying that the guilty verdict had been settled upon only 10 minutes after the panel went into deliberations, but they were emotional and needed time before returning to the courtroom. In the penalty phase, it took the same jury 30 minutes to recommend that Oba Chandler should be executed in Florida's electric chair.

Oba Chandler had a smirk on his face when he entered the courtroom for his presentencing hearing on October 8. That day, he was not dressed in the gray suit he had worn during the trial. His attire was the dark-green jail garb. Judge Schaeffer asked Chandler if there was anything he wanted to say to the court at that time. Chandler politely said no.

Chandler sat at the defense table, fingering his reading glasses, sometimes putting them on, sometimes just holding them in his hand, while his attorney argued that he be permitted to live rather than be put to death in the electric chair. While the lawyers talked, Chandler would cock his head first to one side, then to the other. He put on his glasses and seemed to be following along on a copy of cases his attorneys quoted from.

Then the defense attorneys brought up Chandler's troubled childhood, telling of how his father had committed suicide while Chandler was just a boy.

But Executive Assistant State Attorney Doug Crow could not see showing Chandler any mercy for the heinous killings he was convicted of. "The jury's verdict was reasonable," Crow said to the judge, pointing out that a unanimous decision by a jury to impose the death penalty on a convicted killer is a "rarity."

Crow restated how horrifying the experience must have been for Joan Rogers and her daughters, Michelle and Christe. He went over how Chandler charmed them onto his boat, and then, out on the dark bay, where the women were alone and helpless, he gagged them with duct tape, stripped them from the waist down, and tied their hands and feet. Finally, he tied a "noose" around each of their necks and weighted them down with concrete blocks.

"We can only imagine how it was on that boat," Crow said. "While three people had nooses around their necks, duct tape on their mouths, bound, and weighted down with concrete blocks, then a sibling, or mother—or even worse for Joan Rogers—to be in that state while she awaited the deaths of her daughters, tossed one by one over the boat into the bay."

Chandler showed no emotion as he heard Crow say, "This is an overwhelming case for the death penalty."

Judge Schaeffer agreed. At Chandler's sentencing on Friday, November 4, 1994, Schaeffer said, "Oba Chandler, you have not only forfeited your right to live among us, but under the laws of the state of Florida, you have forfeited your right to live at all."

Judge Schaeffer ordered that Oba Chandler, now age 48, be transported to the Department of Correction in northern Florida, to be held on death row while awaiting his rendezvous with Florida's electric chair.

"CATCH THE PERVERT WHO PREYS ON JOGGERS!"

by Peter Depree

As she glanced outside her apartment's bay window over-looking Georgetown, Jennifer Coruzzi wrinkled her nose. There they were, the same muck of purplish clouds that had hung stubbornly over Washington, D.C., all that Saturday, March 31, 1990, imbuing everything with an awful and chilly dampness. It couldn't have been more than 40 or 50 degrees. So, even though it was only a 10- to 15-minute ride by bike to her boyfriend's apartment in Rosslyn, Virginia, the 25-year-old recent college grad pulled on a pair of sweatpants over her knee-length spandex bicycle pants and a sweatshirt over several layers of T-shirts, then laced up her Reeboks. It was 6:55 P.M. and the sun had already gone done by the time Jennifer wheeled her blue mountain bike onto the sidewalk and hopped on, but there was a swatch of afterglow in the sky, and if she pedaled hard, Jennifer might just make it before dark.

Five minutes later, at seven o'clock, a 24-year-old woman was jogging down the Martha Custis bike trail in Rosslyn, Virginia, opposite the sound wall that buffered off the Lee

Highway. At the same moment as the first stars began to appear, the woman heard footsteps behind her. There was something frantic in the particular cadence, and when she glanced around, she noted a heavyset, muscular-looking black male in a navy-blue sweatsuit. The woman picked up her pace. The man picked up his. She went from a fast jog to a hard run. So did the man. She began to sprint. The man matched her. No other runners were around. And he was gaining on her.

The woman slammed into the security entrance of her apartment in the 1600 block of North 21st Street, burst in, and locked the door behind her. Collapsing hysterically into tears, she ran up the steps and double-bolted herself in her apartment. For a long time she couldn't erase a mental picture of herself, violated, leaves in her hair, staring up helplessly at the figure in the sweatsuit. And he had no face. The woman grabbed the phone and punched in the emergency number.

Meanwhile, Jennifer Coruzzi sighed blissfully as she stepped into the early-spring twilight and drew in the cool air. The nubbed gumwall tires of her bike raced over the cobblestones as she cut down one of Georgetown's side streets, then raced across Key Bridge with traffic whizzing past. As she crested each hill, Jennifer didn't see any of the joggers, power-walkers, or cyclists who usually peppered the popular Custis trail on warmer days. Her path clear, Jennifer gunned the mountain bike, pedaling furiously to build up momentum before the next hill.

As she picked up speed for the next hill, Jennifer barely noticed a man on the other side of the path strolling toward her. As they approached each other, they made brief eye contact, but the only thought that registered in Jennifer's mind was that the stranger had "an unthreatening face."

Before Jennifer knew what was happening, the man clotheslined her off her bike. Jennifer went sprawling across the blacktop and into the grass, almost landing in the ditch.

"And then," she would later recall, "I was jumped on from behind. I tried to say something. I didn't really scream a lot because I was more scared than anything else. I attempted to talk to this person, but anytime I tried to turn my head around, he would hit me or push my head away so I couldn't see."

Pressed flat, with the man's full weight atop her, Jennifer's heart pounded with fear. "And he began to hit me in my head, my sides, my face. Hard enough that I thought that he was trying to knock me out. But I kept trying to turn to him to see who it was, or to just reason with the person. But anytime I did that, he'd hit me again. With his fists. Both of them, because, depending on how I'd squirm, he'd have to hit me with the other hand and also close my eyes. He would never let his hands off my eyes.

"And then I said a few times, 'Please don't hit me anymore.' I mentioned that I had a purse connected to my bike. I said, 'There's money in my purse, please go get that. Don't hurt me.' But he didn't care. And when I stopped squirming around, he began to pull at my pants. I had two layers on, but he got my pants partway down."

At that same moment, coming from the other direction and heading east, Georgetown Law Center student Bob Hoyt was racing his bike. Late for a banquet he was supposed to attend at Georgetown University at 7:30, Hoyt, too, was in a hurry. As he passed the yellow stanchion at the start of the sound wall, Hoyt was pedaling as fast as he could, hurtling downhill. Barely glancing up as he shot by Jennifer and her assailant, he merely jigged his bike over to the left momentarily. There was a man kneeling over near a fallen mountain bike. They made eye contact as he passed. Nothing more. But then as the mental snapshot registered, Hoyt's curiosity was aroused. Still not braking, he briefly glanced back over his shoulder. Then he saw it. In that one split second glance, he saw the man throw a punch at the ground. Reacting instantaneously, Hoyt jettisoned his bike and sprinted back.

"Initially he didn't spot me as I was going up the path toward the bike and where he was," Hoyt would later tell police. "Then he saw me. He picked up a purse and proceeded up the path where I had just biked. He was running and I was racing after him."

Chasing after the assailant as far as the crest of the hill, Hoyt lost him as he made a right onto North Quince. Pumped on adrenaline, puzzled, and still not having seen Jennifer, Hoyt headed back for his bike and walked right past the other blue mountain bike ditched on the side of the path before he heard a rustling sound. He turned. There was a girl, face and sweat-shirt covered in blood, pants and panties down around her ankles.

"I asked her to put her sweatpants and panties on," Hoyt would recount to police, "then she started screaming how she was attacked by someone. I didn't want to touch her because I felt she'd been assaulted, so I tried to look her over to see if she had any stab wounds or bleeding from anyplace I hadn't seen." Reassured that she would survive, Hoyt helped Jennifer hobble up the hill to the nearby Fort Georgetown apartment complex where they sought help.

Although a police cruiser was dispatched to respond to the 1500 block of Lee Highway, Officer Stuart Chase, of the Arlington County Police Department, was in the neighborhood and volunteered to take the assault call. Flagged down by a tenant, he arrived at the apartment at 7:20, within two minutes of the call and less than 10 minutes after the assailant had been seen supposedly fleeing.

Chase frowned as he noted the obvious trauma to Jennifer Coruzzi's face—her left eye was already starting to goose-egg, blood was pouring from her swollen nose and one of her ears, and deep abrasions marked her face, elbow, and legs. Her sweatpants were shredded and her hair was mussed.

After clearing his radio and calling for a medical unit, Chase worked with the hysterically crying victim to try to get a description of her assailant—an urgent requirement. Jennifer and Hoyt concurred on all points. The attacker was a black man with medium-to-dark-complected skin, 25 to 30 years old, standing 5-foot-9 to 5-foot-10 with a stocky upper build, probably somewhere around 195 pounds. He had, they told Officer Chase, no facial hair, no obvious scars, no jewelry, no eyeglasses. His hair was short, with no signs of receding hairline or baldness. He wore a plain navy-blue matching zippered sweatsuit (they couldn't recall if it had a hood or not), and light, perhaps white, sneakers. There was no distinctive cut to, or brand name visible on, the shoes.

Officer Chase paused for a moment, deep in thought about the details he'd just been told. No identifying lettering on the assailant's shoes or sweatsuit. Navy blue to blend into the night. No distinctive jewelry. Didn't say anything so his voice wouldn't give him away. It sounded as though the attacker had planned it all out, premeditated.

Along with the thumbnail description, Chase immediately broadcast the supplementary BOLO information that the assailant had last been seen fleeing west. Two more Arlington County uniforms entered the bike path at the Lion Village area west of the attack site and began walking east in hopes of intercepting the attacker. Meanwhile, other officers in cruisers were circling the block and surveying the surrounding areas while a K-9 officer from the Falls Church Police Department tracked his German shepherd through the area in an attempt to pick up a spoor.

There was only one glitch here, one factor that nobody could have been aware of at that moment: The assailant had never fled the area. He was right there, almost next to them!

Not a quarter of an hour later, pretty paralegal Anne Elizabeth Borghesani grinned to herself as she trotted down the concrete steps from her one-bedroom unit in the Fort Bennett garden apartments on North 21st Street and onto the Custis trail. A bunch of Anne's friends were getting together to throw her a belated 23rd birthday party in Crystal City, and she didn't want to be late. Not owning a car, Anne had learned this five-minute shortcut to the Metrorail's blue and orange lines station at Rosslyn by rote. She was barely paying attention to where she was going, her head filled instead with visions of the good cheer ahead, with her as the center of attention.

The man in the matching sweatsuit seemed to blend into the darkness at the base of the sound barrier buffering the bike trail for Lee Highway. It was now only 20 minutes after the attack on Jennifer Coruzzi and not 100 yards from the site. Although not overly large, the attacker's muscles were thick and powerfully developed, and he moved with a congested tension as he paced slowly back and forth. Jennifer's blood was still crusted across his knuckles, and psychosexual fantasies were mushrooming in his brain.

Coming over the small rise in the concrete bike path, Anne could see only impenetrable blackness below, a sharp-edged shadow cast by the sodium-vapor lights of the highway beyond. The bike path itself was poorly lit, and Anne picked her steps more from memory than sight. Her friend had promised cake and ice cream.

In the pooled shadows below, the powerful man ran one stubby finger down the zippered front of his sweatsuit and paused at his emerging erection, then his hand slid on and withdrew an object from his waistband.

Anne could only have believed that she was now on the crest of an exhilarating new independence in her life. As her first year in the Washington area was drawing to a close, the nervous energy that had accompanied her move the previous spring from the dorm at Tufts University was mellowing out. An international relations major, Anne had gone on to prove herself at her demanding position as a legal assistant with a downtown D.C. law firm and was settling into the refreshing camaraderie of a coterie of friends as dedicated and idealistic as herself. Just the month before, Anne had excitedly informed a family member that she had decided to apply to law school.

The assailant felt all his muscles tense as he fingered the sharpened edge of the Stanley-brand awl he drew from his waistband. An ice-pick-like instrument used for punching holes in leather, it was a sturdy length of steel riveted into a spherical bulb of knurled cherry that fit neatly into the coarsened palm of his hand. The punching-tine of steel jutted comfortably between his index and middle fingers when he made a fist.

Meanwhile, at that exact moment, the force of Arlington officers who had responded to Jennifer Coruzzi's beating was running field interviews in the apartments on the hill above this little valley, while others were still combing in sweep-searches through the underbrush and thickets. Incredibly, the assailant was actually operating inside the area that was crawling with police and K-9 rottweilers!

As Anne Borghesani passed the yellow center stanchion marking the beginning of the sound wall and the switch from concrete to blacktop, she glanced at the posted sign warning cyclists to reduce speed to five miles per hour. This last length of bike path, no more than 30 yards long, was a final enclosed stretch before the trail opened out onto Lee Highway. Four overarching lights threw weak cones of sodium light on the path and, further on, a faint glimmer shone from the smoked-glass windows of the terraced Air Force Building at the path's end, on the corner of North Oak and Lee Highway. What the waiting assailant knew—in fact had now thrice chosen this spot for—was that this last stretch was completely and dangerously bracketed in. The 20-foot-tall sound wall blocked in one side. Then, two to three feet from the path on the other side was a meandering V-shaped concrete drainage ditch, a thicket of brambles, stinging nettle and gooseberry, then a steep hill banking up to a six-foot-tall Cyclone fence that hedged in the other side of the trail. Anyone trying to suddenly flee the area would find the other two ends hemmed in, as well. The path curved up another steep hill to one end, while the other side narrowed abruptly at the adjacent Air Force Building to create a bottleneck before opening onto Lee Highway.

At the exact moment that Anne reached the bottom of this deadly basin, the man in the dark sweatsuit stepped into her path, trembling violently with excitement. The sweat that streamed down his face diluted the back-spattered blood from his ferocious beating of Jennifer Coruzzi 20 minutes earlier and ran it in rivulets (tinctured a cobalt-green under the sodium-vapor light) through the creases of his cheeks. Anne could barely see the man's tiny eyes socketed in the deep declivity under his massive brown eyes that seemed spaced too far apart, like a hammerhead. Anne's mind made the traumatic jag from anticipated images of cake, birthday candles, and laughing friends to this stranger with the blood-spattered face, lunging for her, the odd spike of sharpened steel pointing from his fist, the menacing bulge in his blood-caked sweatpants.

But in the millisecond it took for a mental picture to register and before she even realized it, Anne had bolted toward and past the predator.

Taken completely by surprise, the man spun around in a crouch and sprinted after Anne. At the last second, he grabbed out, his trembling fingertips lingering for the briefest moment at the collar of Anne's plaid shirt, a moment when she must have realized that only four more steps would have brought her out onto the busy highway and freedom, past the Air Force Building and into the open.

But the assailant's fingers caught hold, wrapped over a handful of plaid collar, and jerked Anne back with almost superhuman strength. Although the sound wall did a poor job of masking the roar of six lanes of traffic, Anne's screams were so loud and piercing they were heard by residents of the apartments overlooking the path from atop the steep hill, some who had just been interviewed by officers responding to the Coruzzi attack. They all shrugged it off.

Anne kicked, bit, and scratched her attacker ferociously, but to no avail. Inexorably, the muscular man in the bloody sweatsuit pulled Anne back over the concrete ditch and around the foliage at the side of the building, then wrestled her past an open-air cafeteria patio and down an L-shaped fire stair. When Anne resisted, the assailant smashed her in the face and head full force, battering her features into bloody disfigurement.

And here it all ended in a fusillade of 21 excruciating punctures from the sharpened awl. The attacker punched the weapon through Anne's breastbone, burying the awl down to the chrome-vanadium steel of the hex shank, ripping through her flesh with such force that pathologists would later find carve marks on her bones.

Grabbing futilely onto the salmon-colored handrail, Anne left long smears of blood as her assailant pulled her down, step by step, to the final landing, still stabbing and puncturing. For the tough spots, he leaned his weight into the awl. One thrust was so ferocious that the awl went in the back of Anne's neck and came out through her open mouth. As Anne bit down instinctively on the blade, the attacker calmly pushed at the base of her skull with the heel of his hand to free the wedged spike.

Anne's trembling hand left clear palm prints on the mustard-colored steel fire door to the underground garage as the assailant tore her panties completely off, mounted her, and raped her. Anne might have been trying in one final vain attempt to summon help, a last pounding on the fire door to alert someone, or her hand might have simply flopped there. Perhaps she had already gone into seizure, or perhaps she was dead. Her attacker, oblivious, continued to thrust.

Sated finally, the savage assailant ripped off Anne's earrings, tearing the lobes, and twisted off her two rings. Then, snatching up her purse and tucking it under his shirt, he trotted up the steps and began jogging. . . .

Meanwhile, in their shared Crystal City apartment, a classmate of Anne's from Tufts and her roommates had finished cleaning up and baking Anne's birthday cake and were almost ready for the evening. Anne was due at eight o'clock. The friends had phoned Anne that afternoon to make sure she would make it, but the three young women lost track of the time as they became absorbed in decorating the birthday cake.

When the doorbell rang at 8:20, two other friends came in. They expressed surprise that they were the first guests there and wondered where the birthday girl was. One woman glanced at the clock and concurred. She would later say, "We figured by twenty after eight, Anne should probably have been there because she was a very on-time person who definitely wouldn't be late for her own birthday."

At about the same time, around 8:30, a scattering of residents on 21st Street who happened to be glancing out their windows spotted a man running from an abandoned house to a garage and then into the inky-black woods toward the Potomac River.

Back at the Crystal City apartment, more time passed as other guests arrived. The fact that everyone invited had been late for the party didn't offset the worry they were beginning to feel. They picked up the phone and dialed Anne's apartment in Rosslyn to find out if she had been delayed somehow. They got no answer and figured it meant that Anne was on her way.

"I don't remember at what point we became really concerned," one friend would later recall, "but it was very unlike her not to just show up or call. We started taking some action, calling the Metro police to see if there had been an accident on the subway. Eventually, we all went out looking. Some friends walked to the Metro. Other people cruised around Crystal City in the neighborhood. And two of my friends actually drove all the way to Rosslyn to check Anne's apartment. We tried to come up with scenarios for why she was late."

Several of Anne's friends were still walking the bike path after the sun had risen the next morning. At 8:25 A.M., a male friend of Anne's was kicking through the brush next to the Air Force Building when he heard a dull moan and turned. It was another friend whose voice was quaking. "Can you come here?" she asked. "There's something really gross down here. I think it might be a vagrant."

The male friend rushed over and gazed down into the stairwell. It was no vagrant.

"I knew it was Anne," he would later say. "I'd figured out which coat she would've been wearing because I looked in the closet and figured out it was blue. And I saw that color blue coat, unfortunately. And Anne was there, as well. There was blood all over the place, coming out of her mouth."

At 10:15 A.M., Detective Stephen R. Carter arrived to supervise the crime scene. A 24-year veteran with the Arlington County Police Department, Carter had eight years with robbery-homicide, eight years that didn't make this scene one bit easier. It was hard not to turn and bolt. Permeating the air was the familiar "old iron" stench of blood, along with the creepy feeling that the site now had a numen, a "bad soul," that would linger at the scene of the violence that had taken place here, haunting it.

After conferring with Detective Robert Carrig who gave him a quick overview, Carter ducked under the yellow crime-scene ribbon and descended the two tiers of steps. It was a nasty one all right, a long duration killing, a virtual abattoir in the open air. On the bottom landing, sprawled on the concrete at a diagonal to the drain, was the deceased, a white female, nude from the waist down, on her back with her hands raised up in cadaveric spasm. She was in plus-four rigor mortis, her heather-gray eyes staring up unseeing, her complexion blue. Insect activity had already begun. She was the apparent victim of massive cerebral-cranial blunt force trauma and pronounced hematoma. Blood was streaked everywhere, in the cracks of the firebaked brick, squirt lines 15-feet high across the landing ceiling. It had dripped geometrically along the grout lines. If you looked hard enough, it seemed to make words.

Flashbulbs were going off as forensic technicians photographed the high-speed-spattering tracks crisscrossing the stairwell walls. Other techs spooned up blood samples for transport to the evidence-room refrigerators. Detective Carter trudged back up the steps for a breather, but the evidence of how ferociously Anne Borghesani had fought for her life was everywhere. Bloody hanks of her hair, ripped out by the roots, littered the lawn. More gaudy palm prints patterned the brick and railing. Skidmarks from a pair of bare heels had dug divots up out of the lawn and left blood and skin across the sidewalk.

With a baggage-style tag figure-eighted and snapped over the big toe, the corpse was wrapped in plastic sheeting, zippered into a rubber body bag, strapped snugly into a collapsible gurney, and loaded into the coroner's refrigerated van for transport to the morgue's freezers.

Detective Carter thought to himself. The victim's earrings had been torn from her lobes but were on the ground next to her. Two white bands around her fingers suggested that the killer had made off with a couple of rings. And her purse was missing. Tough as it was, the next order of business was to contact Anne's roommate and family and get a description in case the valuables turned up. Carter discovered that Anne's purse was designed by Liz Claiborne, light gray, about five-by-eight inches. One of the rings was a Tufts graduation ring with her name inscribed on it.

At the autopsy, Detective Carter observed as Dr. Francis P. Field, a coroner with the Northern Virginia Medical Examiner's Office, found a pubic hair on the sheet Anne was wrapped in. Another negroid pubic hair that had become tangled up in Anne's pubic hair was tweezered out and sealed in a small ziplock Baggie.

Studying the small puncture holes after cleaning the wounds, Dr. Field dictated into her suspended mike about angles, depths, probable thrust force, and blade-edge characteristics, surmising that they could have been caused by any one of a multiplicity of weapons: penknife, sharpened screwdriver, a nail or spike of some sort, one blade of a scissors, perhaps. An ice pick, she told the detectives, would have been too thin to make these wound "mouths." Her best "guesstimate" was that the weapon was a blade or a shaft three and a half to four inches long and not more than a quarter of an inch in diameter, with an extremely sharp tip. And Detective Carter had been right. It had been a protracted long-duration killing. But, although some of the thrusts had reached the big veins (the ca-

rotid and left and right ventricular jugulars), only three of the
stabs (one to the heart, one to the throat, and one in the left
lung) were necessarily fatal. "Insanguination," the M.E. scribbled; Anne Borghesani had drowned in her own blood.

Meanwhile, another medical examiner took vaginal swabs.
After testing with a Woods light showed the smears positive
for acid phosphotase, indicating the presence of semen, they
were signed over to another uniformed officer who rushed
them to the property-room refrigerator.

The victim's mother took the murder brutally hard. She
would later write, "The mother-daughter relationship was especially strong between us. Anne was my best friend. We
laughed and cried together, had our silly private jokes, worried
over family problems, planned and cooked for holiday cele-
brations."

Devastated, too, was the emotional tranquility of the usually
placid Arlington community, the triple almost back-to-back attacks ranking big front-page headlines in local papers for
weeks. Many women now carpooled instead of walked, most
avoiding the bike trails entirely.

To further tie the three incidents together into a mini-spree,
six days after the assaults and slaying, the purses of both Jennifer Coruzzi and Anne Borghesani were found together in a
homeless area on a hill nearby. More than two dozen officers
in slickers and galoshes had been exhaustively picking through
the marshy grass and over the trails, quadrant by quadrant,
from Quinn to Rhodes Street on both sides of Lee Highway.
They were into the thick underbrush and woods near the Scott
Street Bridge, two blocks from the killing, when they came
across the handbags.

But it would be a full four and a half months after the Custis
trail triple attack, on the swelteringly hot morning of August
18, when the assailant would strike again on another recreational path, this one in South Arlington. About 9:30 that morning, 42-year-old Rosslyn lawyer Kathryn Hutton was
power-walking briskly past the mile-2 marker on the Washing-

ton and Old Dominion recreational trail in South Arlington, when, suddenly, she felt someone reach around her neck and begin pulling her violently over to the side of the trail and into the woods. The man's left arm was around Kathryn's waist, his right arm around her neck, and when Kathryn looked down, she could see a small knife about the size of the largest blade on a Swiss Army knife in his right hand. "Come with me!" the man hissed as he continued dragging Kathryn about 20 feet off the trail.

"Okay, okay, okay," the terrified lawyer just kept repeating.

"I got very scared," Kathryn would later recall, "so I peed in my pants and I told him this, told him how scared I was, and he dropped me. I ran back to the paved trail and started screaming."

The crowd of concerned runners who gathered around Kathryn Hutton discovered she was relatively unharmed and called police, who sped to the scene. But all Kathryn could tell the officers was that she thought she had seen part of a red sleeve. That was it.

Echoing the briefness of the lapses between the three attacks on March 31, the assailant was back in action two hours later.

Cynthia Ingersoll, an energetic 39-year-old computer programmer, was at that time finishing up what was to be a four-hour hike that morning. By 11:30, she had already walked up to Route 65 on the Washington and Old Dominion bike path and over to Best's, where she had bought some videotapes.

The man jogged past Cynthia, then instantaneously came up behind her and grabbed her with a knife pressed tight to her throat, forcing her off the trail. Cynthia had only one chance and she used it. With all her might she began to slam at the man's face with the bag of videotapes she carried, over and over again.

"He must have tripped on a rock or a root or something," she would later tell police, "because we fell to the ground. But he never lost his grip during that time. When we were falling, he never loosened his grip, and when we were lying on the ground, I thought I pretty much had him pinned down. But he somehow never loosened his grip. He managed to get up and pull me up with him. So I think he's tremendously strong.

"After lying there for a few seconds, he pulled me up, and I yelled for help a couple of times. And several people jogged into sight, and he ran. Two joggers coming down the path scared him away."

At the top of the hill in front of the Park Lane condominiums overlooking the bike path and the water, Margery Litton was sorting articles in the trunk of her car and had just stood up to wipe the sweat from her brow when, as she later told police, "This guy came running back of my car, right off the bike trail, running really hard. And I turned around and he about knocked me down and just kept on running. If he'd come any closer, he would've fallen over my jack and tripped."

As Margery watched him tear up to the back of the apartments, it struck her as odd that on a day as scorchingly hot as that one, a jogger would be sprinting, in sweatpants, no less. And Margery was somewhat miffed that he hadn't even paused to apologize for almost knocking her head over heels.

Meanwhile, Cynthia Ingersoll picked up her tapes and told the assembling joggers that her attacker was a black man who was wearing red sweatpants, white T-shirt (possibly with some red lettering on it), and black fanny pack, or waist wallet. She thought he stood a little taller than her 5-foot-four, but she couldn't guess his weight since she only saw his back as he was running up the trail. Nor could she even approximate his age. No, she hadn't glimpsed his face, either, but she did recall that he had a "high-topped" Afro.

Cynthia's legs were scraped and bruised. Later, she would discover a couple of knife nicks under her chin. She was in rough shape, and two fellow joggers supported her as they walked up the bike trail in the direction the attacker had fled toward.

The second time Margery Litton glanced up, she saw Cynthia Ingersoll being supported between the two joggers. Litton grimaced at Ingersoll's badly skinned knees and listened to their breathless account of the attack. She immediately made the connection with the sprinting man she had seen in the sweatpants and took the injured woman back to her apartment where they phoned the police.

Approximately 40 minutes later, Yetta Cohen, a department coordinator for Hughes Network Systems, was jogging in the lower half of the bike path between Walter Reed and George Mason. "I was in there because it was so hot and it's a shaded area," she would later tell police. She paced herself as she came up through the picnic area and onto a small footbridge over a creek, veering around a man who was sitting on the bottom rung of the bridge.

She would later tell police, "As I passed him, I can't explain this, I have said it to several people, I didn't feel comfortable . . ." In addition to the creepy vibes, Yetta, too, noticed his odd clothing. "It was an extremely warm day and I had a T-shirt and shorts on and I was very hot. And he had sweatpants on, and the first thing that crossed my mind was: if I was in those sweatpants, I'd be very, very hot."

Yetta began to run faster. "I didn't feel comfortable; I can't explain why, I just didn't. So I picked up my pace and went down the path and I turned around to see the man who was sitting on the bridge had now gotten up and he started to run."

James Lee Page, a motorcycle officer with the special operations section of the Arlington County police, was scheduled to work the county fair that Saturday morning but arrived late and snagged the assault call. Page mounted his 1000cc Harley-Davidson and screeched out of the back of the station. He headed west down Route 50, then cut south down George Mason Drive over Four Mile Run Drive, and then left onto the Barcroft bike trail. It was 12 minutes past noon.

Yetta Cohen ran faster. Almost automatically, the man following her picked up his pace, as well. He had a razor-sharp opened lockblade wrapped in his T-shirt, and he began to pant heavily as he struggled to overtake the jogger ahead. But Yetta had seen him, and knew how much closer he was. Fear began to beat in her chest. "So I picked up my pace again and I turned around, and the last time I saw the man that had been sitting on the bridge, he was about twenty yards behind me," she would later say.

Roaring down the narrow wooded trail, motorcycle officer Page picked up speed as he made a couple of turns heading toward Walter Reed and Shirlington Shopping Center. He zoomed past a female jogger running in the opposite direction with what he immediately spotted as "a look of fear in her eyes." It was Yetta Cohen. In the brief instant as he made the corner, Page spotted a black man running about a foot or two behind her who answered the description of the suspect in the assault.

"I was fairly new to the motor unit," Page would explain later, "and these motorcycles are enormous. I couldn't turn it around in that confined space. So I went down to the picnic area across a wooden bridge and turned around there and then raced back up the bike path."

Officer Page may very well have saved Yetta Cohen from the same sort of fate that befell Anne Borghesani. "I looked up again," Cohen would say, "and there was a motorcycle officer coming my way! I can't even tell you how happy I was to see him. I just took off."

Even as Yetta Cohen sprinted off, Officer Page corralled the suspect on the hanging bridge over Four Mile Creek, telling him that he was a suspect in an assault and asking for his ID. The exaggerated manner in which the suspect reached into his waist wallet and unzipped it using only his right hand struck the motorcycle officer as odd. The man had a sweat-soaked T-shirt wadded up in his left hand and appeared to be trying to make it inconspicuous around his side. When Page studied the driver's license for a Michael Charles Satcher of the 200 block of 38th Street, Southeast D.C., he was immediately suspicious.

By far the most drug-ridden and crime-infested quadrant of the District, Southeast produces almost all the homicides for the city. Whereas Arlington had only one murder in 1989—Borghesani's was the first of 1990 and a record-breaking 10 Arlington homicides that year—the Southeast quadrant of D.C. alone would come close to 400.

"Let's start with a simple one. What are you doing in Arlington on the bike trails when you live in Southeast?" Officer Page asked the suspect.

Satcher mumbled vaguely that he was visiting a friend who was busy doing something, so, naturally, he'd decided to go for a run.

Page shook his head and radioed for backup. When Arlington County Police Detective Brian Cammarata arrived, he also noted the nervous way Satcher was clutching his T-shirt to himself. "What's in the shirt?" he asked. But Satcher only squeezed it closer to his hip. Again he asked, and again the suspect clutched the shirt closer. Finally, tiring of the game, Cammarata snatched for it. An opened lockblade clattered out onto the bridge.

By now, other officers were arriving, including Detective Stephen Carter, who had helped work the Borghesani slaughter scene. And although the gathering uniformed officers were making the obvious connection here, they all kept a tight lip.

At noon, the police picked up Cynthia Ingersoll from her house and Margery Litton from her apartment and drove them back to the site where the suspect was being held for identification. Margery asked the police to have the suspect put his shirt back on. When he complied, Margery nodded. That was definitely the man, she said. And further corroboration was forthcoming.

Criminal Investigator Marion Douglas Triplett, of Arlington County, loaded the handcuffed Satcher into the back of the paddy wagon and drove him downtown to the Arlington County Detention Center.

After pulling into the jail's underground parking area, Triplett would later recall, "I unlocked the rear gate of the wagon to let Mr. Satcher out. When I was helping him down by holding his arm, with my other hand I patted him on the back and said, 'What's up?' Based on my experience and working in corrections, police feel that you want to ease [the tension] somewhat, so [a suspect] won't be a problem when you bring him in to fingerprint and photograph him." Triplett could hardly believe his ears when he heard Satcher's immediate and spontaneous response. "He said, 'The police are trying to frame me for a murder or something, or a rape.' "

Knowing full well that not a single officer had mentioned one word to Satcher about a possible link with the Borghesani case, Triplett was stunned.

Charged with two counts of abduction and one of malicious wounding, Michael Satcher was held on $40,000 bond, well out of his financial reach. He was staying put as detectives tried to figure out what they had here. Unmarried, with two children, Satcher, detectives discovered, was a 22-year-old mover for a furniture and storage company, with a lightweight arrest record. None of his priors (two felony PCP possession convictions in the District) hinted at the rage and sickness required to carry out the kinds of crimes they suspected him of. But he couldn't tell detectives where he was the night Anne Elizabeth Borghesani was punctured 21 times with a carving tool, then sexually penetrated—before, during, and after death.

"Naw, it ain't like that, homey," he told the detectives. Too much time had gone by for him to recall where he was on the night of August 31. Maybe he was at his girlfriend's crib in Southeast, maybe not.

But the sleuths had done their homework. They had combed through Satcher's 1984 Volkswagen Jetta and they had interviewed his family, friends, coworkers, and acquaintances. So they pressed on. Wasn't it true that he'd been scheduled to work that day? they asked Satcher. They had already conferred with Satcher's superiors at the furniture store in Capitol Heights, Maryland, who had checked payroll records and personnel files and seen his name on the schedule. His bosses had told sleuths that Satcher was regular as clockwork. It was very unusual that he'd miss a day like that without at least calling.

Did anything out of the ordinary happen that Saturday? detectives asked. Any wacky feelings that made you decide to play hooky?

Satcher just glowered, beads of sweat trickling down his pronounced forehead and glittering on his bushy eyebrows.

Detectives produced the Stanley-brand awl sealed in a transparent ziplock Baggie and slapped it on the table. "Maybe you could tell us just what this was doing in the glove compartment of your car," they said.

Satcher shrugged. "Every time it rains, the radio would drain the battery. It was the only thing I had to take the radio out."

Where'd he get it? they wanted to know. From a relative, he replied. When? Oh, around March or so, he said.

The detectives glanced at one another; Anne Borghesani was multiply punctured with a sharp instrument on March 31. This guy was either innocent or stupid, and he wasn't innocent. But, although Medical Examiner Field had assured them that the awl was perfectly consistent with Borghesani's fatal wounds, Amy Wong, the state serologist, in Fairfax, had been unable to discover any blood traces on it.

Their suspect was obdurate, but detectives had other ways of tying him in to the rape-murder. They took blood, hair, and saliva samples from Satcher, which they express-mailed to the Northern Virginia Forensic Laboratory in Richmond. There, serologic tests indicated that Satcher's blood was consistent with the rare type, found in only seven percent of the population, discovered in a pool near Borghesani's body almost five months before and carefully refrigerated.

On August 23, when the blood test results arrived, Satcher's bond was promptly revoked. Oddly, however, four days later, another batch of results would arrive indicating the "foreign" hairs combed from Borghesani's pubic area did *not* match Satcher's, so his bond was reinstated. The next, and conclusive, bioforensic step now was to compare the DNA in the sperm swabbed from the victim's vagina with Satcher's DNA.

Other than fingerprinting, DNA profiling is believed to be perhaps the most certain and foolproof way of linking a suspect to a crime. The genetic material in all living cells is purported to be unique from individual to individual, with the sole exception of identical twins. The state of Virginia spearheaded the use of DNA profiling in criminal cases, and convicted felons in Virginia are now required to give their blood up for testing and categorizing in a DNA data bank.

Virginia state serologist Richard Guerrieri at the forensics lab in Norfolk ascertained that the semen on the vaginal swab was intact, unadulterated, and not degraded by any moisture. After satisfying himself that the basic genetic material was in mint condition, he ran it through a series of exhaustive tests. The result was a clear match with the characteristics of the double-helix in Satcher's blood. Guerrieri tested it three more times to ensure an accurate reading, then, for additional confirmation, he had his supervisors test it all over again themselves. It would be two months before the key DNA results were back from the Norfolk lab, but they were worth waiting for, linking Michael Satcher to the crime scene beyond a shadow of a doubt. The suspect's bond was once again revoked.

On July 17, 1991, Circuit Court Judge Benjamin N.A. Kendrick slammed down his gavel and the trial began. It was reckoning time.

All too cognizant that their client was facing Virginia's electric chair, court-appointed Defense Co-counsels Richard McCue and John C. Youngs went all out to muddy the water, throw in red herrings, and raise the specter of reasonable doubt. They called a relative of Satcher's to the stand who testified that she always did Michael's laundry and he certainly didn't own any navy-blue sweatsuit. She said she never saw bloodstains on his clothes or found any women's jewelry in his pockets.

Cautioning jurors against "a rush to injustice," McCue tried to poke holes in the eyewitness identification, the DNA fingerprinting, and the serologic test results. He repeatedly underscored the fact that the foreign pubic hair had not matched Satcher's and that the blood test only limited the killer to seven percent of the population.

Targetting Jennifer Coruzzi and Bob Hoyt's joint description of the attacker as "clean-shaven" and weighing around 195 pounds, McCue put two of Satcher's relatives on the stand to say that at the time of Borghesani's murder, Michael was wearing a light beard and weighed no more than 150. Sensitive skin, they insisted, prevented Satcher from shaving closely.

After attempting to impeach the eyewitness testimony, McCue snatched up the composite sketch done by a police artist after the attack on Jennifer Coruzzi and paraded it before the jurors: "Look at it! The hair's too long, the face much too large, the neck way too wide. It's not even close."

The urgent tone underscoring their arguments was understandable. Both McCue and Youngs knew that although some southern states sentenced more men to the chair than Virginia did, the Commonwealth had a reputation for actually carrying out a much higher percentage of their death penalty convictions.

The jurors—five women, seven men, and two alternates—listened carefully but appeared unimpressed.

Then, as cleanly as picking the wings off an overbroiled turkey, Commonwealth attorney Helen F. Fahey began to take Satcher's defense apart piece by piece. "Do you happen to remember where you were August thirty-first?" she asked. "What you did that day?" No, he sure didn't. Starting to turn away, Fahey shrugged briefly, as though willing to concede the point, then spun around and slammed a glossy eight-by-ten crime scene photo in front of Satcher. It was Anne Borghesani at the bottom of the stairs. "Why don't you take a good look at that picture?" Fahey snapped, staring Satcher in the eye. "See if it helps to refresh your memory."

The prosecutor wanted to make it crystal clear to the jurors that with the ejaculant that Satcher left at the crime scene, and the incredibly delicate genetic DNA code held in that semen, he had signed his own death warrant. "It's better than if he had dropped his driver's license by the body."

Fahey recapped testimony of the state's expert witnesses who had set the odds at 40 million to one that the particular DNA profile found in the sperm in the victim's butchered body had come from someone other than Satcher. And all the myriad other evidence must factor in, as well. "And who had an awl? He did. Do other people have awls? Sure, I suspect that some of you have an awl in your tool chest. How many of you carry one around with you? How many people do you think there are in the Washington metropolitan area who carry awls around with them?

"Does that rise to the level of the DNA evidence? No. But does it add something to your assurance? I suggest to you that it does. The serology. Here we're talking about another factor of ten. . . ."

And on and on. One bone at a time. Pick, pick, pick, until little was left of the defense team's turkey of a defense. Fahey, unflinching, relentless, even masterful at moments, choreographed each minute detail into its place in the totality of the case, building an ominous momentum. Then, turning to the state's ace in the hole, the relentless prosecutor apologized for the monumental amount of DNA theory and countertheory the jurors had suffered through. "We've all been here a long time and I'm sure, especially during the last week, it seemed at times that you were in the middle of a class on microbiology or probability theory." But, she continued, it was vital to understand the impact of the bio-forensic results on the question of guilt: "If you wanted to," the Commonwealth's attorney continued, brushing a strand of hair back from her eyes, "you could take that forty-million-to-one number and you could multiply by ten and make it forty billion."

The data, Fahey stressed over and over again, was irrefutable: "The only way I submit to you that you could sensibly, scientifically challenge that information is to come up with a Michael Satcher subpopulation which has a different structure, which has different gene frequencies than everybody else. Perhaps some kind of unknown genes."

After deliberating for two hours on Monday evening, the jury was spirited off and sequestered at an undisclosed motel overnight. Seven more hours of grueling testimony the next day, and they were ready.

They nailed him.

On Tuesday, July 30, 1991, the jurors found the young furniture-mover guilty of all charges. After unsealing them, Judge Kendrick handed the verdicts to the court clerk who crisply intoned one verdict after another. On the Jennifer Coruzzi matter, the jury recommended 12 months for the assault and battery, a decade for the attempted rape, and a term of life behind bars for the robbery. In the case of Anne Borghesani, they recommended a second term of life imprisonment for her robbery and a third for her rape. For the actual killing—a capital murder since it carried the "special circumstances" rider of having been performed in the commission of felony rape—they now had to decide whether Satcher would serve life without possibility of parole or burn in Virginia's electric chair on the capital charge.

On July 31, the defense co-counsels and the prosecution team presented their arguments against and for the chair.

Reminding the jurors that Satcher already had three life sentences, his counsel struggled to save their young client from the chair. "If they send that fatal charge of electricity through him," McCue said sternly, "the lights won't flicker on and off in your homes, but you'll know your role in the process. Take away his freedom, but don't take away his life."

Prosecutor Fahey countered, reminding the dozen jurors that Satcher was nothing less than a "vicious predator."

Satcher's relatives had their brief moment to beg for his life. One told the jurors that the defendant was gentle to a fault.

"Never was the type of kid who was violent. You had to push him hard before he'd fight back. Look, that person who committed those crimes is still out there. [Michael] just happened to be at the wrong place at the wrong time."

Tears streaming down his cheeks, the prison chaplain who had come to know Satcher recited the prisoner's "favorite" biblical piece from Psalm 31: "Have mercy on me Lord, for I am in trouble. I am forgotten like a dead man. Deliver me from mine enemies. Let lying lips be put to silence."

But it took less than three hours of debate for the jury to come back with a recommendation of the electric chair.

On December 16, Judge Kendrick concurred and passed the sentence of death upon Michael Charles Satcher, scheduling an execution date of June 26, 1992. Maintaining that the slaughter of Anne Borghesani exhibited "torture and depravity of mind beyond the minimum necessary to accomplish murder," and that it was an act "outrageously and wantonly vile," the judge appeared to have no doubts about his action.

Satcher, for his part, sat calmly in his denim shirt and new blue jeans, betraying (as he had throughout the trial) not the slightest flicker of emotion one way or the other. No, he had no last words, he shrugged. His lawyers had said it already. Attorney Youngs managed a brief pat on his shoulder as sheriff's deputies led the condemned man away to become the 45th prisoner on Virginia's death row.

If the Virginia average of a decade's delay for death sentence appeals holds true, Michael Satcher will be put to death in the year 2001.

"THE HUNT FOR POLLY KLAAS'S BRAZEN KILLER!"

by Turk Ryder

The search for Polly Klaas, the 12-year-old who was abducted from her home in Petaluma, California, in October 1993, set off one of the most massive manhunts since the Lindbergh kidnapping, involving dozens of investigators from the FBI, the California State Police, the Sonoma County Sheriff's Office, and the Petaluma Police Department. Additionally, Hollywood celebrities joined hundreds of volunteers in distributing millions of posters and collecting a reward fund that topped $300,000

In the end, however, the credit for breaking the case and bringing it to its tragic conclusion went to an unlikely pair of crimebusters: an ordinary mom out for a stroll and a beat cop who took the time to look through some trash in the woman's backyard.

It began shortly after 11 P.M. on Friday, October 1, 1993, when the pretty seventh-grader was reported abducted. Petaluma police sped to a modest home on Fourth Street, where they heard a bizarre story.

At 10:45 that evening, Polly and two friends were having a slumber party in the living room, while her mother and her 6-year-old half sister were asleep in the back bedroom.

The girls were engaged in a board game, when a man suddenly appeared in the living room, brandishing a knife. "Just do as I say and everything will be all right," he said menacingly.

The girls said they first thought it was one of Polly's infamous practical jokes. But one look at the man's face told them that this was no joke.

The man tied up Polly's two friends and put pillowcases over their heads. He told them not to move or make a sound until five minutes after he left. He took Polly with him.

The girls freed themselves and woke Polly's mom, who was sound asleep until they roused her, and told her what had happened. She called the police.

After questioning the two girls and assessing the situation, the patrol officers radioed headquarters. More police quickly arrived at the Klaas home and began an intensive search of the comfy, middle-class neighborhood.

The girls described the abductor as Caucasian, about 30 to 40 years old, with a beard and thick, wavy hair that hung shoulder-length. They had no idea who he was.

"We really thought this was one of Polly's practical jokes," one of the girls said. "But when we took the pillowcases off, they were gone."

The search continued well into the morning hours. A description of the pretty 12-year-old and her abductor was broadcast to law enforcement agencies in surrounding counties.

"Later in the day, the FBI entered the case, and a massive search was launched. Hundreds of volunteers participated in the field search and hastily printed posters bearing the kidnapped girl's likeness and a police sketch of the suspect.

The late-night abduction stunned the residents of Petaluma, a community of 45,000 north of San Francisco, which is such a picture of Middle America that Ronald Reagan used it to film TV ads in his 1988 presidential campaign.

No one was more surprised than Petaluma Police Chief Dennis DeWitt, who made the case a top priority and assigned 12 investigators to work the probe full-time. It turned out that every one of those investigators was needed, as news of the abduction spread, and tips flooded the special hot line set up by the police department. Within 24 hours, the detective team was fielding as many as 80 tips an hour. But none of the tips led to the whereabouts of the missing girl or the identity of the bearded, wavy-haired abductor.

The search was the largest in Petaluma history and one of the largest ever conducted in Sonoma County. A small group of residents, however, decided that they couldn't stand by doing nothing, so they began organizing a private effort to find the girl. It quickly mushroomed into a community phenomenon, with dozens of volunteers quickly signing up. With funds and organizational help from a San Francisco-based Kevin Collins Foundation, the group opened an empty storefront on Kentucky Street in Petaluma, which they called the Polly Klaas Volunteer Center. The group installed phone banks and, with the help of a local printer, began distributing posters of the missing girl and a sketch of her abductor.

As the center went into action, 600 volunteers began a second massive ground search, this time focusing on ranchlands, creeks, and fields in the Petaluma area that had not been previously searched. Led by tracking hounds, they combed the hilly, forested terrain, looking for anything that might lead them to the missing girl.

Meanwhile, psychologists offered free assistance to the students at the Petaluma Junior High School, where Polly had been a seventh-grader.

Just about everyone found it hard to believe that the friendly, popular student had fallen victim to such a shocking crime. They knew her not as the focus of a massive police search, but as the happy pal who liked to make up practical jokes and did a mean rendition of Elvis singing "Hunka Hunka Burning Love." She also did a hilarious imitation of a Chihuahua in which, according to one chum, "She'd stick out her tongue and move her eyes around."

"When I first met her she was shy," said the classmate who'd planned to take Polly to their school's winter dance. "All of a sudden, she blossomed into this hyper-fun person."

Polly was a good student who played the piano and clarinet and had joined the Petaluma Junior High band. "We thought the world of little Polly," one teacher lamented.

As students struggled to understand why their world had suddenly been turned upside down, the Petaluma investigators, now aided by local agencies and FBI agents, waded through the hundreds of tips that had been phoned in.

The avalanche of clues increased after the two girls who were tied up but left unharmed in Polly's room appeared on a special segment of *America's Most Wanted*. The segment was followed by a plea for help from the show's host, John Walsh, who had led a crusade against crime after his young son was abducted and murdered.

One person who was touched by the Polly Klaas story was Winona Ryder, the elfin, doe-eyed actress whose appearances in such glossy movies as *Bram Stoker's Dracula* and *The Age of Innocence* have made her one of Hollywood's hottest young stars. Ryder was more than just another celebrity hoping to gain a few headlines out of a big story. Ryder grew up in Petaluma and, like Polly, had been active in student drama courses.

On October 9, Ryder entered the investigation when she offered a $200,000 reward for anyone with information that would lead to the young girl's safe return. "We want Polly back," Miss Ryder told an assembled crowd of media hounds who had been covering the story since it first broke. "I am making a special plea to anyone who has seen Polly or knows something about the kidnapping but perhaps is afraid to come forward and tell what she or he might know. I hope that you will now do the right thing and come forward."

The response to the plea swamped telephone lines at the center, with many of the calls coming from anonymous tipsters who said that they had been too embarrassed to come forward because they did not think the information they had might prove valuable in the search. A few calls were placed directly to the task force of detectives who had been assigned to the Polly Klaas investigation.

The reward offer was followed a few days later by a detailed, life-size portrait of the abductor, released at a press conference. The portrait, which showed a square-faced man with thick, gray-streaked brown hair and a mustache and beard, was based on information given by Polly's two friends to a forensic artist.

"The girls had a good look at the man," said a detective who accompanied the artist at the media conference. "We are sure this is an accurate likeness of the kidnapper."

The sketch generated almost as many responses as the $200,000 reward fund. But it was one phone call in particular that got most of the attention. It came from a man who called the media center on October 19 and told the volunteer who picked up the receiver, "I know where the girl is. I kidnapped her."

The caller said he had been following the story in the newspapers and on television. He said the girl was unharmed, but he wanted $10,000 before she would be released. He wanted the money in small bills and he detailed a plan on where the money could be dropped. Once he got the reward money, he said, the girl would be released. He told the volunteer to follow the plan as he laid it out and not to call the police.

Later that afternoon, the police arrested a 20-year-old man in Petaluma on suspicion of extortion. After questioning him at headquarters, they determined that he had nothing to do with the kidnapping and was only trying to cash in on a quick $10,000.

Police continued working on other leads already developed in the three-week-old case. Another ground search was conducted, but it proved to be no more successful than the first one.

On October 25, Hollywood celebrities crowded the Burbank

Center for the Arts in Los Angeles and raised $30,000 for the Polly Klaas Fund, pushing donations to $250,000.

Some of the money was used to hire a famed San Francisco private investigator. The gumshoe conducted his own investigation, but he was unable to turn up any clues.

The departure of the San Francisco detective was the latest setback for police investigators and the Polly Klaas Foundation. In its one month of operation, the foundation had managed to raise $300,000, which was used to distribute over 8 million posters worldwide, and generate national interest which had produced almost 1,000 tips. Despite the whirlwind of activity, nothing had worked out. Polly Klaas was still missing.

The mood was no better at the Petaluma Police Headquarters. Task force investigators had spent thousands of man-hours pursuing clues and conducting searches, yet their efforts had led to only one arrest—that of a mindless numbskull who had purportedly tried to extort a quick 10 grand.

Perhaps no one was hit harder than Sergeant Mike Kerns, who met the daily barrage of news media at press conferences, whenever he was not personally involved in the field investigation. Kerns had tried to remain positive during the month-long search, and when he was asked if he thought Polly was still alive, he answered truthfully that he had no information to suggest otherwise.

The investigators, he said, were still working the case as if the pretty seventh-grader was still alive. He himself was still positive that the girl would be found.

But if she was, it would be by a task force that had been greatly reduced since it was formed almost a month earlier. At the height of the search, more than 50 police officers and FBI agents had been involved in the case. But by October 20, most of the FBI agents had been pulled from the search, saying that the "labor-intensive" phase of the investigation had been completed, and they could do nothing more. A week later, eight Petaluma detectives were reassigned to other cases, leaving just four to work the pile of dwindling tips.

No one wanted to admit it, but it appeared that the Polly Klaas abduction would soon join other cases in the steel file cabinet in the detective detail reserved for those cases that had not been solved.

What prevented that was the action of an unlikely pair of case-cracking sleuths—a mom out for a stroll and a cop who didn't mind nosing around garbage.

On Sunday, November 28, Laurie Berk, a 40-year-old Santa Rosa woman, was taking a walk near her home on her 188-acre ranch outside Santa Rosa, when she found some trash stuck partly hidden in waist-high grass.

She looked at the items, then stopped cold. Her mind flew back two months earlier to the evening of Friday, October 1. That day, she had been walking on her property when she encountered a man standing by a car stuck alongside her driveway. The man was sweating heavily and told her that he had run off the road.

The stranger so frightened her that she rushed into her house and called the sheriff's office. The stranger was questioned by deputies and let go, but she never forgot the expression on his face.

A few hours later, she learned about the search for Polly Klaas. Now she wondered if there might be a connection. She didn't know, but she figured that the discovery of the discarded items was worth a phone call.

Sheriff's Sergeant Mike McManus took the call. He could have dismissed it as just another dead-end tip from a well-meaning citizen, but instead, he went out to the ranch to check out the tip himself.

He met with Laurie Berk, who took him to the spot and told him about the stranger who had bothered her almost two months earlier. The discarded items included a dark-colored, adult-sized sweatshirt, several white cloth strips, and a used condom.

Sergeant McManus checked the files and pulled out the old field report. It showed that at 11:42 P.M. on October 1, Sonoma

County deputies had logged a call reporting a trespasser on Berk's property. The deputies responded at 12:08 A.M. on October 2 and found a man, identified as Richard Allen Davis, in his white Pinto stuck in a ditch. Davis told the deputies that he'd run off the road while sightseeing in the neighborhood.

The deputies were immediately suspicious—what was someone doing "sightseeing" at midnight? They ran a routine check to see if Davis was wanted by other law-enforcement agencies and for outstanding warrants. Upon finding none, they searched him and his car, checking the trunk for bloodstains and other evidence that might indicate foul play. Still not satisfied, the lawmen kept him at the scene, administering a sobriety test and questioning him for 38 minutes before finally telling him to get going.

It was, as Sergeant McManus noted, just a routine stop.

A criminal records check, however, revealed that the 40-year-old "sightseer" had a lengthy record that showed previous convictions for kidnapping, assault, burglary, and robbery. He had been on parole when he was stopped and questioned.

"Kidnapping!" McManus exclaimed, nearly jumping off his seat. He got another jolt when he obtained a Department of Motor Vehicles picture, which showed that Davis bore a striking likeness to the sketch of Polly's abductor.

Sergeant McManus contacted the Petaluma police and told them what he had. Investigators searched the spot where the items had been found and then turned the evidence over to the FBI, which sent them immediately to the agency's forensic experts in Washington.

The next day, the report came back that threads from the white strips matched the strips that were used to tie up the two girls in Polly's home.

On Tuesday, November 30, Petaluma police and FBI agents raided a house on the Coyote Valley Indian Reservation in Mendocino County, 100 miles north of Petaluma, and arrested Richard Davis, who was staying there—it was the home of a relative of his.

Davis had been living on the reservation since an arrest on a drunk-driving charge earlier in the month. He appeared surprised when the police burst into the wood-frame home where he was living, but he offered no resistance.

He was held for violating parole.

Davis appeared unruffled when he was returned to Sonoma County later that day. He was no stranger to the judicial system, after all. The report from the Department of Justice that had made Sergeant McManus almost leave his chair was a frightening document that portrayed the tattooed loner as a time bomb ready to explode.

One of five children, Davis had grown up in suburban San Mateo County, where he made a name for himself in the neighborhood by stealing checks from mailboxes and then forging them in his name.

By age 17, Davis had racked up a long list of arrests, and he was given a choice of going to juvenile hall or entering the Army. He enlisted, only to be discharged 23 months later because he fought with other soldiers and was unable to adjust to the discipline of barracks life.

In 1973, Davis's girlfriend committed suicide virtually in his presence. "I flipped out after that," he reportedly told a psychiatrist. "We were having fun at a party, and next thing I know, she croaked herself."

Davis claimed that he started suffering headaches and blackouts after his girlfriend's suicide and that she started talking to him from the grave. Sometimes she told him to take it easy and not blame himself for what happened to her. But at other times, the voice instructed him to commit crimes, including rapes against several women, because, secretly, "they wanted to be assaulted and robbed."

After a string of burglaries in San Mateo County, he was sent to state prison in 1975. Released after one year, he was quickly arrested again for kidnapping a woman from a Bay area subway station, placing a knife to her neck, and attempting to sexually assault her. The terrified woman broke free, and Davis was arrested.

During a psychiatric interview, Davis said he attacked the woman because he had the feeling that she wanted something done to her. "But I guess I was wrong," he said.

Davis was sent to jail in Alameda County, where he attempted suicide by trying to hang himself. That got him sent to the Napa State Hospital, where he escaped and was later arrested for assaulting a woman with a fireplace poker.

Davis spent five years in prison before he was released in 1982. Three years later, he was arrested again, this time for robbery and kidnapping. According to the police reports, Davis and a woman companion forced their way into another woman's apartment, attacked and beat her, then forced her to give them money from her bank account. Davis again went back to prison, this time for 16 years. He served eight years and was paroled on June 27. According to the State Department of Corrections, Davis had complied with the provisions of his parole, and there were no further indications of trouble until he failed to return from a family visit to Ukiah on November 15.

The police questioned Richard Davis about the disappearance of Polly Klaas. Initially, he declared that he didn't know what they were talking about. When they reminded him that he had been questioned outside Santa Rosa just hours after the girl had been abducted, he simply shrugged.

"You told the two deputies you were sightseeing?" one investigator asked.

"That's right," Davis replied, with a smirk.

"At midnight?" the detective shot back.

"I had nothing else to do," Davis said.

The convicted kidnapper did not give anything away. Having spent half his life behind bars, he knew the drill—if you have anything against me, fine, prove it.

The evidence against the reticent con quickly mounted. Fibers taken from the cloth strips used to tie up Polly's two friends matched the strips found near the spot where Davis had run his car off the road. The two girls also picked Davis out of a lineup as the man who had abducted Polly. But the icing on the cake came when the FBI matched Davis's left palm print to one found in Polly's bedroom.

Davis's shoulders slumped when he heard the bad news. Later that afternoon, he drew a primitive map on a sheet of paper. "She's there," he said, marking an "X" with the tip of his lead pencil.

The map led to a wooded area near U.S. 101, south of Cloverdale, 35 miles north of Petaluma. After scraping away brush and tree branches, the investigators found the mummified remains of Polly Klaas, still wearing the clothes she had on when she was abducted almost two months earlier.

On Sunday, December 5, while FBI agents searched for clues around the site where the girl's body was buried, hundreds of volunteers streamed into the search center in Petaluma, mourning the death of the town's adopted daughter. Vigils were held in the town square and Cloverdale, drawing hundreds of mourners. At the Polly Klaas Foundation Center, volunteers hugged each other and cried openly after they received the grim news. "We knew this was a possibility," one volunteer said. "But we were hoping for a miracle, that somehow there would be a happy ending to this ordeal."

Davis was arraigned on kidnapping and murder charges in Sonoma County Municipal Court. Spectators passed through metal detectors and under the watchful eye of sheriff's deputies to get their first live glimpse of the suspect.

A few minutes later, Davis made his first appearance. Wearing an orange jumpsuit, with his hands manacled and secured to a chain wrapped around his waist, he entered the courtroom with a jaunty bounce to his step. He smirked as the charges were read, his dark eyes glassy with merriment as he stared at the full-house reception. After pleading not guilty, he was hurried back to his cell. A defense attorney later said that Davis was very sorry and disgusted with himself for what he had done.

To the investigators, however, Davis did not appear disgusted when he recounted the murder of the young girl in his confession.

Davis said he was high on booze and drugs, driving aimlessly around Petaluma on the night of October 1. "I passed by this house and saw these girls through the window," he said.

He said he went to the house and, not seeing any adults, stormed inside. He tied up two of the girls and then took the third one from the house at knifepoint.

"Man, I was flying on all the dope and booze!" Davis said, describing how he pushed Polly into the car. He said he was still "flying" when he passed through Santa Rosa, then accidentally drove off the road at Pythian Road.

Davis claimed he left Polly unbound and ungagged about 60 feet from the car while he talked with deputies who arrived in response to a complaint.

"Man, I couldn't figure out why she didn't scream," Davis said. "She wasn't gagged or tied up. She could have come out any time."

He said that after the deputies left, he went looking for the girl and found her asleep. "I thought you had left me," he quoted her as saying.

Davis said he took the girl to an abandoned sawmill south of Cloverdale, where he strangled her and buried her underneath some scrap lumber.

Davis gave no motive for abducting the girl and insisted that he had not sexually assaulted her, even though a used condom was found in the items linked to Davis and the abduction. He said he thought he was initially going to be arrested for bank robbery when he was arrested, not the kidnapping.

The investigators believe that Davis killed Polly, but they don't believe many details of his story. "Polly would have screamed if she was able to," one of her relatives insisted. "If she had known that sheriff's men were only sixty feet away, she would have got their attention, that is for sure."

On Friday, December 10, Polly Klaas came home again—for one last time—as her grieving family and friends gathered at a memorial service at St. Vincent Catholic Church to honor the little girl whose honesty and decency had captured their hearts.

"We remember Polly, whose life and death brought our entire community to a whole new height of caring and love," the pastor of the church told the gathering. "It is a mighty legacy for a twelve-year-old girl to have given us."

More than 1,500 people held red roses and listened solemnly, sometimes in tears, as family, friends, politicians, a police officer, and two singers tried to ease the pain and make sense of the senseless kidnapping and murder.

Outside the Spanish Romanesque cathedral, a soft rain fell on a flotilla of TV remote trucks and nearly 4,500 people who overflowed onto the surrounding streets.

Among those attending the service were California's governor, Pete Wilson, Senator Diane Feinstein, and Representative Lynn Woolsey, who read a message from President Bill Clinton and Hillary Clinton.

"Her death is a terrible tragedy, unbelievably difficult to accept," the letter said. "We must draw strength from the knowledge that so many people bound together to help Polly and her loved ones during her moment of need."

Singer Joan Baez opened the service with the 19th-century hymn "Amazing Grace." The investigators struggled to fight back tears as Governor Wilson said, "For sixty-five days, we held our breath, hoping that the outpouring of love and support for Polly alone could bring her back. We know now that God had already called Polly home."

Pop singer Linda Ronstadt concluded the service when she took the podium with Polly's sisters and several of the slain girl's closest friends to sing several of Polly's favorite songs.

Polly's tragic death has led to a citizens' demand for tougher sentencing and lent a voice to California's "Three Strikes and

You're Out" initiative, which would mean a mandatory life sentence for anyone who is convicted of three felonies.

One of the promoters of the ballot is a man whose daughter was murdered in June 1992 by two prisoners out on parole. He described the killing as something "that poisons you forever. It leaves a hole in your heart that won't heal."

If the "Three Strikes" law had been on the books, Polly's alleged killer would have been behind bars, not loose roaming the streets on that cold October night, and the death of the innocent seventh-grader might never have happened.

Richard Davis is being held under tight security at the Sonoma County Jail, charged with the first-degree murder and, if convicted, facing a possible death sentence. Meanwhile, in accordance with his constitutional rights, he must be presumed innocent of the charges against him until and unless he is proven otherwise before a jury of his peers under due process of law.

"FIVE RAPED/MURDERED BY THREE-TIME SEX OFFENDER!"

by Christy Nash

Fear was growing in East Orange, New Jersey, with the news of yet another black woman savagely murdered. The city of 73,000 people borders Newark, which is one of New Jersey's largest cities. The crime occurred in a working-class neighborhood where decent people had to struggle to make ends meet from day to day.

Jamillah Jones, only 16 years old, was found dead at 2:49 A.M. on Friday, April 10, 1992, at the corner of Main and North Maple Streets in East Orange, her body covered with stab wounds.

Her family was devastated by Jamillah's death. "She was such a sweet girl, and so popular," said one of her relatives.

Jamillah had been out with her friends on Thursday night. They said she'd started back to her home at about 10 P.M. A male friend said he walked her part of the way. He left her at Main and Grove Streets. When he got to his own house, he telephoned Jamillah to see if she got home safely. To his dismay, she had not.

The friend immediately alerted Jamillah's family, who in turn called the East Orange Police Department. Officers responded right away. Detective Joseph Ash was put in charge of the case.

Usually, a 24-hour wait is required before a missing-person report may be filed officially. However, with so many murdered women having been discovered recently, Detective Ash knew it was important to move quickly in Jamillah's case.

Police officers went to the area where she was last seen and fanned out to begin a search. They scoured the streets, alleyways, dark corners, interiors of buildings, and any areas where a person's body could be stashed.

They issued a missing-person bulletin over the police teletype, alerting other local police departments of Jamillah Jones's description, hoping that she might still be alive. She could have encountered a carload of friends and have gone for a joyride. She was at an age at which she was very social, and her friends were beginning to get driver's licenses.

A few hours later, however, police found Jamillah's dead body. They discovered the corpse within feet of where three other bodies had turned up the day before.

Jamillah Jones was 4 feet 10 inches tall and didn't weigh more than 100 pounds. She had been stabbed repeatedly and raped.

"She was such a good person. She had lots of friends, and we always knew where she was," one of relatives remarked. In tears, she asked, "Why would someone want to hurt her?"

Jamillah Jones was only one of many victims in the past 10 days.

The previous Friday—April 3—two other women had been found within 100 yards of Jamillah Jones. One of them had been missing since February 1992. Their decomposed bodies were discovered on an embankment near Interstate 280.

The first one was found by a local person who was taking a walk and notified the police. The other body surfaced with the help of police cadaver dogs, which are trained to detect the smell of human remains.

These victims were identified as Elizabeth Clenor and Stephanie Alston, both 30 years old. Both bodies were in an advanced state of decomposition, and it took dental records to make positive identifications.

The East Orange police had their work cut out for them.

On Wednesday, April 8, just two days before those two bodies were found, and Jamillah Jones's murder was discovered, the body of another woman was found in the basement of an abandoned building only one mile from the interstate highway in the area.

She was quickly identified through dental records as Denise Gaskins. A grim twist was added to the situation when the police realized that another victim, Maria Ferguson, had been found strangled to death in that same abandoned building the previous August.

Now little Jamillah Jones was dead.

On Saturday, the corpse of another young victim, Shakia Hedgespeth, of East Orange, was discovered on the same embankment along Interstate 280 where the bodies of Clenor, Alston, and Carter had turned up. Hedgespeth, found deep in foliage, was 14 years of age and had been sexually assaulted before being killed.

The New Jersey authorities now realized that a serial killer was on the loose. They asked the FBI to step in to help the local and state police in this investigation.

The FBI has the funding and the manpower to solve large, complicated cases such as these. They have the latest technological resources at their disposal and are educated on the newest psychological discoveries that help catch killers and rapists. The FBI has always been a great help to local law-enforcement agencies because the agency distributes information from other crime areas.

Moreover, the FBI keeps a file of fingerprints for instant access. The agency also operates the National Crime Information Center (NCIC), which lists 23 million items of interest to law enforcement that can be identified by serial number—stolen vehicles, license plates, guns, boats, securities and cash, as well as missing persons, fugitives, and even people who have threatened the President.

From the differences in two of the murders, it seemed apparent to FBI experts that they could be dealing with two different killers. What they were sure of at this point was that six black female bodies turned up in East Orange, New Jersey, since the previous August, five of them in the course of a week.

The residents of East Orange were scared and angry. Now the streets of their town were desolate. Usually they were bustling with people, but the residents now heeded the advice of Mayor Cardell Cooper and the police: "Avoid walking alone, especially after dark."

One worried resident declared, "This just isn't that sort of town. I can't believe this is happening in East Orange!"

But the police knew, just because the town had always been relatively safe, that didn't mean it was safe now.

"In addition to the FBI's violent crimes task force, New Jersey State Police set up a special task force to investigate the killings. They have a hot-line number for people to call if they know any information leading to the killer," State Police Sergeant Daniel Cosgrove said.

Upon hearing the terrible news, members of New York City's Guardian Angels posted a 24-hour patrol in East Orange. They dispensed fliers on safety and self-defense and provided escorts near the sites where the bodies were found.

Meanwhile, many members of the East Orange community went to great lengths to make sure that the women of the town were protected. People set up car pools so that nobody had to walk home after their evening outings.

A community meeting was held on Sunday, April 12, 1992. One parent, a father of five children said, "It's getting so I don't let my kids out of my sight. I even worry about them going to school." Several other residents at the meeting voted to ask the city council to establish a community patrol and seal the underpass where two of the bodies were found.

The police had spent days at the underpass with cadaver dogs, looking for more bodies. This operation had apparently upset the townspeople. But it was not only necessary, it was also instrumental in cracking the case and catching the killer.

The hot line turned out to be the most helpful tool of all. Two women called the police and said that they had escaped a knife-wielding rapist with their lives.

Police dispatchers, trained in the details of the murder cases, instantly noted similarities when the two living victims had called. The women's stories were similar, and yet both were apprehensive about whether their information was helpful, because their painful ordeals had occurred months before.

Both victims said that the incidents happened in the same working-class neighborhood in East Orange and both were black women.

They both also said a man approached them, nicely first, and when they refused his advances, he attacked. One he overcame and sexually assaulted; the other was able to escape before anything happened to her.

Lead detective, Joe Ash questioned the living victims extensively and realized that the pattern of their assaults fit what must have happened to the dead victims discovered previously.

Detective Ash showed the witnesses evidence he had gathered from the other cases. One of these witnesses was able to identify a knife found at the Jamillah Jones death site. This woman was 26 at the time. She said it happened on Thursday, December 12, 1991. The perp sexually assaulted her and threatened her with that very same knife.

The other witness was a 22-year-old woman who said she was threatened on Sunday, February 22, 1992, and had managed to run for her life and escape.

Both women described their attacker as a stocky black man in his 20s, with short hair and no mustache or beard. Both said he had come up from behind them while they were walking alone on darkened streets.

Together the women helped the police develop a composite sketch of the suspect. The composite led to a mug shot, which was included on a poster that they circulated in the tri-state area.

The East Orange police combed through their files of suspects, looking at names of outstanding sex offenders, and other violent criminals. One name in particular stuck out.

It was Jerome Dennis, a 25-year-old who had been paroled in November 1991. He was listed as currently working in a nearby bakery.

His name stuck out because he had a long string of sex offenses, since the time he was 14 years of age. He had just served 10 years of a 30-year sentence for two rapes, an attempted rape, and a robbery he had committed with his brother, William Dennis, who was still serving time in the East Jersey State Prison.

The authorities realized they had to question Jerome Dennis because he fit the physical description the two escaped victims had given and because even though he lived in West Orange, he worked in the East Orange area.

The police came to his door on Sunday, April 12, and brought him in for questioning. Then the press was alerted that an arrest had been made.

Acting Essex County Prosecutor Peter Francese refused to answer press questions about the case evidence, a possible motive for the killings, or what had led the police to Dennis.

"I can assure you, he was not plucked out of thin air," he told information-hungry reporters.

The truth was, at this juncture, the case became very simple. Jerome Dennis confessed to murdering some of the women.

Much to the surprise of the authorities, Jerome Dennis also confessed to a fifth victim, 41-year-old Robyn Carter, who had been found similarly murdered in nearby Newark the previous December.

Jerome Dennis told the cops that ever since being paroled in November and getting a job in the East Orange bakery, he'd been cruising the streets at night, searching for female prey. Within a month of his release, therefore, he was out committing the same crimes he had been incarcerated for previously.

Dennis said he could not control himself. He admitted that he killed five women and sexually assaulted three of them. He also signed a written confession.

The authorities described Dennis as a virtual walking time bomb ready to go off. Once let out of prison, he started raping again, and his attacks escalated into murder. Meanwhile, the time span between his attacks got shorter and shorter, and the violence increased dramatically. By April 1992, he had burst out with full-fledged lethal violence.

Dennis was not charged with two other recent slayings in East Orange, those of two women whose bodies were found in the abandoned basement. That case was being concurrently investigated, but now it was considered a completely different case.

The FBI experts studying Jerome Dennis's confession knew that he fit the profile of a serial killer. His confession confirmed that he selected a particular kind of victim consistently and used specific methods to kill the women found near the embankment. All had died of strangulation, bludgeoning, or stabbing; some had been sexually assaulted. They were all of the same ethnic background and body type.

Dennis was even consistent with location. All the victims had come from within the same neighborhood. All were dumped at the same spot and left in similar positions.

In profiling the personality of a serial killer, the FBI experts realized the patterns were so similar in five of the seven deaths that five had to have been caused by one suspect and the other two by a completely different suspect.

The FBI behavior specialists have deduced that there is a correlation between what sleuths see at crime scenes and the people who commit the crimes. Criminals generally leave a "signature" at the scene by the way they kill. The patterns are most pronounced in sex-related crimes, which account for most serial killings, an FBI spokesperson said.

The other killer had strangled his victims and left them both in the same place, the abandoned building. However, those killings did not involve the same modus operandi that Jerome Dennis used on his five victims.

Jerome Dennis was arraigned on Monday, April 13, in Essex County Superior Court in Newark on five murder charges. The prosecutor asserted in open court that Jerome Dennis had confessed to the five murders.

Nevertheless, the suspect's lawyer entered a not-guilty plea.

The confessed killer was wearing a dark-green sports jacket with his collar turned up. He kept his head bowed and covered his face with handcuffed hands. He remained silent except to give his address and Social Security number to Judge Joseph A. Falcone, who set bail at $2 million.

Jerome Dennis was remanded to the local jail. He was now charged in the murders of Jamillah Jones, 16; Elizabeth Clenor, 30; Stephanie Alston, 30; Robyn Carter, 41; and Shakia Hedgespeth, 14. In addition, he was charged with sexually assaulting Jones, Alston, and Hedgespeth.

Dennis was also charged with sexual assault and attempted murder for one of the escaped victims, and with attempted murder for the other escaped victim.

His trial followed almost exactly a year later.

As the trial got under way, there was a dramatic development. The defense team informed Judge Falcone that their client now wished to enter a guilty plea.

Judge Falcone said he was satisfied that the psychiatric examinations of Dennis taken while he was waiting for trial in prison showed that he fully understood the consequences of his guilty plea. While in prison awaiting trial, Dennis had been hospitalized twice for two suicide attempts.

However, when the judge asked Dennis if he remembered confessing to police in April 1992, the plea agreement almost broke down. One of the public defenders, Alfred Kapin, told Judge Falcone that Dennis suffered from a "memory dysfunction" and couldn't remember committing the violent crimes. The judge then asked First Assistant Prosecutor Norman Menz to read from the confession form the legally required "factual basis" for the plea.

The judge ordered a recess to allow Kapin and another public defender to confer with Dennis in private. When Dennis came back before the judge, he answered in the affirmative all of Falcone's questions about the case.

Ultimately, Dennis pleaded guilty, on Friday, February 26, 1993, to four counts of murder, one count of manslaughter, and two counts of aggravated assault. This was in satisfaction of a total of 30 charges against him. He pleaded rather than facing the death penalty. The prosecutors accepted the plea bargain rather than trying a risky capital case. The victims' families were therefore spared the long and painful process of a trial by jury.

As the judge read the names of the victims, their relatives sobbed loudly in the courtroom.

The sentencing was held on Monday, April 12, 1993.

Relatives of three of the victims gave emotional speeches before the sentence was passed and many were crying in the courtroom.

Prosecutor Norman Menz said, "It is indescribable the sense of loss that all of the families of the victims expressed. There is not only one of loss, but a sense of pain."

Judge Falcone sentenced Jerome Dennis to life in prison with no parole for 60 years for killing five women and assaulting two others in his gruesome spree. The judge agreed with the prosecutor that it was necessary to protect the public from Jerome Dennis by giving him two consecutive life sentences, each with a mandatory 30 years in jail.

Judge Falcone observed that Jerome Dennis, who grew up in the slums of Newark and had only a seventh-grade education, had unleashed a "reign of terror on the citizens of Essex County and East Orange."

With his age at 26 and a 60-year mandatory sentence to serve, Jerome Dennis will be at least 86 before he has a chance to see the light of day again.

At first, the arrest of Jerome Dennis did not allay the fears of some East Orange residents. Some had doubts because the murders of Maria Ferguson, found on April 8, 1992, and that of Denise Gaskins, found on August 28, 1992, both in the abandoned building, remained unsolved.

One local resident demanded, "Tell me—how do you know he is the right guy? We just can't be happy with the first one you get."

Through skillful police work, the East Orange detectives have since made fantastic progress on one of those other cases. Since that time, a suspect has been charged with killing Maria Ferguson. Police could not provide details of the other case because it was still in progress. No arrests have been made in the slaying of Denise Gaskins, but the police are confident the streets of East Orange are now safer than they were.

Jerome Dennis has begun serving his sentence.

"CRYSTAL'S KILLER WAS HER PALLBEARER!"

by Richard Devon

The morning of Sunday, November 17, 1991, was crisp and bright blue, typical for late autumn in coastal South Carolina. The temperature had dropped to 50 degrees the night before, but already the mercury had started creeping back upward. The two men, their red deerstalker caps bright against the brown foliage of autumn, reached a narrow dirt road that cut through the scrubby woodlands and came to a dead end against a thick stand of hardwood timber. The pair were brothers, accustomed to acting and thinking in concert. They paused stealthily, watching for any movement across the road to indicate that their fleet quarry was about.

As his eyes scanned the area, one of the hunters saw a peculiar dark spot in the white sand of the rutted road. He walked closer, bent down, and then motioned to his brother.

"Blood," he said. The two later agreed that at first they'd thought it was from some wounded animal. As they straightened up and looked toward a nearby ditch directly in their line of vision, however, they realized the blood had not come from any wounded animal. A small human foot and slender ankle were protruding above the tangled growth of the ditch bank.

Nervously the hunters moved closer, then turned away suddenly, overcome by shock and nausea. Sprawled in the ditch was the most gruesome sight either of them had ever come across. What lay there was the bloodied, partially clothed body of a young woman. From her appearance, there was no way that she could be anything but dead.

A relative of the two brothers lived nearby, and it was to her home that they went on the run to call the police. A short time later, Wade Petty, a uniformed patrolman with the Horry County Police Department, and Lieutenant Gilbert Lewis responded to the emergency summons. After viewing the scene and preparing to cordon it off, Lewis called the dispatcher and asked that the homicide detective on call be contacted.

Bill Knowles had the duty that weekend. At 34 years of age, he was a stocky man with a mustache and receding hairline. A native of Mobile, Alabama, Knowles had grown up in the coastal regions of South Carolina and graduated from Conway High School. He joined the Horry County Police Department in 1979, and has been accorded the local distinction of being only one of three members of his force to have graduated from the famed Federal Bureau of Investigation Academy in Quantico, Virginia. On that particular morning, Knowles was nearing the completion of his sixth year as a homicide investigator.

A family man and churchgoer, Knowles had to abandon his plans for worship that day. He arrived at the death scene a short time later.

The corpse had been found off State Road 813 in the Glass Hill section of Horry County, about 10 miles west of Myrtle Beach. Knowles was soon joined at the ditch bank by the assistant coroner Gerald Whitley.

The murdered girl had lost an incredible amount of blood. Her slender body was awash in crimson from head to toe. She had obviously been stabbed and slashed a great number of times with some sort of sharp instrument. The consensus of the investigators was that the murder had taken place at the spot where the corpse was found.

The sleuths immediately figured this was a sex crime because the victim's slacks were unzipped and pulled down below her buttocks. Her torn shirt, a stylish garment of good quality, had been pushed up under her armpits, exposing her breasts. The body was so mutilated that it was impossible for the experienced coroner to arrive at any reasonable estimate of the victim's age, but it was obvious from her lustrous hair and firm flesh tone that she had been quite young.

When he had first arrived and looked at the pitiful corpse, Officer Petty had an immediate suspicion that he knew who the victim was. Earlier that same morning, he had responded to a local home where a distressed woman reported that a teenage family member had not returned the previous evening after attending another relative's birthday party and, later, another party for teenagers.

The worried woman had previously contacted several friends of 17-year-old Crystal Faye Todd, but none of them acknowledged knowing anything about her disappearance. The woman also reported that her young relative's automobile was missing. It was a new metallic-blue Toyota Celica, which the teenager had received as an early graduation present. The missing girl was a senior at Conway High School, Petty was told, and her prized new car bore a personalized license plate that identified its driver as "C TODD."

Before talking with Crystal Todd's nervous relative, Officer Petty had spotted what turned out to be the girl's missing car parked in an elementary school yard on Elm Street. For fear of further alarming the woman unnecessarily, the officer said nothing about it to her until he could check further. He left the house and went back to the school yard, where he checked and confirmed that this was indeed Crystal Todd's vehicle. It was—no doubt about it. Officer Petty reported the find to Crystal's relative, who then went to the school and drove the vehicle back home. Nothing suspicious was found in the car—no evidence in it or on it of any kind of foul play.

The Horry County police dispatcher was personally acquainted with Crystal Todd. He was asked to come to the scene in the woods to see if he could make an identification of the corpse. The veteran officer winced as he peered closely at the brutalized body. He could not be positive, he said, but it did look a little like Crystal. Pressing his fingers against the bridge of his nose, the dispatcher turned away, feeling sick from the bloodied and mutilated body in the ditch. He breathed deeply to ward off a sudden wave of nausea.

When the crime scene team arrived to process possible evidence, they removed a high-school class ring from the victim's bloody hand. Engraved inside was the name Crystal Faye Todd.

Other than the body itself and the large bloodstain on the sand of the lonely woodland road, the investigators found little evidence to be collected. There were some impressions in the sand left by automobile tires. This was a known "lovers' lane," however, and more than one vehicle had driven over its rutted surface, including the truck belonging to the hunters who had found the body.

While the crime-scene search proceeded, the body was photographed from several angles, and plaster casts were made of the tire impressions.

Meanwhile, word spread rapidly about the discovery of the body, and the lawmen faced an immediate problem in keeping curious onlookers away. They immediately cordoned off the area with yellow police tape. After a thorough search of the immediate vicinity was completed, the corpse was removed and taken to the Medical University of South Carolina in Charleston for autopsy.

As officers arrived for duty that Sunday at the county's law-enforcement center and learned about the crime, a growing number of them collected at the murder scene. Detectives Knowles and Wiggins left for the Todd residence, where they gently informed the victim's relative about the murder. Knowles was seized by the instinctive opinion that whoever killed the young beauty must have known her. Her pocketbook was discovered behind the front seat of her vehicle, its contents apparently undisturbed. No evidence was found in or about the car to indicate that Crystal Todd had not willingly gotten out and gone with someone she knew from the school yard on Elm Street to meet her horrible fate.

By now, every member of the Horry County detective division had been called to duty. The investigators immediately began seeking out and interviewing persons who had attended the two parties at which Crystal Todd had been a celebrant.

One young girl, the victim's high school friend, informed Detective Knowles that she and Crystal had been together at the second party. The two had met at the Coastal Mall about 9 P.M., where they decided to leave the friend's car at the mall and go to the party in Crystal's Toyota Celica. The two teenagers left the party at about 11 P.M., and Crystal dropped her friend off by her car at the Coastal Mall about 11:15 P.M. From that point, the saddened friend could not say what had happened to Crystal.

A canvass of the neighborhood around the school where the car was found turned up two witnesses who said they had noticed the vehicle parked in the school yard about 11:30 P.M. This meant that whoever had killed the pretty high-school senior had made contact with her within a span of 15 minutes.

Detective Knowles obtained permission from the victim's family to conduct a search of Crystal's neat bedroom. Among the items he removed were a diary and a booklet containing telephone numbers. From these, the investigators compiled a list of persons they wanted to interview in an effort to get a line on who might have killed and mutilated the popular young girl.

From the beginning, the investigators believed that the killer had to be known to someone. Whoever knifed Crystal Todd could not have escaped being heavily stained with her blood. By the same token, the vehicle that had carried the young beauty to her horrible death would certainly have traces of blood in it, even if the actual attack took place outside the car. The victim's blood had stained the ground around her body.

Anyone who stepped in that soil would have carried traces of blood on his shoes and onto the floor mat of his vehicle.

As the probe continued, the authorities got in touch with school officials and counselors to allow them to prepare the student body for the fact that one of their own had been brutally murdered. In turn, the school staff asked the students to contact the authorities with any information they felt might be useful to the investigation. Assurances were made that the identity of any person who gave information would be securely confidential.

That Monday, a pathologist at the University of South Carolina Medical Center in Charleston conducted an autopsy on the body of the murdered high-school senior. All told, he counted 35 wounds, of which at least 20 were potentially fatal.

Three of these were slashing-type injuries to the neck that ran from ear to ear, measuring 10 inches in length, and had all but decapitated the girl. The only thing that had kept the victim's head on her body was her spinal column, the pathologist reported. He said that these wounds were made with a carving motion, cutting through the victim's esophagus and windpipe. From the moment the first slash was made, her killer, even if he had been standing behind his victim, would have been working in gushing blood.

There were three penetrating wounds to the skull, three inches deep. Driving a sharp instrument through the skull bone required considerable strength, the doctor believed. For a grisly touch, the killer had apparently reinserted his weapon into one wound on the left side of the girl's skull after having made the first deep penetration. The killer must have been in a frenzy.

"It's extraordinary that so much power was used to penetrate the skull, not once, but three times," the pathologist reported.

The double-entry skull wound was something that neither he nor any other doctor in the pathology department had ever seen, the pathologist said, even though together they had performed countless autopsies.

The victim had also suffered five penetrating stab wounds to her right lung. Another wound sliced through the sternum, or breastbone, and cleaved into the girl's liver. Yet another sliced into the left lung.

Three wounds to the girl's lower abdomen measured six inches long and three inches wide, exposing her intestines. These wounds, the pathologist ruled, had been made after the victim was dead. It appeared that a maddened killer attempted to disembowel his dead or dying victim—and very nearly succeeded.

There were three stab wounds to the back, one of which cut through to the aorta. Another was deflected slightly when the weapon struck a bone in the teenager's spinal column.

Three slashing wounds marred the girl's once pretty face, one below the inside corner of her right eye, one below the eye, and one slicing the right eyebrow. Small cuts were also found on her left thumb, middle finger, and left ring finger— these were probably defensive wounds received when the helpless girl threw up her hand to ward off the knife—in vain.

Besides the knife wounds, the pathologist discovered seven significant bruises, principally to the victim's face and genital area. He also found sperm in the vagina and rectum.

Despite the apparent frenzy of the injuries inflicted on the helpless girl, "it was," the pathologist observed, "a very controlled and deliberate attack."

Weighing the information developed through the autopsy, the investigators considered the possibility that more than one attacker had been involved. They reasoned that, taken together, the number of wounds, the severity of the trauma, and the postmortem slashing of the abdomen, as well as the quantity of sperm discovered, were all cause to consider the possibility that more than one person participated in the barbaric attack. Yet, as likely as it seemed, the serology tests would eventually dispel this theory. If two men were involved, only one of them had raped the girl, the medical experts declared.

With the pathology report—and other information developed by investigators—in hand, David Caldwell, a behavioral scientist with the State Law Enforcement Division (SLED), came up with a profile of the killer. It was Caldwell's opinion that the killer was in his early 20s and had to be well known to the victim and her family.

On Tuesday, a total of $10,000 in reward money was posted for information leading to the arrest and conviction of the killer. Horry County posted a $5,000 reward in the case, as did CrimeStoppers.

On the Wednesday following the discovery of the body, an estimated 1,000 people attended the funeral of Crystal Faye Todd. Horry County police and SLED investigators were on hand to observe and photograph the mourners, hoping to come up with something that would lead them to a suspect.

Not until months later would they learn that they had indeed captured their quarry on film. On the day of the funeral, however, the sleuths saw nothing to indicate that the individual was a killer.

After the initial investigation, which involved just about every member of the Horry County Police Department, a team of 10 investigators was formed to follow up leads obtained in the early interviews. The group was comprised of Chief J. Gordon Harris, Detectives Bill Knowles, Russell Jordan, Dale Long, Mike Cannon, and Kim West, and SLED investigators Campbell Streater and Mike Anderson, as well as Lieutenants Ben Thomas and David Caldwell. This investigation, which concentrated on the victim's friends at school, resulted in 50 teenagers giving statements and offering opinions about the case.

Despite the investigators' efforts to conceal certain details of the vicious, perverted attack, a rumor quickly surfaced suggesting that the murder had climaxed a satanic ritual. Chief Harris eventually quelled this gossip, but not before it had caused widespread alarm in the area.

The Crystal Todd investigative team was putting in 16-hour days in their efforts to close in on a suspect. Despite their concentrated efforts and the full cooperation of students, school officials, and parents, each promising lead fell flat on its face.

A number of parents voiced concern for the safety of their children, but Chief Harris stressed that no one was in danger unless he or she was withholding information that might help identify the murderer.

A week after Crystal's body was discovered, the police decided to release to the press the information that she had been raped. At the same time, Harris told newsmen that no less than 200 leads had been checked out since the investigation began. The chief also said that his department was receiving assistance from the Conway city police, Myrtle Beach city police, and a team of crack investigators of SLED's Coastal Division, headed by Lieutenant Anderson.

Among their efforts, the investigative team returned to the murder scene with metal detectors to look for a weapon. Despite tedious hours of combing the area, they found no weapon there.

One frustrating aspect of the investigation was that some witnesses had seen a man in the vicinity of the school yard on Saturday night at about the time the car was spotted. He was described as being in his late 40s, with an olive complexion and salt-and-pepper hair. The suspicious-looking man was wearing a dark jacket and a plaid shirt.

Detective Knowles stressed that the man was not a suspect, but maybe he could provide some information about exactly when the car was parked in the area. He might even have seen what vehicle Crystal Todd had entered, only to be driven to her death. A public appeal requesting the identity of such a person proved to be fruitless.

As November came to a close, the team tried another measure. They began obtaining blood samples from anyone who was acquainted with the victim and who fit aspects of the profile developed by psychology experts.

As this phase of the investigation progressed, a reenactment of that fateful Saturday night's known events was videotaped for broadcast on area television stations. It was hoped that the reenactment would trigger a memory in the mind of someone who had seen Crystal Todd in her new metallic-blue Toyota between 11:15 P.M. and 11:30 P.M. on the night she was killed.

As Christmas came, the grieving kin of the slain girl placed a Christmas tree on Crystal's fresh grave. Even in the dead of winter, the soft southern climate allowed a tender growth to begin spreading its green veil over the mound.

The investigators, hoping that the killer would visit Crystal's grave, set up a hidden camera in the cemetery. When they viewed it later, however, the film only showed frame after frame of a brokenhearted woman family member bent over the girl's final resting place.

By now, more than 3,000 man-hours had gone into the investigation, and every lead had been eliminated.

On Thursday, January 23, 1992, a patrol unit spotted a suspicious vehicle going north on U.S. 17. When the car turned off on a dirt road, the police gave chase. Suddenly, the driver of the pickup stopped his vehicle, leaped out, and fled into the woods. Nine hours later, the scratched and exhausted suspect, who had gone more than 20 miles on foot through the briar-tangled woods, was finally run to earth.

He was identified as a parole violator from Alabama and was immediately viewed as a suspect in the Crystal Todd murder, since he fit the profile developed by SLED. Originally held under $100,000 bond, the man was cleared in the case two days later by a blood test. He was greatly relieved when Alabama lawmen arrived to escort him back south.

Unknown to the investigators at the time, their long chase and the new blood testing had been unnecessary. They had already sent a blood sample to their state capital that would nail their killer.

The investigative team was making periodic reports to the victim's family regarding their progress. On one visit, at which point more than 40 blood samples had already been provided to SLED's scientists for testing against the semen recovered from the girl's body, a grieving family member told the sleuths about a conversation she'd had with a family friend. This young man had been a pallbearer at Crystal's funeral, and a regular visitor to her home since then.

At one time, blond, stocky Ken Register had dated Crystal Todd, the woman told police, and on that fateful Saturday night, it had been Register she had called first to seek his help in locating Crystal. Register, who was aware of the blood samples being taken, had told Crystal's relatives that it would be a simple matter for the killer to fool police. "All you would have to do," she quoted Register as saying, "would be to substitute someone else's blood."

Like more than 50 current and former students at Conway High School, Register had been interviewed by police early in the investigation. He'd told the probers that during the time frame of the murder he had been at a go-cart track in the neighboring small town of Aynor. When that interview had been conducted, Register had not been a suspect in the developing case investigation.

Like a number of Crystal Todd's acquaintances, Register had been scheduled for a re-interview. It wasn't until January that the investigators got around to him again. Their initial purpose for that second interview was to try to develop possible information they might have missed the first time concerning Crystal Todd's acquaintances.

SLED detectives Dale Long and Campbell Streater spent 45 minutes on this subject before asking Register to submit to a blood test. At that point, Register's demeanor changed, and he asked, "What's it going to be used for?" Then he said he wished to speak to a family member before agreeing.

"You can talk to anyone you want to," Detective Streater responded, suddenly alert to the young man's obvious reluctance to submit to the testing.

And that was when the sleuths confronted Register with his reported statement about fooling or beating blood tests. Faced with the probers' knowledge, Register admitted having said that test results could be falsified by carrying someone else's blood as a sample.

"That's not the way it works," Long informed the young man. "You would personally go to the hospital with a police officer to have the blood sample taken."

After further conversations, Register consented to having his blood sampled. With that, his blood followed 47 other samples to SLED headquarters in Columbia, where the DNA testing was being conducted.

Register was not the first young man to have become nervous when asked to give a blood test. Thus, the fact that he seemed at first hesitant didn't set off any serious alarm bells for Long and Streater, although it did give them pause to think.

Ten days later, however, Detective Knowles got a call from Columbia reporting a first positive step from the beginning test on Register. It wasn't enough to cause any excitement, and the request for blood samples continued with others who fit any aspect of the profile developed for the killer.

On Saturday, February 15, a SLED scientist finally called to say that a positive match had been made with Register's blood sample. Chief Harris and Detectives Knowles, Long, and West, whose narcotics division had furnished several investigators during the probe, kept that knowledge to themselves. They placed Register under surveillance while they worked out a plan for his peaceful arrest.

On Monday, February 17, the regular team and five other investigators met to plan the arrest. They decided that Ken Register's family and Crystal Todd's kin would be informed of the arrest as it was taking place.

Detectives Russell Long and David Avant of the Horry County police were assigned the task of arresting Register. They arranged to meet him at an electric company in Garden City, where he was employed. At 9:31 A.M., the two detectives asked Register to sign a statement from his earlier interview in January.

Again, Register was nervous and anxious. Several times, he asked, "What's this?" Register read the statement and, at one point, he laughed and said, "Yes. That's what I said." Finally he asked, "How's the investigation going? What's happening?"

Meanwhile, the two detectives had quietly moved to flank Register to prevent any sort of disturbance. Now, each grabbed one of his arms. Smoothly, they handcuffed the startled young man's hands behind his broad back.

"You are under arrest for the murder and rape of Crystal Todd," Detective Jordan told him, and proceeded to read the suspect his rights.

"I was not even around that night!" Register yelled. "I want to call my mom. If I had killed her, why would I have given blood?"

Back at the homicide office, Detective Knowles was waiting, having just returned from informing the dead girl's relative of Register's arrest. As the sleuth waited, he saw Register being hauled out of a police vehicle, struggling and protesting loudly, "I didn't do it! I didn't do it!"

It was decided that Detective Knowles and SLED Agent Streater would conduct the interrogation of Ken Register. After they brought the suspect to the homicide office, they gave him a few minutes to compose himself.

Register appeared to be very nervous. His legs kept trembling, his hands shook, and tears welled up in his eyes. Knowles and Streater waited for him to compose himself. Finally Knowles quietly began to ask questions.

"We want to know where you were when Crystal Todd was killed," Knowles began.

"I told you before," Register replied. "I was at the go-cart track in Aynor, and then I drove straight home."

Detective Knowles persisted, pointing out various discrepancies in Register's two previous statements, including his saying that he had stopped at the Coastal Mall and had spoken to a friend there.

Finally Agent Streater said point-blank, "We know you killed Crystal Todd—we just want to hear your side of it."

Again Register's ruddy face flushed red. He ground his teeth together and rose halfway out of his chair. (Later, Streater would say he thought for a moment that the suspect was preparing to rush him.)

But Register sank back into his seat and repeated what he had said in the two original interviews—that he had not seen Crystal for three or four days prior to her death.

Finally, at 1:27 P.M., after maintaining over the course of more than two hours of questioning that he had not been involved in the girl's death, Register said, "I'm not going to tell you about it until I talk to my [relative]."

The two detectives left the room and conferred in the hall. It was decided they would go and speak to Register's relative. Investigators West and Streater would keep the very nervous Register company while the arrangements were made.

Then Detective Knowles went to review the events with members of Ken Register's family and requested that one of them write Ken a note asking him to tell the truth. She did write a note, but instead of a request for him to tell the truth, the note declared, "I love you. I know where you were. I'll stand by you. I love you."

Investigators Caldwell and Knowles returned to the homicide office at 2:20 P.M., but they decided not to give the note to Register just then. Instead, Knowles took a different tack with the suspect.

"Have you asked God to forgive you for what you've done, Ken?" Knowles asked quietly.

Register covered his face with his hands and began crying. The seconds ticked off as Knowles and Caldwell waited for an answer. The only sounds in the room were Ken Register's wracking sobs.

After some three or four minutes, Knowles posed the question again in a low voice.

This time, Register nodded his blond head up and down and answered, "Yes."

"Explain it to us," Knowles urged him.

In a halting voice, Register told the lawmen that on the night Crystal Todd was murdered, he had gone to the go-cart track in Aynor and had driven back through the little farm-market town of Conway. At a stoplight on Ninth Avenue, he had spotted Crystal's car and tooted his horn at her. Both had then driven to the Elm Street Middle School, where, he said, Crystal joined him in his car.

From the middle school, Register drove Crystal out to the Glass Hill section of the county and onto the dirt road where her body was eventually found.

"We started kissing, and one thing led to another," Register said. "I didn't have a rubber, and when I shot off in her, she got mad and started saying if she got pregnant, she would say I raped her." Then, he said, she got out of the car and started putting her clothes back on, still screaming and saying that if she got pregnant, she would say Register had raped her.

"I reached down between the seats and got a knife my dad had given me," Register said, pausing almost between every word. "I don't remember what-all I did. Then I dragged her to the ditch—and drove home as fast as I could."

After he had arrived home, Register said, a family member commented to him that he was home early. It was 12:15 A.M.—and his home curfew was 12:30 A.M., he explained to the sleuths.

Ken watched television for a while and, at 1 A.M., Crystal's relative called him, asking if he'd seen Crystal. Register said he called the Conway Hospital and inquired if any automobile accident victims had been brought in that evening. Then he called back Crystal's relative and told her he didn't know where Crystal was, but he felt sure she was all right.

The following day, he said, a friend tried to get him to ride out to the place where Crystal's body was found, but Ken begged off, telling his friend he couldn't do it because he was so upset.

Having gotten his admission out, Ken Register now appeared to the two detectives to be relieved and calmer. They asked him if he would sign a statement concerning the slaying. He agreed.

While the statement was being reduced to written form, Register inquired as to what kind of sentence he would get—20 or 30 years?

"I had a good job—I was about to get the boat I always wanted, and I'm probably going to lose my girlfriend," Register said ruefully, apparently lacking any depth of feeling about his dreadful act and its likely consequences.

At 4:10 P.M., Register signed the transcribed copy of his statement, as well as the rights form, declaring that he had freely consented to the questioning that had resulted in that statement.

The announcement that Johnnie Kenneth "Ken" Register II had been arrested after one of the most intensive murder investigations in Horry County history hit the community like a bombshell. Register had been a popular student at Conway High School and an outstanding player on its football team—a regular teenage heartthrob. Many citizens of the county recalled that on the day of Crystal Todd's funeral, Register had been one of the pallbearers, and a TV cameraman had filmed him in his neat, dark suit, placing a solitary rose on her coffin. That film would be subpoenaed for use at his murder trial.

The investigators would learn, too, that on September 23, a scant couple of months before Crystal Todd was raped and killed, Ken Register had been arrested by Georgetown Community College campus police for exposing himself to two female students there. That case from another county's jurisdiction had not come to the attention of Horry Police or SLED investigators, or to the active gossips of the area.

Soon after Register's arrest for the murder of Crystal Todd, solicitor Ralph Wilson announced that he would likely seek the death penalty when the case came to trial. It would be the first time in the state's history that DNA testing would figure in a capital-murder case. Wilson had already successfully prosecuted a rapist using DNA evidence.

On Wednesday, February 26, the investigators searched Ken Register's home. Among the items they seized were numerous newspaper clippings pertaining to the Todd murder and investigation, a green blanket, a pair of red socks, a pair of red-and-gray socks, a shirt, and two sweaters.

The next day, Morgan Martin and W.T. "Jim" Johnson, who were named as Register's attorneys, announced that they would probably ask for a change of venue for his trial, inasmuch as the case had drawn nationwide attention. Two national television shows would develop segments to be aired before the trial.

On Tuesday, April 21, 1992, Ken Register was formally indicted for first-degree murder, criminal sexual conduct, kidnapping, and sodomy. Three days later, Solicitor Wilson gave formal notice that he would seek the death penalty. Circuit Judge Edward Cottingham, a 63-year-old jurist from Bennettsville, would hear the trial. He scheduled it for September 14, some 10 months after the murder.

Register went to trial on Wednesday, September 23, in Darlington County on the indecent exposure charge brought by the Georgetown Community College police. He was found guilty and sentenced to a year in jail.

Meanwhile, the defense requests for DNA test results forced a delay in the scheduled murder trial. On December 11, Judge Cottingham agreed to a change of venue for the trial: the jury was to be selected and brought in from Bennettsville, the Marlboro County seat. The trial itself, however, would be held in Conway, in the Horry County Courthouse. Because feelings in the community were running so high, the lawmen decided to station metal detectors at the entrance to the courtroom, in case someone tried to enter carrying a weapon.

Register was arraigned on Thursday, January 7, 1993. The

following Monday, jury selection began. A panel of seven men and five women, with two alternates, was seated the following day. Meanwhile, tight security measures were being taken in Conway, where testimony was set to begin on Thursday, January 14. Several threats against Solicitor Wilson and Detective Knowles had been received in the months following Ken Register's arrest.

With a metal detector set up at the courtroom door, armed sheriff's deputies accompanied the prosecutor on his walk from his office to the courthouse.

In weighing a motion to suppress evidence in the accused man's indecent-exposure conviction in Georgetown, Judge Cottingham agreed with the defense that the jury, sequestered in a Conway motel, would not hear of Register's arrest and conviction on that charge. The judge did rule, however, that the confession Register had given Detectives Knowles and Caldwell could be read to the jury.

Solicitor Wilson brought forward 57 witnesses to present the state's case, with the most striking evidence coming from the pathologist who had performed the autopsy on Crystal Todd. Although the jury was not allowed to see photographs of the victim's mutilated body, the pathologist gave graphic testimony, illustrated by poster-sized drawings and a Styrofoam replica of a human head.

The shocking testimony drew gasps from the packed courtroom. One woman juror broke down and wept while listening to the pathologist's painful testimony.

To the surprise of a lot of people, Ken Register took the stand in his own defense. He denied that he had killed his former girlfriend and declared that the police had coerced his confession.

After Register took the stand, Defense Attorney Tommy Brittain stunned the courtroom by slapping his hands together loudly and asking the defendant, "Did you kill Crystal Todd?"

"I did not kill Crystal Todd," Register replied. He also denied raping the girl or seeing her on the night she was murdered. Later, as Brittain read each line of his signed confession, Register responded, "That's a lie."

The jury did not believe him, however. On Friday night, January 22, after deliberating for 4 hours and 40 minutes, the panel returned at 11:40 P.M. with their verdict. They found Ken Register guilty on all counts of the indictment.

Judge Cottingham said the penalty phase of the trial would begin the following Monday. For that, he would allow the testimony regarding Register's indecent-exposure conviction, and any earlier offenses.

This time, the jury was out only an hour and a quarter before coming back with a recommendation of mercy. One juror later commented that the convicted man's youth had moved the panel to spare him the death penalty.

Judge Cottingham sentenced 19-year-old Ken Register to serve life in prison for the murder, and an additional 35 years on the rape and sodomy charges. He will become eligible for parole in 30 years.

Register was assigned to the Allendale Correctional Institution, a medium-security facility in South Carolina's prison system, where he is currently serving his sentence.

"KILLED EIGHT FOR HIS EIGHT YEARS IN JAIL!"

by Barbara Geehr

Every year in the waning days of August, the city of Gainesville, Florida, home of both the University of Florida (UF) and Santa Fe Community College, gets turned upside down. Its student population catapults from 15,000 during the summer months to 34,000 as incoming students settle into residence halls and off-campus apartments to get ready for the start of the new academic year.

The week before classes begin has always been a happy one—until the waning days of August 1990, that is, when a ghastly nightmare held the city in terror for 72 hours and, in its wake, left five students brutally murdered in their off-campus apartments.

It was 3:30 on the Sunday afternoon of August 26, when the bodies of 17-year-old Christina Powell, of Jacksonville, and 18-year-old Sonja Larson, of Deerfield Beach, were discovered in the town house they shared at Williamsburg Village.

Powell's parents had driven from Jacksonville earlier in the day to bring Christina some things to comfort her in her new home away from home. The Powells were already concerned about their daughter and her roommate, for they had been unable to reach either one by phone for the previous two days and nights. Now, with no answer to their repeated knocking on the town house's door, and with the vehicles of both girls standing in the parking lot, Christina's father returned to his car and contacted Gainesville police on his cellular phone.

Twenty minutes later, a responding deputy who had the foresight to stop at the office of the complex to pick up a maintenance man with a key, arrived at the town house where Christina's parents were waiting outside.

"Better stay out here while we make sure everything inside is okay," the officer advised. "We shouldn't be more than a few minutes."

It was a ghastly sight that greeted the officer and the maintenance man inside the town house. The bloody nude body of Christina Powell lay on the living-room floor, her bloody clothing, which appeared to have been cut from her body, nearby. Her face, with a double-wide strip of duct tape covering her mouth, had been turned toward the sofa, her hands had been taped behind her back, and the nipples on her breasts had been cut off. Her body appeared to have been sexually posed.

Upstairs, the bloody body of Sonja Larson lay atop her bed. Her mouth had also been covered with a double-wide strip of duct tape, and she, too, had been stabbed multiple times. Slash marks on her arms and left thigh indicated she had tried to defend herself against her killer's deadly blows.

Returning outside, the deputy told Mr. Powell, "You and your wife better wait at the office. There's something very wrong here."

As the maintenance man escorted the Powells to the manager's office, the police deputy radioed for homicide investigators and crime-scene technicians to come to the scene.

The detectives, after viewing the bodies and talking with the Powells, theorized that the two murders had taken place sometime between 5:30 on the Thursday evening of August 23—the last time Christina's mother had reached her by phone—and 4 P.M. on Friday—when Mrs. Powell began getting no answers to her phone calls.

In the initial search of the crime scene, technicians found evidence indicating that the killer may have broken into the town house by prying open the sliding glass door at the back. They also reasoned that the intruder had spent an unusual amount of time in the residence after the killings: he had apparently cleaned up the two areas where the bodies were found and had posed the bodies of both young women in sexually explicit positions.

At midnight on Sunday, while crime-scene technicians were still searching for evidence in the town house, a deputy from the Alachua County Sheriff's Office was dispatched to check on a records clerk who had failed to show up for her midnight-to-8 A.M. shift. The deputy discovered that 19-year-old Christa Hoyt, a daytime Santa Fe Community College student who lived alone in a duplex about two miles west of Williamsburg Village, had also become the victim of a grisly murder.

Sheriff's investigators called to the scene discovered that Hoyt had not only been murdered but mutilated and decapitated, as well. Nude and sprawled across her bed with her hands taped behind her back, her breasts had been monstrously slashed, and her body had been deeply sliced from her lower abdomen to her breastbone. Her decapitated head, the mouth sealed with duct tape, had been propped atop a bookcase so it would be in clear view of anyone who chanced to look through the front window. The bookcase appeared to have been deliberately moved from some other spot to serve as a base for the display.

Investigators estimated that the Hoyt slaying had taken place 8 to 24 hours after the Powell-Larson killings. Crime-scene technicians found evidence indicating that the killer may have gained entry by breaking or dislodging the locking mechanism on the sliding glass door at the rear of the duplex with a screwdriver.

At eight o'clock on Tuesday morning, August 28, at Gatorwood Apartments, a student complex near Williamsburg Village where Powell and Larson shared a town house and about two miles from the duplex where Christa Hoyt lived alone, a maintenance worker discovered the bodies of two more University of Florida students: Manuel Taboada and Tracy Paules, both 23, and both from the Miami area.

Alachua County sheriff's investigators responding to the scene theorized that Taboada, whose body was found on his bed, had been awakened when the attacker began stabbing him. The tall, powerfully built young man had apparently fought desperately. The fingers on both of his hands had been stabbed to the bone, and he had deep cuts on his arms and legs.

Paules's nude and sexually posed body, with three obvious stab wounds in her back and the nipples on her breasts cut off, lay on the floor of the hallway separating the two bedrooms in the apartment. Once again, the killer had used double-wide strips of duct tape to seal the victim's mouth and to hold her hands behind her back. Paules's T-shirt had been either cut or torn off; it lay on the floor near her body.

Crime-scene technicians found evidence indicating that the killer had probably gained entry to the first-floor apartment by prying open the sliding glass door at the rear—possibly with the same screwdriver that he had used to pry open the sliding glass doors at both the Powell-Larson and Christa Hoyt crime scenes.

Upon completion of the autopsies, the Alachua County medical examiner officially released the cause of death for each of the five victims. According to the report, Sonja Larson and Christina Powell had died as a result of stab wounds. Powell had been raped before being killed; Larson had not. Christa Hoyt had also been raped before being turned facedown on the bed and stabbed in the back with such force that her aorta was ruptured. Manuel Taboada had been stabbed with such force that the knife entered his solar plexus region and penetrated through to his thoracic vertebrae. Tracy Paules, after being sexually battered, died from one of the many stab wounds her attacker had inflicted.

With the bodies of the five students found between 3:30 on the Sunday afternoon of August 26 and 8 A.M. on Tuesday, August 28, investigators from both the Gainesville Police Department and the Alachua County Sheriff's Office feared the similarities in the slayings indicated that a serial killer was on the loose in Gainesville. All five murders had taken place in off-campus residences in the southwestern part of the city. Except for Taboada, the killer had targeted young white females.

Powell, Larson, Hoyt, and Paules were all petite and attractive brunettes, ranging in age from 17 to 23. Their assailant had bound and gagged them with tape, sexually assaulted three of them, poured detergent or disinfectant over their bodies, and savagely mutilated the body of one of them. Before leaving each of the apartments, the murderer had picked up and taken with him a photo of each of his female victims—an act commonly practiced by serial killers, according to psychiatric experts.

Investigators found no identifiable fingerprints at any of the victims' apartments and believed the killer had worn gloves. They also theorized that he had spent a long time after the slayings—perhaps several hours—posing the bodies, getting rid of evidence, and cleaning himself up. The efforts, however, were not completely successful, for at each of the crime scenes, technicians took into evidence samples of semen from which they hoped to get DNA "fingerprints."

As hometown funeral services were being held for each of the victims over the next few days, national media representatives began to stream into Gainesville. The story of the student murders hit the front pages of every major newspaper in the country. The immediate question everyone wanted an answer to was: "Why? . . . Why had these particular college students been chosen by the knife-wielding killer?"

Christina Powell, an incoming freshman from Jacksonville, was a typical American teenager: a good student, an excellent athlete, a terrific softball infielder. She had written for a literary magazine in high school and been popular among her classmates. Considered hardworking, well adjusted, and "a little straight-laced," she didn't drink alcohol or use drugs.

Sonja Larson, from Deerfield Beach, had wanted to become an elementary-school teacher. At high school in Pompano Beach, she was a National Honors student and managed the girls' basketball team until finally making the team herself. Involved in "Students Against Drunk Driving," she was popular and well liked.

At the time of her murder, Christa Hoyt was enrolled in chemistry honors classes at Santa Fe Community College on a scholarship. Friends and family said Hoyt was a perfectionist who seemed always full of energy. At the Alachua County Sheriff's Office, where she worked as a records clerk, Hoyt was active in a program that helped young people begin careers in law enforcement.

Tracy Paules, of Hialeah, was another attractive, athletic, goal-oriented honors student. When murdered, she was in her senior year at UF. She was planning to enter law school after obtaining her political science degree. Highly attractive, Paules had been a homecoming queen during her high-school years.

Manuel Taboada and Tracy Paules had been friends for at least five years and had attended American High School in Miami together. Taboada had already graduated from Santa Fe Community College and was about to enter UF's College of Architecture. Powerfully built, he was expected to make the UF's rowing team. The crew coach described Taboada as "just a great guy. If you were with him for a couple of hours, you felt like you'd known him all your life." Friends of Taboada and Paules said the two were not romantically attached.

Professional criminal profilers and psychiatrists from several parts of the country offered opinions on the kind of suspect investigators should look for in the gruesome murders. Common among them was the belief that he was a person driven by anger brought on by years of failure and futility, someone whose life was on the rocks, who was directing his rage and frustration against college students whom he considered successful and privileged.

By Wednesday night, August 29, 1990, a 100-member task force, headquartered at the Gainesville Police Department, had been formed. The following morning, investigators from the police department, the Alachua County Sheriff's Office, the Florida Department of Law Enforcement (FDLE), and the FBI began the multifaceted task of tracking leads, sifting evidence, discounting rumors, and keeping the public aware of safety precautions they needed to take for themselves and their homes.

In interviews throughout the campus and neighborhoods surrounding the three crime scenes, the name Phillip Earl Porter surfaced many times. From the information gathered, investigators learned that Porter—described as 18 years old, 6 feet tall, and weighing 200 pounds—had first entered the university at the start of the 1990 summer session.

After living briefly in a coed residential hall on campus, Porter moved into an off-campus apartment with two male students he had not previously known. After only a few days, he fought with the roommates and in one incident in the dorm's parking lot, behaved irrationally. A carelessly thrown basketball bounced off the hood of his Cadillac and so infuriated him that he grabbed a chain and began chasing everyone from the area.

Porter's 79-year-old grandmother, who had come to his rescue many times in the past, came to Gainesville and spent three days hunting for another apartment for her grandson. In mid-August, Porter moved into another off-campus complex, where he chose to live by himself.

The parking lot incident with the basketball was one of many examples of Porter's erratic behavior that sleuths learned about. On the whole, those who knew Porter expressed a feeling of uneasiness when in his presence. The fact that he often dressed in military fatigues, carried a knife on his thigh, and went on "reconnaissance missions" in nearby woods frightened them. The young man's acquaintances described him as "silent, sullen, and spooky"; a person who hated life"; and "someone capable of extreme violence."

On Wednesday morning, August 29, a little more than 24 hours after the discovery of the bodies of Tracy Paules and Manuel Taboada, the investigative task force put Phillip Earl Porter under 24-hour surveillance.

The operation had barely begun before Porter walked out of his off-campus apartment, got into his Cadillac, and began driving south. FDLE agents followed by plane on what turned out to be a 180-mile trip to Porter's grandmother at her home in an upscale Brevard County community. That very night, Porter was arrested for beating his grandmother. Charged with aggravated battery on a person over 65, he was booked into the Brevard County Jail and held under a $1 million bond.

The FDLE agents who had tracked Porter from Gainesville went to the jail to question him about the student murders. Asked why he had left Gainesville, Porter explained that the murders had put him in a panic about his own safety, and, as at least one-third of the student population had done, he fled the city.

Though the youth's answer seemed simple enough, Porter made several statements during the questioning that the agents considered incriminating. He also gave signs of having multiple personalities, one of whom he referred to as "John." When asked directly if he knew who had committed the student murders, Porter answered, "John did it."

Gainesville investigators, informed by FBI agents about the interview, hoped Porter's statement would enable them to obtain a warrant to search the youth's off-campus apartment. It didn't, so they settled for picking through the Dumpsters outside the building in the hope of finding something of sufficient evidentiary value to get such a warrant. They found little besides garbage, empty pizza boxes, pieces of clothing, and papers.

Under pressure to make some kind of headway in the investigation of the student murders, task force members were desperately seeking evidence incriminating enough to make an arrest. Phillip Porter had become the number-one suspect in a pool bubbling over with suspects. Held in the Brevard County Jail under a $1 million bond for the beating of his grandmother, Porter wasn't going to be going anywhere soon, so the task force began following up on the next most promising leads.

On the Wednesday morning of August 29, the day following the discovery of the last two bodies, the *Gainesville Sun* ran a photo and story on Walter Wesley, a 58-year-old Ohio fugitive wanted by the FBI for the stabbing death of 52-year-old Phyllis Elam. According to the news report, the woman, whom Wesley had been dating for years, dropped him unceremoniously and began dating other men. Wesley hadn't accepted the situation lightly. He began harassing Elam at her home and at the store where she worked. When those tactics failed to improve the situation, he threatened to take her life.

On August 10, Elam's mutilated body was found in a wooded area in a nearby county. She had been stabbed so many times in the face and throat, it was impossible to make out her facial features, and she had to be identified through dental records. Photos and descriptions of the woman, except for her age, closely matched the descriptions of the four female victims in the student murders. She was good-looking, well built, small, and dark-haired, and she had been murdered in a similar way: viciously stabbed, her body mutilated.

On August 14, a U.S. magistrate issued a warrant charging Wesley with unlawful flight to avoid prosecution for the brutal slaying of his former girlfriend. The fugitive had last been seen at a Fairfield, Ohio, automobile dealership where he worked. On that day, he told his employer he had pneumonia and was going to check into a hospital. He told coworkers, however, that he was going on a trip and asked them where he should go to have a good time. They had suggested Orlando.

In the newspaper article, the FBI was requesting that everyone in the cities Wesley would have to pass through to get to Orlando should be on the lookout for him. Gainesville and Ocala were among those cities. Wesley was described as a 205-pound white male with brown hair and brown eyes. When last seen, he was carrying a briefcase containing a shotgun and a large knife.

The *Sun* had barely got off the press before people who had seen Walter Wesley's photo and read the story began calling the student-murder task force to report sightings of, or dealings with, the fugitive during the week before the student murders. A sales employee at an Ocala Chevrolet dealership told of taking a phone call from a man identifying himself as Dr. James Curtis, a surgeon at Monroe Regional Medical Center.

"The doctor complained he hadn't been able to get help from a salesperson during a recent visit to our showroom," the salesman said. "I apologized for the incident and told him I would personally help him if he would come back. He explained he couldn't come that day because he was scheduled for surgery.

"But he did show up around noon the following day," the salesman continued. "He had on a smock, and he did look like a doctor. He liked a white van we had on display and wanted to test-drive it alone. As he was about to drive off, he gave me a beeper number and said if anyone at the medical center called for him, I should say he was on his way back to his office."

The employee explained that no one at the dealership got concerned about the van until the "doctor" had been gone more than a couple of hours. "We checked the medical center that evening and were told there was no Dr. Curtis on the staff there. After seeing that photo in the paper this morning, I'm sure Dr. Curtis is none other than Walter Wesley."

An employee at the Chevrolet dealership in Gainesville related a similar experience to task force investigators. A man fitting Wesley's description had pulled the same scam there the very next day, Thursday, August 30. This time, however, instead of identifying himself as a surgeon at a medical center, he said he was a veterinarian at the University of Florida Veterinary School. The vehicle in which he had driven away was an S-10 Blazer.

The information from the automobile dealers placed Walter Wesley in the Ocala-Gainesville area only days before the murders of the first two victims in the student murders. He was known to be carrying a knife, the kind of weapon used in all the killings. And the four young women slain in Gainesville were of the same type as the one he was believed to have killed in Ohio.

FBI agents working on the Gainesville murders flew to Ohio to check Wesley out. At the automobile dealership where he had worked, the manager said Wesley had been a good worker and his experience selling vehicles would obviously have helped him in carrying out the automobile scams in Ocala and Gainesville. A salesperson at the dealership described Wesley as "a quiet man but weird in his own way.

"He shook constantly," the salesman said. "It was probably due to his heavy drinking."

The Ohio sheriff described Wesley as an alcoholic. "He has literally haunted the bars and lounges around here for years. But he does not have a criminal record here, except for some bad checks that he tried to pass."

Concerning the possibility that Wesley had murdered his girlfriend, people who knew the couple well commented that the woman had rejected Wesley so many times that he "must have just gone over the edge."

The FBI agents headed back to Gainesville, wondering just how far over the edge Wesley may have gone.

Meanwhile, other members of the task force had gone to the south Florida community where Phillip Porter, his brother, and his mother had been living at his grandmother's home since his mother's divorce from his father. The sleuths wanted to find out more about the teenager's background, to question Porter's hometown friends and acquaintances about his activities and state of mind during the time he was there, and to find out whether he had had any brushes with the law.

They learned that Porter had been a B student in high school, had played on the football team, had served on the student council, and had been an all-around normal teenager. However, his whole pattern of behavior had changed two years before when he got mononucleosis and was put on lithium, a medication prescribed for manic-depressives. Reportedly, he sank into deep depressions, acted and reacted irrationally, and talked about suicide.

Family members and close friends believed Porter was trying to take his own life when he became involved in two automobile accidents, which left him with disfiguring facial scars and serious physical injuries, the most noticeable of which was a heavy limp. He underwent therapy for a year and a half and was still taking lithium in the summer of 1990 when he first started classes at the University of Florida.

The investigators quickly learned that practically everyone in Porter's circle of friends and acquaintances had become aware of the drastic changes in Porter's behavior. Many of Porter's friends were not surprised when they learned he was a suspect in the Gainesville student murders. Others, who readily admitted that Porter's behavior was sometimes pretty strange, could not believe he would ever commit murder. "It would be completely out of character," they said.

Many psychologists agreed and stated they did not believe Phillip Porter fit the profile of a serial killer. "Serial killers are rational, calculating, and methodical people," they said. "Porter, by contrast, seems to be more prone to sudden, angry outbursts than to calculated violence. And it's highly unlikely that a serial murderer would draw attention to himself by beating his grandmother only one day after killing five college students."

During the time the background check on Porter was being carried out in Brevard County, other task force members were following up on a lead from the Polk County Sheriff's Office.

Thirty-year-old Barry Murphy, a short-order cook, had turned himself in one day after the last two bodies in the student murders were discovered.

In a case completely unrelated to the murders, Murphy had fled charges of aggravated assault and battery in a knife attack on a mother and daughter whose home he had allegedly broken into during the night. Neither of the two women had been seriously injured; but, during the past 10 years, Murphy had been arrested several times on charges of aggravated assault, petty larceny, carrying a concealed weapon, and resisting an officer. He was also wanted in Pasco County for violation of parole.

In jail on a high bond, Murphy had given information to Polk County investigators that made them believe he may have been involved in the student murders. They forwarded a set of Murphy's fingerprints, along with his arrest record, to the Gainesville task force.

On Thursday, August 30, task force investigators, with Murphy's consent, searched his home. The search yielded a hangman's noose, two pairs of women's panties, pornography, satanic writing, and a book on Jack the Ripper—but nothing linking Murphy to the student slayings. Nonetheless, sleuths took body samples from Murphy, and made efforts to obtain his medical records, which were being held at a Lakeland blood center. He was still officially considered a possible suspect in the Gainesville slayings.

Early on Saturday morning, September 1, 1990, Gainesville authorities held a media conference at the city's largest shopping center, the Oaks Mall, to bring reporters up to date on the status of the investigation. An official spokesperson announced that various pieces of "extremely critical evidence" taken from the crime scenes had been sent to the FDLE crime lab in Jacksonville, but it would take "a long time" to get the results on various tests.

Concerning the current status of the investigation, the spokesperson stated that investigators had already received more than 1,500 leads—some from as far away as California—and were still receiving about 400 phone calls and 30 letters a day.

The spokesperson also stated that Walter Wesley, the Ohio fugitive, had been dropped from the suspect list and that Brian Murphy had been added. After briefing reporters on Murphy, the spokesperson said that sleuths were presently trying to obtain records on Murphy from a Lakeland blood center.

Asked when a search of Phillip Porter's Gainesville apartment would take place, the spokesperson said that investigators had not yet been able to obtain the necessary warrant. "Officers will, however, be searching Hogtown Creek in the area where it passes behind the apartment tomorrow. They do not need a warrant to do that."

On Sunday, investigators wearing hip boots and carrying metal detectors waded through Hogtown Creek's muddy waters, but they came up empty-handed.

In early September, a crime-scene specialist with a high-tech fingerprint device was brought in from Hattiesburg, Mississippi, to search the residences of the murdered students for fingerprints and other subtle evidence missed by traditional crime-scene analysis methods. Despite the use of the advanced technology, the expert was unable to find any fingerprints he could identify as belonging to the killer. He attributed the negative results to the three crime scenes being "the most difficult" he had ever seen. "The killer was very methodical and very neat," he said. "He didn't leave any trace of his presence."

Meanwhile, investigators had received information from the crime lab that tests performed on a pubic hair found at one of the crime scenes could belong to Phillip Porter. Though a hair match does little more than narrow down a field of suspects to a class of people having the same characteristics, there are some cases in which additional DNA testing can more positively link the hair to a specific suspect. In this instance, it would take six-to-eight weeks to perform the tests necessary to do that.

Gainesville investigators, more anxious than ever to search Porter's apartment, used the possible hair match as the evidence necessary to accompany the required list of what investigators hoped to find at the apartment to obtain the warrants.

Among the more interesting of the items on the list were a black hood, black clothing and gloves, women's undergarments, flesh, a knife with a blade four inches or longer, liquid soap, and a Bible with passages highlighted or with handwritten notations.

However, the search of Porter's Gainesville apartment failed to turn up any of the hoped-for items. Nevertheless, investigators did not leave the apartment empty-handed. They confiscated several things for processing. "It's going to take lab technicians time before they can let us know if any of the items will be useful as evidence," they noted.

In Brevard County, the pubic hair was also just the evidence detectives needed to obtain warrants to search not only Porter's Cadillac and his grandmother's home, but also to take body samples from Porter. Investigators there encountered no problems in obtaining the body samples from Porter at the Brevard County Jail.

At his grandmother's home, one team of investigators sealed Porter's black Fleetwood Cadillac and towed it off to the FDLE crime lab in Jacksonville while another team began the search of the house itself. After some eight hours, they carted away 15 cardboard boxes, a trash can, and several paper bags filled with items of possible evidentiary value. The cardboard boxes, which contained items possibly relevant to the student murders, were taken to the FDLE crime lab in Jacksonville. Material in the paper bags and trash can was taken to the Orlando crime lab for sorting and checking.

Investigators were unsure as to where the student murder case would go from there. In little more than a week's time, Phillip Earl Porter had been catapulted from an obscure part-time college student to a household name as the media continued to focus on him as the chief suspect. Investigators had uncovered plenty of situations in which the youth had demonstrated violent and erratic behavior. They believed some of the evidence taken from the crime scenes, his off-campus apartment, his Cadillac, and his grandmother's house appeared to be "promising." However, the search for physical evidence that might link him to the murders had really only just begun.

Because it was known that Porter enjoyed dressing up in military clothes, strapping on a knife, and slipping into woods for "reconnaissance" missions, investigators organized a search of the wooded areas near the Gainesville apartment where he had lived at the time the five murders were committed. On Thursday, September 13, 1990, about 200 members of the Army and Navy Reserves, the Florida National Guard, and the State Game and Fresh Water Commission helped "deep-woods experts" conduct a grid search through 10 square miles of swamps and trees. Using mine detectors and dog teams, they gathered many items but did not know if any would have evidentiary value.

Efforts to find evidence continued with searches of two large ponds—one at the apartment where Porter had lived, and the other at a pond at Gatorwood, scene of the last two murders. The recovered items were less than interesting: the remains of three bicycles, a television set, several bottles, gold balls, and a 16-pound bowling ball.

Determined to leave no stone unturned, investigators next targeted a Sebastian Inlet state park where Porter was known to have taken a rest break on the drive to his grandmother's home on the day following the discovery of the last two student murders. Well over 100 searchers, made up of National Guard troops from Lake City, naval trainees from Orlando, and task force investigators from Gainesville, combed through several hundred acres of dunes and underbrush looking for a knife or anything else that would support suspicion of Porter's possible involvement in the Gainesville slayings. Again, nothing of that kind was found.

Nonetheless, 40 task force investigators dressed in camou-

flage fatigues waded through the shallow marshes of Bivens
Arm Nature Park in Gainesville and scanned nearby grounds
with probes and metal detectors. As in the other searches, they
retrieved some articles for examination but none of them
looked particularly promising as evidence.

A spokesman for the task force cautioned that these searches
should not be taken to indicate there was only one suspect in
the student murders. "Porter is just one prong in a mul-
tipronged investigation," the spokesman explained. "Actually,
we're working on a list of eight possible suspects. Some don't
know they're suspects; some are suspects in similar cases elsewhere; some of their whereabouts are unknown; and some
would be picked up promptly if investigators could find them."

A reportedly authentic crime-lab report leaked to a Tampa
newspaper stated that technicians had now found physical evidence from two different men at two of the three crime scenes.
That gave rise to speculation that the students' killer had carried out the crimes with a partner.

Task force investigators let it be known that they had already
worked on a "two-killer theory" and discarded it at the end
of the first week. "We've begun pursuing leads in eleven other
states," they pointed out.

In talking with investigators who had come forward from
Shreveport, Louisiana, task force interest had been briefly
aroused by a triple murder that had taken place there in November 1989. It was now more than a year since neighbors
had discovered the bodies of Thomas Grissom, 58, his daughter
Julie, 24, and his grandson Sean, 8, in Grissom's Shreveport
home. Julie, who lived with her father, was believed to have
been the actual target and the first to be slain. Raped and
stabbed in the chest and back, her nude body, cleansed with
vinegar, had been found draped over the end of her bed, with
her feet on the floor and her hair seductively arranged over
the bedspread.

Sean, stabbed once in the back, lay on the living-room floor.
Grissom, also stabbed in the back apparently while trying to

escape, was found near a utility-room door. A large, military-type knife had been used in all three killings. Investigators believed the weapon had been precisely aimed, for it had either pierced or come close to each victim's heart. With no sign of forced entry, the sleuths also theorized that the attacker had probably known Julie and been readily admitted to the house.

Gainesville investigators more or less discounted the similarities between the Shreveport and Gainesville cases when they learned that Phillip Porter could not possibly have been in Louisiana at the time of those slayings. And so it went with dozens of other multiple murders checked out in other states. State Attorney Len Register issued a statement that the search for the killer of the five Gainesville students had become "a massive whodunit" involving dozens of suspects. He also acknowledged the possibility that the killer probably would not be identified and apprehended any time soon.

On Friday, October 5, Phillip Porter celebrated his 19th birthday in the Brevard County Jail. Three days later, October 8, he went to trial on charges of aggravated battery in the beating of his 79-year-old grandmother. After two days of testimony, the six jurors took just under an hour to find the defendant guilty of battery of a person over age 65, a lesser offense than the original charge. On October 10, a judge sentenced Porter to 22 months in prison and assigned him to the Florida State Mental Hospital in Chattahoochie.

With the person considered to be the top suspect in the student slayings imprisoned, task force investigators flew to Shreveport to talk again with Shreveport investigators about the similarities in the Grissom and Gainesville student murder cases. They found several. Twenty-four-year-old Julie Grissom, a brunette, had been a student at Louisiana State University-Louisville. The four female college students in Gainesville had also been brunettes and between the ages of 17 and 23.

The Shreveport killer had directed his violence toward Julie Grissom but had also killed her father and her nephew who happened to come into the home at the wrong time. The

Gainesville killer targeted women, but he also killed a man at one of the scenes because, sleuths believed, the man just happened to be there.

The weapon used in all the killings was a large knife.

The Shreveport killer posed Julie Grissom's body to shock whoever found her. He used tape during the killing but removed and took it with him afterward. He also used a liquid to cleanse Grissom's body and to destroy evidence. On the whole, the Gainesville killer did these same things.

The chief difference between the two multiple slayings was the mutilation of the bodies. The bodies of the Shreveport victims had not been mutilated, but in Gainesville, they had.

Experts quickly pointed out that it was not uncommon for the degree of brutality in serial killings to escalate from one series of murders to the next. Still, at that time, Gainesville investigators decided there were not enough similarities among the slayings to make a connection likely. A spokesperson for the Gainesville task force said, "The Shreveport killings are not any more significant than any other cases the Gainesville task force is looking into."

By mid-December 1990, most people believed it would be months, possibly even years, before the student slayings would be solved. Task force investigators were becoming so discouraged that they feared they would not be able to solve the case until the killer struck again.

But midway into January 1991, preliminary results of some DNA testing looked positive enough to renew hopes of a major breakthrough. Initial comparison of some blood taken from the bedroom floor of the Shreveport crime scene showed enough similarity to semen found at two of the Gainesville crime scenes for investigators to explore again the possibility that the killer in both the Shreveport and Gainesville slayings was one and the same. They named 36-year-old Danny Rolling as the new chief suspect in the student murders.

Task force investigators immediately began delving into Danny Rolling's background. The deeper they dug, the more unbelievable their findings became. There seemed no way to explain how a boy reared in a neat, middle-class neighborhood, in an economically sound river town of about 200,000, could grow up to become a suspect in a series of gruesome sex-slayings.

Rolling dropped out of school at the 10th-grade level, worked at odd jobs, married a local girl, and was divorced a year later. He was 25 at the time of his first recorded crime, a robbery in Montgomery, Alabama. He served five years, between 1979 and 1984, of the eight-year sentence for that crime in prisons in Alabama and Georgia. In March 1986, Rolling was sentenced to 15 years for armed robbery and grand larceny in the holdup of a Kroger grocery store in Mississippi. He served only three years before being released in July 1989 with a probation period of five years. He was granted the right to serve the period of probation in his home state of Louisiana, so he returned to his parents' home.

The Grissom slayings took place that November and the nonfatal shooting of Rolling's father six months later, in May 1990. Rolling fled. In doing so, he was running not only from the charges he would likely face in the Grissom slaying and his father's shooting, but also for breaking parole. He had served less than a year of the five-year probationary period he'd been given as a condition of his release in the armed robbery of the Kroger grocery store.

Shreveport police, unable to track Rolling down, issued a warrant for his arrest in the shooting of his father.

The immediate questions the task force now needed to find answers to were: Where had Danny Rolling gone and what had he done in the three months between the time he left his parents' home in Shreveport in May 1990 and that August 26, the day the bodies of the first two Gainesville victims were discovered? Through the cooperation of many people and the tireless efforts of investigators, Rolling's movements were tracked as methodically as footprints at a crime scene.

He had fled first to Kansas City, Kansas, where, during the

nearly two-and-a-half week period between June 12 and June 20, 1990, he was suspected of robbing two Kansas City grocery stores and of stealing the ID of a Vietnam veteran who had died in 1975.

On July 17, Rolling was in Tallahassee, Florida, where he purchased a 9mm semiautomatic pistol and a Marine Corps Ka-bar utility knife, the type of weapon believed to have been used in the student murders.

On July 22, Rolling showed up in Sarasota, Florida. During a stay of nearly a month there, he dated two women and purchased a gold chain and an amethyst ring at a jewelry store. He paid several thousand dollars in cash for the jewelry.

In mid-August, Rolling checked into a Gainesville hotel, registering under the name of the dead Vietnam War veteran whose ID he had stolen.

It was August 14, 1990, when a lone gunman walked into the First Union National Bank on Archer Road and handed a teller a bag and a note instructing her to put all the bills from her cash drawer, excluding singles, into the bag. The employee had been smart enough to include a pack of bills containing an explosive red dye.

One week later, August 21, two men walked into the Southeast Bank, gagged and handcuffed two employees, and took off with all the money they could grab.

On the morning of August 23, Rolling, still known by the name of the dead Vietnam veteran, checked out of his hotel room and was later seen at the Wal-Mart on Archer Road. There, according to a witness, he purchased a pup tent and a foam mattress and also stole some athletic gloves, a large-handled screwdriver, and several rolls of duct tape. Upon leaving the store, he went into a wooded area near Archer Road and 34th Street and set up camp. On the Monday morning of August 27, another bank was robbed.

Found in the camp in the wooded area near Archer Road and 34th Street were a gold chain, an amethyst ring, and a pair of men's pants stained with red dye. Investigators now believed the three robberies had been carried out by the same person. If they could find the person who fit the dye-stained pants, they believed they would have their bank robber. If the robber turned out to be Danny Rolling, they would have substantial proof of his presence in Gainesville during the time of the student murders.

Continuing with the tracking of Danny Rolling, task force investigators now rechecked a stolen car incident on August 30. It had been reported by an engineering student who lived in a single-family house located about three miles away from the Gatorwood Apartments where the bodies of Tracy Paules and Manuel Taboada were discovered two days before. At the time he filed the report, the student told investigators that his Buick Regal had been driven from his driveway between the hours of 11 A.M. and 2 P.M. while he was away playing tennis.

"Someone popped the screen on my open bedroom window, climbed inside, ate oatmeal, watched television, and probably even played with my six-month-old puppy," the student had stated. "Whoever it was, stole the keys to my Buick Regal and left the television on and the front door partially open when he went out."

A week later, the student reported the return of the car. "It was riddled with bullets, and such a wreck, I couldn't do anything but sell it for junk," he said. "I was told it had been used for a Save 'N' Pack grocery story robbery in Tampa."

Investigators had the foresight at the time to have the vehicle's steering wheel processed for fingerprints before the student sold it for junk. Those fingerprints matched Danny Rolling's

Following up on the information that the Buick Regal had been used in the grocery store robbery in Tampa, a Gainesville task force investigator drove to the Hillsborough County Sheriff's Office to obtain some firsthand information about that crime. There, an officer turned over the file report on the robbery, explaining, "All the basic information is pretty well contained in this report."

According to the report, a masked man entered the Save 'N' Pack store at twilight on Sunday, September 2, 1990, threw paper bags at four cashiers, and ordered them to empty their registers. Another employee and a customer managed to run to an adjacent restaurant to call for help and, by sheer luck, found and alerted three law officers who happened to be eating there. As the officers responded to the emergency, the robber fled down a nearby alley, carrying the paper bags that the store cashiers had stuffed with currency and food stamps. As a female corporal confronted the thief with her gun drawn, he jumped into the Buick and, with his own gun drawn, warned, "Back off, lady! I don't want to shoot you!"

A second officer, approaching the scene on foot, diverted the robber's attention, causing him to veer the Buick away and head toward a third officer, who was firing his gun from a standing position with his back against a wall. Again, a split second before the officer would be pinned to the wall, the robber turned the vehicle away from the store property. All three officers had the vehicle under a hail of gunfire as it sped down the road.

When deputies later found the vehicle crashed and abandoned two blocks away, they discovered that in the gun duel with the robber, they had riddled the body of the vehicle with 17 bullet holes and shot out its windshield. A witness to the crash scene related that the car had careened off a cement wall and struck a nearby mobile home. "It was a miracle the driver wasn't killed," the witness stated. "But he just jumped out and fled into the surrounding woods."

The robber was described as a white male, 6 feet 2 inches tall, weighing about 180 pounds, with hazel eyes, a thin mustache, and curly, longish brown hair. He was wearing Bermuda shorts, deck shoes, a T-shirt, a floppy fisherman's hat, and sunglasses.

"I have to say the guy had plenty of guts," one task force investigator commented.

"Or experience," the sheriff's officer agreed, adding, "we

now know that the guy who escaped from the robbery at the Save 'N' Pack store was the same guy who stole a 1984 silver-colored Ford Mustang from a garden complex here in Tampa later that very night. The owner of the vehicle told us the thief had to be pretty cool; he'd taken his time going about his business. He'd pried open the sliding glass door facing the woods at the back of the apartment, taken a banana out of the refrigerator, eaten it, and hung the peel over the back of one of the kitchen chairs. He'd apparently managed to find the key to the Mustang without too much trouble. He picked it up, along with a couple of watches. When he got what he was looking for, he just casually walked out the door, climbed into the Mustang, and drove off. We learned the vehicle was used in the robbery of a Winn-Dixie store in Ocala that next night."

In following up on the Ocala robbery, task force investigators learned there were no miracles this time. The robber, dressed in the same Bermuda shorts, deck shoes, fisherman's hat, and sunglasses, entered the store, put a .38-caliber gun to an employee's head, and demanded money. After grabbing cash and food stamps from the cashier, the robber fled in what turned out to be the silver Ford Mustang stolen from the Tampa garden apartment complex the night before. He managed to elude officers only until he wrecked the car, jumped out, and ran into a store near Bridge Street Station. Officers lay in wait until the thief, apparently believing the coast was clear, walked out the door. His luck ran out. The officers apprehended him.

Processing of the Mustang yielded the .38-caliber revolver used in the holdup, numerous tools, a denim bag containing a large screwdriver, two pairs of gloves, a black T-shirt, and two rolls of undeveloped film.

At his arraignment on the Winn-Dixie robbery the following morning, Danny Rolling, asked by the judge if he had an attorney to represent him, answered, "No, sir, I don't need one. I'm guilty, and I'd like to clear my record. I'm also wanted in Shreveport for shooting at my father. So I'd like now to put myself at the court's mercy and let y'all judge me as you see fit."

The magistrate had Rolling held in the Marion County Jail under a $25,000 bond and ordered that he undergo psychiatric evaluation.

To Gainesville and Shreveport investigators alike, Rolling's confession meant he was hoping that imprisonment on a known crime would keep him from becoming a suspect in crimes of a more serious nature.

In prison, Rolling whiled away his time reading books about war and karate, playing spades after breakfast, talking about music, and professing devotion to God. Though he made two suicide attempts—once with a razor and another with an overdose of a prescription drug—he attracted little attention.

Gainesville task force investigators contacted the Marion County Jail. They asked to have a note put in Rolling's file to notify them immediately if Rolling was ever released.

Following that, task force investigators and Shreveport police officers investigating the Grissom slayings literally rushed to the Marion County Jail with warrants to take blood and other body samples from the prisoner. When results in the DNA testing indicated a match to body fluids taken from both the Grissom and student murder scenes, investigators in both cases now focused on Danny Rolling as their prime suspect.

Anxious as task force sleuths were to charge and arrest Rolling for the Gainesville slayings, State Attorney Len Register wanted to proceed slowly. "When you have a suspect who is already in prison and in no danger of fleeing the jurisdiction of the court," he explained, "an arrest is to be made only after a grand jury indictment has been returned. There is no grand jury at this time, and to convene one requires a minimum two-week notice. Furthermore, evidence not yet fully processed indicates that *two* men may have been involved in the student slayings."

During the first months of the new year, 1991, task force lawmen directed their efforts to Shreveport, where they subpoenaed Rolling's school records and interviewed family members, friends, neighbors, and former employers. According to family members, Rolling had been an abused child from the day he was born. One relative stated, "His father was jealous of him, never wanted anyone to hold him or show love for him. He told Danny from the day Danny was old enough to understand that he would be dead or in jail by the time he was fifteen."

Comments from friends and neighbors were mixed. Friends recalled the special rapport Rolling had with children. Several remembered how well he played his acoustic guitar, wrote his own lyrics, and enjoyed playing and singing for groups of kids. "He was pretty much on a kid's level himself; he did all kinds of things you wouldn't expect an adult to do," one of them commented.

Neighbors described Rolling as a disturbed youth who often behaved in strange and bizarre ways. "His strength was legend," they said. "Wearing Army fatigues, Army boots, and a bandanna around his head, he practiced martial arts by sparring with trees and jogging with a heavy piece of wood across his shoulders."

One neighbor described Rolling as "the strongest man" he'd ever seen. "I once saw him carry an automobile transmission across a parking lot on his shoulders," he said.

Former employers described Rolling's job performance as "terrible."

While many of the people interviewed thought Danny Rolling "wasn't quite right," they did not believe he could be connected to any murder, let alone such gruesomely methodical ones as the Grissom slayings in Shreveport and the student murders in Gainesville.

Weeks later, preliminary results of some DNA testing looked positive enough to renew hopes of a major breakthrough for both Shreveport and Gainesville investigators. When initial comparison of some blood from the Shreveport crime scene showed similarity to semen found at two of the Gainesville crime scenes, and when the semen from the Gainesville crime scenes matched genetic material found in Rolling's blood, investigators began exploring again the possibility that the Shreveport and Gainesville killers were one and the same.

Shreveport investigators now wanted to have saliva swabbed from a bite mark on Julie Grissom's breast put through a new testing method which would develop a DNA fingerprint that could be compared to DNA samples from Rolling. "We're planning to travel to the prison in Ocala armed with search warrants to take body fluids from Rolling,"Shreveport investigators announced. "The tests will either give us evidence to proceed with charges against Rolling in the Grissom slayings or completely eliminate him as a suspect. Unfortunately, it will take up to a year for the tests to be completed."

Meanwhile, FDLE agents working on the three Gainesville bank robberies held a lineup consisting of Rolling and six other men of physically similar appearance. Witnesses culled from each of the three bank robberies viewed the lineup. Every witness pointed to Rolling as the robber. Those identifications and the dye-stained pants found at his campsite established his presence in Gainesville between August 14 and August 27, 1990, the dates of the first and last bank robberies, as well as the time frame during which the student murders were committed.

By the end of 1991, Rolling had been convicted and sentenced for his Tampa and Ocala crimes, arraigned on the Gainesville bank robberies, and indicted in the Gainesville student murders.

For the 12 charges stemming from the Tampa crime spree—three counts of aggravated assault on law-enforcement officers, three counts of robbery, three counts of burglary, and one count each of attempted robbery, grand theft, and petty theft—Rolling was sentenced to three life terms plus 170 years. Though the Tampa crimes were not directly related to the August 1990 Gainesville slayings, they were significant because the Buick

Regal used in the getaway had been stolen in Gainesville two days after the last two murders.

Charged as a habitual offender in the robbery of the Winn-Dixie grocery store in Ocala, Rolling was given another life sentence.

A three-count indictment in the First Union National Bank case charged Rolling with bank robbery, federal firearms violations, and possession of a semiautomatic pistol by a convicted felon. The indictment was significant in the investigation of the student slayings because of the timing and the proximity of the bank to the student-murder scenes.

The indictment on the student murder cases charged Rolling with five counts of first-degree murder, three counts of sexual battery, and three counts of armed robbery. He was ordered held without bond on the murder counts, placed under a $700,000 bond on each of the rape charges, and under a $100,000 bond on each of the burglary charges. At the hearing, grand jurors also returned a "no true bill" on any possible involvement of Phillip Porter in the student murders.

Porter, now 19, had been released from the state's Reception and Medical Center at Lake Butler after serving 13 months of the 22-month sentence he'd been given for the August 29, 1990, beating of his grandmother. He looked different now from the shackled, handcuffed young man, with wild hair and lithium-tired eyes, who had pleaded guilty to beating his grandmother.

He was slimmer, his blond hair was neatly trimmed, and he was casually dressed in khaki pants, a red striped white shirt with a red tie, and a navy-blue blazer. He was met by members of his family, his attorney, and a swarm of reporters. Asked about his plans for the future, he said only that he wanted to be left alone so he could get on with his life.

His attorney answered the question a little more specifically. "Phillip will live in Orlando with a close relative for a while and eventually return to college. For the present, however, he is scheduled for a couple of surgeries—one to remove his facial scars and another to remove the rod in his leg, which causes him to limp. His family has also hired a public relations consultant to redo his image."

As attorney's began the tremendous job of getting Danny Rolling ready to face trial in the student slayings, reporters began doing a little sleuthing on their own. One managed to interview a Marion County Jail inmate who had shared a cell with Rolling for six days at the time Rolling was arrested for the Ocala-Winn-Dixie robbery.

"Rolling was always practicing how to act crazy," the inmate told the reporter. "One time he unscrewed the toilet in his cell and heaved it at the cell's plastic window, trying to break it so he could escape from the jail. But the toilet bounced off the window and hit Danny on the foot before breaking into pieces. As Danny began picking up the pieces and throwing them at the window, guards stormed the cell. They put him in solitary under twenty-four-hour watch."

Asked by the reporter if Rolling had ever admitted committing the student murders, the inmate answered, "No, Danny never admitted that. But he did mention offhandedly one time that he had wiped everything down in the three apartments and knew how to do it because he'd learned law-enforcement procedures. He also said one time that the only way he could possibly be traced to Gainesville was through the damned Buick Regal he was driving at the time of the Tampa Save 'N' Pack robbery. But he never admitted killing anyone."

Danny Rolling went to federal court in Tallahassee on Monday, March 16, 1992, to face trial for the Gainesville bank robberies. A federal jury, after two and a half hours of deliberation, found him guilty on all charges. Before handing down a sentence on May 21, the U.S. judge who had presided over the case asked Rolling if he wanted to make a statement.

Rolling asked, "I have the opportunity now to speak?"

The judge nodded.

Rolling then turned to face the courtroom, and, after asking everyone there to be patient, he started singing a religious song, which he had introduced as one written by himself. The performance lasted three minutes. He then thanked Jesus Christ for coming into his life and setting him free.

The judged sentenced Rolling to 25 years for armed bank robbery, five years for the use of a firearm in the commission of a dangerous felony, and life in prison for possession of a firearm by a convicted felon. Unlike life sentences in the lower courts, which carry a possibility of parole after serving 25 years, life sentences handed down by a federal court have no chance for parole. Also, federal sentences are served in a federal prison. Accordingly, Rolling was transferred to the Florida State Prison in Starke.

When Rolling's conviction in the bank robberies placed him in Gainesville during the time period of the student murders, preparations to arrest and formally charge him in those slayings got under way. On Tuesday, June 9, 1992, Rolling, in his cell at the state prison, was formally charged and arrested for the five murders and the many related crimes.

In the 10-minute hearing that followed in the prison's tiny courtroom, Rolling sat quietly in handcuffs as his public defender entered innocent pleas to all 11 counts with which Rolling was charged. The judge formally ordered that Rolling be held without bond on the five murder counts and placed under bonds of $700,000 for each of the rape charges and $100,000 for each of the burglary charges.

Following formal arrest for the student murders, Rolling attempted to commit suicide in his cell by wrapping a sheet around his neck. Though the attempt was considered a fake, he was transferred to the Florida State Mental Hospital at Chattahoochie where he remained until the end of December.

Upon his return to the Florida State Prison, Rolling resumed his friendship with Harry Hart, a convicted murderer who had befriended Rolling at the time he was sentenced there on the bank robberies. Hart had become Rolling's father-confessor then; Hart now resumed being Rolling's father-confessor.

It was generally believed but never proven that Hart, based

on his close relationship with Rolling, had asked for a reduction in his own sentence in return for asking Rolling questions about the murders and reporting his answers to task force investigators.

Hart, in two meetings between the end of January and the first week of February 1993, told task force sleuths that Rolling had also told him that the murder weapon was a Marine Corps Ka-Bar utility knife and had said that a pair of gloves that he had used in the murders was buried in an abandoned deer pen across the road from the Gatorwood Townhouses. This was where Christina Powell and Sonja Larson were slain and about a half-mile from the duplex where Christa Hoyt was murdered. "But Danny did not actually confess to the murders," Hart said, "because he is a born-again Christian who believes that confession, like suicide, is a sin and that the case should be tried in court."

After a week of futility in digging and excavating the area where the murder weapon and the gloves had reportedly been buried, the search was called off. Rolling was still maintaining his innocence in the student murders.

In early March 1993, circuit judge Stan Morris appointed a Gainesville psychologist and neuropsychologist to determine Rolling's competency to face trial, his competency at the time of the five murders, and the possibility of any factors that could affect the sentencing if he were convicted. The state had already let it be known that they would be seeking the death penalty. In Florida, a person cannot be sentenced to death if found to be mentally incompetent.

The defense asked for more time to prepare for trial. Public defender Rick Parker told Judge Stan Morris during a pretrial motion hearing, "The amount of information received in this office on the student-murder case has equalled all of the information received in this office on all other cases combined during the course of a year."

Judge Morris reluctantly granted the motion. "It's about the last thing I want to do," he stated. "Just as much as the public and the state want this case over with, believe me, so does the bench." He set a new trial date of February 15, 1994. He again imposed strict deadlines for both the prosecution and the defense for scientific tests and pretrial motions.

Then something incredible happened. On Wednesday, January 26, Danny Rolling contacted public defender Rick Parker to say that he now wanted to plead guilty to the five Gainesville student murders.

"That's a very serious decision," Parker told him.

"I know. But I've got to thinking about honesty, about being honest about the things I've done," Rolling said.

"Okay," Parker said. "But I want you to be sure about this decision. The trial is nearly a month away. Think about it some more. Pray about it. Make sure that this is what you really want to do."

It apparently was; for on Thursday, February 10, 1994, at the Florida State Prison, Danny Rolling signed a confession to the five murders. Parker advised Judge Morris of the confession shortly afterward, and Prosecutor Rod Smith was informed that evening. Smith was cautious and asked that the information be withheld from everyone but lawyers on the case until Tuesday morning, the day the testimony was scheduled to begin.

"A plea is not a plea until it happens," Prosecutor Smith warned. "I, myself, will proceed with caution. I will personally have my own attorney take care of the paperwork on the guilty plea so my clerical staff will not know anything about it, and I won't even tell anyone on my own staff what has happened."

On Tuesday, when jurors who had been selected to hear the evidence against Rolling heard him plead guilty to the five murders and related charges, they were literally shocked.

"There are some things you can't turn from," Rolling told them in entering a guilty plea on all counts, "this being one of them."

On March 24, 1994, after routinely deliberating on the sentence for several hours the previous night and again in the morning, the 12 jurors returned a unanimous guilty verdict on all counts. They recommended a sentence of death in the electric chair for each of the murders. On April 20, 1994, Judge Morris followed the jury's recommendation.

In the aftermath of the sentencing, a simple three-sentence notice of appeal was filed in Gainesville Circuit Court. The notice signalled what would be a 10-year effort to keep Danny Rolling out of Florida's electric chair. Additionally, the civil rights of Phillip Porter, the first prime suspect in the Gainesville student murders, were restored; and Shreveport investigators announced they did not have sufficient evidence to charge Rolling in the Grissom slayings.

"RAPED GIRL OF 11 DIES . . . BUT HOW?"

by Charles W. Sasser

A warm spring sun glinted brown against the muddy waters of the Arkansas River on Wednesday, May 20, 1992. At 3 P.M. in Van Buren, Arkansas, 11-year-old Amanda Dee-Ann Craig and a friend left King Elementary to walk home together. They were still excited by a school field trip they'd taken that day to the historic Fort Smith courthouse of the legendary "hanging judge" Isaac Parker.

Still chatting and giggling, the little girls split up a few blocks from the Jesse Turner Terrace Apartments where Amanda, better known as "Mandy," lived with her parents. Brown-haired, brown-eyed Mandy was large for her age at 5-foot-1 and 105 pounds. That warm afternoon, she wore a light-blue blouse embossed with the image of an elephant, pink shorts, socks, and high-topped sneakers.

Mandy, said her mother, was one of those youngsters so excited by life that sometimes she could hardly sleep. In fact, mother and daughter had sat up together the previous night talking until about 2 A.M. Mandy so anticipated becoming a teenager. She was an avid reader who also enjoyed cooking, skating, and collecting teddy bears.

Mandy, on that May afternoon, waved good-bye to her chum—and then disappeared in broad daylight, off a busy street, with no trace.

"Everything we ever feared for her happened," cried Mandy's distraught mother, who notified police about 5 P.M. She had already telephoned the school and Mandy's classmates.

"When she would come home from school, she would ask if she could go out and play," continued her mother. "I would say, 'Sure, just be sure to be in by dark.' This time, she didn't come home at all."

Van Buren police led by Assistant Police Chief Wayne Hicks and Detective David Cate immediately launched a search for the missing girl. Mandy was a well-adjusted child, happy with her home life, with no history of juvenile problems. She would not have wandered off with friends or run away from home.

Nightfall that Wednesday found detectives issuing regional police computer alerts on Mandy Craig's description and questioning students and teachers at King Elementary. They checked with friends and family in the vicinity, hoping Mandy may have gone to one of their houses. No one had seen her since she parted from her schoolmate.

Tips started trickling into police headquarters on Thursday in response to police requests for public assistance in locating the missing grade-schooler. A number of people reported seeing little girls of Mandy's description wandering the streets or getting into cars. These kinds of sightings were expected; most proved groundless, but each one had to be carefully checked out.

At noon, still with no firm clues, one detective drew his own conclusions: "That little girl was plucked off the street by some child-molesting pervert. We're going to be very lucky if we find her alive."

Nothing significant developed the rest of that Thursday. Mandy's parents had been up most of Wednesday night, searching, and stressed to the limits. They faced another long night.

Friday morning dawned without developments. Little Mandy had been missing 45 hours at noon that day when the focus of the search abruptly shifted 120 miles west of Van Buren to Chouteau, Oklahoma.

Chouteau, a town so small locals referred to it as "a wide place in the road," lay in Mayes County, south of Pryor Creek on IS-69. Some years before, in 1977, Mayes County had become nationally notorious as the site of the brutal murders of three Girl Scouts on their first night at summer camp. For 10 months afterward, lawmen chased a convicted rapist and escaped prisoner through the rugged Cookson Hills before they finally nabbed him and charged him with the slayings. Some folks in Mayes County thought this was about to be a replay of that case.

A group of children were playing in the Guy Williams Park less than one block from Chouteau Elementary School, chasing each other through a thick patch of trees and brush, when suddenly, one of the children screamed. That instantly summoned parents—and, eventually, Chouteau's police chief, Leroy Linam.

Chief Linam found the body of a young girl lying curled fetal-like in the bushes. Fully dressed, she wore a blue blouse with an elephant on it, pink shorts, and high-topped sneakers. Her clothing was not torn, except for a small rip in the seat of the shorts. Her little fists seemed to be clasping foliage. Decomposition of the body indicated she had lain there for some time.

"We can't tell if she crawled under the bushes and pulled up her knees, or if someone threw her under and pushed her feet in making her appear to be in a fetal position," Chief Linam said. "Her hands were outstretched, but I can't say she was holding on to any of the branches.

"There was considerable insect activity, but there was no sign of animal activity. There was some amount of fluid containing blood around the area of the nose and mouth. . . . It appeared she had been there some time."

"[The killer] may have been unfamiliar with the area and thought he was hiding the body in the tree line of a field and that the body wouldn't be discovered until the next time someone baled hay," Mayes County A.D.A. Terry McBride surmised.

Although Mayes County assumed jurisdiction over the death, other agencies had interest in the case. Modern rapid communications quickly attracted Van Buren authorities, who confirmed the corpse's identity as that of Amanda Dee-Ann Craig, the missing Arkansas fifth-grader. The interstate aspects of the crime drew FBI agents along with Van Buren police, the Arkansas State Police, and agents of the Oklahoma State Bureau of Investigation (OSBI) to work the crime scene.

The cause of death was not readily apparent. Mandy had not been shot or strangled or beaten or stabbed. Detectives were puzzled. Only an autopsy could determine the method of Mandy's dying.

"We treat all unexplained deaths as a homicide," said Chief Linam.

Forensics experts admitted they recovered virtually no usable evidence from the park and surrounding areas. There were no signs of a struggle. Apparently, the girl had either been dead or unconscious and near death when someone dumped her in the park.

While the crime scene yielded few clues, an autopsy by the Oklahoma State Medical Examiner's Office eventually told a dark story of a night of horror through which Mandy Craig must have lived before succumbing to death.

First of all, analysis of the contents of her stomach revealed that the last meal Mandy had eaten was the school lunch her mother prepared for her on Wednesday, May 20. She had died within 12 hours or so after eating. That meant that she was dead and taken to the park sometime Wednesday night or before dawn on Thursday morning.

"There were some marks on the vaginal and anal areas," noted OSBI spokeswoman Kym Koch, "but [medical investigators] can't really tell if activity occurred in those areas because of the decomposition."

However, sperm found in oral samples confirmed that Mandy had been raped, at least orally.

"What she must have endured . . . ," muttered one grim detective.

The exact cause of death proved difficult to pinpoint, even for skilled pathologists. Mandy had been murdered, no doubt of that—but how? Medical examiners ran a series of tests on blood and other body fluids, trying to pick up traces of foreign poisons, drugs, or chemicals. A great many materials fatal to human beings require specific tests in order to detect them, but a forensics pathologist must know exactly which foreign agent to test for in order to find it.

To prove a legal case of murder, the cause of death must first be established. Without that important element, no killer can be convicted.

Still, while the cause of Mandy's death remained a mystery, there could be no doubt that she had been kidnapped, transported out of state, sexually molested, and then murdered by some unusual means.

Police said only a monster could do such a thing to a little girl.

"Why did he want to hurt my baby?" Mandy's mother mourned. "Why would someone want to do this to any child?"

To answer that question and the more important ones of "Who" and "How," lawmen from two states, two municipalities, and the federal government formed a task force. No crime causes as much concern and anger as a crime against a helpless child. Van Buren detective David Cate and OSBI agent Dennis Franchini worked together with other law-enforcement officers in the task force. They initiated a probe that spread from tiny Chouteau to the nation at large.

Chouteau's Guy Williams Park encompasses about 10 acres. A raised railway bed shields it from IS-69 on the east. A line of trees and underbrush further shield it from the scattering of houses on the west and north. Nonetheless, detectives tramped to virtually every home in Chouteau asking questions about anyone or anything unusual people may have seen in the park starting late Wednesday.

"I saw a man walking down between the park where the child was found and the cemetery Thursday evening," one witness volunteered. "He was right near where the body was."

"Can you describe him?" police requested.

"He was a stranger, but I'd know him if I saw him again. He was white, about fifty or so, thin, not real tall."

The witness saw the same man a day or so later at a local convenience store asking directions for "back roads to Arkansas."

A second witness described a similar individual driving through the Chouteau park at about the same time Mandy Craig's body was discovered.

"The guy seemed in a hurry. He left right after the body was found."

A June 1 regional broadcast asked lawmen in Arkansas, Oklahoma, Kansas, and Missouri to keep an eye peeled for the 50-year-old stranger.

Over the days following the grisly discovery in the park, the Mandy Craig Task Force chased down dozens of leads. They questioned anyone arrested in the vicinity for sex offenses. They sent fliers nationwide asking other law-enforcement agencies to assist in the search. Paroled child molesters living in the area between Van Buren and Tulsa, as well as other known sex criminals, became grist for the probe.

"There is no telling how many people we have talked to," said Detective Cate.

FBI agent Ron Wolfe, of the Little Rock office, requested that the Bureau's National Center for the Analysis of Violent Crimes in Quantico, Virginia, develop a profile of the killer based on forensics and psychological evidence. The behavioral science unit had been featured in the 1991 movie *The Silence of the Lambs*.

"It's a psychological profile based on the crime scene," explained Wolfe. "I do not anticipate any arrests in the immediate future."

Meanwhile, in Van Buren, Mandy Craig went to her grave while her killer remained unidentified and at large.

Her stepfather was certain Mandy must have put up a fight when she was abducted and assaulted.

"She took tae kwon do for five years and was good at it."

Her mother agreed. "I think she did fight. I saw scratch marks on her hands . . . and her fingernails were all broken off. Whoever did this is a psycho . . . with no conscience whatsoever. Anyone who could do this and go on living is as coldhearted as Satan himself."

Meanwhile, on June 1, 35 miles west of Chouteau in Tulsa, another 11-year-old named Roxie Moser left her home near Admiral Place and Zunis Avenue at about 1:30 P.M. to walk with a girlfriend to a nearby grocery store. The girlfriend returned to Roxie's house at 3:30 P.M. saying she had lost contact with Roxie at the store's entrance.

"She went into the store to get some change or something—and she never came out," the girl cried.

Roxie's family searched the neighborhood, then notified police.

Tulsa police detective Dean Finley said the disappearance of the 11-year-old was of grave concern. "I think something is wrong," he said.

One witness told police that she saw Roxie at about 5 P.M. walking near the grocery store with two men in their 20s. Another report had Roxie in a car with two men at about 8 P.M.

The police all-points bulletin described Roxie Moser, 11, as 4-feet 11-inches, 110 pounds, with blue eyes and blond hair. When last seen, she was wearing a large blue sweater and blue jeans.

Police could not help but make comparisons between the

kidnapping and death of Mandy Craig and the disappearance of Roxie Moser. Was there a connection?

Maybe. If so, however, days passed, and then weeks—and Roxie Moser, either dead or alive, remained missing with no clues as to her whereabouts.

On July 16, 1992, the task force received encouraging news. Florida was holding a man on charges of lewd molestation and attempted sodomy. The man matched a description of the mystery man who was spotted at Guy Williams Park the day before and the day of the recovery of Mandy Craig's body. He was from Tulsa, Oklahoma, and at the time of his arrest, drove a vehicle similar to the one the suspect drove when he asked the Chouteau convenience store clerk for "back roads to Arkansas."

"Contact . . . and find out what he knows about the manhunt," began a task force log, "and [check] for that guy that raped and killed that little girl in Van Buren. . . . OSBI and FBI records note extensive criminal history. . . . Wanted by Tulsa County and Oklahoma City FBI for several warrants."

Kym Koch, of the OSBI, cautioned newsmen that the communication was merely "gossip between law-enforcement agencies," and that the Florida arrest should not yet be regarded as a breakthrough in the case.

"This one looks good," conceded a Van Buren spokesman, "but we've had several others who looked good, but they all folded in the end."

A week later, following an intensive check of the Florida detainee and his whereabouts during the critical days around May 20, detectives reluctantly admitted that this suspect, too, had folded.

Almost two months had passed since the beginning of the investigation. The task force had no solid leads, and time was running out. Homicide detectives subscribe to an unwritten rule that the first 48 hours of an investigation are the most critical. After that time, the chances of apprehending and convicting a slaying suspect decline rapidly.

"[Time] was on our side at first," Kym Koch pointed out. "Then it began to slip away."

"Anytime time elapses," added Chief Leroy Linam, "you run the risk of losing what might have been crucial evidence. The trail gets colder and colder. Some evidence will be there forever, and some is gone in a short time."

"We will solve this case," promised Assistant Chief Wayne Hicks in Van Buren.

In the meantime, Roxie Moser remained missing. And Mandy Craig's death remained a mystery.

The dog days of summer arrived. And, then, apparently, came a crucial and unexpected break.

Around August 4, 1992, an Arkansas truck driver named Brian Long was traveling back through the Van Buren area when he happened to overhear people at one of his truck stops talking about a little girl who had been kidnapped in Van Buren and left murdered in Oklahoma. Long stopped the first policeman he saw and related an incredible story.

"If people get out like I do and watch stuff," Long explained, "it would help a lot. But a lot of people don't do it."

Long had made it a habit of jotting down details of anything he saw that struck him as suspicious during his travels about the country. On May 20 in Van Buren, not far from King Elementary School, he had jotted down notes on a man he saw on the street talking to a little girl. As soon as he described the little girl—blue shirt, pink shorts, and socks—Detective David Cate gave a whoop.

"You've just described Mandy to a T."

Long told police what had happened: "I was taking a load of vans from Springdale to Van Buren when I saw this bluish pickup and an ol' boy standing there. The first thing I noticed were the tags on the pickup. They weren't Arkansas tags.

"[The man] was talking to [a girl] and when he reached into his back pocket, I slowed down real slow because I wanted to see what was going on. He pulled out a badge and showed it. . . . That's when I knew something wasn't right. Before I turned the corner, I saw [the girl] get into the pickup. So I stopped and got the license-plate number."

Long then drove on and thought nothing else about it—until over two months later when he overheard the conversation about murder.

The truck driver described the man he had seen as a white male in his early 30s, skinny, of average height, with brown hair cut fairly neat. His vehicle was a blue 1975 Chevrolet pickup truck bearing New Mexico plates 099-CGK.

Lawmen's hopes rose that this lead would not fold. Van Buren police ran a make on the tag number and notified other members of the task force. The license plate checked to a Vernon Lynn Hopper Jr. at an address in Roswell, New Mexico.

Roswell police honored a request from Arkansas and soon determined that Vernon "Buddy" Hopper, 32, was no longer in New Mexico with his pickup; he was in south Texas, in jail pending trial on rape charges.

How long had he been in the Texas jail? Before Mandy Craig disappeared and was murdered? Or after?

Hopper held up as a likely suspect when the task force learned that he had been arrested in Port Lavaca, Texas, on June 8, 1992, more than two weeks after the Van Buren abduction slaying. Not only that, but authorities learned that Hopper had recently lived in Tulsa where he had worked for a security agency. When arrested, he carried an ID card from the "A&A Detective Agency" and a gold security officer's badge, which detectives assumed may have been the one shown to Mandy to lure her into the pickup with him.

"We taught Mandy to respect the law," said the victim's mother. "Children are not afraid of a police officer in or out of uniform as long as he shows a badge."

In Texas, police accused Vernon Hopper of two rapes, two kidnappings, robbery, and one attempted abduction involving three young women in separate incidents. Allegedly, he lurked outside Corpus Christi taverns where, on two different occasions, he kidnapped a young woman and took her to a nearby motel room and raped her. Each time, he showed his victim a leather strap and growled, "I've used this to kill before and it depends on how you act if you live or not. It don't make any difference to me."

Hopper's third intended victim, a jogger in Port Lavaca, escaped before the suspect could get her into his pickup. She notified police of her attacker's description. Officers arrested him soon thereafter.

In addition to confessing to his Texas crimes, Hopper also alluded to a possible fourth girl in Oklahoma, saying, according to police, that "he had asked her to go to a motel room with him."

The same way he "asked" the Texas women? Was he referring to Mandy Craig? To Roxie Moser?

On August 7, Investigators Bobby Walker and Dale Best, of the Arkansas State Police, and D.A. Gene Haynes and A.D.A. Terry McBride of Mayes County, Oklahoma, traveled to Texas where they interrogated Hopper about Mandy Craig and Roxie Moser.

Meek and diffident, the thin Hopper denied any knowledge about Tulsa's missing Roxie Moser, but he hesitated only momentarily before admitting responsibility for Mandy Craig's slaying.

According to his confession, Hopper said he picked up a girl named "Mandy" off a Van Buren street by posing as a police officer. He then drove her to Oklahoma where he rented a room at the Travelers Inn motel on IS-69, four miles north of Chouteau and Guy Williams Park.

While he confessed to raping the child, he vehemently denied otherwise abusing her. Marks found on Mandy's decomposing body, he said, must have been the results of "play karate fighting" between the two of them in the motel room.

How, then, had he killed Mandy? That still remained a crucial point in the homicide investigation.

Hopper cleared it up by saying that on Wednesday night, after he finished with Mandy, he used a syringe and needle to

inject her with a dosage of one cubic centimeter of Acepromazine and two ccs of Rompun, drugs used by veterinarians
as tranquilizers for large animals. The dosage Hopper gave
Mandy, police said, was enough to "drop a horse on its nose."

"He doesn't actually say she died," said D.A. Gene Haynes.
"He tells us he got her in the pickup and drove to Oklahoma.
He says she was asleep when he carried her out to his truck
[after assaulting her at the Travelers Inn], that he drove down
by the [Chouteau] school, turned and drove down by the cemetery, and placed the body in the bushes."

Back in Oklahoma, forensic pathologists corroborated Hopper's confession now that they knew the specific drugs that
had killed Mandy Craig. They identified Acepromazine and
Rompun in samples of the victim's blood and tissue preserved
for evidence.

OSBI agent Dennis Franchini showed a photo lineup to the
clerk who had been on duty at the Travelers Inn the night of
May 20. Although Hopper had used an assumed name, the
clerk remembered his face. Investigators then recovered a
syringe from a sandpile outside the motel where Hopper said
he had thrown it after filling Mandy's veins with lethal drugs.

"There have been doubts of [the killer's] ever coming to
justice and justice being served," exclaimed Mandy's mother.
"When I got the call from McBride, I got the best news I've
had all year."

Hopper stood accused of a half-dozen serious crimes in
Texas. Arkansas authorities charged him with kidnapping
Mandy Craig. As all these charges were sufficient to hold Hopper in jail without bond, Oklahoma prosecutors delayed filing
murder charges against him until they could obtain the results
of DNA comparisons between the suspect's body fluid and
those he left inside his victim.

As for Roxie Moser, A.D.A. McBride explained, "Evidence-
wise, there is nothing at all linking him to any other disappearances."

Little Roxie Moser remained missing, with no clues as to what may have happened to her.

On December 15, 1992, and then again on January 27, 1993, Vernon Lynn Hopper Jr. was found guilty in Neuces County, Texas, of raping the two women he abducted in Corpus Christi. He received two 99-year prison sentences, to be served consecutively. Even then, however, he would still be eligible for parole in the year 2007.

On April 16, 1993, D.A. Gene Haynes in Mayes County, Oklahoma, having secured DNA results positively linking Hopper to Mandy Craig's death, filed a charge of first-degree murder against the now-convicted rapist. Charges of kidnapping in Arkansas and assault in Port Lavaca, Texas, were still pending.

A year later, on May 5, 1994, Hopper stood before District Judge James Goodpaster in Mayes County District Court in Pryor Creek and pleaded guilty to first-degree murder.

"I want to apologize to the victim's family," Hopper muttered. "I'll never be able to forgive myself for what I did to that little girl and her mother."

Judge Goodpaster sentenced Hopper to life imprisonment without the possibility of parole.

"This man may spend the rest of his life in prison . . . but it's not going to bring Mandy back," said the victim's mother. "He deprived me and my family of life's most precious memories, as well as watching our beautiful girl grow into a young lady."

Vernon Lynn Hopper Jr. is presently in the Huntsville, Texas, penitentiary serving his sentences for rape. He must serve them before he begins serving life in Oklahoma for the injection slaying of Amanda Dee-Ann Craig.

"TEXAS'S SAVAGE FATHER-SON MURDERING SEX-FIENDS!"

by Bill G. Cox

Pretty 16-year-old Gracie Purnhagen and her cute little sister, 9-year-old Tiffany, were happy kids who were looking forward to an evening of fun when their folks dropped them off at a shopping center on Wednesday, June 13, 1990. With a $10 bill their parents had given them, the girls intended to eat at a nearby restaurant, maybe go to a bowling alley, and then take in a movie. In a sense, Gracie was "baby-sitting" her younger sister on the outing.

They preferred doing this together rather than accompanying their folks and two brothers to the car races at a track in nearby Houston, Texas.

The girls promised to be home by the 11 P.M. curfew set by their parents. The shopping center was not far from their home in the small town of Oak Ridge North in Montgomery County, only a short distance from Houston.

When the rest of the family got home from the races after midnight, they were surprised and extremely anxious to discover that Gracie and Tiffany had not returned yet. The girls were dependable and always stuck to their curfews; they were not the types to dawdle with friends or overstay their curfew.

After a brief search in the immediate area the worried parents notified the Oak Ridge North Police Department at 2:50 A.M. on Thursday that the girls were missing. Officers Andrew Walters and Robert Lovelace took the initial report and obtained descriptions of the sisters. City patrol units were notified to be on the lookout for the two girls and were told what both girls were wearing when last seen. Young Tiffany was wearing a black shirt, blue cutoff jeans, and black deck shoes without laces. Her older sister Gracie was clad in a white striped shirt, gray shorts, and light-colored, high-top tennis shoes.

The police officers told the worried parents that it wasn't all that unusual for youngsters to stay out with friends longer than intended and that they usually showed up later. But the couple emphasized that their daughters would not do anything like that and certainly had no reason to run away from home. They had never done such a thing before. And even if they might have gone somewhere with someone they knew, they were now long overdue.

"If they had gone willingly with anyone, by now it's not willingly," one of the girls' relatives said. "Tiffany would be scared. She gets afraid. I think something bad has happened to them."

The sisters were described by their family as "normal, happy-go-lucky kids who are friendly and trusting and would never think that anything could happen to them."

With the girls still missing at midmorning on Thursday, Police Chief George Biernesser of the Oak Ridge North Police Department intensified the search. Investigators checked at the restaurant and other places where the sisters might have gone the previous evening.

The investigators learned that the girls had been seen at the eatery about 6:30 P.M., and again an hour later at a local convenience store. At a bowling alley near Interstate 45, an employee told the sleuths that Gracie often stopped by to visit with friends or play in the game room. Several teenagers recalled seeing Gracie and her little sister at the bowling alley about 8:30 P.M.

The sleuths came up with one witness, a school friend of Gracie's. He had seen the girls emerge from the bowling alley and had talked briefly with Gracie. Gracie mentioned to him that she was waiting for a boy named "Delton" to come and pick her up.

Another teenager remembered that he had seen the sisters talking to two men near a pickup in the bowling alley parking lot. The pickup was white, with a blue stripe on the side, the teen said.

But no one remembered seeing either girl after that.

On the possibility that the sisters might have been abducted, two FBI agents joined the investigation, working with the Oak Ridge police.

When the detectives asked the members of the girls' family if they knew who "Delton" might be, they said they knew of an individual named Delton Dowthitt who was an acquaintance of Gracie's. But there had been no serious relationship between them, one family member said, and they had no idea that Gracie intended to see the boy that evening.

Gracie was not allowed to "car date," as the relative described it. She only socialized in a group of school kids, since she was not considered old enough to have regular dates. Gracie had talked to Delton Dowthitt on the phone several times, the family member recalled, and he had once visited at the house.

With the investigation turning up no leads as to the sisters' whereabouts, the family had posters printed and distributed them around Oak Ridge, including the bowling alley that was a favorite teenage hangout. The posters bore photographs and the descriptions of the missing sisters.

Shortly before 4 A.M. on Friday, June 15, Montgomery County deputy Mickey Worley was patrolling along Rayford

Road near the Imperial Oaks Subdivision when he spotted a dusty 1975 Malibu Classic station wagon bumping along on a flat tire. The station wagon was occupied by two men.

His suspicions aroused, the deputy stopped the station wagon and talked briefly with the driver. While looking over the vehicle, the officer noticed several cinder blocks and some rope in the back.

Deputy Worley did a radio license-registration check with his dispatcher. He learned that the driver, 20-year-old Ben Fulton, was wanted on outstanding traffic warrants.

The passenger in the car was identified as 16-year-old Delton Dowthitt, a friend of Fulton's. Both young men were employed at an area construction company.

Deputy Worley took the pair to the county jail in Conroe, where Fulton was confined on the traffic warrants for failure to respond to past traffic citations. The station wagon was towed into Conroe by a wrecker and impounded.

Since he was a juvenile and not involved in any known offense, Delton Dowthitt was released. He phoned his family and was soon picked up by a relative.

At the time, Deputy Worley was unaware that Dowthitt was wanted by the Oak Ridge North Police Department for questioning about the disappearance two days earlier of the Purnhagen sisters. The Oak Ridge investigators had been looking for young Dowthitt since the witness at the bowling alley recalled Gracie saying she was waiting for "Delton."

Later, Ben Fulton was bailed out of jail by his employer, Max Smith, the owner of the construction firm for which both youths worked.

The next day, the Montgomery County Sheriff's Department received a phone call from Smith. Smith said that one of his employees had called him to say he was scared because he knew something about a killing.

"He's at my house now and wants to talk to an officer," Smith said.

The sheriff's department dispatched Deputy Heather Drennan to the Smith residence, where a young and frightened construction worker named Pete Brown related a shocking story.

Obviously worried, Brown said that one of his coworkers, Ben Fulton, knew about the murders of two girls. A nervous Peter Brown related that Fulton had said that Delton Dowthitt had bragged about raping and killing a girl "named Casey" and her little sister. Moreover, Fulton had led Brown to a wooded area along a pipeline in south Montgomery County where he had seen the bodies of two females. At the deputy's request, Brown agreed to direct Drennan to the spot.

Accompanied by Brown and Smith, the deputy followed directions to a location along a pipeline near its intersection with West Welsford Road in the Imperial Oaks Subdivision. The site was on Rayford Road, the area where Ben Fulton and Delton Dowthitt had been stopped by Deputy Worley. Brown led the way and pointed to the bodies of two young females lying head to head in the brush.

The deputy radioed the sheriff's office, asking that the homicide-response team be sent to the scene. Shortly thereafter, deputies and crime-scene technicians, including Sergeant Tracy Peterson, arrived, along with a justice of the peace who was the acting coroner under Texas law.

Examining the badly decomposed bodies, the officers saw that the older girl was nude. The smaller victim, who appeared to be about 10 years old, was clothed. She had apparently been strangled with the rope that was still twisted around her neck. Neither girl was wearing shoes.

From the descriptions of the missing Purnhagen sisters and the clothing they were wearing when last seen, the investigators had little doubt that they had found the girls. On the wrist of the younger victim was a multicolored bracelet that matched the description of one mentioned in the missing-person report.

After the bodies and scene were photographed and searched for possible evidence, an ambulance transported the victims to a hospital, where the autopsies would be performed.

Meanwhile, Montgomery County detectives Frank Hidalgo

and Dan Norris took an audio-video statement from Pete Brown, who had directed the deputy to the bodies.

According to Brown, Ben Fulton told him that on Friday morning, Fulton and Dowthitt were on their way to pick up the victims' bodies to dispose of them elsewhere when they were stopped by Deputy Worley.

Fulton told Brown that he and Dowthitt planned to weigh down the bodies with cinder blocks and dump them in a creek, but they were interrupted when the flat tire on the station wagon drew the deputy's attention.

Fulton also told Brown that Dowthitt had forced a bottle inside Gracie Purnhagen during the assault.

Max Smith gave the detectives some additional information that bolstered the growing circumstantial evidence against Delton Dowthitt, a handsome, long-haired youth with tattoos.

Smith recalled Fulton's bragging that he and Dowthitt had picked up two girls at a bowling alley and had sex with them.

"I didn't pay any attention to it then," Smith said. "These guys are always blowing hot air and bragging about stuff like that."

Meanwhile, Detective David Moore passed along to Detective Hidalgo the preliminary findings from the autopsies on the victims. Because of the advanced decomposition of the body, the cause of Gracie Purnhagen's death had not been determined immediately. The pathologist found cuts and other evidence of anal assault that was consistent with some type of object having been forced into the girl's anus.

Tiffany Purnhagen did not appear to have been sexually assaulted, but the cause of her death was believed to be ligature strangulation, because a rope was still knotted around her neck when her body was found. More details would be forthcoming from additional tests, the medical examiner told the probers.

The identification of the victims was confirmed later in the day through the comparison of dental records with the teeth of the slain girls.

Based on the witness statements and the accumulated evi-

dence, Detective Hidalgo and A.D.A. Anthony Benardino prepared affidavits seeking an arrest warrant for Ben Fulton and
a search warrant to search his station wagon.

Because the other suspect, Delton Dowthitt, was a juvenile,
and the county attorney's office had jurisdiction over juvenile
offenses, Hidalgo conferred with Assistant County Attorney
Mary Szilagi-Ovaitt to obtain an order to have Delton Dowthitt
held in detention on allegations of sexual assault and capital
murder. Meanwhile, the detectives searching for the out-on-bail
Ben Fulton learned that he was staying at a motel in Porter,
Texas. Since the suspect was not at home when officers showed
up, the sleuths set up a surveillance on the motel. Later, the
suspect was taken into custody there.

When Ben Fulton was grilled by Detectives Hidalgo and
Norris, he denied having taken part in the slayings or assaults
of the victims. He gave the probers the names of witnesses
who could verify where he was when the murders were thought
to have been committed. However, Fulton admitted that he'd
agreed to help Delton Dowthitt dispose of the bodies and that
they were sidetracked from this plan when the deputy stopped
them early Friday morning in Fulton's pickup. Fulton said the
two had returned to finish the job the next day, but they
changed their minds about moving the victims because of the
bodies' deterioration.

According to Fulton, Delton Dowthitt had left Montgomery
County with his father to visit relatives near New Orleans.
Fulton was jailed on the capital-murder charge and ordered
held without bond while the investigators checked out his
story. The alibi witnesses named by Fulton later verified that
he was elsewhere and could not have been involved in the
murders.

After an investigator obtained the address of a relative of
Delton Dowthitt's in Metarie, Louisiana, the teenager was
nabbed there by Jefferson Parish sheriff's deputies. The youth
was arrested when he attempted to flee.

Delton Dowthitt was returned to Montgomery County the

next day by Detective-Sergeant Peterson and Detective Moore. Confronted with the case against him, the youth gave a video-taped statement to detectives. In his account, he said that he picked up Gracie and Tiffany Purnhagen at the bowling alley late on Wednesday night, June 13. The trio decided to go for a drive. At a secluded spot on Rayford Road, Delton and Gracie got out of his vehicle to discuss their "relationship."

When the girl told him that she was ending their so-called relationship, and that she and her family were moving to North Carolina in three weeks, they began to argue. Delton became enraged and attacked Gracie, choking her with his hands and then raping her. Then he stabbed her with a pocketknife and cut her throat.

When Tiffany got out to see what was going on, Delton strangled her to death. After placing the bodies in the woods, he drove to his apartment in Humble, a small community in the area.

One investigator told reporters that Delton and Gracie had apparently had "a stormy relationship." The sleuth said, "It seems he's very possessive of his girlfriends. He became en-raged."

A relative of the victims told reporters that he knew of no relationship that Gracie had with Dowthitt. "He was at the house one time months ago," the man said. "If it was a rela-tionship with Gracie, it was a secret one. I don't know where this 'big relationship' came from, unless it's in his mind."

Delton Dowthitt was arraigned on charges of capital murder and aggravated sexual assault under provisions of the state ju-venile code. However, the prosecutor said he planned to seek a hearing to have the youth certified for trial as an adult rather than as a juvenile. At the same time, the district attorney noted that the capital-murder and sexual assault charges filed against Ben Fulton would be dismissed. "Texas has no accessory-after-the-fact law," he explained. "To be an accomplice of any kind, Fulton would have had to be involved in the slayings. Covering up the crime doesn't make him an accomplice." He added that

Fulton would be placed under a material-witness bond to make sure that he was available to testify against Delton Dowthitt when Delton was tried.

The day after confessing to the two brutal murders, Delton Dowthitt led Detectives Hidalgo and Hal McElroy and Officer George Tones to the site where the bodies had been found.

After obtaining a search warrant for the blue-and-white pickup in which the teenager had driven the sisters to the secluded area, the officers had it transported to Austin to be gone over thoroughly by specialists at the Texas Department of Public Safety crime lab.

In processing the vehicle for blood and trace evidence, the lab specialists found blood on the pickup seat and on the door handle on the driver's side. Hairs and other trace evidence were found, according to the lab report given to Detective Hidalgo.

Though Delton Dowthitt had admitted to both killings, Hidalgo and the other investigators were still not convinced that the teenager was telling all he knew about the murders. Their doubts were bolstered by information they received from a family member of Dowthitt's.

The relative reported that Delton Dowthitt and his father, Dennis Thurl Dowthitt, had been together on the evening of June 13. Father and son had reportedly set out for Conroe to repossess a vehicle from a customer who was delinquent in payments. "They both were in a blue-and-white pickup," the relative said.

In addition, the sleuths turned up two other witnesses who had stopped at the Dowthitt car lot about eleven o'clock that night. These witnesses noticed blood on the clothing of both the son and father. Delton had blood on his pants and Dennis had spots of blood around his shirt pocket, the witnesses told the investigators.

Having received this new information, the sleuths requested that Delton's father come to the sheriff's department for questioning. The 45-year-old Dennis Dowthitt came in voluntarily.

After some preliminary questions, Detective Hidalgo told

the used-car dealer that he had been seen with his son in the pickup on the night when the victims disappeared and were slain.

Dennis Dowthitt agreed to make a statement.

He said that he drove his son to the bowling alley in Oak Ridge North on the night of June 13, and watched as Delton talked to Gracie Purnhagen in the parking lot. Father and son then went back to the auto-sales lot in Humble, where Dennis stayed while Delton returned to the bowling alley in a truck borrowed from the car lot to pick up Gracie for a prearranged get-together.

When Delton came back, about 11 P.M., he had blood on his clothing, acted distressed, and would not tell his father what had happened.

About the same time that Delton returned, two couples, relatives of Dowthitt's, came to the car lot. When they spotted the blood on Delton and also on Dennis's shirt, they asked what had happened.

In response, Delton told them that he had been in a fight. Dennis said he had gotten blood on his own shirt when he hugged his upset son.

Dennis Dowthitt voluntarily agreed to submit to a lie-detector test, which was administered by Kelly Hendricks, a polygraph examiner from Houston. After failing several polygraph tests and being quizzed further by Hendricks and Hidalgo, Dennis Dowthitt now said he had lied about staying at the car lot and admitted to being present when his son killed the two sisters. He denied any direct involvement in the murders, but he admitted that he'd helped destroy evidence of the crimes.

Polygraph expert Hendricks told Detective Hidalgo that Dowthitt showed strong reactions, indicating that he was not telling the truth when asked if he had actually taken part in the slayings.

Upon making a formal statement confessing that he had been present during the girls' deaths, Dennis Dowthitt was booked for investigation of capital murder after Detective Hidalgo consulted an assistant district attorney.

The next day, Detective Hidalgo brought young Delton Dowthitt to the Criminal Justice Center to be reinterviewed and informed about his father's admission that he had been present at the scene when Delton killed the victims.

Delton Dowthitt reacted with a surprising new statement of his own. Not only had his father been there, the youth said, but it was his father who had sexually attacked Gracie Purnhagen, jabbing a bottle into her anus and then stabbing her to death. Delton added that his dad ordered him to kill Tiffany Purnhagen, and he had done so out of fear of the older man.

Delton told Detective Hidalgo that he and his father picked up the sisters at the bowling alley and drove in the pickup truck to the isolated area where the slaying took place. Delton said he was talking with Gracie at the rear of the truck when, suddenly, Tiffany screamed and came running around the pickup, with Dennis in hot pursuit.

According to Delton's statement, his father said they had to kill both girls because he had "messed up." The son quoted his father as saying, "I've done something very wrong. Now they both have to die!"

Delton confessed to choking Tiffany with his hands and then with a thick rope to make sure she was dead after being ordered to kill her by his father. Delton remembered Gracie screamed at the time that he himself tightened the rope around Tiffany's neck.

Dennis Dowthitt tried to rape Gracie, then cut her throat and stabbed her in the chest. He also sexually assaulted her with a beer bottle, the youth said. The father-son killers then moved the bodies into the brush.

Later, Delton Dowthitt, accompanied by his attorney, led the officers to a wooded area behind his apartment. There, he pointed to the location where his father had thrown the knife used to kill Gracie. After a brief search, the lawmen found it.

The knife was sent to the Department of Public Safety crime

lab for examination, which subsequently reported that blood was found on the knife. Now the sleuths obtained a warrant to search Dennis Dowthitt's office. While sorting through a bag of trash there, they recovered a beer bottle that appeared to be bloodstained and two pieces of rope that had been fashioned as ligatures. The rope was the same kind that was found knotted around the throat of Tiffany Purnhagen. A subsequent examination of the bottle by crime-lab technicians revealed a bloody fingerprint on it. The blood was the same type as Gracie Purnhagen's and the fingerprint was identified as Dennis Dowthitt's.

Charges of capital murder were filed against Dennis Dowthitt, along with a charge of aggravated sexual assault for the brutal attack on Gracie Purnhagen. The bearded suspect was denied bond.

Eventually, Delton Dowthitt, who had been certified to be tried as an adult, entered into a plea-bargain agreement with the state. He pleaded guilty to the murder by strangulation of Tiffany Purnhagen and was sentenced to 45 years in state prison. Delton agreed to testify against his father when he was brought to trial, in return for which the state would drop the capital-murder charge filed against him in the stabbing and sexual attack of Gracie Purnhagen.

On September 28, 1992, Dennis Dowthitt, now 47, went on trial in the 221st State District Court in Conroe, with Judge Ervin Ernest presiding.

It was the lurid and bloodcurdling testimony of Delton Dowthitt that transfixed the packed courtroom. Testifying for over two hours in a voice choked with emotion and barely audible, the teenager related that he had moved in with his father a short time before the murders occurred.

He told the jury that he and his father were giving the victims a ride home from the bowling alley when his father suggested they drive to a remote place and drink beer. After Delton and Gracie Purnhagen got out of the pickup and walked to the rear, the witness said, the chilling chain of events began.

Delton said he was kissing Gracie when her younger sister ran up screaming. Tiffany was being chased by Dennis Dowthitt, who had a knife in his hand. Delton left Gracie and went over to Tiffany.

"I remember he said, 'Man, I made a mistake. Now we got to kill them!' " Delton Dowthitt testified about his dad.

Delton said he didn't see it all in the darkness, but he heard a "thudding," which was Gracie being pushed to the ground by Dennis. After trying to sexually assault Gracie and stabbing her, Dennis walked over to where Delton and Tiffany were standing and twice shouted to his son: "Do it! Do it!"

In a choked voice, Delton Dowthitt testified, "I then turned around. I leaned over and kissed her [Tiffany] on her forehead. I told her I was sorry."

Delton then strangled Tiffany with his hands and tied a rope around her throat to make sure she was dead.

"I heard Gracie scream while I tied the rope around Tiffany's neck," Delton said.

Delton said his father continued the sexual assault on Gracie and cut her throat a second time. Later, his father warned him not to implicate him in the murders, Delton said.

"He just told me I'd never better snitch on him, and if I did rat on him, he would rat on me."

His father even visited Delton in jail, reiterating his warning. During that jail visit, the elder Dowthitt stressed that he wasn't the only one out of jail—so were Delton's other family members. The youth took this as a threat on his relatives' lives.

A woman relative of Dowthitt's, who described the Purnhagen sisters as "real good friends of mine," testified about a telephone conversation she'd had with Dennis Dowthitt about 10 P.M. on June 14, 1990, the night after the slayings. Fighting back tears, the witness recalled the phone call.

"He asked me how I was doing . . . I said fine. And he asked me if I'd ever forgive him for what he had done. I said, 'About Sunday?' He said, 'No, about what I did yesterday.' "

"Yesterday" was June 13, the date of the murders, as the jury knew by now.

The witness identified a hunting knife, the one recovered from behind Dowthitt's place, as Dennis's knife. She said he had used it when she'd accompanied him on hunting trips.

Answering a question from the prosecutor, the woman confirmed that Dowthitt was impotent. At that point, it was not clear how she knew this.

The question set the stage for part of the testimony of the next witness, the medical examiner who had conducted the autopsy on Gracie Purnhagen. He told the jury that Gracie was sexually assaulted with an object the size and shape of a beer bottle. The state offered into evidence the beer bottle found in the trash at the defendant's car-lot office.

Sheriff's department fingerprint expert Buster Emmons testified about the results of the tests he'd run on the beer bottle. He explained that he had found Dennis Dowthitt's fingerprint on the bottle, in blood that was identified as the same type as Gracie Purnhagen's. The expert witness said that with the help of the FBI, he was able to use an innovative new technique to enhance the fingerprint.

The state also called as a witness the woman relative whom Dennis and Delton Dowthitt had visited in Louisiana after the double murders. She testified about a conversation she'd had with Dennis Dowthitt four days after the killings. She said that during a walk, Dennis Dowthitt told her, "I did it and made Delton do it."

He refused to explain his comments and started talking about something else, the witness said. At that time, she had no idea what he was talking about, but the remark took on ominous and pertinent meaning after Dowthitt was arrested and charged with the slayings.

The defense had little offer in the way of testimony, except to try to attack the credibility of the state's key witness, Delton Dowthitt.

The defendant's lawyers called to the stand a psychologist,

who two years earlier had been among those who recommended that Delton Dowthitt be certified to stand trial as an
adult. The psychologist said that after examining the teenager,
he'd diagnosed him as a remorseless sociopath. "I came to the
conclusion he showed more regret for being incarcerated than
for what happened to the girls," the witness said. "He was
worried and preoccupied by having to go to prison."

The defense attempted to show that young Delton pinned
the murders on his father to escape more prison time, since
the prosecution had agreed to dismiss the murder charge
against him in Gracie's death in exchange for his testimony
against his father.

Also taking the stand for the defense was a friend of Dennis
Dowthitt's for 40 years. The witness testified that Dennis had
told him that he needed to hide a truck which had been used
in the murder of two young girls. Dennis had indicated that
the truck could be used to link his son to the crime. Dennis
had told him that he threw away a knife used in the murder,
the witness said, but he never admitted involvement in the slayings.

In closing arguments, lawyers for the state and the defense
told the jury they would have to believe the testimony of Delton Dowthitt in order to convict his father.

On the other hand, the defense contended that the youth was
lying to save his own hide through the plea-bargain deal made
with the prosecution.

But Prosecutor Barbara Hale said she had no apologies to
make for the deal that gave Delton Dowthitt 45 years behind
the walls. She said, "I would make a deal with the devil himself to keep Dennis Dowthitt off the streets."

Hale told the jury that the elder Dowthitt was the one who
had reason to take the lives of both girls. She said that the
father, in his statement to the investigators, said it was Delton
who had tried to have sex with Tiffany while the four were
parked in the wooded area. But, she pointed out, Dennis Dowthitt stumbled briefly in his statement and indicated that he

was the one who had tried to sexually molest the 9-year-old child.

"He just told us why the girls were killed," said Hale. "He didn't mean to, but he slipped."

The prosecutor theorized to the jury that the elder Dowthitt, who had admitted to being impotent for 15 years, exploded into a frustrated rage after the young girl fought off his advances and jumped out of the pickup.

"The defendant is impotent and that makes him angry," the prosecutor said. "You can see that anger in pictures of Gracie Purnhagen when he got through with her."

The jury deliberated about four hours before they returned their verdict. They found Dennis Dowthitt guilty of capital murder in the death of Gracie Purnhagen.

The same jury would decide his fate: either life in prison or death by lethal injection.

In the penalty phase of the trial, the state set out to show the jury what kind of man Dennis Dowthitt was. To assess the death penalty, the jury would have to agree on three questions: whether he had deliberately killed the girl, whether he would be a continuing threat to society, and whether there were no mitigating factors in the commission of the murder.

A prison psychiatrist characterized Dennis Dowthitt as a sadistic rapist, one who gets pleasure from causing pain through sex. He would be a continuing threat to society, the doctor testified.

A female relative of Dennis Dowthitt's told the jury that he'd raped her only four days before the murders. The brutal sexual assault occurred at a camping ground while others on the trip, among them Delton Dowthitt, were away from the campsite, the witness said.

"He started hugging me and trying to kiss me and he started grabbing my private parts," she related. "I told him to stop."

But he continued the attack, she said, throwing her to the ground and taking off some of her clothing. The victim related that he pulled a knife, which she said was identical to the one identified as the knife that killed Gracie Purnhagen, and placed it against her wrists and then her throat.

"He put the knife to my throat and said he would kill me if I didn't do it," she testified. "I just told him to go ahead and do it because I didn't want to deal with this anymore." She said that Dennis Dowthitt had been assaulting her with his hands, broomsticks, and bottles since she was 11 years old.

Another relative testified that Dennis Dowthitt had fondled her when she was four years old and again when she was a teenager. She said the last incident caused her to move from his home.

In closing her remarks to the jury, Prosecutor Hale said, "We are dealing with a man who feeds on inflicting pain, and he knows he is doing it, and he doesn't care. He is a sadistic rapist. He is dangerous. I submit to you that he is a serial murderer who was caught the first time."

The jury deliberated less than four hours before returning their verdict, mandating death for the convicted killer.

After Dennis Dowthitt was sentenced by the judge, he was taken to death row at Huntsville, where he is currently awaiting the automatic appeal of the death verdict.

As for Delton Dowthitt, he continues to serve his 45-year sentence.

"THE KILLER DEFILED, BLUDGEONED, THEN CALLED 911!"

by Harry Spiller

On Saturday, January 18, 1992, Dispatcher Bruce Graul, of Illinois's Herrin Police Department, was enjoying a quiet morning when the phone rang.

"Nine-one-one, cmergency," Dispatcher Graul said into his mouthpiece.

"Yes, ah, there's been a rape and murder at Herrin, on the—uh, dry—in the—at the dry-cleaning place," the caller muttered.

"A rape and murder?" Graul asked.

"Yeah," the caller replied.

"Uh-huh. Whereabouts, sir?"

"I don't—I don't know the—the, uh—the address or nothing to it."

"Okay. It is at a residence or . . . ?"

"It's—it's in Herrin."

"Okay. Can you tell me where the body and everything's at?" Dispatcher Graul asked.

"Uh . . . it's in the back of the place," the caller said. "You go in there. You go through a door. Seen this, you know. It freaked me out. It looked like she was, you know, she was stripped down. But there's blood everywhere. Looked like somebody bumped her."

"It's in a gas station?"

"No. It's in—it's in the dry-cleaning place. It's right next to it."

"Okay. It's in the dry-cleaning place."

"Yeah," the caller responded.

"It's inside the building?" Graul asked.

"Yes," the caller replied.

"What is your name, sir?"

"I can't tell you. This is nine-one-one. I don't want to get—"

"I've got to have your name, sir."

"I'm sorry, buddy—it's real! Go check on it!" the caller shot back impatiently just before he slammed the receiver down.

Dispatcher Graul immediately put a trace on the call.

Sergeant Frank Vigiano and Detective Mark Brown were both in the dispatch office when the call came in. They scurried out to the dry cleaners on Park Avenue to check out the possible murder and rape.

As the lawmen pulled into the parking lot, they spotted a gold Dodge parked in front of the bay doors of what had once been a gas station, but was now converted into a dry cleaners. They quickly got out of their vehicle. Detective Brown looked through the front windows of the building while Sergeant Vigiano checked the two doors on the south side. Both doors were locked.

Vigiano continued around the building to check for other open windows or doors. When he got to the southwest corner of the building, he noticed a nylon stocking lying on the ground. He continued around the building until he met Detective Brown at the front door.

"There'a woman's stocking on the ground at the back of the building," Sergeant Vigiano informed his colleague.

Both officers cautiously entered the building. The front

lobby was empty. The officers moved to a door at the north side of the room. Slowly, they opened it. On the floor a few feet inside the room beyond, they saw a black purse lying there with its contents scattered all over.

The officers moved through the door but saw no one in the bay area of the building. Suddenly, however, both sleuths' stomachs tightened with knots as what had been only the possibility of a prank call now turned into the reality of murder and rape.

Near the furnace at the back of the chamber lay the body of a white female, facedown. The victim was nude except for a bra. Her head was turned slightly to her left. Her arms were underneath her chest. A mass of congealed blood matted her hair and covered the left side of her face. Next to the body lay a pair of pantyhose and a pair of panties. A pale-yellow plastic garbage bag was beneath the victim's legs.

Detective Brown walked over to the body, bent down and felt her neck. There was no pulse.

"She's dead," Detective Brown said. "Let's secure the crime scene and call dispatch." His partner nodded.

Sergeant Vigiano secured the store while Detective Brown called the dispatcher. He asked that the crime-scene technician from the Illinois Department of Criminal Investigation be sent to the scene. Just as the sergeant finished his request, Dispatcher Graul informed him that the 911 call had been traced to a pay phone on the corner of Cypress and Park Avenue, four blocks south of the crime scene. Brown immediately went to the phone booth and secured it.

At 9:30 A.M, crime-scene technician Gary Otey from the Department of Criminal Investigation of the Illinois State Police (ISP) arrived at the crime scene. The dry-cleaners building consisted of a small salesroom directly inside the front door. Upon entering, Otey noticed a small counter, a small table, and three racks for hanging clothes. On the countertop, Otey found a personal check made out to the cleaners and signed by a Milly Mason. On the table sat a partially eaten Pop Tart and a half-filled cup of coffee.

Otey discovered a purse, apparently the victim's, which had been dumped in the bay area of the building. Then he moved to the south end of the bay and behind the furnace, where the nude body was lying.

Technician Otey photographed the corpse and the scene. Then he collected more than 100 pieces of evidence from the scene, including blood, hair, fingerprints, palm prints, clothing, a pair of eyeglasses, a plastic garbage bag, and a mop wringer.

After the crime scene had been processed, the coroner's assistants transported the body to a local hospital for an autopsy.

Technician Otey drove to the phone booth from which the 911 call had been made and processed it, too. He lifted two latent fingerprints off the telephone receiver.

Meanwhile, Chief of Police Tom Cunduff initiated a canvass of the four-block area around the murder scene.

A gas station attendant told officers that he'd seen a white male with short brown hair, wearing a white hat or cap, white coat, and blue jeans, talking on the phone at the booth to which the 911 call had been traced. The attendant did not see the man leave the phone booth.

A woman in the four-block area said that she saw a man running down Park Avenue around 9 A.M. The only thing she could remember about him was that he'd been wearing blue jeans.

Technician Otey contacted Chief Cunduff and informed him about the personal check found at the crime scene, apparently written by a Milly Mason of Herrin. The chief and Captain Tom Horn immediately obtained the address and went to the Herrin residence of Milly Mason.

Mason told the lawmen that on Saturday, January 18, between 8 and 8:15 A.M., she'd gone to the dry cleaners to pick up some laundry. No one was behind the counter or in the room. So she wrote the check, picked up her clothes, and then walked to the back of the store, looking for the employee. There she encountered a brown-haired white male who was between 30 and 35 years old, 6 feet 2 inches tall, weighing 220 pounds. He was wearing a blue sock hat, blue work shirt and pants, red-plaid insulated vest, and brown lace-up boots. The man was walking toward Milly from the back of the building.

"I told him I laid a check on the counter for my clothes," she said, "and then I left. I thought he was an employee."

Chief Cunduff quickly realized that Milly Mason must have come face-to-face with the killer. He immediately contacted Technician Otey and asked him to do a composite drawing of the suspect based on Mason's description. Copies of the composite were immediately distributed to businesses throughout the area.

In the meantime, the police found out through the owner's registration of the vehicle at the crime scene and from the manager of the dry-cleaning business that the murder victim was Kathy Anne Woodhouse, a 40-year-old mother of two children.

At 10:30 P.M. that same day, forensic pathologist John Heidingsfelder performed an autopsy on Woodhouse's body. The pathologist concluded that the victim was sexually assaulted, based on her nude condition, the bruising of her vaginal area, and the presence of dried semen stains on her skin. The doctor determined that at some point during the assault, the victim was placed on her abdomen and received a blunt-force blow to the left side of her head, just above the ear, resulting in extensive skull fractures. The pathologist concluded that the cause of death was a result of cerebral disruption and brain-stem compression, along with compound skull, orbital, maxillary, faacial, and mandible fractures due to the blunt-force injury to the head.

The doctor also examined the mop wringer found at the crime scene. The wringer was bent and covered with blood. The doctor told the sleuths that the wringer was heavy enough to have been the blunt instrument that caused the victim's injuries.

The sleuths continued the probe by interviewing Tammy Edwards, who also worked at the dry cleaners. Tammy told them that she and Kathy took turns working the Saturday 8 A.M-to-noon shift and that this Saturday had been Kathy's turn to work. Tammy had last seen Kathy on Friday, January 17, at 6 P.M., when she'd relieved Kathy at work. At that time, Kathy told her she had received a disturbing telephone call in the afternoon. A person with a gruff male voice had asked Kathy what color toenail polish she wore.

Tammy said that the only other unusual incident Kathy told her about had occurred about three weeks earlier. That was when a white male, about six feet tall, weighing 200 pounds, with a large build and brown hair, came into the cleaners and asked to use the phone. It was raining outside and he led Kathy to believe that he needed to make an emergency call. After he dialed and began talking on the phone, Kathy realized that the call was personal. A few days later, the same man came in again to use the phone. Kathy told him that she was expecting a call, so he could not use the phone. He left and never returned. For the past several days at about noon, Kathy saw the same man walk by the store. However, she did not see him on Friday, January 17.

A relative of the victim's told the police that Kathy had not appeared to be apprehensive about anyone. The relative said that when Kathy was living in Marion, Illinois, there were three or four occasions when she came home and heard someone leaving from the rear of the house. She never saw anyone and never found anything missing. Kathy's relative had contacted the police on two of those occasions, and then the incidents stopped.

Meanwhile, Herrin officers rounded up six people who fit the description of the suspect given by Milly Mason. The police asked the suspects to stand in a lineup. All agreed.

On January 19, a Sunday evening, Milly Mason attended

that lineup and attempted to identify one of the men as a suspect. One of them looked similar to the man she'd seen in the dry cleaners, she told police, but she wasn't sure.

The police were quickly able to eliminate that man as a suspect, however, when they determined that he'd been at work at the time of the murder.

The probers were beginning to get frustrated and worried. They had investigated the case continuously for three weeks. Every day they checked out leads called in by citizens. Yet they weren't any closer to a suspect than they'd been on the day of the murder.

On Tuesday, February 4, the sleuths received an anonymous call that gave them their first lead to a suspect. The caller told them to check out Paul E. Taylor, a parolee from Louisiana who was currently living with relatives on South 16th Street in Herrin. Taylor had been released from prison around Christmas. He had been serving time for aggravated attempted sexual assault.

Detectives Mark Brown and John Allen, of the Southern Illinois University Police, drove to the residence on South 16th Street. A relative of Taylor's told the lawmen that on Saturday, January 18, when she'd left for work at about 6:30 A.M., Paul had still been in bed. When she returned, about 9:30 A.M., she'd found Paul in the living room watching television or playing Nintendo.

The lawmen had found out that Paul Taylor worked at a local fast-food restaurant, so they asked the relative when the best time would be to talk with Paul. She said she was going to pick up Paul at a friend's house around 6:30 P.M. She promised the sleuths that she herself would bring Paul to the police station.

At 7:15 P.M., Detectives Brown and Allen met with Paul Taylor at the Herrin Police Department. They informed him that he was not under arrest.

"This is a voluntary interview," Detective Brown explained. "You can leave at any time."

The sleuths told Taylor that they were working on a homicide that had occurred on January 18, and Paul's name was one of many brought up, so they were simply checking out all the names.

"Paul, we would like to run a number of tests on you. Would you consent to being fingerprinted and photographed?" Detective Brown asked.

"Sure," Taylor responded.

"We would like to get blood, saliva, head and pubic hair samples, as well," Detective Allen added.

"Okay," Taylor responded once again. Then he signed consent forms, and the lawmen took him to the local hospital for the tests. After the tests they all returned to the police station. There, the sleuths began to question Taylor.

"Paul, do you know why we asked to talk to you?" Detective Brown asked.

"Yes. Because you are investigating the murder of Kathy Woodhouse," Taylor answered.

"Did you kill Kathy Woodhouse?" Brown asked.

"No!" Taylor snapped back.

"Do you have any idea who may have killed her?"

"No. I don't know anyone around here."

The sleuths asked Taylor why he thought someone would name him as a suspect. He said he didn't know, unless it was because of his height. Taylor also told the detectives that it did not bother him that he was being questioned about the murder, but he did hope that there were other people being questioned, too.

"Why would someone want to kill Kathy Woodhouse?" one of the sleuths asked Taylor.

"Because they are sick!" Taylor answered curtly.

"Paul, have you ever thought about doing something like this, even though you didn't go through with it?"

"No, because it is wrong and I wouldn't have the nerve," Taylor replied.

"What do you think should happen to the person that did this?" Allen asked.

"Fry him!" Taylor shot back.

"What did you do on the morning of the murder?"

Taylor said that he was home until approximately 8:45 A.M. Then he left the house, went to a local grocery store to buy a pack of cigarettes, and returned home about 9:15 A.M.

"Is there any reason you would have for killing Kathy?" one of the lawmen asked.

"No," Taylor replied.

"Have you ever been in the dry cleaners where the murder took place?"

"No."

"Have you ever been questioned about doing something like this before?"

"No!" Taylor fired back.

"Would you be willing to take a polygraph examination?"

"Yes," Taylor responded.

With that, the sleuths ended their interview with Taylor. They were suspicious of him and felt sure that he had lied about his past sexual offenses.

The next morning, the investigators went to the dry cleaners to review customer receipts. They discovered that someone from the restaurant where Taylor worked had recently taken some shirts to the dry cleaners. The sleuths called the restaurant and asked if Taylor had been the person who'd delivered those shirts. The manager told them that Taylor had worked for the eatery for about three weeks, that he had indeed taken shirts to the dry cleaners, and that he had just turned in his resignation, saying he was going back to Louisiana.

In the meantime, the sleuths heard from the crime lab, which had conducted tests on the saliva standard taken from Taylor. The results showed that Taylor was a nonsecretor. Interestingly, the person who'd raped and murdered Kathy Woodhouse was also a nonsecretor. However, the lab did not have enough head

and pubic hair standards for testing. The sleuths would therefore have to bring Taylor back for additional samples.

Detectives Allen and Brown went to the 16th Street residence and asked Taylor's relative if they could talk with Taylor.
Then Taylor himself came to the back door. The detectives told
him that the crime lab had requested more head and pubic hair
samples from him to carry out the proper testing.

"I don't know—maybe I should talk to an attorney," Taylor
said.

The relative urged Taylor to cooperate with the police, but
Taylor stood silently staring at the detectives.

"Do you plan on leaving town?" one of the sleuths asked
him.

"No. I just got off work," Taylor replied.

"No, you didn't Paul—you just quit your job and told the
boss you were moving to Louisiana," Detective Allen told him
pointedly.

"What's going on?" the relative asked Taylor.

At that point, the detectives asked the suspect's relative if
she would give them permission to search the house. She
agreed. Then the sleuths asked Taylor if he would grant them
permission to search his room. He also agreed.

After Taylor and his relative signed permission-to-search
forms, the sleuths went to Taylor's room. There they found a
pair of stone-washed blue jeans lying on Taylor's bed. The blue
jeans appeared to have some small bloodstains on them. Taylor
said that those were the jeans he'd been wearing on January
18. In the closet, the sleuths also discovered a white-and-black
sweatshirt that Taylor had worn on the morning of the murder.
When Detective Brown lifted the end of the mattress at the
foot of the bed, he found a pair of pantyhose with one leg
missing lying on top of two porno magazines. The sleuths
found another pair of bloodstained blue jeans in a dresser. They
found no other evidence in Taylor's bedroom.

The probers continued to search the rest of the house and,
while doing so, they asked Taylor's relative if Taylor had a hat.

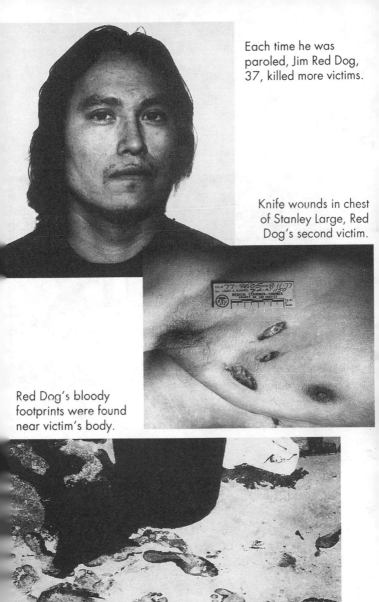

Each time he was paroled, Jim Red Dog, 37, killed more victims.

Knife wounds in chest of Stanley Large, Red Dog's second victim.

Red Dog's bloody footprints were found near victim's body.

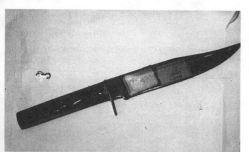

Police believe Red Dog used this knife to kill his fifth victim, Hugh Pennington, 30.

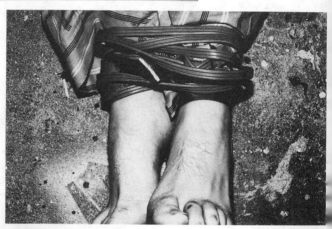

Pennington's feet were bound nine times with electrical cord and his hands eleven times with duct tape.

Polly Klaas, 12, was abducted from her California home in 1993.

Police sketch of suspected kidnapper bore a striking resemblance to Davis.

Richard Allen Davis, 40, was on parole when he was arrested for kidnapping Klaas.

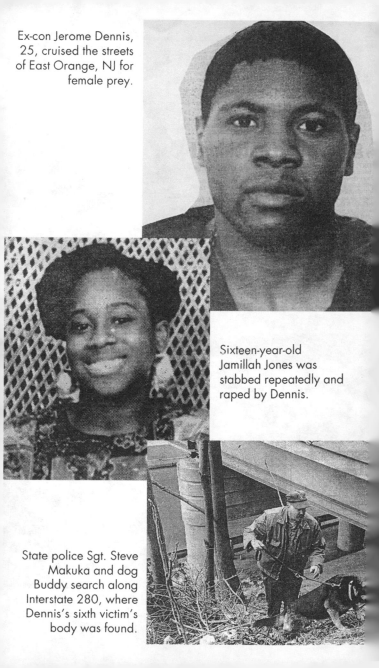

Ex-con Jerome Dennis, 25, cruised the streets of East Orange, NJ for female prey.

Sixteen-year-old Jamillah Jones was stabbed repeatedly and raped by Dennis.

State police Sgt. Steve Makuka and dog Buddy search along Interstate 280, where Dennis's sixth victim's body was found.

Twenty-year-old Todd Mendyk's stuck pickup was spotted by helicopter search crew.

The body of missing Lee Ann Larmon, 23, was found 400 feet from Mendyk's truck.

Mendyk tied Larmon between two scrub oak trees after molesting her.

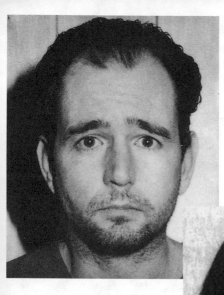

Danny Rolling, 36, confessed to killing five Florida college students during the summer of 1990.

Student victim Christina Powell, 17.

Student victim Sonja Larsen, 18.

Student victim
Christa Hoyt, 19.

Student victim
Tracy Paules, 23.

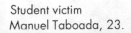

Student victim
Manuel Taboada, 23.

Gracie Purnhagen, 16, and her sister disappeared from a shopping mall.

Tiffany Purnhagen, 9.

The Purnhagen sisters' killers intended to use cinderblocks to weight their bodies for dumping in the creek.

Delton Dowthitt, 16, confessed to strangling Tiffany Purnhagen at his father's insistence.

Dennis Dowthitt, 48, received the death penalty for sexually assaulting and murdering Gracie Purnhagen.

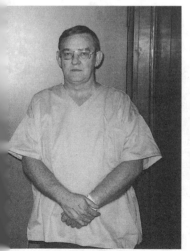

No one suspected civic leader Charles Lord, 59, was an embezzler and murderer.

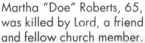

Martha "Doe" Roberts, 65, was killed by Lord, a friend and fellow church member.

Shot in the left temple, Hong Thi Nguyen, 26, was left for dead beside a Dumpster.

Police learned ex-Marine Timothy DePriest, 29, was on parole after he was arrested for Hong's murder.

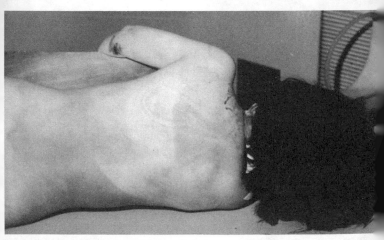

Police found bruises, scrapes and dirt on Hong's body.

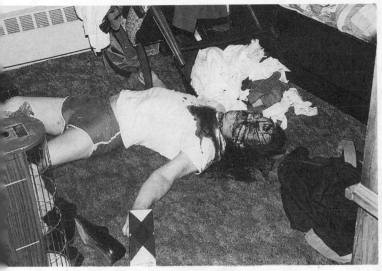

Investigators found forty-year old Gerald Trottier's viciously slashed body amidst signs of a struggle.

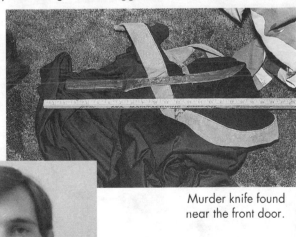

Murder knife found near the front door.

Fingerprints from ex-con Paul Stephen Reese, 28, linked him to Trottier's murder.

Victim Debra Owen, 20.

Cement ball court where Owen was stripped, beaten, raped and killed.

Jesse Ray Moffett, 20, said his bloody prints were at the scene because he'd tried to help the injured Owen.

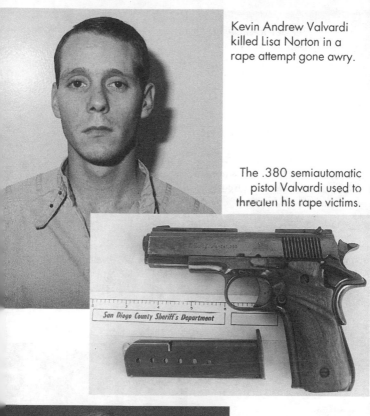

Kevin Andrew Valvardi killed Lisa Norton in a rape attempt gone awry.

The .380 semiautomatic pistol Valvardi used to threaten his rape victims.

San Diego County Sheriff's Department

Horace Benjamin Beach, Jr., 39, raped and killed two eighty-six-year old women.

Serial rapist and killer Nathaniel White, 32.

Aerial view of the farm where the bodies of two of White's six victims were found.

Victim Julianna Frank, 29.

Victim
Christine Marie Klebbe, 18.

Victim
Laurette Riviere Huggins.

Victim
Adriane M. Hunter, 27.

Lois Haro, 26, died of a gunshot wound to the head.

Haro's credit cards and keys were found on Ronald Anthony Jones, 19.

George Marvin Trone, 18, killed Haro after he and Jones raped her.

She said that he did and went to another bedroom where she pulled a blue hat from a dresser drawer. Handing it to the sleuths, she said Taylor did not like to wear the hat.

With the search ended and no other evidence found, the lawmen asked Taylor if he would go to the hospital and give them more hair samples. He agreed.

At the hospital while the samples were being taken, Detective Eric Frattini, of the Williamson County Sheriff's Department, came into the examining room and asked Taylor if he would come down to the police department for further questioning. Taylor told the detective that he preferred to go home because he was going to a rock concert and wanted to get cleaned up.

Taylor was free to leave the hospital, and Detective Allen gave him a ride back to the 16th Street residence.

Meanwhile, the sleuths put a surveillance team on Taylor, even as other lawmen took the evidence to the crime lab for analysis.

Taylor left his residence and went to the Southern Illinois University Arena for the concert. The surveillance team followed.

On Wednesday evening, February 5, Detective Frattini contacted the crime lab. Serologist Grace Johanson told the detective that Paul Taylor's blood standards showed a P.G.M. of (1+). (P.G.M. refers to phosphoglucomutase, a protein that serves as a "genetic marker" and is useful on a more detailed level of blood-typing.) Johnson explained that these results, coupled with the earlier results showing Taylor to be a nonsecretor, increased the chance of his being Kathy Woodhouse's murderer.

Detective Frattini then spoke with Glenn Schubert from the microscopy section. Schubert told the sleuth that the stocking taken from Taylor's bedroom was similar not only in color, but also in fabric, to the one found near the crime scene. Schubert had also compared pubic hairs from the scene with those taken from Taylor. The hairs were similar.

When Frattini spoke with latent fingerprint technician Mike Pittman, he learned that the fingerprints found on the telephone matched Taylor's.

The case investigators immediately contacted Williamson County state's attorney Chuck Garnati to make sure they had enough evidence to show probable cause for an arrest. Garnati adivsed them to wait until Taylor was back within Williamson County jurisdiction, and then make the arrest.

That same evening, Illinois State Trooper Daren Lindsey and Sergeant Bob McCluskey drove to the Williamson County line and waited for the suspect. Taylor left the rock concert and crossed the county line at 10:30 P.M. Trooper Lindsey and Sergeant McCluskey pulled Taylor's vehicle over and arrested him for the rape-murder of Kathy Woodhouse.

At 11:54 P.M., the detectives read Taylor his Miranda rights. Taylor waived them and agreed to talk with the police. He told the investigators that on Saturday, January 18, at about 8 A.M., he walked from his home to the dry cleaners. When he got there, he walked in and told the attendant, Kathy Woodhouse, that he was going to rob her. Then he took her to the bay area of the building. At the rear of the chamber, he picked up a mop wringer, hit Kathy twice in the head, and then left.

"When did you take Kathy's clothes off?" Detective Frattini asked.

"She was fully clothed when I left," Taylor replied.

Now the sleuths told Taylor about the physical evidence found at the scene. Taylor looked down at the floor for a few seconds, then he looked up, directly at the detective. "I raped her," he said.

"Okay, Paul, now tell me exactly what happened," Frattini prompted.

Taylor said that after walking the victim to the rear of the building, he ordered her to take off her clothes and lie down on the floor. Kathy lay down on her back. Then, Taylor said, he pulled his pants halfway down, got on top of the victim, and had sexual intercourse with her. He said that he told the victim he was having an orgasm.

Then, he said, Kathy asked him, "Did you hear that car pull up?"

Taylor told her that he didn't hear anything. He got up and told Kathy to turn over on her stomach. Then he walked toward the front of the store, where he saw a woman standing at the counter. She told him that she was there to pick up her laundry and was going to leave a check in payment.

"Fine!" Taylor told her curtly.

The customer then walked out.

Taylor said he walked back to the rear of the building and picked up a mop wringer on the way. He hit the victim twice over the head with it. Then he went to the front of the bay, took $4 from the victim's purse, and dumped the rest of the contents on the floor.

After that, Taylor said, he walked down Main Street south of the cleaners. He found a pay phone and called 911 to report that there had been a murder and rape at the cleaners. Taylor said that the officer on the line sounded as though he didn't believe him, so Taylor told him, "It's real! Go check it out!" Taylor then hung up the phone and went home.

On Friday, April 10, 1992, Paul Taylor pleaded guilty to the murder and rape of Kathy Anne Woodhouse. On Thursday, October 15, 1992, a 12-person jury sentenced him to death. Taylor is now sitting on death row, scheduled for execution by lethal injection on January 23, 1993.

UPDATE:

Paul Taylor is now sitting on death row, his execution temporarily on hold as the lengthy appeals process grinds on. For his victim, of course, there were no such similar amenities.

"BOUND SEX SLAVE HAD HER THROAT SLIT!"

by Patty Shipp

Sheriff's deputy Carlos Douglas was on routine patrol in the early-morning hours of April 9, 1987, making the rounds at businesses in Spring Hill, Florida. The community was one of the fastest growing areas in Hernando County, about 60 miles north of St. Petersburg.

Douglas, a handsome, young deputy with a friendly manner and a ready smile, slowed the cruiser as he neared one of many convenience stores in the area. The area had been plagued recently by a rash of abductions of store clerks working the night shift. Some had even wound up murdered.

Douglas kept an eye on several different convenience stores in Spring Hill. He would pass the Presto store on U.S. Highway 19 and Forest Lakes Boulevard at about the same time every night he was on duty. At about 2:55 A.M., the beautiful, young store clerk on duty would always come to the window and wave to assure Douglas that everything was fine.

On the morning of April 9, 1987, Douglas pulled into the parking lot and glared at the store. Instantly, his gut feeling told him something was wrong. The store looked empty. The girl's truck was parked near the store, but he could not see her. The deputy knew that the conscientious store clerk would never go away and leave the store unattended. He pulled his cruiser closer to the store and manipulated the vehicle's spotlight so it shined inside. When the clerk did not come into view, Douglas parked his cruiser and went into the store. Perhaps the girl was in the washroom, he reasoned, or maybe she was stocking beer in the cooler.

With his hand on the gun that rested on his hip, Deputy Douglas walked cautiously through the store. As he peered around the aisles, he called out the young woman's name. "Lee Ann, you there? Lee Ann?" But 23-year-old Lee Ann Larmon did not answer.

As Deputy Douglas walked about the store calling out for Lee Ann, he became more anxious, hoping any second to see the pretty woman with light-brown hair and the smiling face, laughing and chatting about country-western singers, or quietly engrossed in her studies.

Douglas walked behind the cash register and looked around. Lee Ann's multicolored purse and jacket were lying there. Pinned to the purse strap was a button proclaiming Lee Ann's enthusiasm for country-western star Conway Twitty. Lee Ann would never leave the store willingly without her purse, Deputy Douglas thought to himself.

Douglas walked from behind the cash register to the counter where a microwave oven sat. A hot hamburger on the counter was still steaming, and a container of relish was sitting beside it. It appeared as if someone had just left the store. Could that person have kidnapped Lee Ann? Douglas wondered. Fear, already worrying the officer, now made his heart pound. He knew something had to be done quickly. Lee Ann Larmon had surely been kidnapped.

Deputy Douglas hurried from the store and got on his radio with the police dispatcher. "The girl that works the night shift here is missing," he explained. "She knows what time I make my rounds. I think she's been kidnapped. It's very suspicious."

Spring Hill is an unincorporated area with no police department of its own. The area, which is made up of thickly populated sections of new homes and shopping centers, lies in the county's southwest corner and covers most of the area to the southwest of Brooksville, which is located in the center of the county. Except for a couple of small communities in between, Spring Hill is separated from the Gulf of Mexico by the Weeki Wachee and the Chassahowitzka Swamps. Except for Brooksville, all law enforcement in the entire county is handled by the Hernando County Sheriff's Office (HCSO), the Florida Highway Patrol, and the Florida Department of Fresh Water Fish and Wildlife.

Upon receiving Douglas's call, sheriff's deputies were dispatched to comb the county. We've got to find her, Douglas thought while he waited for backup officers to arrive at the store. He knew Lee Ann could not have been gone long.

Officers went to Lee Ann Larmon's home and awakened her relatives. She had not come home, they said, and the had no idea where she might have gone. They said that a friend of Lee Ann's had mentioned that a former boyfriend of Lee Ann's might have returned to town. He could have picked her up at the store and they could have gone out someplace to talk. Perhaps they were getting back together. Perhaps she left with him in his vehicle. That would explain why Lee Ann's truck was still at the store's parking lot. But if she had left with him willingly, why would she have left her purse?

Lee Ann's relatives told officers that they knew nothing about Lee Ann leaving work with anyone. They had heard nothing from her since she had left the house to go to work. At that time, everything had seemed normal. Lee Ann had dressed as usual in a pair of jeans and shirt. She had slipped her multicolored purse over her shoulder, got into her truck, and hurried off to work at the convenience store. She had said nothing about going away somewhere else. Lee Ann would not have left the store to go anywhere, relatives assured the officers. She took her job seriously and was working her way through Pasco-Hernando Junior College.

"Lee Ann Larmon did not leave on her own accord," deputies concluded. "She was kidnapped."

Sheriff's lieutenants Jerry Calhoun and Royce Decker were awakened at their homes by telephone calls. "You've got to do an air search," they were both told. Both men quickly got dressed and hurried through the fog to the sheriff's office airplane hangar, located at the Brooksville Regional Airport, about five miles south of Brooksville.

Through the wee-morning hours, both officers sat impatiently in the helicopter, wishing the thick fog that covered the west end of the county would lift. If they tried to take the chopper up in such a white cloud, they would not be able to see their hands in front of their faces. They had no choice but to wait and pray that the fog would lift soon.

Deputies in patrol cars circled through Spring Hill parking lots, where young people had partied in the night hours. In Spring Hill and other areas in Florida, parking lots are popular hangouts for teenagers who stay out late at night and have nothing else to do. Often, young people will meet in parking lots, and from there, they will go to secluded sinkholes that have filled with water and become lakes, or to houses where they can drink beer and smoke marijuana, without the threat of cops or parents popping in on them.

Sheriff's detectives and deputies looked in every direction, checking out every road that might possibly lead to Lee Ann Larmon's whereabouts or to her abductor. There was one other possibility, detectives acknowledged—the newspapers, which were delivered in the early-morning hours, had been delivered to the store as usual. Maybe the carrier who brought them had seen something.

Sleuths contacted and questioned the newspaper carrier. Yes, he said, he had been at the store at 2 A.M. that morning. Lee Ann had been on duty. When he left the store, she was fine, he said.

Another person deputies felt they should contact was the store manager. He told officers that Lee Ann was a nice girl.

He said he knew she was working the night shift at the store so she could go to school during the day. But he was unaware of anything that might have happened that night.

HCSO detective Jim Blade also knew Lee Ann Larmon. Blade went into the store occasionally and drank coffee while Lee Ann was on duty. He knew no one who would want to hurt her.

Meanwhile, the helicopter's propeller whirred with an impatient whining hum. And as sheriff's lieutenants Calhoun and Decker waited for the fog to lift, they, too, became more and more anxious. Radio communications with the Sheriff's Office convinced the lieutenants in the helicopter that Lee Ann Larmon had been kidnapped from the Presto store. Officers were swarming western Hernando County in search of Lee Ann. And as day started to break, Calhoun felt he could wait no longer. Although there was still too much fog to go up safely, Calhoun decided he would have to risk it.

The chopper was soon hovering over areas near the Presto convenience store where Lee Ann had last been seen. It then veered to other areas where new construction was going up, to housing developments and shopping centers.

The chopper then headed slowly up the east side of U.S. 19, a well-traveled highway that runs down Florida's west coast, from the northernmost part of the state south to Naples. At night, U.S. 19 in Hernando County north of Spring Hill is dark and eerie. The country is scantly populated, with deep woods marked by signs that warn of bears. Sinkholes and dusty lime-rock roads lie to the east, and wildlife preserves and swamps to the west.

If Lee Ann had been kidnapped, which officers believed was the case, her abductor might have left her someplace along the highway. She could be trying to get back from some isolated place at that very minute. Lieutenant Decker climbed out of the helicopter and positioned himself on its runner, in order to get a better look at the ground below. Through the thick mist, both officers kept their eyes looking downward, combing the ground over which the chopper hovered slowly. Reaching the northern part of the county, Calhoun turned the chopper, swooped across the highway, and started back south on the west side of U.S. Highway 19. There the swampy area was mostly wooded with scrub-oaks, dressed with Spanish moss, and thick, prickly palmetto bushes.

At about 10 A.M., while flying over the long swampy area adjacent to the gulf, deputies in the helicopter spotted a pickup truck that appeared to be stuck in the swamp. With Decker still sitting on the helicopter runner, Calhoun made a sweep, passing over the blue Ford truck. Two men were trying to get the vehicle out of a mud hole. A woman stood near a car behind the truck. She looked up at the helicopter and waved.

Calhoun got on the radio and reported the incident. The sheriff's dispatcher sent a patrol car to the scene. Without help, the people involved could be stranded in the swamp indefinitely.

While patrol deputies were still searching throughout the county for Lee Ann Larmon, deputies were dispatched to the swamp where the people were stranded. The middle-aged woman identified herself as a relative of the truck passenger. The owner of the truck was an acquaintance who had been to her house before, but she did not know him too well. The two men had come to her home earlier that morning to ask for help, she said. They needed equipment to free the truck. The dirt road through this part of the swamp was often used by people to illegally dump garbage.

A deputy walked in front of the car to the pickup truck. "Y'all have a problem here?" he asked.

"Yeah," both men agreed. The truck was stuck in the mud and had been for some time.

"What were y'all doing out here this time of morning?"

"We've been mud-bogging," they both replied.

"Mud-bogging," or driving a truck through a swamp for sport, was a popular form of recreation around the Florida wetlands.

With Lieutenant Decker still on the helicopter runner, Lieutenant Calhoun made another sweep over the truck. He saw that help for the people below had arrived. Still, Calhoun put the helicopter in hovering mode and stared down at the swampy area around the stuck truck.

Suddenly, Calhoun's eyes widened. Below, about 400 yards from the stranded truck, a female form was lying in a cluster of palmetto bushes. "Take a look down there," Calhoun said, but Decker's eyes were already focused on the nude girl. Portions of her body were bound with wire, and she was curled up in a fetal position. Looking closely, the men could see the girl was wearing nothing but socks.

Without hesitation, Lieutenant Calhoun got on the radio. "Don't let those two men out of sight," he ordered. "Keep them there. They might be involved in what has happened out here." Calhoun felt that even if the men were not involved, with a girl lying in the bushes only about 400 feet away, they might have seen something.

While other police cars were dispatched to the swamp, deputies kept the woman and the men talking.

My God, officers thought when they went to the palmetto bushes where the girl lay. Who could have done such a thing? The men at the truck, when asked moments later, shook their heads. They didn't know anything, they said. They were out mud-bogging. They had seen nothing.

The men identified themselves. The one with long, straggly light-brown hair, peach-fuzz mustache, and goatee said he was Phillip Frantz, of Spring Hill. The other with shorter, wavy black hair, black piercing eyes, and a thick black goatee, identified himself as Todd Mendyk of Shady Hills, an area south of Spring Hill in adjoining Pasco County. Both men were 20 years old. Neither one had much to say to police.

While officers from the Sheriff's Office started gathering evidence, Jeff Cario, an assistant in the State's Attorney's Office, and Jane Phifer, an investigator for the State Attorney's Office, were sent to view the crime scene and watch officials gather evidence.

As they walked alongside the yellow crime-scene tape that stretched across a large area of ground around the stuck truck, Phifer, who had been to many crime scenes previously, felt a cold chill come over her.

Investigator Phifer could not make any sense of what had happened. The beautiful girl lay nude except for a pair of socks. She was bound with electrical wire and gagged. Phifer thought about her own daughters. The sadness that had been coming over the investigator deepened. The beautiful girl had been discarded in this illegal dump, as if she was no more than garbage. On the victim's face, Phifer could see the torture the girl had suffered.

Detective Jim Blade, who had known the victim, was called to the scene. He identified the dead girl as Lee Ann Larmon. He followed the ambulance to Lykes Memorial Hospital morgue in Brooksville, where the body was turned over to Dr. John Sass, pathologist and assistant medical examiner for the state's 5th Judicial Circuit.

The Presto store manager was called to the morgue to identify the body. He, too, identified the dead girl as Lee Ann Larmon, the store's night clerk.

In the swamp where the body had been found, Detective Ralph Decker (no relation to Lieutenant Royce Decker), of the HCSO, found articles of clothing. These were later identified as having belonged to Lee Ann Larmon and had been thrown into the swamp. The clothing was sent to the FBI lab in Washington, D.C., to be analyzed.

A knife was found in the mud underneath a truck wheel; it, too, was sent to the FBI. They subsequently determined that it had been the knife used to cut the electrical wire that had bound Lee Ann's neck, wrists, and ankles.

Other FBI agents became involved in the case. Raymond Rawalt, an expert mineralogist, compared soil samples taken from the bottom of the stranded motorists' shoes with samples taken from the area where Lee Ann's body had been dragged and tied to a tree and from the palmetto bush where she was later ditched. The FBI found that the soil samples at the scenes matched the soil samples taken from the bottoms of Todd Mendyk's shoes.

FBI agent Michael Malone determined that hair that had been vacuumed from Todd Mendyk's truck had been taken from Lee Ann's head by some act of force.

As Sheriff Thomas Mylander, detectives, and deputies dug into the incident, Phillip Frantz and Toddy Mendyk were ordered to be held for the murder and kidnapping of Lee Ann Larmon. The men were then indicted by the grand jury.

Frantz and Mendyk were held in jail until the case went to court in October 1987. Phillip Frantz agreed to exchange a guilty plea for a life sentence, which would put him in jail for 25 years without parole, rather than be subjected to the electric chair. In order to get this deal, Frantz had to agree to testify against Todd Mendyk, who, detectives said, was the "mastermind" of the crime.

But there would be no plea bargaining for Mendyk "unless he wants to plea for high voltage," Assistant State Prosecutor Tom Hogan said to reporters outside the courtroom on the day of Frantz's pleas.

Hogan kept his word. No plea agreement was offered to Mendyk. Due to enormous publicity about the case, the trial was moved from Brooksville to Tavares, in Lake County, about 60 miles northeast of Brooksville. There, an impartial jury was selected.

On Monday, October 12, 1987, a chained Todd Mendyk was escorted to a black vinyl court chair where his shackled feet were locked to the defendant's table. He made some type of a facial gesture to Prosecutor Tom Hogan. Hogan walked toward him and asked Mendyk what he had said. "I thought you were talking to me," Hogan said, visibly annoyed.

Mendyk replied, "I'll get out, and I'll be back to get you. Your court clerk can put that on her record."

During the proceeding, Mendyk sat with a pen in his hand, drawing what appeared to be a dagger. And during the trial, he would point the "dagger" at the judge, at witnesses, at jurors, and at cops and reporters in the courtroom.

But a hush came over the courtroom when Prosecutor Hogan made his opening statement. "April ninth was the last day of Lee Ann Larmon's life. She was twenty-three, working the night shift at a convenience store and going to junior college."

Hogan described the kidnapping, telling how Lee Ann had walked around the counter to get relish for Mendyk, how he then grabbed her around the neck, how he forced her into his truck and held her on the floor while Phillip Frantz drove away. Hogan told how Lee Ann had begged for her life, and how Mendyk told her to shut up.

The most damning evidence against Mendyk was delivered by Detective Ralph Decker. Decker had worked on the kidnapping and murder case from the beginning. On October 16, he was called to the witness stand to testify against Mendyk.

Decker used a toy truck to pace over a poster-size drawing he had made to show the route the truck belonging to Mendyk had taken on the night of the kidnapping and murder.

Mendyk's public defender, Alan Fanter, objected to that type of testimony, arguing that the drawing and the toy truck were not to scale. However, Judge L.R. Huffstetler Jr. agreed with Hogan that the demonstration would help the jury in knowing where the incident had occurred. The judge allowed the testimony.

Decker testified that Mendyk told him that he and Frantz had been riding around looking for a "target" when they went to the Presto store. The two men hung around the parking lot for a while, waiting for a customer to leave the store. The time was approximately 2:40 A.M. This was not the first time Mendyk had been in the store; he knew what the clerk looked like, Decker said.

According to Decker, once inside the store, Mendyk ordered a hamburger. Then he grabbed Lee Ann around the neck, hit her to "make her know he meant business" and, holding her upright, he forced her to the truck.

While in the truck, Larmon was asking, "Where are you taking me? What are you doing?" Mendyk told Lee Ann to be good and everything would be all right.

Frantz drove the truck into Pasco County while Mendyk tied Lee Ann's wrists together with stereo speaker wire. Mendyk continued to fondle Lee Ann in the truck while she begged and pleaded.

They went to a place familiar to Mendyk in Shady Hills, where Mendyk had hoped to rape Lee Ann. Finding the gate into the property locked, they went to an area in the swamp that was familiar to Frantz.

After reaching the swamp, Frantz parked the truck near the illegal garbage dump. With the headlights shining, Mendyk made Lee Ann bend over a sawhorse he had taken from his truck bed and tied her wrists and ankles to it. While she was tied helplessly to the sawhorse, Mendyk sexually molested her with a stick and forced her to perform fellatio. Mendyk then dragged her to two scrub oak trees and using electrical wires, he tied Lee Ann's wrists to the limb of one tree and her feet to the other. Her body formed a quartermoon against the dark night.

With Lee Ann tied to the trees, still alive, Mendyk and Frantz decided to find a shovel and bring it back to bury Lee Ann, in case they decided to kill her.

At this point, the two men had not decided whether to kill Lee Ann. The idea of keeping her there, tied to the trees, and making Lee Ann their sex slave appealed to them.

Mendyk started to drive the truck out of the swamp, and on the way out, the wheels bogged down in the mud. Mendyk left Frantz to work on the truck, and went back to the trees where Lee Ann was mercilessly tied with electrical wires. Mendyk talked to Lee Ann, telling her he was unsure about what to do with her. Should he kill her, or should he make her his sex slave?

Lee Ann kept saying, "Trust me. I won't tell anyone. Please don't kill me. I'm too young to die." But, Mendyk told Lieutenant Decker, the idea of her begging him not to kill her excited him. Mendyk left Lee Ann again and went back to the truck where Frantz was still trying to get the vehicle out of the mud.

"She's still there," Mendyk said to Frantz. And then in a little while Mendyk went back to check on Lee Ann again.

"Trust me, trust me, I don't want to die. I'm too young to die," was Lee Ann's final plea.

After telling this story to Lieutenant Decker, Mendyk said, "Anyone will say anything to get out of dying." That was when he put a bandanna around the victim's neck, and using his knife as a tool, he tightened it slowly. Lee Ann was shaking, so Mendyk wrapped her neck with wire, cut her down from the tree, and took her to the palmetto bushes, where he stabbed her in the throat.

Killing the helpless girl gave him an "incredible high," Mendyk told Decker.

One day, while Mendyk was in the county jail awaiting trial, Detective Kim Curlew asked Mendyk how he felt about killing the young girl. Mendyk responded that he wasn't sorry. He told Curlew that he would do it again if he had it to do over, Curlew testified.

When codefendant Phillip Frantz testified, he corroborated Decker's testimony. Frantz, who had pleaded guilty to first-degree murder and to being a principal to kidnapping and a principal to sexual battery, said he did not help kill Lee Ann and did not sexually batter her, although he admitted that he stood by and did nothing to stop Todd Mendyk from committing the crimes.

According to Frantz, he and Mendyk had been looking for a girl before they stopped at the Presto store on the morning of April 9. Frantz said that on April 8, the day before the murder, he was in his room playing his bass guitar when Mendyk showed up uninvited.

At about 10:30 that evening, the two decided to go out.

Frantz said he drove Mendyk's truck because he didn't trust Mendyk's driving when he was drinking.

They picked up a six-pack of beer, then went out looking for the house of a female friend in Brooksville. When they could not find her, they went to Spring Hill in the hopes of finding a party someplace. They drove by a couple of 7-Eleven stores where kids usually hung out in parking lots, but they couldn't find a party. By this time, their beer was gone.

The two men then drove to a friend's house and partied there for about half an hour. When they were ready to leave, their truck wouldn't start, so they stole a battery out of a car and put it in Mendyk's truck. When they left, they went to they Presto store to get something to eat.

"As we were getting out of the truck, Todd said, 'Let's grab this babe,' and jokingly I said, 'Yeah, right.' "

Inside the store, they went to the cooler and looked at sandwiches. "Todd got a hamburger and put it in the microwave. I was talking about wishing we had money to get beer." Frantz said that about that time, a man came into the store and looked him directly in the eyes.

"Todd asked the girl for onions, and she said she didn't have any. Then he asked for relish. When she got the relish for Todd, Todd stepped behind her and grabbed her around the neck. She asked what he was doing and he walked her out the door. He told her to get in the truck and she did," Frantz added that Mendyk told him to drive to Shady Hills.

Public defender Alan Fanter asked Frantz if he knew what was happening at the time. Frantz replied, "I had a good idea. We were kidnapping the girl. We were going to do something. She wanted to know if we were gonna kill her. Todd said, 'No. Just be a good girl.' "

After going down a road near Mendyk's house off Shady Hills Road and finding a No Trespassing sign and a locked gate, the men drove to the swamp where Lee Ann Larmon was later sexually battered and murdered. Frantz claimed he stood about six feet away while Mendyk tied the victim to the sawhorse with black guitar strings, sexually battered her with objects, then tied her to the trees.

When they were ready to leave the swamp, Mendyk insisted on driving. When the truck got stuck and Mendyk went back to kill Lee Ann, Frantz said he did not try to stop him.

After the killing, Mendyk appeared to be the "normal Todd," Frantz testified. Frantz said he never went back to look at the body. But together, he and Mendyk threw the victim's clothes in the swamp, locked the truck, and started walking to find help in getting the truck out of the mud.

Evidence showed only one set of footprints going to the trees where Lee Ann had been tied. They belonged to shoes worn by Frantz, while tracks made by shoes worn by Mendyk had left several sets of prints between the stuck truck and the trees. Evidence also showed prints belonging only to Mendyk's shoes going to the palmettos where the body was found. This evidence showed that Phillip Frantz was telling the truth about what had happened in the swamp.

Upon delivering his closing statement to the jury, Prosecutor Hogan walked rapidly across the courtroom. With an angry look on his face, he pointed to Todd Mendyk, who sat comfortably in the vinyl chair, his feet still shackled to the legal table. "This is the last face Lee Ann Larmon ever saw," he said, with a raised voice. "This is the face Lee Ann Larmon saw while she begged for her life. While she pleaded that she was too young to die!

"Three hours of terror for Lee Ann Larmon. Why?" Hogan asked. Then he answered his own question. "So Todd Mendyk could practice his domination. His lust."

In less than an hour, the jury of three women and nine men returned to the courtroom with their verdict. While Judge Huffstetler read the verdict over to himself, the courtroom was full of anticipation. Huffstetler handed the written verdict to the court clerk to read aloud. While she read the verdict, four bailiffs moved closer to where Mendyk sat shackled. Mendyk laughed lightly and whispered something to his public defender. The bailiffs never took their stare off Mendyk while they heard the verdict.

Mendyk was found guilty as charged of first-degree murder, two counts of sexual battery, and the kidnapping of Lee Ann Larmon.

The same jury recommended unanimously that Mendyk be sentenced to death in Florida's electric chair.

Todd Mendyk was sentenced by Judge Huffstetler to die in the electric chair for Lee Ann Larmon's murder. The judge called it "heinous, atrocious, cruel, cold, calculated, and premeditated."

Mendyk has been on death row at the Florida State Prison in Starke since his 1987 sentencing. The case went to the Florida Supreme Court in June 1989, at which time, the death sentence was unanimously upheld.

"THE OKLAHOMA SEX FIEND RAPED AND 'DOUBLE-KILLED' THE VIRGIN COED!"

by Charles W. Sasser

The 911 alert in Stillwater, Oklahoma, went out to patrol officer Glen Westberry at approximately 10:30 P.M., Friday, October 22, 1993. "Possible homicide," the dispatcher said, giving an address on North Boomer Road, and specifying a unit in the Forty North Apartments, not far from the Oklahoma State University (OSU) campus.

Officer Westberry kicked his cruiser into high gear and stepped on the gas. When he arrived at the darkened blocks-long sprawl of apartments, he found a team of paramedics leaving the scene.

"Young female," one of the paramedics informed the lawman. "She's already dead. Nothing we can do for her now."

Some police officers had come to refer to that area as "the most dangerous three blocks in Stillwater." Two OSU coeds had been murdered at the Forty North complex in the last three years. Karen Lauffenburger was slain on December 19, 1990;

her killer, Kelly Lamont Rogers, was on death row. Nancy Wanless was strangled to death a year later, on October 2, 1991; her estranged husband, William, was doing life without parole.

And, now, it seemed, a third coed victim had been claimed at Forty North.

Officer Westberry immediately sealed off the victim's apartment to preserve the crime scene. Lieutenant Ron Thrasher, the night-shift supervisor, assigned Corporal Randy Dickerson to ramrod the investigation with the assistance of veteran detective Kyle Gibbs. Gibbs had worked on the previous coed slayings at the Forty North complex.

After nearly nine years' service on the Stillwater Police Department, the last five as a plainclothes investigator, Randy Dickerson had recently been reassigned as a uniformed supervisor. He was a tall, dark-haired man with a soft voice and a reputaton for cracking difficult cases.

"You're into plainclothes again for this investigation," Lieutenant Thrasher informed him.

Stillwater was normally a peaceful little college town that averaged less than one homicide a year.

Patrolman Westberry corraled two female witnesses for the sleuths. The pair identified themselves as OSU foreign students from Indonesia who were friends of the victim's. The dead woman, they said, was 21-year-old Sri Sedjati Sugeng, also from Indonesia. In America, she went by the nickname "Jati."

"We all planned to go to the movies tonight," one of the witnesses said. "She didn't come for us. We tried to call her on the telephone, but she did not answer." The two friends therefore drove to Forty North at about 10:15 P.M. to check on Jati.

"We knocked on her door, but she did not answer still. We heard the television playing. Her door was unlocked."

The young women cautiously entered the apartment, where they immediately discovered that Jati's dog, a young rottweiler, had made a mess on the floor. They took the dog outside for a few moments, then returned, calling out for Jati. When Jati failed to answer, they started to search the apartment.

They found Jati in the bathroom. She was half floating face-down in the bathtub, naked except for a black ski jacket. Her friends quickly dialed 911.

Detective Dickerson directed crime-scene specialists in scouring the apartment for fingerprints and other trace and latent evidence. The on-scene probe lasted most of the night. Specialists inched from room to room, looking for clues as to what had led to Jati's death and who might have murdered her.

The young victim was a slender and beautiful Asian, about 5 feet 6 inches tall, with shoulder-length black hair. Emergency workers who dragged her out of the bathtub to work on her left her on her back on the bathroom floor. Her bare legs were hooked over the side of the tub with her feet in the water.

The unbuttoned ski jacket, the only clothing on her, gaped open to reveal bruises and lacerations on her breasts and upper torso. Before bagging her hands to preserve possible evidence, Dickerson and Gibbs noted numerous other bruises on her face, neck, hands, and knees. The water in the tub was slightly stained with blood and fecal matter. The blood in the water, as well as blood in other areas of the apartment, apparently originated from the victim's vagina, which the state medical examiner later determined was forcibly torn and ripped. From all indications, the victim had been a virgin.

"She was not taking a shower," Detective Dickerson decided, "not in her jacket. And there's no soap or anything in the bathwater. But why would she be wearing a coat and nothing else?"

He soon answered his own question. The victim's shirt, bra, and jeans turned up crumpled on the living-room floor; her underpants lay discarded on the floor at the foot of the bed. The clothing had been torn and ripped as though the rottweiler had shredded it—which the detectives soon determined was not the case. No, it was a two-legged beast who had done the shredding.

Young Jati Sugeng, of Indonesia, had been attacked by some individual so insane with lust and rage that he had literally torn her clothing off her body.

"She came in from outside wearing her jacket," Dickerson theorized. "The assailant somehow surprised her. He tore her clothing out from underneath her coat, then later dragged her to the bathroom, filled up the bathtub—and drowned her."

The detectives ruled out forcible entry. The apartment did not appear to have been ransacked. From all appearances, nothing had been stolen. That meant that the motive for murder was probably not robbery or burglary.

Then what was it? Rape?

"There are indications of sexual assault," Lieutenant Thrasher remarked, "but that has not been confirmed by the medical examiner."

Another detective voiced a stronger opinion: "The perp came to her door with only one thing on his mind—sex."

"Whatever animal did this either followed the victim into her apartment—or she voluntarily admitted him," one officer at the scene concluded. "This means she may have known her assailant."

Small amounts of blood had stained the victim's torn clothing and the bed. Drops of blood also glistened on the bedroom floor and in the living room leading to the bathroom. Detectives Gibbs and Dickerson speculated that Jati was first assaulted in the living room, then forced into the bedroom, where she was raped. Afterward, bleeding from the vagina, battered from being beaten, Jati found herself dragged to the bathroom, where she met a brutal death.

A blood-specked "foam cap" around the dead girl's nostrils indicated a fluid buildup in the victim's lungs and trachea prior to death, said Dr. Larry Balding of the State Medical Examiner's Office. He explained that pinpoint hemorrhaging in her eyes normally resulted from cutting off the blood supply to the brain. In the pathologist's opinion, the victim had been forcibly raped.

"Bruises all over her body," he reported. "She had severe acute lacerations of her vagina and hymen. That injury would require a good amount of force. If [sex] were consensual, it would be fairly violent sex—rough activity."

Dr. Balding cited the "foam cap," the water in her lungs, and the bruising around her neck, noting that all this was "consistent with a chokehold." In other words, Jati Sugeng had been double-killed. He ruled the cause of death to be asphyxia from *both* manual strangulation and drowning. She had been drowned in the bathtub at the same time that she was being strangled. Dr. Balding said that it might have taken up to four minutes for her lose consciousness.

The pathologist's best estimate as to the victim's time of death was sometime between 7:40 P.M. and 9:20 P.M. on that Friday, October 22.

Crime-scene specialists carefully collected and preserved blood samples from the victim's apartment. They located and saved semen stains on the bedclothes and on a soiled towel in the bathroom. They detected and collected more than 20 hairs that were obviously not the victim's. Jati's hair was black; the nonmatching hairs were a rather distinctive strawberry blond.

The hairs came from the bed, from the victim's body, from the floor, from the soiled towel, and from a baseball cap left on the living-room floor. The baseball cap, the detectives decided, was probably a vital link to the perpetrator. It was a dark-blue nylon cap with white lettering advertising a tool company.

Door-to-door canvassing of the surrounding apartments failed to turn up a single witness. Apparently, no one had seen or heard anything suspicious on Friday evening. On Saturday morning, Detectives Dickerson and Gibbs found themselves with a dead coed and a reasonable hypothesis about why she was murdered—but not a single suspect.

In checking the dead student's background for a possible connection between her and her killer, the probers learned that she was majoring in interior design at OSU and was vice president of the Indonesian Students Association. Her priest at St. John's Catholic Church in Stillwater described her as a "very spiritual" young lady whose death had left "the whole parish in shock. . . . She had a nice, but firm personality. . . . She really enjoyed sports . . .

"You send your daughter to a foreign country and hope she comes home with a bright future," the priest said. "This is such a tragedy—really sad."

Jati's family was from Jakarta, where her father was branch manager for an international construction company. Lieutenant Thrasher explained how the authorities caught up with the victim's parents in San Francisco, where they were en route to Toronto by air. With the help of an interpreter from the Indonesian embassy, the San Francisco police were able to notify the couple of their daughter's slaying. The shocked parents immediately changed their destination from Toronto to Stillwater.

"She was a very nice, kind, loving, humorous young lady," the victim's sister said. "When I heard that my sister was murdered, I felt like I was being struck by lightning."

Investigators Gibbs and Dickerson tramped from door-to-door at the massive sprawl of the Forty North Apartments, asking questions, trying to uncover some clue as to who might have committed such an atrocity against an innocent virgin from across the seas. They also ran computer checks comparing the M.O. (modus operandi) in the present case against those of known sex offenders in the region. They rousted underworld informants. They tried to pinpoint possible suspects for routine questioning.

Nothing substantial surfaced. Lieutenant Thrasher's only comment to the press was that the police had developed "numerous viable leads."

On Sunday, October 4, Dickerson prepared hair, blood, and semen evidence samples for shipment to the well-equipped forensics laboratory of the Oklahoma State Bureau of Investigation (OSBI) in Oklahoma City. Not only did he want to know what the lab might tell him about a suspect, but he also requested FBI assistance in formulating an offender personality profile.

In the afternoon of that same day, the sleuths picked up some information that they thought might prove to be useful. It wasn't much, but at least it was something. . . .

Police interrogations had turned up two separate witnesses who stated that Jati Sugeng had been afraid of someone in her apartment complex for the past several months. One of those witnesses was 21-year-old Verna Hendricks, a former OSU coed from Ames, Iowa. Hendricks said that she had been Jati's best friend. She had immediately flown to Stillwater upon learning of the murder from a TV news broadcast.

"Her fears started about three months ago," Hendricks told the police. "She was telling me she was getting very nervous, very scared. She said some white man had started talking to her when she went out to walk her dog. He asked her to go out with him several times. She said he was asking a lot of questions that scared her—Was she married? Did she have a boyfriend? She said he made her feel very uncomfortable."

The second witness, Jati's Indonesian friend, Arfan Santos, recalled that Jati had remained uncomfortable about this "white man" up until just a few days before. She telephoned him one night earlier in the week to complain that "someone was outside staring at her through her window." Santos said, "I told her to lock her door."

"Did she know who this man was?" Detective Dickerson asked. "Did she describe him?"

Both witnesses looked abashed that they hadn't thought to ask her.

"She said only that he was a white guy," Santos finally replied. "He was always standing outside among the apartments, smoking cigarettes and watching her window."

He hesitated for a moment, then added, "She did say that he had a dog also."

Dickerson grasped for the clue he could sense was just within reach. "Did she say what kind of dog it was?"

"I'm sorry. No," Santos said.

Forty North Apartments housed several hundred tenants. At least 20 percent of them were dog owners. Still, the detectives took that single, isolated clue and ran with it. Again they went pounding door-to-door, asking about a "white guy" with strawberry-blond hair who smoked cigarettes, owned a dog, and might be described as "weird acting."

"Almost everyone around here seems weird-acting to me," one tenant remarked.

Temporarily roadblocked in his efforts at running down the white guy with the dog, Detective Dickerson turned to the blue baseball cap from the crime scene as a possible link to Jati's killer. The name of the tool company on the cap led the sleuth to Ponca City, another small town a few miles north of Stillwater.

"We had a hundred and forty-four of these caps made and distributed to construction workers," a company representative informed the investigator. "We didn't keep a list of who we gave the caps to."

Great. That meant the police had 144 potential suspects.

Again thwarted, Dickerson returned to Stillwater and the Forty North Apartments. Both he and Detective Gibbs expressed their conviction that the solution to the mystery lay somewhere in the apartment complex. All they had to do was ask the right questions of the right people to uncover it.

This time, instead of canvassing the residents, the sleuths rounded up apartment complex employees and asked them the same question, slightly modified, they had been asking the tenants since Friday night: "Who lives in the apartments who owns a dog, smokes, once wore this blue cap, and has strawberry-blond hair?"

Each of the employees pondered the question. Finally one of them said, "You might talk to Lloyd Mollett. He has that color hair."

Lloyd Edward Mollett lived in an apartment two buildings north of Jati's building. Before confronting the man, the sleuths requested a records and background check on him. The check revealed him to be an ex-convict, 29 years old, with three prior felony convictions—two of them in 1984 and 1985 for knowingly concealing stolen property, and the third in 1986 for burglary in Tulsa County. He'd served two years of a seven-year sentence for the burglary before being paroled from prison in 1988.

His crimes were all considered "nonviolent."

About 9 A.M. on Monday, October 25, Detective Dickerson rapped on Lloyd Mollett's door. A short man, about 5-foot-4, came to the door. Muscular but wiry, Mollett sported a mustache and shoulder-length hair—both of which were a strawberry-blond.

So far, so good.

With Mollett was a dog, a rottweiler almost identical to the victim's.

Later, Dickerson commented that the entire scene was almost like a script that had been written for some TV detective show.

"Mollett did not ask why I was there," Dickerson observed. "I find it strange that the police come to your door and you don't ask why they're there. It's like he already knew and might have been expecting us."

The impromptu interrogation lasted about 15 minutes. Detective Dickerson asked several questions before advising Mollett that he was investigating the homicide of Mollett's neighbor, Jati Sugeng. The sleuth deliberately avoided any mention that the victim had been sexually assaulted.

The diminutive ex-con appeared to be "extremely nervous," Dickerson later remarked. "I could actually see his hands shaking."

Mollett conceded to the lawman that he knew the dead girl. He said they'd met in a field adjacent to the apartments where they both sometimes walked their dogs. They often encountered each other there, talked, and gradually became casual friends.

He was quick to say, however, that he knew nothing about her death. He hadn't even heard about it until now, he declared, since he had left town on Saturday morning and had not returned until Sunday night.

"Do you own a blue baseball cap?" the detective asked, describing the one found in Jati's living room.

"It's mine," the little man admitted. Detective Dickerson did not tell him where he found the cap.

"I gave it to her," Mollett added as an explanation.

"Have you been to her apartment?" the sleuth inquired.

"Never!" Mollett quickly responded.

"How did the cap get inside her apartment?"

"About a week ago, we were walking our dogs together in the field," Mollett told the lawman. "I was playing with her dog with my cap and he chewed it up. So I gave it to her for the dog."

Now Dickerson's questions grew sharper. Mollett's responses came with increased agitation. Finally he exploded.

"Why would I do something like that when I have a perfectly good woman at home?" he snapped.

The way Dickerson saw it, Mollett had now obviously alluded to the fact that the murdered victim had been raped. The only persons who knew that Jati was raped were the investigators—and the actual killer himself.

His suspicion aroused, Detective Dickerson made an appointment to meet Mollett at police headquarters at 3 P.M. to resume the interview. Before taking his leave, he learned that Mollett was rooming with a young woman named Molly Brown, who was presently away from home. The investigator made a mental note to question her later.

The police now had a suspect.

To the detectives' surprise, Mollett was punctual in keeping his appointment at 3 P.M. on the dot.

"I looked at your cap again," Dickerson began, "and it hasn't been chewed on at all."

Mollett stammered his response. "Well, uh, what I meant was, the dog slobbered on it."

Accounts of Mollett's second interview describe how he began to waver in his answers. It hadn't really been a week ago, he said, that he gave his baseball cap to Jati. What he meant to say was that it had been a week ago from the present time. In fact, he gave the cap to her at about five o'clock on the Friday afternoon before the evening that she was murdered.

"But I still had nothing to do with what happened to her," he declared.

Lack of hard evidence at the moment forced Detective Dickerson to release his prime suspect.

The next day, Tuesday, Mollett refused to submit to further questioning. Neither would he agree to relinquish any hair samples and body fluids for comparison with the forensic evidence recovered at the crime scene. The little man later asserted publicly that he felt he couldn't talk to the detectives because they didn't want to listen to the truth.

"He didn't want to listen to me!" Mollett complained about Detective Dickerson. "I'm speaking to a man who wants a confession."

Dickerson, to be sure, did want a confession. He confided to his colleagues that all the evidence so far pointed to Mollett as the perpetrator. As the week dragged on, the investigator worked hard to develop new support for his belief that he was on the right track.

That was where the OSBI crime lab came in with the needed help. Forensic experts reported that the hairs found on the victim's body and on her bed and towel all matched the hairs tweezered from the baseball cap Mollett admitted he owned and gave to Jati on the afternoon of her death. The hairs—all of them, said the criminologists—had a common source.

Was that common source Lloyd Edward Mollett?

"We need body fluid and hair from your suspect in order to make comparisons," OSBI forensics expert Mary Long told Detective Dickerson. At the moment, however, Dickerson was unable to obtain the needed samples. That part of the probe would have to be put on hold until he could dredge up sufficient probable cause against Jati's diminutive neighbor.

The detective began to anticipate any alibis the suspect might offer and took them apart beforehand by questioning his friends and his live-in girlfriend.

Subsequently, Mollett's best friend at Forty North Apartments remembered that on the night of the slaying, Mollett "left my apartment about seven-forty P.M. and returned to my apartment at nine-twenty P.M."

"Where did he go?" Detective Dickerson asked.

"I have no idea," the friend replied. "He didn't say and I didn't ask him."

That left Mollett's whereabouts unaccounted for during the critical time period in which Jati Sugeng was murdered.

The sleuths also established that Mollett's girlfriend, Molly Brown, could not provide him an alibi. She said she'd left on Friday afternoon to spend the weekend with relatives of hers in Woodward, Oklahoma. Mollett joined her there the next day. When the probers asked her if she recalled anything unusual about him physically or emotionally when they rendezvoused on Saturday, the young woman said that she had not.

Somewhat later, however, she amended her statement. There had been something unusual, after all. She said Mollett had had a scratch on his chest and another deeper scratch wound on his wrist.

"He told me he got them at work," Brown said.

Mollett was employed as a printer for a Stillwater printing company. The detectives asked management and employees if Mollett had been injured on the job that last Friday. None of them recalled any such thing.

On Thursday, October 28, with the evidence continuing to mount against Mollett, Detective Dickerson petitioned the district court for a search warrant. The warrant allowed him to obtain body hair and fluid samples. Dickerson said he had probable cause to arrest the suspect, as well.

Detectives Gibbs and Dickerson caught up with the suspect at his job.

"Is this a first-degree murder charge?" Mollett asked the sleuths.

"It is," one of them replied.

"Does that mean the death penalty for me?"

If that question wasn't a tacit admission of guilt, Dickerson wanted know, then what was?"

After that one spontaneous statement, Mollett clammed up tight and refused further discussion. Doctors at the local hospital collected the necessary body samples authorized by the warrant. As Detective Dickerson waited, he noticed some half-healed abrasion on the little man's chest and wrist.

"I got them last Saturday night working on my girlfriend's car," Mollett explained casually.

As far as Dickerson was concerned, that had to be a lie.

Nearly a week had passed since the slaying. Payne County district attorney Paul Anderson reviewed the evidence on Thursday afternoon before approving charges of first-degree rape and first-degree murder to be filed against Lloyd Mollett. The D.A. said he would ask for the death penalty.

While an impressive array of evidence had helped produce the murder charges against the defendant, his conviction depended largely upon the physical evidence from the crime scene. The OSBI laboratory began feeding the Stillwater police the results of the scientific analysis.

Criminologist Long reported that the hairs recovered from throughout the victim's house matched or were "microscopically consistent" with Mollett's hair. But it was DNA fingerprinting that cinched the case. DNA analysis proved conclusively that the semen stains left on the victim's bed were deposited there by none other than Lloyd Mollett.

Faced with the DNA evidence, Mollett had no choice but to take the witness stand at his trial, which began on Monday, January 16, 1995, in order to testify that he had indeed had sex with Jati Sugeng.

But it was consensual sex, he insisted, before going off into what was regarded as a far-fetched alibi. The defendant said that while they were in Jati's bedroom that fateful Friday night, two Indonesian men burst into the apartment. One of them, armed with a knife, poked Mollett in the chest with the blade and cut him on the wrist.

Then the two angry intruders began pushing Jati around. Mollett said he left the apartment because he figured that Jati would be better able to defuse the situation without him there.

Mollett's defense attorney argued in his closing statements that the defendant was an "innocent victim in the war on crime . . . [The death penalty] should be reserved for truly bad crimes. . . . You can't compare this to Ted Bundy. . . ."

A.D.A. Laura Thomas responded by saying that Mollett was "evil to the core. . . . Jati Sugeng looked evil in the face and it leisurely took her life."

The jury bought none of the defendant's alibi. On Thursday, January 19, the panel deliberated less than 75 minutes before reaching their verdict. They found Lloyd Mollett guilty of first-degree rape and murder and recommended that he be executed.

On Tuesday, February 28, 1995, district judge Donald Worthington asked Mollett if he had anything to say before sentencing.

"I can't think of nothing to say," Mollett slowly replied. "I don't think it's fair—I didn't get a fair trial. I didn't do it."

Lloyd Edward Mollet is currently sitting on death row in the Oklahoma State Penitentiary.

"SILVER-HAIRED SEX-STRANGLER!"

by Charles Patrick Justyce

While investigating a series of more than 30 sexual assaults and slayings in eastern San Diego since 1985, the Metropolitan Homicide Task Force called upon the best minds available in criminal detection and relied on an uncanny knack for putting themselves in the place of the sex criminal. By "becoming" the criminal, so to speak, they managed to peer inside his twisted mind. By seeing the world through his eyes and anticipating his moves, the task force was well on its way to zeroing in on the fiend whose rape spree had been terrorizing residents of San Diego for nearly five years.

In November 1986, the Metropolitan Homicide Task Force had yet another sex assault to handle. It began one day as 26-year-old Kathy Bell stood alongside the shoulder of Interstate 8 with her thumb stuck out. She'd had an argument with her husband that morning and decided to hitchhike to her grandfather's house in Florida.

Kathy was standing on the side of the heavily trafficked highway, lugging all her worldly possessions—clothing, a walkie-talkie, a radio-cassette player, and a box of country-western tapes. One other fact that lingered in the memory of one motorist who passed her by was that the pretty hitchhiker appeared to be about eight months pregnant.

Finally a handsome silver-haired man in a white van pulled over next to Kathy. "I'm going as far as El Centro," the soft-spoken man offered.

"Sure," Kathy said, beaming as she climbed into the van. The driver was considerate enough to help her load her belongings aboard.

The van crossed the lonley desert lands of El Cajon, bathed in the fiery rays of the red sun, and swung off at the exit adjacent to Imperial County. Slowly the van dipped down into the biker-scarred foothills and seemed to depart from civilization. Then the driver bluntly told the young woman that he had to relieve himself. He pulled the van over, got out, and promptly disappeared amid some sage.

Suddenly Kathy felt someone's fingers close tightly around her throat from behind. All she knew was that she was being strangled as she blacked out. When she regained consciousness, she found herself stretched out in some brush. Her belongings were gone. Her blouse was open and her bra was pulled above her breasts. And the fiend who had choked her into unconsciousness was long gone from the scene.

Stunned, Kathy managed to get up and started to scramble up the side of the mountain. She made her way over the remote, snakelike biker trails, and crossed to the other side of the freeway. Waving frantically, she flagged down a passing motorist, who then drove her to notify the police.

One morning in February 1988, as cirrus clouds drifted over El Cajon and a heavy wind stirred up dust near the Buckman Springs on-ramp on Interstate 8, two women were hitchhiking along the highway. Both were from Arizona, both in their early 20s, and they were heading from Los Angeles to Tucson. Suddenly a white van pulled over to the shoulder of the road. The driver was a silver-haired man with a smooth silver mustache, and a silver tongue.

"I'm going as far as El Centro," he said with a smile.

Both women hopped in.

The van plowed blindly through the windstorm. An eerie groaning caused by the wind whipping against its sides filled the vehicle as it rolled eastward on the road through the desert growth. One of the hitchhikers was sitting up front with the handsome, elegant-looking driver, chatting amicably. The second woman was in the back, nodding off to sleep.

The white van unexpectedly swung off the main approach and dipped into the shadows of Creastwood Summit. Suddenly the driver muttered something about having to relieve himself. Nothing seemed out of the ordinary as he got out and hurried into the stunted brush nearby.

When the driver returned, he jerked open the passenger-side door, startling the women. He ordered them out of the vehicle. "I have a gun," he said. "Do as I tell you!" Then he leaped on the first woman and choked her until she passed out. When he seized the second woman, she fought frantically, but he quickly subdued her with his superior strength. Finally she, too, felt herself being choked into unconsciousness.

Sometime later, when the two women came to, they realized that they had been sexually molested.

The women struggled to their feet and made their way to the freeway, where they flagged down a passing couple who took them to the nearest police barracks.

As the two victims described their attacker and his vehicle, the officer nodded in recognition. It was an all-too-familiar pattern. The description of the driver and his congenial manner was always the same. He was always on his way to El Centro. He always stopped off at a secluded roadway where he said he had to relieve himself. And he always rendered his victims unconscious long enough to sexually attack them, without actually killing them.

The officer figured the rapist to be a frustrated man whose ability to perform normal sex was inadequate. Tensions were no doubt building within him to the point that he vented his anger by abducting and raping hitchhikers. The officer noted the areas where the female victims were picked up and discarded after the attacks. Matching them with a timetable of the attacks, the officer suggested to his superiors that it was possible the rapist might be an outpatient at a mental hospital, someone able to leave the premises for his sex-assault forays.

Crimefighters began a check of institutions where sex deviates received treatment. The difficulty facing the probers was that there were many people who fit the rapist's description, and there were countless white vans in Southern California. Besides, the circumstances of the rapes weren't as strange as the newspapers tried to make them out to be. Southern California, particularly the beach areas of San Diego where most of the victims had been abducted, was a mecca for hitchhikers. At almost every freeway entrance, young men and women could be found with their thumbs outstretched.

A spokesman for the El Centro PD observed that checking on known sex offenders was a monumental task. He explained that there were some 7,500 registered sex offenders in Southern California, up from 6,000 in 1980. A recent study showed that 1,100 persons were arrested for sex offenses in California in 1987. Of that number, less than half had wound up with felony convictions. Of 504 convictions, only 43 resulted in the offender spending more than one year in a prison or mental facility.

California has a number of institutions for the confinement and rehabilitation of sex offenders. Two of the largest—except for the prisons—are the state hospital with maximum security at Atascadero, and the California Men's Colony at San Luis Obispo. Both facilities had recently come under severe criticism because of the number of parolees who committed vicious sex crimes within months of their release.

The local police, sheriff's departments, and state police started a drive to warn hitchhikers that they were risking their lives in seeking rides on the roadways. It was almost an exercise in futility. A typical response was, "I know a creep when I see one. If a guy looks suspicious, I won't get in with him."

Other hitchers shrugged off the warning with "I haven't got any other way to get around," and, "I can take care of myself."

As the weeks passed, and still more similar assaults were reported in one San Diego County police agency or another, the law-enforcement officers in three towns pooled their information and created a dossier on a man they were almost positive was the same sex fiend. He drove a white van, his victims were all female hitchhikers who were picked up along Interstate 8, each abduction occurred during the early-morning or early-afternoon hours, and most of the victims were driven within five to 10 miles from where they had been picked up. In a few cases, the rapist went "all the way," but in most cases, his attack went no further than fondling the victim.

The puzzle was, why hadn't he strangled the victims to the point of actually killing them? His technique hardly fit the M.O. of the rapist who murders his victims to avoid leaving behind someone who can identify him.

"It will only be a matter of time," one officer commented, "until someone puts up a frantic fight, and our man will kill them to silence their screams."

As the number and frequency of the attacks increased, the news media gave the crimes more and more attention. Now citizen groups began to cry out for more action from the police.

One of the detectives involved in investigating the numerous cases plaguing the area responded by saying, "People cannot comprehend the complexity of a case like this. They watch television detectives like Columbo, Kojak, and Rockford. They get the idea that we should pick up some clue and have it all solved in sixty minutes. Real-life police work doesn't work that way."

The next attack came one morning in 1988. Alesia Garrett had checked out of a La Mesa motel, had coffee at the coffee shop and, carrying a backpack containing her worldly goods, she climbed the hill to the shoulder of the Interstate 8 Freeway. One by one, cars zoomed past the lonely 27-year-old woman who stood there with her thumb in the air.

Not everyone was indifferent, however. A silver-haired man in a white van was more sympathetic than the other early-morning commuters. He screeched to a halt at the side of the road, his wheels kicking up loose pebbles. Alesia, her eyes glistening, hopped in at his invitation.

"I'm going as far as El Centro," the driver said, with a smile. Alesia gratefully accepted his ride.

It was when the car detoured off I-8 near Alpine that an almost palpable tension gripped Alesia. "Nature calls," the driver said, chuckling. "You don't mind, do you?" Alesia was in no position to object, but her woman's intuition warned her that something was wrong as the van dipped down into a bed of dry wash off the freeway.

Once they were out of sight of the freeway and he stopped the van, the driver suddenly turned on Alesia. He punched her in the face, choked her into unconsciousness, then raped her. When he was done, he tossed her into the nearby brush. Later, when Alesia came to, she found her clothes disarranged and realized she'd been raped.

An old couple in a camper, returning from a Las Vegas trip, picked up the battered girl on the side of the freeway. While the elderly woman calmed Alesia down in the back of the camper and treated her cuts and lacerations, her husband steered toward the nearest hospital.

The detectives assigned to the case immediately recognized the modus operandi of the assailant who choked his victims and put them to sleep before fulfilling his sick sexual fantasies. Alesia's statement about her attacker telling her that he was a former U.S. Marine, discharged in 1968, jibed with a dozen other reports given to police by other unfortunate hitchhikers. So did the fact that he said he was married, with two kids.

Alesia described her assailant as a husky silver-haired man, about 6 feet tall, weighing 180 or 190 pounds. The battered victim said that he was soft-spoken and very mannerly. These details seemed to correspond with what the police had learned from the other victims of the silver-haired rapist who prowled on Interstate 8.

"What we really need for a break in this case is to locate a witness who got this guy's license-plate number," Sheriff Jim Roache told a group of reporters. "With more than thirty victims, it seems almost incredible that someone hasn't seen at least one of these girls getting into a van and didn't stop to take down his license number. But that's the way it is—but with the amount of publicity on the case we have now, that many change. People become more observant."

Unfortunately, the sheriff's theory never reached the ears of 28-year-old Terry Gourd before she became another one of those girls who hopped into a vehicle with a perfect stranger—a silver-haired stranger.

It was in May 1988 when Terry left her cottage after a terrible family fight and crisscrossed a field leading to the Interstate 8 Freeway. There was no way Terry could have known that at the very same moment, the man the newspapers had dubbed "The I-8 Strangler" was headed in her direction.

The pleasant-voiced man who picked up Terry Gourd said he was going as far as El Centro. Had Terry been reading the newspapers, she might have gotten suspicious when he told her he was a former U.S. Marine whose military training had provided him with the skills to put a person to sleep within seconds by pressing certain nerves in the neck.

"Of course," he told the hitchhiker, "if you don't know what you are doing, you could kill someone easily."

Terry was so captivated by the motorist's conversation and gentlemanly manner that she didn't mind when he told her he'd have to make a quick stop to see some of his hang-gliding buddies before continuing on to El Centro. In fact, it sounded like fun.

Minutes later, the white van swung off at Buckman Springs Road and veered into a remote area of moisture-starved shrubs. Apologetically the lean-featured driver told Terry that he had to answer the call of nature. He got out and disappeared behind a tree.

When the police received the report that another girl had been viciously strangled until she passed out, and that she had suffered the same indignities reported by over two dozen other women, forensic technicians flooded the crime scene to make casts of the tire tracks and shoe prints. Tight-lipped investigators refused to confirm whether the tire tracks and shoe prints matched any of those in the other cases.

In May 1988, the inevitable happened. When it was over, the smell of dead human flesh permeated a pathway accessible to Buckman Springs Road.

Sandra Cwik was a transient who'd left Jacksonville, Florida, after a bad flare-up with her family. Over the past several years, the woman had been in and out of Miami mental hospitals. With a limited understanding of the outside world, the 43-year-old Sandra took to the wandering life.

Like the victims in the other cases, Sandra was hitchhiking along I-8 when she was picked up by a man who said he was going to El Centro. When she realized that she was in a car with a sex fiend, it was too late.

The decomposed female corpse found by hikers in July 1988, in a remote area of Buckman Springs, was sprawled in the dim light, scantily attired. By the looks of the body, the poor victim must have been subjected to a particularly malicious form of physical abuse before she was murdered.

It wasn't long before a medical examiner, crime-lab technicians, and a crime-scene photographer were swarming over the cordoned-off murder site, along with homicide investigators. From the initial examination of the body, the M.E. reported that the woman had been raped and strangled. After the preliminary examination was completed, an ambulance transported the body to the morgue.

"She was down there for over a month," the medical examiner informed members of the Metropolitan Homicide Task

Force. "The flesh was badly decomposed. There wasn't much more left than a skeleton."

The indignities she'd suffered had probably satisfied the killer's yearning to inflict humiliation and pain, a psychologist would later testify. "The thrill of strangling the woman gripped him and became a substitute for the sexual pleasures he so craved," the psychologist would later explain to a jury.

The detectives digested the medical examiner's statement as they looked over the autopsy report. The body had been found about a mile from where the victim was beaten and sexually attacked. According to the medical examiner's findings, the victim died from loss of blood after walking barefooted across the rocky, hard-packed ground to summon help. Her feet had almost been walked to the bone.

Detectives were able to trace a thin trail of blood back to the attack site. There, the San Diego County Identification Bureau's technicians made casts of footprints and went over the entire area, searching and making molds of tire treads at the scene where the victim had apparently been bludgeoned.

At this point, Riverside County detectivbes began to suspect that the unusually large number of young women being attacked—and now murdered—in their vicinity might all be victims of the same man who had been terrorizing San Diego County. At the same time, the families of some of the 43 prostitutes and transients attacked or slain in the Riverside area began comparing newspaper stories, suspecting a link to the same man responsible for the bizarre rape spree plaguing both counties. They conveyed their suspicons to the police.

After sorting things out, deputy district attorney Jeff Dusek announced that there was positively no connection. What the police did indicate, however, was that they saw a connection between the murder of Sandra Cwik in 1988 and the cruel and vicious slaying of 26-year-old Carol Jane Gushrowski in 1986. Both bodies were found near Buckman Springs Road—Gushrowski's two years earlier than Cwik's. Police theorized that the same man, with an incredible ability to beguile and manipulate attractive young women, was responsible for both murders.

Moreover, the police alleged, the same tire tracks linked the same man to the attempted murders of five other women in the same area between 1986 and 1988.

An official announcement from the task force revealed that the bodies of at least 14 victims in the series of 45 slayings under investigation had been dumped in the same general area off Buckman Springs Road.

Then, one day in 1991, a detective who was investigating a hitchhiker's complaint about an assault pricked up his ears as she told him her story. She said that she had been picked up two miles from the Buckman Springs exit and driven to a remote spot where she was raped and choked. The sleuth sat upright in his chair when the runaway told him that her attacker said he would take her as far as El Centro. His memory flashed back to 1989, and the case of a 30-year-old prostitute named Carol Brown.

Like the women in the other cases, Brown said she was picked up by a silver-haired gentleman who said he was going as far as El Centro. But he pulled off Interstate 8 at the same Buckman Springs exit where Sandra Cwik and Carol Gushrowski were murdered. As usual, the driver said he had to stop to relieve himself. Once out of the car, he attacked Brown, ripped at her clothes, and strangled her until she was rendered unconscious.

A sheriff's deputy driving by looked down into the ravine and saw Brown lying in a patch of desert growth. It was obvious to him that she had been attacked. As he pulled his vehicle off the freeway and steered down a dirt road leading to the battered woman, the alert officer noticed a gray Honda leaving the vicinity. Within minutes, a California highway patrolman intercepted the Honda and arrested the driver. At poice headquarters, he was questioned and formally charged with rape.

At the trial, Carol Brown testified that after the man told

her he was going as far as El Centro, he hauled her out of his car near the Buckman Springs exit and dragged her across a dirt road into some bushes. When she started to scream, he ordered her brusquely, "Shut up! I'm going to rape you, and maybe I'll kill you!"

It was all too coincidental, and the detective handling the 1991 case of the assaulted hitchhiker went to the computer. An inquiry into the previous case brought up the name Ronald Elliot Porter.

Porter, the computer printout noted, had been charged in the Carol Brown case with six felony counts, including assault, battery, and oral copulation. Anxious to avoid a lengthy trial, and the risk of losing a tangled case, the state allowed Porter an opportunity to plea-bargain several days before the trial. Two counts of assault and sexual battery netted him two years in prison. Then, six months after his parole, Porter was picked up and returned to prison on a parole violation.

The detective's research paid off. He learned that Porter was now out on parole. When several of the I-8 victims were shown a photographic laydown, the reaction was the same. In each case came the instant response: "That's him!"

Since the parole board had Porter's address on file, a speedy arrest followed.

Once the suspect had been identified and news leaked out that the respected Escondido automboile mechanic was the rapist who had been terrorizing San Diego County, the local population was outraged. With interest in the case running high, newspaper editors from adjacent cities sent reporters to cover Porter's arraignment in the North County Municipal Court on August 20, 1991.

Porter appeared relaxed and was whispering softly to his attorney, Terry Kolkey, who requested a delay to September 27, to give the defense enough time to confer with Porter's relatives. Judge H. Ronald Domnitz granted the request.

At Porter's September arraignment, overwhelming evidence against him led the presiding judge to rule that the ex-con should be held in lieu of $250,000 bail and held over for a preliminary hearing.

At Porter's preliminary hearing on February 1, 1992, before municipal court judge Joan Weber, deputy district attorney Jeff Dusek, one of the prosecutors assigned to the task force, produced the two Arizona transients as witnesses. They identified Porter as the man who picked them up and then attacked them in an unpopulated area off Buckman Springs Road. Dusek told Judge Weber that Porter had served time in prison for sexually assaulting a male hitchhiker in 1975 and a female hitchhiker in 1988. He said both crimes were committed in a manner that led police to believe he was the same man who had molested other women in the area.

Aside from producing the country-western tapes, the walkie-talkie, and the radio-cassette player taken from Kathy Bell and found in Porter's car after his arrest, the prosecutor also introduced into evidence a forensic expert's sworn affidavit. This affidavit contained blowups of footprints found at the scene of several of the attacks that clearly matched the shoes worn by Ronald Porter.

The charges brought against Porter amounted to five attempted murders, three rapes, and two murders.

Over the next two days, the prosecution tried to show that Ronald Porter had murdered 26-year-old Carol Jane Gushrowski, of El Cajon, in 1986, and Sandra Cwik, the Florida transient, in 1988. The decomposed bodies of both women were found in the same area on the Old Highway 80.

Although the prosecutor said that the forensic evidence and other evidence gathered by the task force clearly showed that Porter was responsible for each of the crimes, Judge Weber disagreed. She said that the evidence produced thus far by the state had failed to show beyond a reasonable doubt that Porter had killed Carol Jane Gushrowski, of El Cajon, in 1986. Those charges were dismissed and the case remains unsolved today.

However, Judge Weber did rule that there was sufficient evi-

dence to charge Porter with the gruesome rape-murder of Sandra Cwik. The judge set a trial date for August 1992.

On August 24, Ronald Elliot Porter went on trial in San
Diego before superior court judge William Kennedy. Porter
was charged with one count of murder and five counts of attempted murder in a series of East County attacks on hitchhikers—cases that had undergone a tedious, drawn-out
investigation by the Metropolitan Homicide Task Force. He
pleaded innocent to the charges.

The defendant, neatly attired on separate occasions in either
a brown or gray suit—always with a white shirt and tie—sat
stiffly at the defense table throughout the trial, never batting
an eye, as one by one the female victims testified that he was
the man who had choked them after they were picked up hitchhiking on Interstate 8.

One victim, a teenage runaway, testified that she attempted
to reach for a knife in her purse while she was being violated,
but she couldn't reach it.

"He put me out by pressing my neck," she said, "and when
I awoke, he was gone.

"I was confused for a while," she recalled. "I didn't know
whether to hide or to start heading down the highway." She
said that two people in a passing car heard her screams for
help and gave her a lift to the hospital.

Pointing to Porter, deputy district attorney Jeff Dusek told
the court, "This man is an extreme danger to anyone in his
wake. He is a sexual predator who preys on women. . . . If
not in prison, this defendant would be a danger to others. He
is a dangerous, violent individual."

In his turn, defense attorney Terry Kolkey told the jury that
mere suspicions about his client weren't enough to justify
sending him to prison for life. He contended that some of the
victims were unable to identify Porter as the man who had
attacked them. He argued that the lineups conducted by the
Escondido and El Cajon police had failed to prove Porter's
guilt. He also maintained that evidence by FBI experts had

failed to conclusively match Porter's shoes and tire tracks with those found at the attack sites.

Defense attorney Kolkey conceded that he wasn't surprised at the verdict returned by the jurors on September 22, 1992. The jury convicted Porter of Sandra Cwik's murder, but acquitted him of charges that he attempted to murder five other women.

"When you're facing this many charges, there's an accumulation of evidence," Kolkey told reporters outside the courtroom. Asked how his client was taking it, he answered, "he's devastated. He still proclaims his innocence."

But Prosecutor Jeff Dusek was surprised at the guilty verdict of second-degree murder and two counts of rape with a foreign object.

"We expected a first-degree verdict," he told reporters. "But we have enough here to protect the community from this man—hopefully for the rest of his life." The prosecutor added that Porter was still a suspect in 10 to 15 other assaults upon hitchhikers.

The jurors who were interviewed said they believed that Porter attacked the five women, but they did not believe that he strangled them with the intention of killing them.

On October 26, superior court judge William Kennedy imposed the maximum sentence on Porter. He sentenced him to 28 years to life in a California State prison.

"FREED TO RAPE AGAIN . . . THIS TIME HE ADDS MURDER!"

by Don Lasseter

The salesclerk stumbled through the back door of a Thrifty drugstore in Garden Grove, California, shortly before 7 P.M. It was the week before Christmas, 1989, and the clerk was seeking a moment of respite from shoppers. It was peaceful and quiet in the dark alley. The sun had set an hour earlier, so the only light came from a single overhead streetlamp and from moving headlights.

Listening to the melodious strains of "Silent Night" from somewhere in the distance, the employee was stepping toward a Dumpster when he spotted something that froze him in his tracks. In the gloomy shadow of the trash bin lay the figure of a small woman, dressed only in a blouse or sweater. Blood oozed from her head.

Dashing back into the store, the wide-eyed employee burst into an office and dialed 911.

Officer Darro Halligan, of the Garden Grove Police Department, sprang from his black-and-white cruiser behind the store at 7:03 P.M. He bent over the supine woman and examined her for life signs. She still had a slight pulse and was shallowly breathing. Within seconds, paramedics screamed to a halt in the alley and hurriedly began trying to save the injured woman's life.

In his subsequent report, Halligan wrote, "I saw in the alcove behind Thrifty drugstore, before the Dumpster, a female Asian lying on her back, and she was nude from the waist down. She wore no shoes or socks. She was bleeding from a hole in her left temple."

While Officer Halligan secured the scene with yellow plastic tape and telephoned the watch commander, the medical technicians placed the unconscious woman on a gurney, loaded her into an ambulance, and rushed away toward Humana Hospital in nearby Huntington Beach.

Another uniformed police officer, James Holder, who had also responded to the scene of the shooting, rode in the ambulance with the victim. He hoped that she would miraculously wake up and describe her attacker.

Detective Ron Shave, of the Garden Grove PD, had finished tinkering with his computer at home and had just sat down to dinner when the call came. Shave had been answering emergency calls at all hours for over eight years as a detective. Standing 6 feet 2 inches tall, slim and trim, with thick hair and a neat mustache sprinkled with gray, Shave didn't look old enough to be a veteran of two decades as a cop, but he was. His meticulously neat image gave him the appearance of a young corporate executive or a successful businessman.

Arriving behind the drugstore at 8:50 P.M. on December 17, Shave listened as Officer Halligan filled him in on details he had observed. Detective Shave carefully scrutinized the area around the Dumpster, where trash had spilled over onto the pavement, while he jotted down entries in his notebook. "I saw blood on the debris and trash," he wrote. "I saw a woman's left shoe, some broken glasses, and some jean-type pants tossed onto a box near the blood."

The jeans were inside out, as if they had been forcibly pulled from the injured woman. According to Halligan, the victim was only about 5 feet tall and weighed roughly 100 pounds. It wouldn't have taken a professional wrestler to have overpowered her. Dirt and scuff marks on her body suggested that she had been dragged across the rough pavement to the Dumpster.

"Next to the jeans, in another box," Shave noted, "there were some female panties, also turned inside out."

In yet another box, just a few feet from the pool of blood that had poured from the victim's head, the investigators found a shiny bullet casing. Criminalist Kenny Wong, who arrived a few minutes after Shave, carefully bagged the shell for future analysis. Wong also checked the pockets in the jeans and found $31 in cash. But his search for anything to identify the victim was fruitless. No purse or wallet turned up.

With Wong and with the help of his partner, 10-year-veteran detective Glenn Overby, Shave expanded the search into the shadows away from the Dumpster. About 70 feet west of the bin, he found a lacy white object that seemed made for a wedding. There was a bridal shop just a couple of doors down from the drugstore. Perhaps the victim had been shopping there.

Detective Shave spoke to the married couple who owned the bridal shop. They were able to tell him that the victim was Hong Thi Nguyen, age 26, a store employee. Hong was a native of Vietnam, as were the proprietors of the bridal business. They told Shave that Hong had arrived at the shop at 5 P.M., dropped of some work she had done at home, and then helped measure some customers who were in the store.

While still in the shop, Hong had telephoned a relative at home. Then, the shaken owners said, Hong had picked up her purse and a white appliqué, a decorative item usually sewn onto wedding gowns. Waving good-bye, Hong walked out the front of the shop at about 5:30 P.M., turned north, and disappeared.

"Do you know where she might have been going?" the detective asked.

Usually, one of the owners said, Hong parked her car to the north. But neither of them had seen the car that day. They just assumed that when Hong left, she was headed toward her vehicle.

Asked to describe what kind of car it was, the couple immediately responded that Hong owned a small white Toyota.

When Detective Shave showed the couple the white appliqué recovered in the alley, they both recognized it as the one Hong had taken with her the last time they saw her.

From the shop proprietors, Shave obtained the home address of Hong Nguyen. Shave and his partner left to notify the family.

In the meantime, Hong's husband and family were sick with worry and fear. As soon as the husband learned that she had been attacked and taken to the hospital, he left immediately to join her. A short time after his arrival, a doctor put his hand on the man's shoulder, and softly announced, "She's gone."

Detective Shave got the bad news from Officer Holder, who had gone to the hospital with the victim. The victim had succumbed to the bullet wound in her left temple. She had never regained consciousness, so she had been unable to say anything about her assailant.

The hustle and bustle of shopping had long since ended and the twinkling Christmas lights had gradually extinguished by the time the investigative team closed down the crime scene.

At Nguyen's home, Detective Shave heard some additional sad news. The 26-year-old victim was the mother of a new baby. She had been performing some of her work as a bridal shop seamstress at home so she could breast-feed the infant. Hong also held a second part-time job at an electronics company in adjacent Santa Ana.

Hong Thi Nguyen had left the strife of Vietnam in 1980 and moved to the region of Garden Grove, known as "Little Saigon," among thousands of fellow immigrants from her homeland. She'd worked hard to carve out a little niche of the American dream.

"Her name meant 'roselike flower,' " Hong's husband sobbed. She'd been to a bridal shower that morning and had happily shown off her new baby.

One of the victim's relatives said she did not have the heart to tell Hong's parents how the poor girl had been killed. Instead, she would save them some pain by reporting that Hong had passed away as the result of heart problems.

After listening with sincere compassion, Detective Shave had to ask some questions. Did the family know of anyone who might want to harm Hong? The answer was a resounding no. They unanimously agreed that she was "loved by everyone."

Hong's husband supplied the detective with details about the car she drove and its license number. It was a white Toyota MR2, and it was missing. Without any more delay, Detective Shave put out a lookout for the car on the national crime information teletype network.

On December 18, Ronald Katsuyama performed the autopsy on the victim, while Shave and criminalist Wong observed. Detective Shave would subsequently report that Dr. Katsuyama "pointed out to me and I was able to observe, the bullet wound near the temple. He showed me the location of the projectile, which had lodged on the inside of the back of the skull. There was a fracture to the skull, bruising to the forehead and the right eye, bruising to the lips."

The appalling inventory of injuries continued. "I saw bruises on both sides of her neck and abrasions in the vicinity of her left elbow. She had dirt and debris along the back side of her buttocks, her thighs, and her caves, and her left foot was abraded."

As Dr. Katsuyama continued the autopsy protocol, he discovered additional bruising to the victim's tongue and thyroid, as well as her vagina, uterus, and endometrium. The neck, he observed, had been subjected to "deep bruising in the muscle tissue."

It was obvious to both the detective and the pathologist that Hong Thi Nguyen had endured an extraordinarily brutal attack in the back alley.

The injuries to her vagina, Katsuyama said, were caused by "penetration with an unknown object, caused at approximately the same time as the gunshot wound to the head."

During the examination of the body, Katsuyama lifted a loose pubic hair from the victim's skin, and Wong carefully bagged it.

Because the slug that was lodged in the victim's brain would be needed as evidence, the pathologist probed for it. He lifted out a copper-jacketed projectile and gave it to Wong.

The cause of death, which occurred at 11:02 P.M. on December 17, Katsuyama said, was the gunshot wound. It had been delivered between 6 and 7 that evening. It was not a contact wound, meaning that the muzzle of the gun had been more than 18 inches from the victim's head upon being fired.

After leaving the autopsy, Shave learned that officers had already arrested a pair of suspects in the case.

In Southern California, as in most urban areas, large numbers of homeless people eke out a living the best way they can. Most of them are harmless unfortunates, but some of them are criminals. Garden Grove had its share of both types.

Along the strip mall where Nguyen was killed, several homeless people were known by the police. Two men were especially noticeable because they frequently harassed motorists and small-business owners by carrying spray bottles of water, along with scraps of dirty cloth, and offering to wash windows for money. Officers categories them as "Window Washers."

The two men had been under police scrutiny for several weeks and had been known to hang out around the Dumpster behind the drugstore. Witnesses had seen them in the area on December 17.

Detective Shave hurried to the police station to look into the possibility that the homeless pair had turned to murder. It didn't take long to establish that they couldn't have been connected to the killing.

But another suspect seemed far more culpable. The youth had been in trouble with the law several times and had recently been convicted of a felony. He was sent to a detention facility but had escaped. Two weeks before the murder, the youth had been spotted by patrol officers visiting a home directly across the alley from the Dumpster. Somehow, the young felon had eluded the cops and escaped to a hideout in Los Angeles.

Eight days after the killing, on Christmas Day, Garden Grove officers again spotted the errant youth. This time, there was no escape. He was handcuffed and brought to the police station.

Detectives Shave and Overby were taking a few days off for the holidays and were in the mountains at Overby's cabin. So other detectives interviewed the suspect.

Fortunately for the suspect, he had an ironclad alibi. He was returned to custody only for his previous infractions, not for murder.

Three days after Christmas, when Shave and Overby returned to work, the news was far better. Hong Nguyen's white Toyota MR2 had been spotted, but not in California. Now, hopefully, it would lead to a suspect.

Just a few days before Christmas, a female patrol officer in Springfield, Missouri, had read the all-points bulletin (APB) and noted the car's description and license number. As she drove into the downtown area, she noticed a car matching the mental picture she'd formed and watched as the driver failed to yield for a fire truck. The officer pursued the white Toyota and recorded its license number, but she was unable to force the driver to stop. She got a good look at him, though, and was able to provide a detailed report of his facial features. When local authorities discovered that the car might be associated with a California murder case, a poster was issued with a likeness of the driver.

Then, on December 23, a few miles from the spot where the Toyota had been seen, someone entered a home, burglarized it, and sexually assaulted the young female resident.

That same evening, the Toyota driver was spotted a few miles west of Springfield, in Republic, Missouri, a small town with a population of only 5,000 people. A patrol officer, investigating allegations that the same man had "engaged in suspicious conduct, trying to pass a check to a local merchant," pulled over a car in which the wanted man was a passenger. The officer asked the passenger to step out and identify himself. Reluctantly the suspect said that his last name was DePriest, but he gave a phony first name. Then he ran. Alone, the officer gave chase, but he couldn't catch the elusive DePriest.

Springfield authorities put together the information and knew they were searching for Timothy DePriest, age 29, a convicted felon. The wanted man ran for five more days.

Just three days after Christmas, December 28, the fugitive was once more spotted by Springfield police. DePriest again ran, this time into an alley where he stopped by a Dumpster, apparently one of his favorite operative spots. He raised a handgun and emptied it in the direction of the two pursuing officers. A slug caught Officer Larry Robinson in the upper right chest, near his shoulder, dropping him to the pavement.

Apparently, when DePriest's weapon was empty, so was his determination to get away. The other cop easily subdued DePriest, slapped handcuffs on him, confiscated the handgun, then called for help for his fallen comrade.

Officer Robinson underwent surgery to have the bullet removed, and survived. He was later featured on the nationally syndicated television show *Top Cops*.

DePriest was arrested for attempted murder of a police officer. He was also connected to the burglary and sexual assault of the young woman, and charged with both crimes. Missouri officials knew that DePriest was wanted in California as a suspect in a murder, but they were determined to convict and punish him for the Springfield crimes.

When Detective Shave received the name of the suspect, Timothy Lee DePriest, he pulled the man's criminal record. Shave was appalled at what he read.

On May 2, 1981, Arlene Gray, the young wife of a Marine who was on duty elsewhere, woke up in the middle of the night in her apartment in Twentynine Palms in California's Mojave Desert. Her heart was racing because she'd heard someone trying to break in. Panicky, Gray jumped out of bed and ran into the kitchen, only to confront a man who'd just broken a window and simultaneously entered the kitchen.

"Oh, my God!" Gray screamed, then ran back into the bedroom and tried to hide by pulling the covers over her head. The intruder followed her, jerked the covers off, and ordered her to remove her T-shirt and panties. Frightened for her life, Gray complied. The intruder then raped her. During the act, Gray nervously told her attacker, "If you don't stop, my husband will kill you."

The assailant ignored Gray's words. When he was finished, he grabbed Gray's purse, ripped the phone from the wall, and fled.

As in so many rapes, the torture to the victim didn't stop when the crime was completed. Arlene Gray never completely recovered. Fear haunted her, preventing her from ever feeling safe enough to be alone at night. Her marriage disintegrated. The tears seemed endless.

Exactly one month later, on June 2, Jennifer Tobin was sleeping with her little daughter in the master bedroom of her Twentynine Palms home. The pretty young woman, who was proud of her long blond hair, missed her husband. He, too, was a Marine who was on temporary duty at another station.

Tobin suddenly awoke, sensing a presence in the room. She turned over, called her husband's name, but saw a strange figure in the dark shadows. A scream escaped her throat, but the intruder quickly told her to stop it or he would kill her.

While Tobin watched in horror, the man undressed himself, and ordered her to move her daughter over. "No," Tobin pleaded, and asked if she could put the child in her crib. Hesitant, the intruder finally agreed, and reached for the toddler, but Tobin pulled her daughter away, and put her in the crib herself.

The intruder started to get into the bed with Tobin, but without thinking, she protested. "It's my husband's bed," she cried. The attacker grabbed her, pushed her to the floor, and raped her. Tobin would later remember pleading with her rapist not to make her pregnant.

When he told her that he planned to spend all night with her, she implored him not to. Tobin desperately wanted him to leave, but was afraid of making him angry. After faking an orgasm, Tobin told the rapist that she didn't want her neighbors to think she was having an affair, and begged him to leave by the back door.

Smirking, the sated intruder pulled $30 from Tobin's purse, and finally left. She immediately ran to a neighbor's house and called the police.

Like the victim one month earlier, Jennifer Tobin would suffer aftereffects for years. Her marriage, too, ended, and her inability to control her emotions caused her to lose her job. She could no longer sleep at night, and was continually terrified to be alone.

Timothy DePriest, a Marine serving at the base in Twenty-nine Palms, was caught and charged with both rapes, then convicted and sent to state prison. But, under a policy that is currently receiving severe scrutiny in California, DePriest was released on parole after serving a few years.

Detective Ron Shave shook his head. He wasn't a believer in early-release programs for rapists. Now, the parolee had apparently tried to rape another woman and had killed her. Shave was determined to collect enough evidence to prove the charges. He hoped the district attorney would extradite DePriest from Missouri to face murder charges in California.

On January 8, 1990, Shave and his partner, Overby, flew to Missouri. It was the first of three trips they would take to the "Show Me" state to try to assemble evidence to convict DePriest.

They were met in Springfield by Detective Larry Asher, who extended the finest of interstate cooperation in providing information and leads to investigate the suspect.

One tip led the sleuths to a relative of DePriest's. The nervous kinsman admitted that he saw "Timmy" on December 19, 1989, driving a white two-seat Toyota. The California fugitive told his relative that he had borrowed the car from a girlfriend and wanted to get it painted black.

Another informant, who identified himself as a longtime friend of DePriest's, said his old buddy brought a white Toyota MR2 to his home on December 23 and asked him to paint it black. DePriest admitted to his friend that he was on the run, but he said it was for a parole violation. The two men put the car in the friend's garage. That was the same day, the officers noted, that DePriest had been spotted in a nearby neighborhood, in the Toyota, where a young woman was burglarized and raped.

After DePriest's arrest for shooting Officer Robinson, Sheriff Wayne Spain, of Dade County, Missouri, located the hiding place of the car and impounded it.

With the help of forensic specialist Marsha MacWillie, of the Garden Grove PD, who flew to Missouri to join Shave, the investigators scoured through every inch of the Toyota and took fingerprints from both the interior and exterior. MacWillie had been trained by the FBI as an advanced fingerprint examiner and had done over a half-million comparisons for identification. When she later obtained sample prints from DePriest, she found they matched several prints taken from the car.

Ordinarily, a car used for a fast trip across country by a fleeing fugitive would be filled with various trash. But the

Toyota was relatively clean inside. That was explained when the sleuths tracked down another friend of DePriest's, who said he had seen DePriest emptying the trash from the Toyota and discarding it by the side of a garage. Detective Asher, the cooperative host, personally located and searched the trash. He discovered a medical prescription receipt made out to Hong Thi Nguyen from a Garden Grove pharmacy.

Some of the strongest evidence turned up when investigators found a trail of credit card purchases, in which DePriest had used Nguyen's cards to purchase gasoline during his 41-hour cross-country flight in her car. Then, before Christmas, he used the same cards to purchase gifts for relatives, friends, and himself. The cards were among his possessions when he was arrested.

Before leaving Missouri, Shave visited a Springfield PD criminalist. Using the handgun confiscated from DePriest, the expert fired several bullets into a water tank. Shave reported, "I saw the ejected casings and personally collected them. [The criminalist] retrieved the projectiles and handed them to me. I packaged them and gave them to Marsha MacWillie for transportation to California."

Even though evidence was mounting to connect DePriest to Nguyen's murder, the state of Missouri wanted him first. They put him on trial, convicted him for rape and attempted murder, and sentenced him to serve life plus 57 years. They would release him for extradition to California, only if he would face the death penalty.

Back in his home state, Shave continued with the investigation. Ballistics tests verified that the bullet and casing recovered from the Nguyen murder exactly matched the ones collected in Missouri, and the pubic hair taken from the victim was found to match a sample from DePriest, but Shave still wanted more.

His determined effort ferreted out a Garden Grove acquaintance of DePriest's who told a revealing story. He and a relative of the suspect's had gone Christmas-shopping on the evening of December 17. When they returned home at about 6:30 P.M., they saw a white Toyota parked in front of the house. Inside, they saw DePriest pack a box and hurry out toward the Toyota. He was sweating profusely. That was the last time they saw him.

Another informant turned up to tell Shave that when De-Priest skipped out from his parole in San Bernardino County, where he'd been convicted of two rapes, he told his girlfriend that he was "going on the run" and was heading toward a relative's house in Garden Grove. Telephone bills from the relative's home revealed that just two and a half hours before the murder, which took place a few blocks from the house, De-Priest called his girlfriend again. Shave tracked the woman down. She reported that DePriest told her that he was going to Missouri, but that since he had no car, he would have to hitchhike or get some money somewhere.

Apparently, DePriest decided instead to sexually attack Hong Thi Nguyen in the alley and steal her Toyota for the Missouri trip.

Shave and his team turned over the evidence against DePriest to the Orange County D.A. The detective had amassed more than 200 pages of notes. There was more than enough for conviction, the D.A. decided. But he was faced with a serious decision.

Capital-murder trials are extremely expensive to the taxpayers. Missouri had sentenced DePriest to serve the rest of his life in prison, so was it really worth it to put him on trial in California? Knowing full well that convicts sentenced to life are often back on the streets in a few years, the Orange County D.A. decided that he didn't want Timothy DePriest to be a free man ever again. He decided to charge the suspect with capital murder and request extradition from Missouri.

In the interim, while serving time in Missouri's Jefferson City State Prison, DePriest was not sitting quietly awaiting his fate. Over the months, he had gradually stolen and concealed parts of various-colored laundry bags, and had managed to weld together a 14-inch, three-pronged grappling hook. He used the bags to weave a 33-foot rope.

Fortunately, on September 20, 1991, a guard discovered the rope and grappling hook wrapped in a gray blanket, covered by dirt in a drainage ditch. DePriest's escape plan was thwarted.

Missouri officials kept DePriest only a few more weeks. In October, he was extradited to California to stand trial for capital murder.

In January 1994, an Orange County jury heard the assembled evidence presented by Deputy D.A. Christopher Evans. Public Defender William Kelley argued that someone else had committed the murder and given the car to DePriest. On February 4, the jury rejected the defense and found the defendant guilty of first-degree murder, with special circumstances.

During the penalty phase, witness Arlene Gray raised her arm, extended it straight at DePriest, and, with her finger pointing steadily, identified him as the man who had brutally raped her in Twentynine Palms in 1981.

Jennifer Tobin described her ordeal when she was subjected to DePriest's savage lust. Trembling and holding back tears, Tobin described the details of how DePriest raped her in 1981. When she rose to walk away from the witness stand, Tobin's legs were shaking so violently she could hardly stand, but she somehow managed to walk out while smiling at the jury.

Prosecutor Chris Evans, in summation, reminded the jurors that Hong Nguyen had been "beaten like a rag doll" when she was stripped, sexually assaulted, and executed in the dark, lonely alley. "He is a predator and a bottom-feeder," Evans snarled. "He enjoys the crimes he does, and does it over and over for the fun of it."

After the jury announced their decision, the foreperson told reporters, "We felt those things the defendant committed were heinous." The 12 jurors had unanimously recommended that DePriest face the death penalty for his crimes.

In California, the judge in a penalty phase has the option

to accept the jury's recommendation or reject it and sentence the convict to life without parole. It was in the hands of superior court judge Everett Dickey.

On May 27, 1994, Judge Dickey delivered his decision with an impassioned speech. Dickey noted that DePriest had committed the murder when he was 29 years old. "In one sense," the judge said, "that means if he were sentenced to life·without parole, he would spend a much longer time in prison than would someone twice his age . . . so life without parole might be a more severe punishment and thus the death penalty might not be as appropriate as it otherwise would. . . ."

Courtwatchers in the gallery held their collective breath. Was the judge going to take the easy way out?

Dickey continued by talking about the victim, Hong Thi Nguyen. "She was strangled. She was shot in the head. She was treated very brutally and for no reason that I can see, except that Mr. DePriest felt that he wanted to have some of her property and her body. There was no reason to kill her and certainly not to kill her in this way. . . . He treated her as though she were a piece of garbage to be thrown out in the Dumpster area. So the overwhelming brutality of these crimes that he committed on Hong Nguyen, in my judgment, outweighs any mitigating evidence."

After a few more comments, Judge Dickey looked at the convicted murderer, and said, "Tim Lee DePriest, it is the judgment and sentence of this court that for the offense of murder as charged . . . that you shall suffer the death penalty, said penalty to be inflicted within the walls of the state prison at San Quentin, California, in the manner prescribed by law, and at a time to be fixed by this court in the warrant of execution."

If the conviction and sentence withstand the test of a battery of appeals, DePriest will, in perhaps 10 or 15 years, have the choice of entering San Quentin's gas chamber, or of lying on a gurney while he is given a lethal injection.

It is still a far better deal than his victim had. Just before Christmas, in 1989, Hong Thi Nguyen had no choice at all.

"THE GOOD WIFE MURDER MYSTERY"

by Jean McGill

When 65-year-old Martha "Doe" Roberts and her husband of 44 years sold their chain of auto parts stores in the Memphis area and moved to a farm in rural Eads, Tennessee, the Shelby County couple immediately fit in. Most of their social life was related to their church, but they also traveled and enjoyed the local dance club.

On August 7, 1992, Doe's husband returned from a business meeting only to find his wife missing. It was just the beginning of a mystery that brought nationwide attention to the area.

Roberts told investigating officers that he waited to call them because he wasn't worried when his wife was missing at noon. The house was in its usual immaculate order, and her car was still parked in its normal space. When he called for her and she was not in the house, he searched for her in the back lawn and her flower gardens. When he did not find her there, he was concerned but not alarmed. Although Doe was recuperating from eye surgery, and could not drive, it wasn't unusual for her to go shopping or visiting with friends.

Roberts had a crew preparing an area for a blacktop driveway, so he put down the sandwich he had bought for his wife and returned to supervise the job.

It was not until he returned in the evening and still found his wife missing that Roberts felt the need to call friends and neighbors. No one, apparently, had seen Doe. She had simply vanished.

The Shelby County Sheriff's Office was notified, and a search for Doe Roberts got underway throughout the community.

A close friend of the missing woman searched through Doe's closet to determine what she was wearing. A black suit was missing, along with a pair of black dress shoes. These were items Doe might have chosen to wear to a business meeting, the friend told Roberts.

The officers could find no evidence of foul play. Roberts seemed sincere in his concern for his wife. They had been married for 44 years and, Roberts declared, "She was everything to me. She was my life."

Although Doe's purse, reported to contain some $700, was also missing—along with her credit cards, her glasses, a pillbox, and some medicine—close friends of the Robertses told the officers that the couple had not argued about anything that would have caused her to leave.

Responding officers notified Shelby County sheriff A.C. Gilless, asking for support and additional officers to aid in their search for the missing Doe Roberts. Gilless assigned 20-year-veteran detective-inspector Romona Swain to the case.

Inspector Swain, commander of the Detective Division, went right to work.

At the time, Swain could not have foreseen that for the next 12 months and three weeks, she would be embroiled in a case so bizarre that at times it seemed impossible to solve. The case demanded, and got, the attention of the Federal Bureau of Investigation, which assigned Special Agent Joe Anne Overall.

Roberts's husband told the officials the same story he had told his friends earlier. On August 6, he said, he received a call from a man who said he was from Indiana and was interested in relocating to the area. The man was interested in looking at some real estate being offered on the Roberts property. An appointment had been set for 10 A.M. on August 7.

Roberts said the man never showed up for the appointment. He waited past the appointed hour, then took care of some other business before stopping to eat lunch at a restaurant where he bought his wife a sandwich.

Roberts told the officers that the day after his wife disappeared, he received a ransom call on his answering machine from a man with a "foreign voice" who demanded $100,000 for the return of his wife. The caller instructed Roberts to destroy the machine by smashing it on the front drive. Therefore, he said, he had no evidence to support his story.

Inspector Swain and Agent Overall recorded 30 ransom calls to Roberts's friends and relatives, however, all demanding various amounts of money for the return of Doe Roberts. One local television station also reported that a "foreign-voiced" caller had contacted them asking for ransom for information about the missing woman.

Swain and Overall put forth their best efforts to quickly obtain a lead that could result in the safe return of the missing Doe Roberts.

"We just never gave up," Swain would later say.

The questions and leads the two officers followed began to cause concern among the relatives and friends of the couple. Although Roberts's husband was obviously suffering from grief and shock, detectives still had difficult questions that demanded to be asked and answered.

According to the initial investigation, Roberts was the last person to see his wife in their home. After he left for his meeting, she had simply vanished.

"Where was Doe Roberts?" was the question being asked by not only the police, but by her neighbors. Fliers with Doe Roberts's picture on them were posted in area post offices and markets. A national television program aired Doe Roberts's picture, asking viewers to help locate her. There was no response.

Eventually the ransom calls subsided, but still the veteran officers watched their files grow thicker as interviews from Doe's relatives and the media kept the case open.

The FBI ordered heavy equipment onto the Roberts property to dig in several areas. Neighbors watched as the searchers dragged three ponds. It was now obvious that the officers were seeking a body, and what had initially started out as a kidnapping case was now being looked upon as a murder.

On March 19, 1993, the federal grand jury convened in Shelby County regarding the Roberts case. Missing from those called to testify was the victim's husband. Those called were under oath and were not allowed to tell Roberts about the questions they were asked.

The implication that he was involved, in some way, with his wife's disappearance, caused Roberts to offer $50,000 for his wife's return and $25,000 for information leading to her whereabouts.

On April 1, the federal grand jury once again convened to review the case, but no indictments were handed down.

Inspector Swain and Agent Overall got their break in the investigation on August 3, 1993, almost a year to the day after Doe Roberts disappeared. That's when a close friend of the Robertses informed the two sleuths that he had also received a ransom call. Following their usual procedure, Overall and Swain ran a routine check to see if the call was valid. With information in hand, they zeroed in on their first real lead in the case.

The man reporting the ransom call was Charles Lord, a 59-year-old retired comptroller for the Memphis Defense Depot. Lord was a friend of the Robertses and a fellow church member.

Lord was well known as a civic leader and chairman of a local church's finance committee. He and his wife lived in an exclusive neighborhood developed near the Robertses' family farm.

Swain and Overall decided to check into Lord's background. They found out that Lord had filed for Chapter 7 bankruptcy on July 1, 1993. Although records indicated that he received a monthly retirement payment of $2,300, he had listed in the Chapter 7 filing $373,000 in liabilities and $128,000 in assets.

Lord's financial difficulties made the sleuths wonder if Lord, who had dined and prayed with the Robertses, was involved in Doe Roberts's disappearance.

Roberts's husband told the investigators about some proposals Lord had made to him. Lord offered to find undercover investigators to help locate Doe for $25,000. Roberts had refused.

Roberts told the investigators that that was Lord's first offer to be a go-between but not his last. Lord had later asked that Roberts meet him in a public parking lot in a nearby town. This time, Roberts brought along a friend, another of his fellow church members, as a witness. This time, Lord proposed to put up $10,000 of the $25,000 to pay the undercover investigators if Roberts would put up $15,000. Roberts told probers that, again, he refused Lord's assistance in the case.

Roberts's witness at the meeting concurred with Roberts's account. He even heard Lord comment to Roberts as they left the parking lot, "You'd better watch your step," apparently implying that Roberts was being watched by officers assigned to the case.

Roberts admitted to the investigators that for the past year, he had viewed every newcomer into the community with suspicion. Roberts also confided to relatives that he felt he was being watched and that it was hard to carry on with his usual lifestyle when he felt that every move he made was being questioned and observed, not only by investigators, but by some area residents.

Roberts told investigators that his friendship with Lord had cooled since the offers of assistance and implications of Lord's comment to "watch his step." But he did speak to Lord when the two met by chance in front of the local post office. Roberts said he even shook Lord's hand as they parted.

Inspector Swain and Agent Overall at last had a suspect, but only a suspect. During the next few weeks, the two officers pooled everything they had on Lord. The case was building. The officers reinterviewed witnesses as they retraced their steps. Neighbors recounted every detail that might connect the Robertses with Lord. One witness revealed that Doc Roberts, an avid gardener, had helped the Lords plant some of their flower gardens. The two couples, on occasions, extended their fellowship from the Eads United Methodist Church by having dinner together.

Although Lord lived only three miles from the missing woman, his home was just inside Fayette County, so on August 26, 1993, Swain contacted Fayette County sheriff Bill Kelly.

Prior to the late-evening meeting, Kelly's department had only conducted a routine search of their county for the missing woman.

"When I left to meet Swain, I had no idea what the meeting was about," Kelly would later reflect about the case. "As she told me she needed me to accompany her and the officers from her department to Lord's home to make the arrest charging him with aggravated kidnapping, I was shocked."

Kelly recalled that Lord, whom he had known for 16 years, was a man he considered his friend.

"When we needed a substation near his home and the Shelby County line, we had a fund-raising, and Lord spearheaded the drive to help finance the substation," Sheriff Kelly recalled.

When the officers arrived at Lord's home, Kelly remembered the warmth of the greeting as the door opened. "Come on in, Bill," Lord said.

"After the charges were read and his rights explained, he was led away in handcuffs by my officers," Kelly remembered, but Kelly also recalled how he felt that it was he, and not Lord, who was shocked by the action.

A polygraph was administered to Lord on the charge of aggravated kidnapping. During the polygraph test, Lord said that he had made a call to the Roberts home on August 6 to set up the appointment with Doe Roberts's husband to inspect some real estate. Lord told investigators that he went to Roberts's home on August 7, 1992, about 10 A.M., the same time that he had set up the appointment to get Roberts out of the house.

Lord said he had called the house before he arrived to be sure Doe Roberts was alone. He had persuaded Doe to come with him by telling her that her husband had been injured. Lord told the officers that a frightened Doe Roberts "had slumped forward in the seat of the car." He panicked. He determined that Doe was not breathing, so he drove to a bridge covering the Wolf River in nearby Fayette County and threw Doe over the railing.

Lord also told the investigators that he threw the victim's personal items out of the car window while driving the three-mile stretch of roadway between the two homes.

On August 27, 1993, with a confession in hand, Inspector Swain, Agent Overall, and Sheriff Kelly arrested Charles Lord. But they still needed to locate Doe Roberts's body.

The search team needed Lord's help in locating the exact spot where he threw the body over the two-foot-high bridge rail. Lord was allowed to leave his jail cell and accompany sleuths to the Spiller Bridge on Chulahoma Road in Fayette County.

As scuba divers in full gear made dive after dive in their inch-by-inch search, onlookers lined the roadway. The group of spectators included the victim's relatives.

Fayette County deputies Ricky Hoskins and Bobby Riles helped during the three-day search.

At the beginning of the search, Lord approached Sheriff

Kelly and said, "Bill, you don't believe that I could do a thing like this, do you?"

"I certainly hope not," Kelly replied.

Lord was then led away by deputies and returned to his cell.

Divers stretched rope across the river to mark the area searched, but Sheriff Kelly said the river had been "up and down" due to rainfall during the past year. Sleuths held out little hope that the victim's body would be recovered. Admitting that the search was futile, investigators dismissed the search team after only animal bones were recovered for the forensic team to examine.

Swain and Overall were joined by Sheriff Kelly as they went back to Lord for a second statement regarding Doe Roberts's disappearance.

The three veteran officers were in agreement that they needed Lord's cooperation if they were ever to find the body. If a kidnapping gone sour had resulted in Doc Roberts's death, they needed to know where her body was, and only Lord would know.

Inspector Swain questioned Lord again on August 30, 1993. This time, Lord admitted that he had killed Doe Roberts and buried her on his property on Great Oaks Drive. He even admitted that a week prior to abducting his victim, he dug an 18-inch-deep pit behind his compost pile in his flower garden. The motive, Lord said, was to demand a ransom from Roberts. As his confession continued, however, it was now apparent that Lord would be facing multiple charges. These included aggravated kidnapping in Shelby County, and first-degree murder and aggravated rape in Fayette County.

Lord was allowed to accompany the officers and medics on August 31, 1993, as they gathered at the secluded Lord home, which was located on a dead-end drive. A flower-bedecked walkway led to the front entrance of the impressive home. Three ponds, reflecting the greenery that surrounded them, were crossed by latticework bridges. A miniature wooden gristmill wheel could be viewed from the garage apartment. A winding paved driveway led to the entrance.

Lord led the medics and officers to the spot in his flower garden and pointed to where he had buried his victim. As crime tape held back the curious onlookers, medics and deputies removed Doe Roberts's body from the 18-inch-deep grave. The body was lying on one side. Although a year had passed, the body was not badly decomposed. Apparently, Lord had placed dirt, lime, and a layer of Sackcrete, a ready-mix concrete with water, over the body before covering it with the compost.

A metal sign, struck in the ground nearby and now surrounded by crime-scene tape, read, "One is nearer God in a garden than anywhere else on earth."

The body was removed and sent for autopsy. It was determined by medical personnel, and by Lord's own admission in his confession, that the victim was killed within hours after her abduction. Estimated time of death was shortly after midnight on August 7, 1992.

When informed of his rights on the multiple charges, Charles Lord waived arraignment and did not request bond. Since Lord had confessed, giving the officers his detailed statement about how he had carried out the crimes with which he was charged, a preliminary hearing was not necessary.

A presentencing hearing was scheduled in Fayette County Court in Sommerville, Tennessee, on October 1, 1993. All interested persons and counsel for Lord were present during the open-court hearing.

Lord was represented by a Memphis attorney while Fayette County attorney general, Elizabeth Rice represented the state. Judge Kerry Blackwood presided.

During the testimony at the presentencing hearing, the public was at last allowed to hear the entire story of Doe Roberts's abduction when Inspector Swain read into the court record Lord's lengthy final account of the victim's abduction and murder.

As told to the court by Inspector Swain, Lord had driven

to the victim's home on August 7, 1992, at 10 A.M. Lord took Doe to his home on Great Oaks Drive. Here, in the garage apartment, he had prearranged restraints to tie her to a chair. Lord had stockpiled a supply of sleeping pills and painkillers to give his victim. When Doe passed out from the pills that Lord forced upon her, he removed her clothing. As his victim lay restrained, he called Doe Roberts's husband to demand $100,000 in ransom.

Lord told how he came back to the garage apartment and lay down on the bed beside the victim. At this time, he discussed with Doe when she thought her husband would be able to come up with the ransom money. Lord told the officers that he began to fondle Doe and eventually had sex with her. Shortly thereafter, he placed a pillow over his victim's head and suffocated her.

Lord told probers that his wife was asleep only a short distance from the garage apartment where he held his victim. The garage apartment is connected to the Lords' living quarters by a hallway. He even told sleuths that he knew his wife was asleep when he killed Doe Roberts because he had tiptoed down the hallway to check.

Sheriff Kelly later confirmed that Lord's actions could be carried out without his wife's knowledge since the home was spacious and a window air conditioner, which would have blocked out the noise, was in use at the time.

Agent Overall testified that it was the investigation by the FBI into Lord's financial background that had provided a motive for the kidnapping and ransom demands. Lord also faced bank fraud and embezzlement charges made by the FBI.

The FBI probe, according to Overall, had been carried out by the department's white-collar-crime unit. Charges against Lord resulted. Lord purportedly had embezzled more than $150,000 from the Memphis Defense Depot during his employment from 1960 until his retirement in 1990. The investigation also revealed that Lord had borrowed almost $500,000 from the depot's credit union, using nonexistent heavy equipment, such as bulldozers, as collateral. Lord had also reportedly taken some $70,000 from Eads United Methodist Church where he served as finance chairman.

Overall testified at the hearing that Lord claimed the money was used to pay off some of his debts and for living expenses.

While the officers testified at the presentencing on October 1, the victim's husband and relatives, the defendant's wife, and his former minister all prepared written statements to be filed with the court records.

"This man deserves to die," the victim's husband wrote. "In lieu of this, he deserves to spend the rest of his life in prison and away from society. . . . Life without [Doe] will never be so fulfilling again."

Lord's wife of 39 years wrote that at the time of the incident with which her husband was charged, he was taking medication that included Clonodine and Accophil. "When his blood pressure gets up high, his mind is not right," her statement read.

Records of the presentencing hearing also revealed that while awaiting the hearing, Lord underwent counseling. The court was informed that the defendant suffered from personality disorders that made him self-consumed and unable to feel empathy for others.

One of Lord's former pastors at the Eads United Methodist Church described the confessed killer as "an honest, upright church member and friend. . . . I am still in total disbelief that he could have committed atrocities of the nature that he has admitted."

"This man has stolen money from the church, embezzled money from the government, and kidnapped, raped, and murdered Doe Roberts in a desperate attempt to extort money from her husband," a relative of the victim wrote to the court. "After he brutally murdered her and buried her in his yard, he invited her husband to his home, pretending to be his friend, while she lay buried a few feet away. We feel that criminals such as Charles Lord should be subjected to the full power of the judicial system."

The victim's family members described the victim "as a warmhearted, gentle woman, who was hardworking, generous, and just an all-around good person."

Only 20 days passed before the sentencing hearing was scheduled on October 20, 1993, in Fayette County Court. During the interim, Charles Lord was held in Shelby County's jail and, by order of Sheriff Gilless, was under suicide watch.

Judge Blackwood sentenced Lord to life in prison, plus 20 years. In a stern tone, the judge faced Lord as he told him, "You are a dangerous offender with little or no regard for human life. . . . No remorse has been shown except the remorse of now being held accountable for your actions."

Blackwood also told those within the courtroom, including the victim's husband and Lord's family, that he was not fully convinced about what really happened in the case would ever be known since Lord had given three contradictory statements.

Although the victim's husband appeared relieved and satisfied with the sentence, he confided to friends that he was eager to put the past year behind him.

As the second anniversary of his wife's death passed, Roberts was still residing in his rural home. The flowers planted by his wife were in full bloom. The estate is behind a security fence, and a gate guards the entrance.

Charles Lord's home is up for sale.

Inspector Swain has been recognized and honored by the Shelby County Sheriff's Office for her "diligent, methodical, hard-driving, never-give-up attitude" in solving the case. The characteristics earned her the in-house monthly award for November 1993.

Lord still faces charges of aggravated kidnapping in Shelby County, and federal charges for bank fraud and embezzlement.

"NATIONWIDE APB: GET THE DEADLY DRIFTER WITH THE DIXIE DRAWL!"

by Stan Munro

"I know he's killed before," Chief William Murray said as he sipped his coffee. "I just can't prove it."

Murray reached under his desk and pulled out two large folders, which he placed on his lap. The assistant chief of police in Albany, New York, leaned back in his chair and flipped through a myriad of reports and documents. The case was several years old, but when he found something that jogged his memory, he cleared his throat to begin the story.

"Sometimes more emphasis is placed on the 'O.J. Simpson' cases and less on the 'Gerald Trottier' cases," Murray said. "But this was the case that probably stopped one of the nation's foremost serial killers."

A small plaque in the corner of Murray's cluttered desk said simply: "REMEMBER—We work for God."

The call came in at 11:50 P.M. on Friday, May 16, 1987. Not surprisingly, the police department in Albany sees more action on Friday and Saturday evenings than the rest of the week. It was, therefore, unusual for Detective-Captain William Murray to be home that night. In a way, he was glad to get the call. Off duty, he didn't know what to do with himself. "I only sleep on Tuesdays," Murray would later muse.

Murray got dressed and headed for the Central Towers Apartment complex in downtown Albany. He had gone through the motions over a thousand times. In his 25 years with the force, Murray had been to about 1,500 crime scenes and worked on over 300 homicides himself.

By the time Murray arrived at the scene, about 30 minutes after the call, Sergeant Jack Nielsen had already placed an entry into the National Law Enforcement Teletype System (NLETS). "Albany, white male stabbed in Central Towers Apartment," the bulletin began, then went on to give a brief description of the scene and the time of the report. Its briefness was due to its urgency; it would be updated as more information was made available.

At the crime scene, Captain Murray stood above the slain body and shook his head in disgust. He crouched beside the body to get a closer look at the deadly damage.

The victim, 40-year-old Gerald Trottier, was wearing shorts and a T-shirt that was now soaked with blood. An empty gift box for a whiskey bottle rested on the clenched fingers of the victim's left hand. He had been stabbed a number of times in the chest and face. His throat was slashed from ear to ear, and a dent in his forehead indicated some kind of blunt-force trauma. Most unsettling of all, the victim had obviously been stabbed in the left eye, which was awash with gore.

The captain looked around the bedroom. The violence that resulted in Trottier's death seemed to have been centered in one corner of the room, which was otherwise in reasonable order. Near the victim's feet, the detectives noticed the apparent reason for the brutal killing: an open floor safe emptied of its contents. Worthless paperwork, most of it evidently from the safe, and other refuse were strewn over the victim's legs, atop a small space heater, and around the floor in the immediate area of the safe. A chair standing on its hind legs leaned back against the wall, and a lamp shade had been knocked from its perch. It appeared as though the violence had occurred before Trottier had retired for the night. The bed was slightly mussed, but only near the pillow.

On the other side of the room from the safe, near the victim's dresser, Captain Murray's eyes locked on a brown leather suitcase with a frayed rope handle. It struck the sleuth as an odd thing to have sitting around, unless someone had just used it or planned to use it. Murray asked the crime-scene technicians if he could examine the suitcase. When they consented, he carefully opened it and discovered that it was empty. Murray wondered if the killer had planned to pack it with something—perhaps with whatever valuables had been in the safe—but for some reason changed his mind.

The other rooms in the two-bedroom apartment showed no signs of ransacking, but detectives scoured them anyway, looking for clues that the killer may have inadvertently left in them. Two beer bottles were on the bar in the next room, and one sat on top of the rifled safe. Crime-scene technicians crossed their fingers, hoping to pull a readable print from them.

The apparent murder weapon, a rusty long-blade kitchen knife stained with blood, was found near the front door. It had been placed on a small duffel bag that contained a few articles of clothing.

When the technicians began to photograph the apartment's interior, all the detectives left to begin their canvass of the neighboring apartments. Nielsen and Murray walked out into the hallway to question the man who reported the crime.

"So who is this guy?" Captain Murray asked Sergeant Nielsen as he pointed to a young man who was leaning against the wall outside the apartment. Two detectives were already questioning him, and their comments were out of the earshot of the captain and sergeant.

"Nicholas 'Nick' Polazzo," Nielsen said as he flipped

through his notes. "He's twenty-two years old and says he's the victim's roommate. He called EMS around eleven-fifty and told the dispatcher that his roommate was bleeding. He says that his roommate is homosexual, but he claims he isn't."

"Where was he this evening?" Murray asked.

"He says he was at work. He's a maintenance man at an apartment complex down the street. We called his employer and his story checks out."

Captain Murray dismissed the two detectives who were with Polazzo and asked the young man to have a little talk with him and Nielsen. Polazzo seemed unusually casual around the detectives, for someone who had just found his roommate dead, but Murray didn't jump to any conclusions about that.

"You can never tell how someone is going to react to a crime scene like this," Murray would later recall. "Just because I've seen it so many times, does that mean I'm supposed to not be affected? And when someone sees it for the first time, are they supposed to fall apart?"

But at the time, Murray wasn't pondering philosophy. His top priority was to get names of people in Gerald Trottier's life—as many names as he could. Unfortunately, Polazzo didn't have many to give.

"I don't know many of his friends," Polazzo told the detectives. "We just didn't talk that much."

The detectives expressed their curiosity about the living arrangements Polazzo had had with the victim.

"It's just business!" Polazzo said, offended by the question. "I'm not gay. Gerry had his own relationships. I was just there to protect him."

"Protect him?"

"Yeah! Gerry was worried about getting attacked. There's been a lot of bashings on Central Street, so Gerry asked if I would move in with him. Plus, he gave me a great deal on the room. That's it!"

Both investigators were familiar with Central Street, where there had been a number of murders and other crimes in recent

years. Muggers and gay bashers preyed on the homosexuals
who frequented the street. But the sleuths couldn't help wondering why, if Polazzo had been Gerald Trottier's "live-in protection," as he claimed, Trottier was lying dead in a room just
down the hall?

Polazzo's emotions fluctuated: One minute he was sad; the
next confused; and finally upset. He didn't like what the detectives seemed to be insinuating. He swore over and over
again that he had nothing to do with his roommate's death.
The detectives took him down to the police station and questioned him well into the next morning.

As the sleuths slowly pried a name out of the distraught
roommate, they would send a detective out to find that person
and ask what they knew about Gerald Trottier. It was three
o'clock in the morning when detectives began knocking on
doors in the Albany area. Surprisingly, many of Trottier's
friends were awake. Some had even been awakened with the
shocking news that their friend had been horribly murdered.

The victim's family was contacted immediately. They had
little information to offer detectives. They said they knew little
about Trottier's homosexual lifestyle, but they provided the
names of his friends. The exhausted sleuths then went to check
on those contacts and were given the names of more contacts,
whom the sleuths would also check out. More than 30 detectives were called in to help out with the early-morning canvass.

Back at the Public Safety Building, Nick Polazzo was drinking cup after cup of hot coffee to stay awake. He still couldn't
think of anyone who had a grievance against his roommate.

"Wait a minute!" Polazzo said, snapping his head up. "There
was this guy . . ." He looked up at the holes in the ceiling,
hoping to find the answer. ". . . Paul . . . something. Or was
it Dave?" He paused in thought a little longer. "It was either
Paul or Dave. I don't remember a last name. Gerald introduced
me once in the living room, but it was only for a second. He
said this guy was going to stay with him for a couple days.

"They stayed on one side of the apartment and I never saw

them. That was two days ago. I bet he was still there. I bet he did it!"

The vague lead was a long shot at best, but the probers would need to know everything about this house guest. Polazzo said the man had been with his roommate that evening at around 8 P.M. when he left the apartment. Polazzo added that he thought Trottier and the stranger were drinking beers together.

"Where was he from?" the detectives asked.

"I don't know. Not from around here. He had a really thick Southern accent, though. I'm not sure where it was from."

Polazzo wasn't able to give much more information on the stranger, except to say the man was clean-cut and very friendly. The detectives hoped someone else would know more about the victim's mystery house guest.

Another NLETS bulletin was put out to the surrounding cities. This report stated that Albany police were looking for a white male possibly going by the name of Paul or Dave with a heavy Southern accent and probably with "homosexual tendencies." The description was thin, but Captain Murray would later recall, "It's easier to look for a white male named Paul or Dave than just a white male. At least it was some kind of start."

New York State police responded to the teletype. Two state investigators arrived in Albany to offer their assistance. "Would you like us to run this description through other states?" one of the investigators offered.

The assistance was appreciated. At the time, Captain Murray had no idea just how important everyone's help was going to be in this case.

The Department of Motor Vehicles gave sleuths a description of the victim's car. Police searched the surrounding garages and could not find it anywhere.

A BOLO (police jargon for "be on the lookout") was put out for a silver 1978 Ford Fairmont with rust on the roof. Normally, only local police are asked to be on the lookout for a certain vehicle, but state investigators offered to send out the description to neighboring states, as well. This was a gesture that investigators would later be thankful for.

Captain Murray got a little bit of much-needed sleep early on Saturday, May 17, but he was up again before 10 o'clock to witness the autopsy performed by Dr. Roberto Benitez.

The doctor reported that the victim had sustained three fatal stab wounds—two to the neck and one to the left eye socket. The skull was also fractured from a blunt trauma to the victim's forehead. Crime-scene technicians would later verify that traces of the victim's blood appeared on the bottom of the floor heater found in the victim's bedroom. It was apparent to Captain Murray that the killer had used the heater to render his victim unconscious and then proceeded to stab him, which would explain the lack of defensive wounds on the victim's arms and hands.

Captain Murray realized the motive was probably robbery. The open safe was a giveaway. Murray played out the scenario is his mind: Perhaps this Paul or Dave forced Gerald Trottier to open the safe, then bashed him on the head with the floor heater, and stole whatever was inside. Then he finished off the job by cutting Trottier's throat while he lay unconscious.

The frenzied nature of the assault made Murray wonder what was inside the safe. Trottier's roommate had no answer. "I never saw him open it," Nick Polazzo told investigators.

Trottier's main source of income was his job at a car dealership downtown. Detectives went to Trottier's workplace and asked the owner about the victim's work habits.

"He was an excellent worker," the owner told sleuths. "He was good with cars. He even made some extra money fixing used cars on the side." The owner said that Trottier had just fixed a car the previous week for about $1,800. Investigators realized that if Trottier had put that money in his safe, it could be very tempting for a criminal.

Perhaps this guy had killed before, Captain Murray thought. He started to look into other murders with similar M.O.s that had occurred in the area, including one of the city's most famous unsolved cases. The M.O. was almost identical. A homosexual had been killed downtown and robbed of all his valuables. But those seemed to be the only connections between the cases. Perhaps the killer dabbled in other homosexual crimes, and maybe this time he had gone too far.

Murray tapped at his computer keyboard and called up files on local extortionists. Among them he found those of several underage boys who hustled local homosexuals. They would lure older men into coming home with them under the pretext of having sex and would then strip them of all their valuables. One address kept popping up. It was a run-down house in a nearby city north of Albany. Murray knew the building as a combination crack house and cathouse. The local cops had tried to shut it down for years.

Three murders were reported at the address: that of an elderly woman, a young female, and a homosexual male. Captain Murray couldn't help but wonder if the underage hustlers had struck again.

With the help of state police, a team of detectives had stormed the building and searched it for clues. Most of the kids had already been fingerprinted, but those who hadn't been were rounded up and taken in. If crime-scene technicians could lift a print, it would then be a matter of finding a match.

Captain Murray waited for nothing. He continued to investigate the homosexual community that Trottier was a part of.

"Homosexuals have their own world," Murray would say in describing his tactics. "The advantage to their closed society is that everyone pretty much knows everyone else." Captain Murray had little trouble finding someone who knew the victim at a bar called the Waterworks.

"Yeah, I know him," one patron said as he finished making a difficult bank shot off his opponent's ball. The man at the pool table put down his cue and walked over to the sleuth asking questions at the bar. "He was in here yesterday."

"Was he alone?" Murray asked as he took out a pen and paper.

"No, some guy was in here with him," the witness replied. "We played pool."

"Did the friend ever mention his name?"

"I think he said his name was Paul . . . Paul Norris, or something. He had a Southern accent. I think he said he was from Texas."

Captain Murray scribbled on his notepad as quickly as he could. The description sounded suspiciously familiar. He wished he had more. Murray also spoke with the bartender, who said Trottier was a good customer who came in frequently.

Murray went on to the other homosexual bars in the area. Most of them were on Central Street. Places like The Rage and The Playhouse got most of the business. But other hangouts, like the State Street Pub, knew Gerald Trottier.

Murray ran into many people who said they saw a man hanging around Trottier. Some said he was from Los Angeles. Some said he was from Texas, and others swore that they heard the man say he was from Nashville, Tennessee. Captain Murray left each bar with an even stronger desire to find this man named Paul or Dave.

Back at the station, Murray discovered that word of Trottier's murder had spread. The homosexual bars in the area all knew of Trottier, and some people who were in the bars the night before were coming forward with what they knew about the victim.

One such man, a local hairdresser, claimed that he introduced one of his friends to Trottier just a couple of days before. Murray's heart skipped a beat. Maybe this would be the "Paul or Dave" he was looking for.

"He only stayed with me one night," the hairdresser began to explain. "I don't remember his name." The idea struck the captain as odd. How could he not know the name of the person who was sleeping in his house? But Murray didn't press the issue and told the witness to continue.

"He had an accent. I think it was Southern," the hairdresser said, pausing for a minute. He looked as if he was deep in thought. "I remember him saying he just got out of prison, and he was just passing through Albany. I could only put him up for one night, and that's when I introduced him to Gerry. They seemed to hit if off."

"And you can't remember his name?" the captain asked again. "Was it Paul?"

The witness thought for a second. "It very well could have been."

"How about Dave?"

"Maybe. It was something like that."

The information was scarce in coming, but again, Murray couldn't wait for the facts to come to him. He remembered a Texas detective he had met at a convention in Nashville, Tennessee. Murray called her up and gave her the limited information he had on his suspect.

"You're kidding, right?" the Texas sleuth asked, regarding Murray's decidedly vague description of the suspect.

"His name could also be Dave," Murray replied, almost fearing her response. "And his last name is Norris, or something like that." He knew it sounded crazy, but that was all he had.

The Texas detective's sigh was a little more reassuring than Murray expected. She said she would call Murray back after she talked to some people at a couple of correctional facilities.

Meanwhile, Sergeant Nielsen came through the captain's door with the most recent development in the case. "CID's got a print!"

The captain followed Nielsen down to the Criminal Investigation Division where the technicians seemed to be celebrating. It wasn't just one print—it was three prints—one from a glass found on top of a small table in the main room, and the other two from the beer bottles on top of the bar. They were all identical. The prints were checked against those of everyone the sleuths knew had been in the room, including themselves,

Nick Polazzo, and the victim. None of the prints matched. It *had* to be the killer's print.

Within a few hours, the Texas detective called back and gave Captain Murray the names of three ex-convicts who had recently been released from prison: Paul Levek, Paul Reese, and Dave Bennett.

Within minutes, Captain Murray had a brief record on the three suspects. Murray though about the second name on the list more than the others. "Reese" sounded a lot closer to "Norris" than the other names. Murray picked up the phone and contacted Reese's parole officer in Texas. Strangely, the parole officer hadn't heard from Reese in a month. His criminal file was not available from either the correctional facility in Texas or Reese's parole officer.

"That's because he wasn't arrested in Texas," the parole officer told the captain. "Orange County, Texas, extradited him from Minneapolis, Minnesota. They probably still have the records."

Murray contacted the department of corrections in Minneapolis late Saturday night. The woman who answered the phone told the captain that no one was there at that time of night, and there was no one available at the prison who could help him. Luckily, a sergeant was walking by at the time of Murray's call. The woman got his attention and asked him if he could pull Paul Reese's file. Murray listened on the other end, silently praying that the sergeant would help. Murray's prayers were answered. The sergeant said he would gladly send the files to Albany.

Now it was a race against time. Murray had a good idea the killer was a drifter who could be halfway across the country by now. The sooner Albany had a print for Paul Reese, the sooner they could eliminate him, or if they matched him, the sooner they could start looking for him. The problem was, the following day was Sunday, and there was no hope of using the postal system.

"By wonderful police methods," Murray would recall with a hearty laugh, "we had those files the next morning."

CID took the files and, within minutes, they had a match. The next step of the investigation would be the most frustrating—they would have to find Paul Steven Reese.

Judging from the little he knew about the suspect, Murray had a feeling Reese was relying on the kindness of strangers. He could be anywhere, but chances were he was staying with someone he'd met along the way. At first, detectives thought Reese might have gone to New York City—it was only three hours away, and it was an easy place to get lost in.

Then Murray made an "unofficial" entry with the NCIC (National Crime Information Computer). A "temporary want" was placed in the computer for any law-enforcement official who came across 28-year-old Paul Reese. This was a way of detaining the suspect without a warrant. "A judge would probably say there wasn't enough evidence for that even," Murray would later say. "I was really going out on a limb."

But Murray wanted this guy—badly. Fingerprints placed him at the scene, he already had a criminal record, and he was wanted in Texas for parole violation.

The entry in the NCIC gave a complete description of Paul Reese, right down to a small tattoo on his right arm that said simply "Debbie." A small note on the bottom of the report stated that the suspect might have "homosexual tendencies." The description was hooked up to every police station and most squad cars in the country.

But Paul Steven Reese had vanished.

On Monday, May 19, three days after the murder, New York State Police contacted Albany detectives about a call that they received from Pennsylvania State Police. A patrol officer in Philadelphia spotted what he thought to be an abandoned vehicle behind a gay bar downtown. The officer called in the license plate, and because of the New York State Police inquiry, the Pennsylvania officials were able to secure the automobile.

Captain Murray sent Detectives Daniel Ryan and Donald Gavigan to investigate.

When the sleuths returned, they weren't able to give the information their captain wanted. The car had been abandoned. There were several homosexual establishments in the area where the car was left, but the probers had found no other clues as to where the driver might have gone from there. The detectives did, however, find a gold ring under the driver's seat—a ring that was identified by a Trottier relative as belonging to the victim.

The information was appreciated, but sleuths were still no closer to finding their man. Captain Murray called the telephone company, hoping a call that had been placed at the victim's home would give sleuths another lead. It did.

Apparently, all of Gerald Trottier's calls were local, with the exception of one, which had been placed on the night of the murder to a small town in Nevada. Murray called that number, not knowing what to expect. A woman answered the phone, and the captain asked her if she knew Gerald Trottier.

"No," she replied. "What is this all about?"

But before Murray would start answering questions, he wanted some answers himself. "Do you know someone named Paul Reese?"

The woman hesitated. "Yes, I do. Why?"

The captain explained his purpose for calling, and the woman remembered Reese's phone call to her.

"I thought it was strange," she told Murray. "I hadn't heard from him in a while. He mentioned that he just got out of prison and that he was staying with a friend."

"Did he say where he was calling from?"

"I assumed he was calling from Houston."

"Well, he wasn't. He was in Albany, New York," Murray said. The detective wondered if Reese was on his way to the woman's home. Murray cautioned her not to trust Reese if he came around and left her his phone number.

As the weeks dragged on, the hopes of finding Paul Reese

dwindled. The Albany detectives prayed for a lucky break, and on July 11, 1987, almost two months after the murder, they got it.

In Portland, Oregon, a branch of the FBI received a call from a man claiming to be Paul Reese. He was calling to see if he was wanted by the government. The receptionist told Reese that it would take time to look up such a request. She put him on hold.

The receptionist was actually looking at Reese's name on the computer screen right in front of her, but she kept Reese waiting long enough to contact Portland police. A trace was put on the call, and the caller's coordinates were radioed to two local police cars.

When the officers converged on the small bar from where Reese had placed his call, they found him in the corner of the room on the phone—still on hold with the FBI. The officers took Reese into custody without incident and brought him to the federal building downtown. From there, police notified Albany officials of the capture.

Captain Murray wanted to send his best detectives on the next flight to Portland, but Portland authorities couldn't allow it. Reese was being held as a "fugitive from justice." Reese would have to waive his extradition rights.

Paul Reese did waive extradition. Murray sent Sergeant Nielsen and Detective Gavigan to Portland on the next flight.

When the two sleuths arrived in Portland, they discovered that the federal building where Reese was held also housed the city, county, and state offices. They reached the federal marshals only to find that their prisoner had been released to federal agents and was taken to the airport.

Nielsen was more than a bit miffed. He felt that the FBI was taking their prisoner right from under their noses. Nielsen and Gavigan raced to the airport and stopped the small charter plane on the runway. The detectives demanded that the agents release their prisoner, but the FBI refused. When they asked the agents to reveal where they were taking the suspect, the agents again refused to answer.

Nielsen called Captain Murray in Albany and asked him, "What the hell is going on here?"

Captain Murray called officials at the FBI headquarters in Quantico, Virginia, and demanded that the agents release their prisoner. When an FBI official said they had first privilege to the prisoner, Murray brought up a small point of order. Albany officials had placed Reese's name with the NCIC before the FBI had. So technically, Albany had first privilege.

Back in Portland, the Albany detectives were finally given their prisoner, but the agents still refused to tell the sleuths where they were taking Reese and why.

The two detectives had to board the next commercial flight they could. An American Airlines pilot approved the detectives' request for transport. Cuffed to their prisoner, the two sleuths were the first on the plane and the last off at Chicago's O'Hare Airport, where they changed planes.

The airline pilot for the remainder of the flight was not as generous as the first. The pilot confiscated the officers' weapons during the trip and warned Reese not to cause any trouble.

But Paul Reese had been no trouble to the investigators. "I actually liked the guy," Nielsen would later say of his mild-mannered traveling companion. "He seemed like a real nice guy."

Reese talked nonstop to the detectives. He told them about his hitchhiking trip across the country after he dumped the victim's car in Philadelphia. First, he went to Los Angeles. Then he traveled back across the country to Baltimore, Maryland. From there, he hitched a couple of rides down to Mexico. "I stayed away from Texas, though," Reese told the detectives. He was still worried about being wanted in that state. "Then I went back to California for a little bit, and finally I went to Portland . . . and that's when you guys got me."

The detectives couldn't help but be amazed by their suspect's candor. He was actually bragging—even a little humorous about it. But his personality soon changed.

Reese seemed to be conversing more with himself than with the detectives. He started talking about his childhood. He grew up in Boys Town, he said, and then he'd been abused by his adopted parents. He told the sleuths that he didn't like homosexuals and that he didn't like being accused of being one. "I'm not gay!" Reese insisted in a shrill whisper.

Passengers on the plane turned to look at the men. Reese was starting to make a scene as turbulence from a violent storm began to rock the plane. The pilot turned off the lights so that passengers could get the full effect of the storm's light show. But the investigators didn't like the idea of being without their weapons as their prisoner escalated into a frenzy aboard the tiny plane.

Sergeant Nielsen calmed Reese down and offered to change the subject. Reese seemed distant, almost schizophrenic. "We don't want to talk about this anymore," Nielsen said. And the rest of the trip was peaceful.

A.D.A. Larry Wiest presented the case to the grand jury. Paul Reese was indicted on first-degree murder charges. Reese pleaded guilty, and the judge passed down a sentence of 20 years to life. By law, the sentence was lowered from the customary 25 to 20 because of Reese's plea.

Paul Reese is currently serving his time in a New York State prison, but even today, as Lieutenant Nielsen thinks about the case, something bothers him.

"The FBI knew something. I think they were going to take him to spots all across the country where they think he [Reese] had killed before."

The lieutenant remembered his experience on the flight with Reese. "He had all the classic signs. He was intelligent, gentle, and psychotic. I know this guy's a serial killer. I can't prove it, but I know he is. It was too easy for him."

" 'GOOD SAMARITAN' SEX KILLER"

by Barry Benedict

The nocturnal slaying of the San Diego coed was first reported on the bright, sunny morning of April 11, 1979, when two small boys ventured into San Diego's Linda Vista Park to spend a quiet morning playing baseball. Those plans were interrupted when one of the youths trotted behind a tennis backstop at the north end of the park and discovered a body.

The victim was a young female, about 18 to 22 years old, with long light-brown hair. She lay nude in the open ditch, covered head to foot with blood.

San Diego police were called to the scene, followed by homicide detectives Dick Carey, Ron Newman, and Lloyd Cox. After examining the body, the sleuths followed a trail of blood to the front of the tennis court and discovered a fresh blood pool in front of the cement tennis backstop. Four bloodstained stones, each the size of a man's palm, lay next to the crimson pool.

Searching the area, investigators discovered a second bloody crime scene, this one between the recreation center and a pottery building 130 feet from the ball court.

It appeared that the victim had been attacked twice: first at the entrance of the recreation center and the pottery building, and a second time at the cement ball court. The killer had then dragged her corpse to the freshly dug ditch.

Police collected a blouse, bra, blue jeans, and other clothing at the crime scene but did not find the victim's wallet or anything else that could be used to identify her. Her identity remained unknown until the next day when a man saw a news story about the slain girl in Linda Vista Park and called police. The description of the murdered woman fit his relative, 20-year-old Debra Owen, of Point Loma.

Later that afternoon, the Coroner's Office confirmed the man's worst suspicion: The victim was his missing relative.

Debra Owen was something close to an all-American girl. A neighbor described her as "a real sweet kid. I knew her for nineteen years. She was very friendly and outgoing."

Debra had planned to enter college the following fall. But those plans ended on a lonely cement tennis court far from home.

Debra's family was devastated. They had no idea what she was doing at the Linda Vista playground. Debra didn't know anyone in the Linda Vista area, they said, and she had no reason to go there when there were several playgrounds in her own neighborhood.

Did she go to the park to meet someone? Or had she been brought there against her will?

Police were still searching for answers when they got another tip from an anonymous caller, who told police, "I was in the park when that girl was murdered. I saw her alive, sitting with her left eye injured."

The caller hung up before the police could get his name, but he called back 10 minutes later and was put through to Detective Carey. The two talked and agreed to meet at the Linda Vista Recreation Center.

Carey arrived at the park at 1 P.M. In the parking lot near the Linda Vista Recreation Center, a young man flagged him down.

The witness identified himself as Jessie Ray Moffett, 20 years old, of Linda Vista.

Detective Carey gave Moffett a hard look. Moffett's face was familiar. Then Carey remembered where he had seen him before. Moffett had stood by with several other spectators while Detectives Carey and Newman searched the pottery building wall for fingerprints.

Short and barrel-chested, Moffett spoke in hyperactive, machine-gun bursts. "I was helping that girl who was killed," he told the detective. "I might have seen who done it."

Moffett said that on the night of April 10, he was walking back from his girlfriend's house, when he stopped at the Linda Vista Jack in the Box. After wolfing down a burger, he passed through Linda Vista Park, headed for home, when he heard a woman crying.

"I went between those buildings," Moffett said, referring to the pottery and the recreation center. "I saw a woman kneeling on the pathway. She did not say anything. I asked if anything was wrong. She tried to walk away."

Moffett said he could see that she was hurt. She had a cut over her left eye and was bleeding profusely. He asked if she wanted him to call the police, or if she wanted to call the police herself.

"She said no to both questions," Moffett said. "I told her my name, and she said her name was Terry. She didn't make a whole lot of sense. I thought she was high on something, some sort of drug."

Moffett said he decided to help the woman, even if she didn't seek his help. He decided that the one thing he could do was wipe the blood from her face.

He took off his T-shirt and pressed it against her eye. He asked who hit her. She said it was her boyfriend. Moffett said she took the shirt away and blood dripped down her clothes. He said at this time he reached up and touched his bloody fingers on the wall of the restroom.

"That is what I wanted to talk to you about," Moffett said,

getting to the point. "You might find my prints there. Also my palm print might be there. I wiped my hand on the wall because I didn't want to get blood on my jeans."

Moffett said he walked the injured woman to the auditorium door and looked at her in the light. He described her as about 5-foot-5, 120 to 125 pounds, with long brown hair that was curly on the ends and hung to her shoulders. "Her eyebrows were pretty and looked natural," he said. "I also saw that her blouse was somewhat open."

Moffett said he felt a wave of compassion come over him, and he grabbed the girl and said he was serious about helping her. The woman, however, screamed and told him to leave her alone. He said he did not try to help her after that and left by going back between the two buildings where he had first seen her.

As he left the park for home, Moffett looked back and saw a man with hair like a surfer's. He was about 5-foot-1 and 220 pounds with wide shoulders. Moffett didn't know if that was the boyfriend who had beaten the girl, but it could have been. He said he did not approach the man, nor did he see where the stranger went after he left the park.

Moffett said he awoke the next morning at 10 o'clock, and a relative told him that police had surrounded the park because there was a dead female behind one of the recreation buildings. Moffett said he wanted to call the police and let them know what he had done with the girl the night before, but he was afraid to because he had just been let out of prison.

"I'm an ex-con," Moffett said. "I was afraid you might think I had something to do with it."

Moffett decided to contact the police anyway because his prints might be on the building and he didn't want detectives to get the wrong idea—namely, that Moffett was involved in the murder.

But that was just the idea that Detective Carey got. He did not buy Moffett's story about aiding the bleeding woman.

Carey believed that Moffett made up the story to explain why his prints were on the pottery building wall.

Moffett claimed he wanted to help the detectives. But he only got himself in deeper.

The next day, Detectives Carey and Newman conducted a second interview with Moffett at the Linda Vista Recreation Center. Moffett said he first wanted to contact his parole officer, then changed his mind and asked detectives if they had found any good evidence.

Bluffing, Carey claimed they had and that they had lifted several good fingerprints off the wall of the pottery shed and that they would have no trouble matching them to whoever had left them.

"I told you so," Moffett said.

Moffett repeated his story to Newman about the bloody girl and the surfer-type stranger. He denied following the girl down the passageway to the ball court.

"I was nowhere near there," he told detectives. "I haven't been near those courts since I was released from prison."

Since the murder, Moffett said he had talked to several other people in the neighborhood. They also told him that they had seen the "surfer" maniac whom Moffett described as lurking around the park. The residents believed that the surfer lived nearby.

"If you want to find the guy who done her in," Moffett suggested, "find the surfer guy. I bet he knows something."

Detectives had bluffed Moffett about the prints. But the bluff turned out to be true. Lab technicians had examined 18 fingerprints lifted from the side of the recreation center and discovered that one of the prints, a partial bloody palm print, matched Jessie Moffett's.

On April 17, investigators met Moffett at his home on Preece Street and collected the pants and shoes that Moffett said he was wearing when he was with the victim. Afterward, they took him down to police headquarters where he was interviewed, as well as processed, as a possible homicide suspect.

Moffett repeated his story that he was "only helping" the woman. He also admitted that he had been the person who asked detectives at the crime scene if it was possible to leave fingerprints on a rock.

Asked how he knew about the bloody rocks—they were 130 feet away at the ball court—Moffett replied. "Everyone was talking about them. I was curious."

Questioned as to why he did not call the police after finding the victim, he replied, "She didn't want me to."

Moffett accused the detectives of suspecting him of murdering the girl when his only involvement was trying to help her.

When told that the detectives would not be doing their job if they did not check him out, Moffett shrugged and said, "Most people think that I'm going to get framed for this thing because I just got out of the penitentiary."

Admitting that he was not a model citizen, the ex-con insisted he was not a murderer; if anything he was only a Good Samaritan, helping a woman who needed help, whether she knew it or not.

Detectives didn't buy the suspect's story. To them, Moffett had concocted a far-fetched yarn to explain what his bloody fingerprints were doing at the scene. And the story had worked—for a while.

After the interrogation, Moffett was released without being charged. Three months later, he was back in police custody, this time for rape.

In July, a waitress at a nightclub left work after it closed at 1:30 A.M. She was returning to her apartment in Mission Beach, when at the corner of Mission Boulevard and Nahant Court, a man jumped into the passenger seat and told her to drive to Tecolote Park.

In the parking lot at the entrance to the golf course, they were joined by two men who trailed them from Mission Beach. The man who jumped in the front seat told the frightened driver that he was a San Diego police officer. He said he had a warrant for the woman's arrest but would let her go if she agreed to have sex with him and his two buddies.

The woman said she wanted to go to the police station. The men ignored her request and repeatedly gang-raped her.

After the men left, the victim went to the police station and reported the crime. She gave sex-crimes detectives good descriptions of the rapists and said she would be able to identify them. She also identified the car that followed her to Tecolote Park and gave detectives a partial license number.

Detectives traced the car to the owner and arrested three men. One of the suspects was Jessie Moffett.

Moffett denied the charge. But after a brief trial, he was found guilty of multiple counts of robbery, kidnapping, and sexual assault and sentenced to a 10-year term in state prison.

Detective Carey wanted to add murder to the list of Moffett's crimes. But the District Attorney's Office said the case had too many holes and declined to prosecute.

So Debra Owen's killer went to prison—but for rape, not murder. That meant that one day he would get out and that somebody else would have to pay the price.

Detective Carey went back to work. Over the years, primarily as a crime-scene investigator, he had compiled an impressive record. By his own estimation, he had investigated over 500 homicides, including a few high-profile "red ball" cases.

In 1989, Carey retired from the police department after 25 years and joined the District Attorney's Office, doing what he did best: investigating murders. Although many years had passed, he never forgot the murder of Debra Owen or her apparent killer, Jessie Moffett.

The crime scene that warm spring day was as vivid in his mind as a snapshot. "It was a brutal murder," he would later say. "It gave off a feeling of pure evil."

Carey was still upset that the D.A.'s office had not pursued the case more aggressively. But, in police work, those were the breaks. You win some; you lose some. Only this time the good guys had lost. However, experience told Carey one thing—they had not heard the last of Jessie Moffett.

That prediction came true on the evening of December 18, 1987, when police went to investigate a shooting of a security guard at the Holiday Inn on Aero Drive. When investigators arrived, they discovered guard Glenn Avery, age 67, lying supinely on the asphalt parking lot. Avery had been shot once in the face, the slug penetrating his skull.

Like most hotel security guards, Avery was unarmed. He had gone into the parking lot to investigate the report of a possible car theft in progress.

While investigators were at the scene, they learned of another crime at the hotel. Hattie Jones, 23, was stepping out for the evening when three men with guns abducted her in front of her Kearney Mesa home. One of the men raped her in the front seat of her car, then, with his two buddies following in a second car, he ordered Hattie to take them to her boyfriend, Wilfred Olney.

She took them to the Holiday Inn, where Olney was hiding out under an assumed name. One of the gunmen in the second car took Hattie to Olney's room, then robbed both her and Olney at gunpoint. Afterward, he ripped the telephone cord from the wall socket, tied the victims up, and threatened to kill them if they tried to get help before he escaped.

Hattie Jones told police that she hadn't seen the gunmen before; she had no idea who they were. Her boyfriend, Olney, was also in the dark about who they were.

"Why me?" he wondered.

Olney, police learned, was no saint. In fact, gunmen had been hot on his trail for almost a month.

On November 22, two men armed with full automatics burst into Olney's Mission Beach apartment. Olney was not in, and a friend of his was house-sitting the apartment. One of the gunmen stuck the barrel of his gun down the terrified man's throat and marched him around the apartment, demanding money and drugs. The man, however, was only visiting and had nothing to offer but pocket change and a couple of beers in the fridge. The gunmen left in a huff.

On December 11, two men threw a barbell through a plate-glass window of a home on Haveteur Way, and jumped through the broken glass, waving automatic weapons. One of the gunmen ordered a mother and her 12-year-old daughter to take off their clothes and hand over their dope and money. When the naked mother did not produce enough loot, one of the gunmen took the naked daughter out to the garage and told her to get in the backseat of her car. Instead, the daughter fled out the garage door and down the street.

Police made a connection between the crimes when they learned that Wilfred Olney and the woman were friends and did business together.

The Mission Beach robbery had been a bust; the Haveteur Way break-in wasn't much better. But the gunmen weren't through.

On December 11, the gunmen used sledgehammers to break through a quarter-inch-thick oak door on Dwight Street, shot to death a 40-pound pit bull that greeted them on the other side, and beat the occupant and a visiting friend with rifle butts.

Four days later it was Hattie Jones's turn.

The robbery investigation had now become part of the larger homicide case. One name that kept surfacing repeatedly in the crime wave was Jessie Moffett.

Moffett had just recently been paroled from prison, after serving eight years for the Mission Beach rape. He was fingered for rape after Hattie Jones identified him in a photo as the man who assaulted her in the front seat of her car. He was also identified as the gunman who attempted to rape the naked girl on Haveteur Way.

Police now believed that the prison-hardened ex-con was very capable of the cold-blooded murder of security guard Glenn Avery.

On December 21, 1987, Moffett was arrested on parole violation. That gave detectives almost a year to bring Moffett up on other charges.

That same month, police arrested Albert Jarrell on a parole violation. A friend of Moffett's, Jarrell had been fingered as one of the gunmen who had taken part in the string of break-in robberies and the abduction of Hattie Jones.

Once behind bars, Jarrell told police that Moffett had murdered Glenn Avery. He offered to give Moffett up if the charges against him were dropped. When the district attorney declined, Jarrell surprised everyone and said he would talk, deal or no deal.

Jarrell told police that he, Moffett, and a third man, Jake Dillon, had been after Wilfred Olney to get money and drugs, which Olney allegedly peddled. When they were unable to find Olney, they decided to abduct his girlfriend, Hattie Jones, instead and force her to lead them to him. Jarrell said they went to the Jones house and confronted her as she was walking to her car. Moffett then got in the car with her, and they followed them to the Holiday Inn.

While Dillon escorted Jones at gunpoint to the hotel room, Jarrell said he and Moffett tried to force the trunk of a Pontiac Fiero that was in the hotel parking lot because it looked like the car that Olney drove. Unable to force the trunk lock, Jarrell said they tried to shoot it off, the way they'd seen it done "in the movies."

They were emptying their guns into the trunk lock when a man in a uniform appeared yelling, "Freeze right there!"

Jarrell said he accidentally fired a shot and the man went down. He said the accidental discharge of the weapon so surprised him that he ran to see if the man was all right.

"He said he was okay," Jarrell told police. "He kept shouting, 'I'm not armed, I'm not armed!' "

Jarrell said that as he went back to the car, he was passed by Moffett, who had his gun out and was walking toward the security guard.

When Jarrell got to the car, he was joined by Dillon, who

was returning from the Holiday Inn with the loot taken from Olney and Jones. Then Moffett appeared.

"He was laughing and working the action to his gun," Jarrell said. "I asked him what was happening and he said that he had shot the guy on the ground."

Jarrell said he wanted to drive back and check on the man to see if he was all right, but Moffett cut him off.

"Forget it," Moffett said in an icy tone. "The fool is dead."

"I can't get it out of my head," Jarrell told detectives. "Jessie shot that guy for no reason at all. And he was laughing about it. I won't ever forget that."

Dillon later corroborated Albert Jarrell's story. In an interrogation with Detective Jamie Bordine, Dillon also helped solve the eight-year-old murder of Debra Owen.

"I wasn't really too surprised that he murdered that unarmed security guard in cold blood," Dillon told Bordine, "because he'd done it before."

Dillon said he and Moffett were playing basketball at the Linda Vista Municipal Gym shortly after Moffett was paroled from prison. During a break, Moffett confided that he had once murdered a woman at the same recreational center.

"I asked him what he was talking about, what murder," Dillon told Detective Bordine. "He said there had been this girl he met at the rec center a long time ago. He said he raped her on the ball court, then dragged her into a ditch and beat her head with rocks."

Dillon knew that a long stretch in prison could make a man say silly things. But Moffett sounded as though he was telling the truth. "He said the police had tried to pin the murder on him, but he was too smart for them suckers and beat the rap."

Moffett was due to be released from probation in 1988. Instead, he was arrested and charged with 20 felony crimes, including murder, robbery, burglary, kidnapping, and assault with a deadly weapon.

At Moffett's April 1992 trial, Prosecutor Al Barret asked jurors for the death penalty, saying that the defendant had a long string of violent crimes that included brutal, unprovoked murders, and as a result, he deserved nothing less.

Over the next three months, jurors heard from 50 witnesses, including others of Moffett's alleged rape victims. Jurors also viewed gruesome crime-scene photos taken at the murder scene.

In August, they convicted Moffett of the rape and murder of Debra Owen and the execution-style slaying of Glenn Avery. Moffett showed little reaction as the bailiff read the verdict to the courtroom.

In the penalty phase, Moffett's court-appointed attorneys asked for leniency, citing Moffett's troubled childhood, which they argued had caused the impressionable young man to become a sadistic killer.

"Mr. Moffett, as a member of society, deserved more," one attorney told Judge William Mudd. "He should have gotten more therapy. He should have received better treatment as a child."

If he had, the attorneys contended, things might have turned out differently. He might not have raped and murdered a young woman. He might not have executed a security guard. With more therapy and understanding, they argued, he might have become a model citizen.

Prosecutor Barret reminded jurors that no one had forced Moffett to murder two people. He did that on his own. Now he had to pay the price, and the price in this case was his own life.

Jurors agreed, taking just under four hours to return a death penalty verdict. On September 3, 1992, Judge Mudd sentenced the 34-year-old killer to die in the gas chamber at San Quentin.

In the event that Moffett's death sentence was overturned, Judge Mudd ordered him to spend 52 years to life in prison for the two murders, plus an additional 29-year prison term for a string of robberies.

"It is the intention of this court to see that you never walk the streets a free man," Mudd told the solemn-faced defendant.

With that, Jessie Moffett left the courtroom, escorted back to his cell. By state law, his death penalty conviction has been automatically appealed to the state supreme court. He is awaiting their decision on San Quentin's death row.

"MURDER IN THE FOG"

by Joseph N. York

Ghosts, goblins, witches, and ghouls looked out from spider-webbed windows. Black cats and fiercely carved pumpkins suspended from chandeliers glared down with evil in their eyes. Outside, the fog hung thick and murky. It was three days before Halloween.

On Saturday night, October 27, 1990, in an upstairs apartment in Imperial Beach, California, Pete Alvarado was making a jack-o'-lantern for his girlfriend. This was the finishing touch to Halloween decorations that would make anyone proud.

About 9:30 P.M., Alvarado heard loud yelling in the street below. It was no big deal. People who live close together are always having differences of opinion. Alvarado then heard three or four gunshots. There was no mistaking that sound. Alvarado stepped quickly to the sliding door and looked out.

In the middle of the street, a full-size pickup truck was parked with the driver's side away from Alvarado's view. A man was standing near the back of the truck, and, about 10 feet from the man, a woman was running away from him.

Alvarado yelled down, "Hey, what are you doing?"

The man in the street looked up at Alvarado, took aim, and shot twice.

Alvarado dove inside and hollered at his girlfriend to call the sheriff.

Although Imperial Beach is an incorporated city, it contracts with the San Diego County Sheriff for police services.

Alvarado's girlfriend dialed 911 and within minutes, Deputy Enrique Diaz arrived. By then the truck, the man, and the woman were gone. However, Deputy Diaz found a bicycle in the middle of the street. He conducted a check of the immediate area and found one spent cartridge on the asphalt.

After finding the bullet casing, Deputy Diaz knew Alvarado was not hallucinating about the gunshots. Diaz checked the facing of the apartment and found the bullet holes. One was only a foot above where Alvarado's head had been. Since the gunman had fired other shots, Deputy Diaz checked the surrounding area for more bullet casings. It was hard enough to find a bullet casing in the daytime. But the night and the fog complicated the search. They were less than a mile from the ocean, and the wind was cold.

Alvarado could only give a general description of the man with the gun: a white male of average height and build. The fog and darkness canceled out any additional information on him. He had been about 75 feet away, and Alvarado only looked at him for a few seconds before diving to safety.

The vehicle was a full-size pickup truck. It had a wide white stripe along the side. The bottom was the same color as the top.

Deputy Pete Martinez joined in the search along with Sergeant Paul Nevills. They walked the area holding their flashlights low and moving slowly.

As Martinez made his way up a sidewalk leading to a house, he saw a woman's body near the front door. The woman was wearing sweatpants, a sweater, and canvas sneakers. She was lying on her side and appeared to be reaching for something, probably the doorbell, hoping for help. Help, if it had come at all, was too late.

Martinez checked for a purse and found none. The victim's

sweater was soaked with blood. He looked around frantically, but discovered he was some distance from the other officers. He quickly shone his light on the house numbers and radioed to Sergeant Nevills that he had found something, and he gave the address on 15th Street.

Martinez saw Nevills and Diaz coming toward him. "I found her," the young deputy said, his complexion ashen. "Sarge, you go up there. You can call homicide."

Diaz waited back with Martinez as Sergeant Nevills checked for a pulse. He radioed dispatch to summon the on-call roll-out homicide team.

From their respective homes, Detectives Russ Oliver, Dave Weil, and Fred Rowe responded. Sergeant Steve Wood came to supervise his crew. Deputy Coroner Ken Bell was also notified, although his office was informed that it would take some time to complete the crime-scene investigation.

Pete Alvarado was reinterviewed to make sure no details, no matter how seemingly insignificant, were left out.

Deputy Martinez found one more expended shell casing in the street. It came from a .380 semiautomatic pistol. Other witnesses and Alvarado said they heard from four to six shots. That meant there were other casings to be found.

While the crime-scene work was being done, deputies were approached by Bud Combs, a man who lived a few blocks away. He said he was expecting his girlfriend to come to his house, but she never arrived. He said his girlfriend, 18-year-old Lisa Ann Norton, had a baby-sitting job. After the job she was going to ride her bicycle to his place.

When the deputy heard about the bike, he ushered Combs inside the perimeter and introduced him to Detective Oliver. With the coroner's permission, he allowed Combs to view the body. Combs turned away in tears. It was Lisa Ann Norton, his sweetheart.

Detective Oliver interviewed Bud Combs. Of course, Combs fell under suspicion. Oliver obtained details of their relationship, and where Lisa had been before her death.

Combs repeated that Lisa was returning from a baby-sitting job that was just two blocks away. This was easy to check out. Detective Oliver learned that the victim had left the house about 10 minutes before her fatal meeting in the fog with a gun-toting killer.

Most importantly, Oliver verified what kind of vehicle Combs owned, a small foreign car. Oliver asked Combs if he had access to any other vehicles. Before Combs answered, Oliver told him to think about his answer before he made it. Oliver said, "I'm going to check your answer out thoroughly. If I find that you regularly borrow, or drive, some other car, and you tell me now that you don't, it will look really bad for you."

Combs only thought for a second. "Mine is the only car I drive. I used my mom's car about two weeks ago for one afternoon while mine was getting fixed. She has an old, faded Chevy Caprice."

Detective Oliver asked Combs if he owned or drove a large pickup truck. Combs answered he did not. Oliver asked Combs if he, or Lisa, knew anyone who owned a large pickup truck. Combs pondered that for a few minutes. He said he could not think of anyone.

Oliver released Combs at about 2 A.M. Oliver knew that most homicides occur between people who know each other. Combs said his relationship with Lisa Norton was good. Oliver would have to check that out. If he learned theirs was a stormy, jealous affair, he would contact the boyfriend later, and the tone of the interview would be different. But for now, Combs appeared to be too shaken up from grief.

Detectives Oliver, Rowe, and Weil worked all night. Around 4:30 A.M., they went to an all-night restaurant for breakfast. They hoped they had a long, successful day ahead of them. Weil would attend the autopsy at 9 A.M.

During breakfast, Oliver thought how he would offer Combs a polygraph examination at their next interview. Combs fit the description given by Pete Alvarado. But then, a large number of men in Imperial Beach fit that description.

Holding steaming cups of coffee from a nearby convenience store, Oliver and Rowe continued their investigation in the street at dawn. The fog was still there, but it was daylight. The fog would burn off in a few hours.

Oliver found two halves of a white button in the street. It could be something, and it could be nothing. He sealed it in an evidence bag after getting an exact measurement of its location.

The patrol deputies had found two more shell casings for a .380 automatic. They had found a total of four, but the witnesses said they heard as many as six shots. So there were two more to be found. Oliver continued to search but never found them in the street.

Meanwhile, Detective Rowe took off to check the neighborhood for the truck. It was like looking for a needle in a haystack, but Rowe felt he had to try. If the killer lived several miles away, it would be in vain. But if the killer lived down the street, the search would pay off.

About an hour later, Oliver received a call to meet with Rowe. He was in the 1300 block of Iris Avenue, which was less than five blocks from where Lisa Norton had been shot.

Rowe pointed down the street to where a full-size Ford pickup truck was parked in a front yard. "What do you think?" Rowe asked Oliver.

Oliver shrugged. "Dunno. It could be, and yet it might not be." The color scheme was the same, and it had the wide white stripe on the sides.

Rowe drove past and obtained the license number. He ran the number in the computer and learned that the truck had been involved in a traffic accident a few months before. It had been driven by an Andrew Kevin Valvardi, who lived on Iris Avenue, where the truck was now parked.

The detectives ran Valvardi's name in the National Crime Information Computer (NCIC) and learned that he had a pistol registered to him. The sleuths swallowed and looked at each other when the dispatcher told them it was a .380 semiautomatic.

They called for a surveillance team to assist in the stakeout of the house. Within an hour, members of the Special Enforcement Division assembled and took over for the detectives.

As Rowe and Oliver returned to the Imperial Beach substation, they were joined by Detective Weil, who had been present at the autopsy. He told them that Lisa Norton had died from a single gunshot wound to her back. It had exited her chest. she had one other wound to her left hand. The hand had probably been hit as she ran away.

Rowe and Oliver told Weil about Valvardi's vehicle and the fact that he owned a .380. The veteran cops sat around for a while and considered their options. "What the heck," Rowe said. "Let's call a deputy D.A. and get a legal opinion."

Marty Martins answered his phone shortly after noon. At first, the lawyer was hesitant. "It's something," he said about the similarity in the truck description and the ownership of the .380. "But, I don't know if we can make that big of a leap." He pondered the situation briefly and resolved his own dilemma. "But, we aren't asking for an arrest warrant. We're only asking to search. Yeah, I'll go for it."

Martins was an attorney assigned to a countywide task force that prosecuted gang members for drug and violent offenses. He not only pored over writs and pondered legal concepts, he also strapped on his 9mm semiautomatic pistol and kicked in doors on search warrants with the other working cops.

Martins arranged for a three-way telephonic hookup between Oliver, Judge Thomas Whelan, and himself. With legal precision, Martins guided Oliver through the niceties of establishing probable cause. Also, the Fourth Amendment of the Constitution requires that the warrant describe the place to be searched and the items to be seized.

Oliver detailed all these things over the phone to Judge Whelan. The conversation was recorded and later transcribed.

When the conversation was over, Judge Whelan said, "Good luck."

Martins drove from his fashionable Chula Vista condominium to meet with the detectives. In the meantime, a woman and man had left the Valvardi residence. They were detained briefly and then taken to the substation. The man was not Kevin Valvardi.

The two, who lived at the house, told the detectives that Valvardi was still inside. They said Valvardi owned a .380 semiautomatic pistol that he always kept on the nightstand next to his bed. Around 9:30 P.M. the previous night, Valvardi had been gone from the residence for a short time.

The woman told the detectives that Valvardi had been wearing a white and gray long-sleeved dress shirt the night before. In fact, she was on her way to the Laundromat when she was stopped by the deputies. She had the shirt with her.

A deputy accompanied the woman to the car where she went through the bag of laundry. She found the shirt and brought it back in to Detective Oliver. The third button from the top was gone. Ripped threads hung where a button should have been. Oliver's pulse quickened involuntarily.

In less than an hour, the surveillance deputies saw a man leave the residence and walk down the street. They notified the detectives who told them to make the stop.

It was Kevin Valvardi. He was not alarmed when two vehicles rolled up and four undercover cops hopped out and showed him badges.

Marty Martins and the homicide detectives drove to the scene of the detention, only a mile from the station. Valvardi was seated in the back of a police car. The door was open and his feet were on the ground. Valvardi was pleasant and composed.

The deputies told him that they wanted to search his residence and his truck. He looked up, smiled, shrugged, and said, "Okay. What's this about?"

Detective Oliver replied, "We'll get into that later. Here, read this." Oliver handed Valvardi the search warrant. Valvardi began to read it. He looked up once and Martins noticed he appeared calm and relaxed.

Well into the warrant, Valvardi came to the part about what the deputies were searching for: a .380 semiautomatic pistol, ammunition, and things relating to the firearm.

Valvardi's hands began to shake so badly that the paper made a loud rattling sound. His legs and knees vibrated, and his whole body trembled. It was then that Martins and the homicide detectives knew they had a "keeper."

The search of Valvardi's house did not produce a handgun. Probers found ammunition, a holster, and a spare clip. The bullets were of the same brand and kind as those found in the street. They found the incidental items described in the warrant such as paperwork proving Valvardi actually lived in the house. The papers were in the form of utility bills and correspondence addressed to him. This is called "D&C," or "items of dominion and control."

The Valvardi residence seemed to be a shrine to his ego. He had scores of trophies and plaques of accomplishments in his youth. He had pictures of himself everywhere. Later, at the time of booking, deputies found that Valvardi had his name tattooed on his bicep.

Valvardi was an electronics instructor in the Navy at the Point Loma antisubmarine base. Sleuths later learned that he had an excellent military record.

The deputies were disappointed not to find the gun. They even exchanged duties and searched the house a second time on the chance that one of them had missed something. No luck.

Detective Oliver had also included the truck in the search warrant. Most of the searching work had been confined to the cab. They didn't find anything helpful to the probe in there.

Marty Martins said, "If this guy had an automatic, and he was firing it while standing outside the truck, there is a good chance the casings went flying back into the bed."

Lawmen turned their attention to the back of the truck. Neither was visible immediately, but, after some probing and looking, two bullet casings were found in the bed of the truck.

The detectives were now more than sure that they had their man. More importantly, they were sure they had enough evidence to convict him. That was all they were going to get, too.

When advised of his rights, Valvardi demanded an attorney. The interview never happened.

The following day, the homicide team sat in the office of Deputy D.A. Gregg McClain, one of the top go-getters in the San Diego office. He trusted the cops enough to know they had been busting their butts, and whatever they brought was all that was out there.

McClain asked, "What do you suppose was the motive?"

The detectives were certain that Valvardi had not met Lisa Norton before. Bud Combs had never heard of Valvardi, nor had Lisa's family.

Detective Weil said, "I think Valvardi is kind of creepy. There's some kind of sexual angle here." Everyone agreed, but they also knew they would never know for sure. Valvardi wouldn't talk, and Lisa Norton obviously couldn't.

McClain issued the case and asked for a million dollars bail. The deputies returned to their office and scoured all of the sex-crime teletypes on the clipboards at headquarters. Detective Rowe did a computer search of reported rapes and attempted rapes for the past year in the county. He narrowed it down to those incidents where a full-size truck was involved and the perpetrator was white.

Weil found a notification alert from Detective Tom Everett, of the Chula Vista Police Department. On February 23, some eight months before, a man abducted a woman as she was walking to her car in Chula Vista. He was armed with a small handgun and he forced her into his full-size pickup truck. He made her cover her face with her blouse to prohibit her from seeing him. They drove a few miles to a secluded area where he raped her. She said her attacker was calm and liked being in control. His physical description was very close to Valvardi's. He spoke with a slight Southern drawl, as did Valvardi.

Detective Rowe found a computer entry on a case from southern San Diego from January of that year, nine months earlier. A man abducted a woman who had just gotten off a bus. He pulled a gun on her, put her into his full-size pickup truck, and drove her away from the area. He also had her pull her blouse up over her head to block her vision of him.

After raping her, he told her not to call the police because he knew she had a young baby. He told her he would watch her place, and if any cops showed up, he would kill her baby. The woman did have a three-month-old daughter and this threat scared her to the point of hysteria. The man spoke with a slight Southern drawl.

Nonetheless, the woman made the report. Detective Al Fragoso assured her that she had done the right thing. When nothing happened for several months, and it looked like the case was going nowhere, the woman was not so sure she had done the right thing.

The homicide detectives started off by showing photo lineups to the women. The woman from San Diego picked out Valvardi right away. She started to cry when she saw the picture.

The woman from Chula Vista was not so sure. She thought Valvardi's picture resembled the man who raped her, but she also picked out another man and said he was a possibility, too.

Pete Alvarado could not pick Valvardi out of the photo lineup. This was not surprising since he had seen him in darkness for only a short time.

On separate occasions, the detectives drove the rape victims to the Sheriff's Operational Center. Valvardi's truck was there, along with several others that needed scientific analysis for one reason or another.

As they drove up with the woman from San Diego, even before the detectives showed her Valvardi's truck, she pointed at it and started to cry again. She told them the truck she was abducted in had a plaid bean-bag ashtray on the console. When they looked inside, it was still there.

When the investigators brought the woman from Chula Vista, she told them which truck was Valvardi's. She also told them the door handle on the passenger side was missing. Sure enough, when they checked, the handle on Valvardi's truck was gone.

Things were looking good. But a thorough homicide detective never gets complacent. A detective might pause and smile a peaceful acknowledgment that a killer is off the streets. But cops know they can never really be happy until the jury foreman stands up and says, "Guilty."

One thing nagging the homicide sleuths was the whereabouts of the murderer's gun. Two days after Valvardi's arrest, Sergeant Wood received a call from a relative of Valvardi's. Valvardi had called another relative from jail and told a story that could have been construed as a justification for his actions.

Valvardi told the relative that he was driving down the street. He saw a girl on a bicycle, and a guy on foot. They waved him over. When he stopped the truck, they came over to him and tried to rob him. The male had a knife. Valvardi resisted and went for his gun. The two robbers ran. Valvardi got off one shot, then he left the area in a hurry.

The detectives knew the story was bogus. They knew it was a desperate story from a desperate man in jail who was trying to save his skin.

Valvardi told his relative that he put the gun under the corner of a large storage shed in the backyard of his residence. Detectives Oliver and Weil went over to Valvardi's house and, after much digging and lifting, found the .380 buried just as Valvardi said it was.

As for Valvardi's story about Lisa Norton and the phantom man trying to rob him, Oliver said, "Not bad on only two days' notice. I think I could have come up with a better one, though."

Valvardi's defense attorney indicated to Prosecutor McClain

that they were going to fight the charges every step of the way. This was no surprise because McClain had filed papers showing he intended to get the death penalty for Valvardi.

McClain knew he had circumstantial evidence, including a button and some bullet casings, that tied Valvardi to the killing. He needed scientific evidence for the rape cases.

The San Diego rape victim was strong in her identification of Valvardi. The Chula Vista victim, aside from successfully describing the interior of the truck, could not be sure the man in the photo was her rapist. McClain knew from his vast experience that juries want more evidence before they find someone guilty of such a heinous crime as rape.

The detectives went back to McClain's office to talk things over. The legal problem facing the prosecutor was seeing to it that Valvardi received a sentence that fit the crime. It was clear to everyone that the killing of Lisa Norton was a rape that went awry. But since she ran away before he could do anything, he never made an overt action other than pointing a gun at her and saying something like, "Get in the truck."

Since the killing had happened so fast, it was likely the state could only get second-degree murder. A murder committed during the commission of an attempted rape carried a much more substantial penalty, like death.

McClain told the homicide investigators that they had to get solid evidence on the rapes. The case involving the Chula Vista woman was shaky due to her lack of identification. The San Diego woman's case was better. But one out of two wasn't good enough for McClain.

He ordered sophisticated DNA testing, or genetic analysis of Valvardi's blood. This would be compared to the DNA from semen collected from the victims after both rapes. This procedure was costly and time-consuming, but McClain and his boss, Edwin L. Miller Jr., could think of no better way to spend the tax dollar.

The weeks turned into months. McClain received other cases that required his time. Detectives Oliver and Weil left the Sheriff's Department to work for the district attorney as investigators. Sergeant Wood trained rookie homicide detectives and turned them into capable probers.

On July 8, 1993, almost three years after the gunning down of 18-year-old Lisa Norton, Andrew Kevin Valvardi pleaded guilty to a host of crimes. He pleaded guilty to the first-degree murder of Lisa Norton, attempted murder of Pete Alvarado, two counts of forcible rape, two counts of armed robbery (he had taken money from both rape victims), kidnapping, and forced oral copulation.

In exchange for the plea, McClain and Miller agreed not to ask the state of California to put Valvardi to death. McClain was not entirely satisfied with this decision, but he knew Valvardi would never be a free man again.

On September 23, 1993, Judge Bernard Revak sentenced Andrew Kevin Valvardi to 67 years to life in prison. He will be eligible for parole when he is approximately 71 years old.

Valvardi surprised court watchers when he addressed the court at his sentencing. Many criminals express remorse that they have been caught and now must go to prison. Valvardi told Lisa Norton's family how sorry he was for what he had done. His remorse was genuine, something rarely witnessed by court personnel.

Valvardi agreed not to file any appeals as a condition of his sentence. He is currently in the California prison system.

" 'MODEL PAROLEE' LET LOOSE, RAPES/KILLS SIX!"

by Dan Storm

Around 9:30 A.M. on Tuesday, March 26, 1991, a brisk wind accompanied the pair as they walked along the rusted railroad tracks near Stanton Street in Middletown, New York, about 40 miles northwest of New York City. The couple suddenly froze. The nude body of a woman was lying directly in their path. The grisly discovery turned their nonchalant stroll into a race to notify the Middletown police.

Ten minutes later, uniformed police cordoned off the area, and detectives began their examination of the body. An apparently young woman, the victim had been stabbed repeatedly in the chest and neck. Detectives noticed that the killer hadn't tossed the body out of a moving vehicle alongside the abandoned railroad spur. Whoever killed the victim had taken the time to lay her carefully on the ground, stretch her legs out, and fold her arms across her stomach. It was almost as though the killer intended his victim to be laid out in a funeral pose.

A preliminary examination of the corpse revealed that a struggle had gone on between the victim and her killer. Her arms showed signs of puncture wounds. She had tried to fend off her attacker, but the killer was relentless. Her once-pretty face was not mutilated, detectives noted. It remained to be seen whether or not she had been sexually assaulted.

With both the woman's clothes and identification missing, detectives tried to determine if she had been killed at the scene or brought there after her death. One thing was certain: whoever killed her must have placed the body alongside the deserted tracks at night, since the area was used during the day by kids riding three-wheelers.

That afternoon, Middletown police chief Thomas Lopez told reporters that the body had been positively identified as 29-year-old Julianna Frank, of Middletown. Described as 5-feet 6-inches tall with brownish-blond hair, Frank was a native of the area who lived downtown, Sheriff Lopez said. Lopez added that her two children did not live with her.

Hoping to protect the sparse evidence found at the scene, the chief would not tell reporters whether or not the woman was wearing any clothes. "I'm not going to release that," the chief said. "Those are things the killer may know."

That evening, Dr. Mark Taff, a Long Island pathologist and consultant to the Orange County coroner, performed an autopsy at Horton Memorial Hospital in Middletown. The forensic specialist made a grisly discovery behind an odd slash across the victim's abdomen: Frank was three or four months pregnant at the time of her death. The fetus, the doctor determined, was male. The victim *had* been sexually assaulted, he concluded.

Dr. Taff noted groups of smaller wounds over the body. While close together, the wounds didn't seem to form any particular pattern, he explained to the sleuths. But they were clearly a sign of a vicious killer. The fatal wounds were inflicted by a sharp instrument that penetrated the woman's chest and neck.

The doctor established that Frank had been dead less than 24 hours. Her body was probably placed by the tracks after dark, between Monday night and Tuesday morning. Lacking more forensic information, detectives left the morgue knowing their work was cut out for them.

The following morning, officers questioned residents along the Stanton Street railhead, while at the Middletown police station, detectives compiled a history of the victim.

Investigators learned that Frank lived at an apartment with friends on John Street until a week before her death. Her two boys, ages five and nine, hadn't lived with her for some time. Known to frequent downtown bars, Frank had been a drifter for the past few years.

Friends and family members recalled that the unemployed woman enjoyed shooting pool. Years before, Frank liked to swim and go bowling. She dropped out of Middletown High School during her sophomore year. According to one family member, Frank had held only one job—at a cleaners—for a short time. Her pregnancy, which surprised the pathologist and detectives, was no secret to her family.

As the days passed, sleuths partially pieced together the victim's travels. The last time a relative recalled seeing her, he told detectives, was between one and two o'clock on Saturday morning at a local bar. "Go home," were the last words she said to him.

One acquaintance said Frank made ends meet any way she could. It wasn't uncommon for her to move from one friend's apartment to another.

Lieutenant Earl Bonnell, of the Middletown Police Department, tracked most of the victim's movements in the days prior to her death. Frank stayed at the John Street residence Thursday night. She helped a girlfriend fix her hair Friday night before the pair went to a local nightclub, the officer learned. From there, they went to another bar.

A male friend told the detective that he and Frank went from the bar to an apartment on North Street. But from there, her movements became sketchy. Someone saw Frank walking up North Street, while other people claimed they saw her in a white car with a group of friends on either Saturday or Sunday night.

"So far we have nobody who saw her Sunday or Monday," Bonnell said, stressing that the last two days of Frank's life remained a mystery to police.

In the five days after the discovery of Frank's body, police interviewed more than 200 people. Seventeen officers from the city's 53-member police department and three New York state troopers were assigned to the case. The more they worked—often around the clock—the less it seemed they un covered.

"I need a little bit of help from the people," Lieutenant Bonnell told a reporter. "With a little help we will crack this case. . . . We need a break."

One week after the discovery of Frank's body on the abandoned tracks, police set up a roadblock. A team of detectives questioned motorists at the intersection of Stanton and Genung Streets. The officers showed occupants of the vehicles a photograph of Frank, asking if they had seen the woman or anything else suspicious a week earlier.

"You always do it a week later the same day," Bonnell later explained to a reporter. "If you don't get it solved in a week's time, this is one of the things you put in service."

In what police thought might be a break, two men, each suspected of fathering Frank's unborn child, were brought in for questioning. After hours of intense interrogation, and a thorough check of their alibis, police cleared them both.

The first week passed, then the first month. Summer came, and the trail got colder. By August, the last full-time detective on the original 20-man task force was pulled off the Frank case. According to Chief Lopez, the task force worked $37,000 worth of overtime, consuming nearly half of the department's $75,000 annual overtime budget.

One year later Lopez, Bonnell, and other investigators were still at a dead end. The last two days of Julianna Frank's life seemed to be something known only to her and her killer.

Lopez thought about the careful positioning of Frank's body and any possible significance it might have had to the killer.

"Could it suggest something symbolic?" he asked. "Does that suggest some sort of remorse on the part of the killer? Who knows? I have no idea. I don't have the mind of a killer. Until we get somebody to tell us, we really don't know."

In an effort to break the elusive case, Lopez asked Orange County officials to consider establishing a fund that would enable sleuths to offer a $10,000 reward for any information leading to an arrest and conviction. His proposal, made in January, was still being considered four months later.

In a concession to the killer, Lopez theorized that Frank was not killed at the Stanton Street site. "We have a victim," Lopez said. "We don't have a crime scene. That's created a severe obstacle."

By July 1992, lacking any significant leads, the hunt for Frank's killer was no longer the priority. So when 14-year-old Christine Marie Klebbe went missing in nearby Goshen, nobody considered that it had any connection to the Frank homicide.

Klebbe was last seen leaving a relative's home on the evening of June 29. According to the parent, she was going out to meet a friend. The 5-foot-4, 118-pound teenager, with brown eyes and hair, was wearing a dark T-shirt, purple shorts, and white sneakers when she left for the evening.

Police had good reason to be concerned about Klebbe's disappearance. Known for her sense of family, her healthy living, and her love of helping people, Klebbe was not the type to run away. Officers distributed fliers with the girl's photo and description, asking anyone with information to contact detectives at the Goshen Police Department.

Back in Middletown, shock waves rattled the community of more than 25,000 residents when another female turned up slain on July 10. A normally quiet dead-end street bustled with activity as detectives walked in and out of the apartment of Laurette Riviere Huggins, a mother of three, whose body police found around 12:30 P.M. after receiving a call from an anonymous friend.

The crime scene had a stark and scary familiarity. Huggins, like Julianna Frank, had been repeatedly stabbed. However, unlike Frank, Huggins had also been strangled. From the condition of the nude corpse, police deduced that she was killed a few hours before the fateful discovery. Police noticed the woman's purse and wallet were missing. There was no sign of forced entry.

Outside the three-story building, detectives combed railroad tracks behind the woman's apartment for clues. Other investigators questioned shocked neighbors. Residents of the middle-class street said Huggins lived in the area for about a dozen years. In August, Huggins was planning to move back to her native island of St. Vincent in the Caribbean.

"Being a single parent was kind of hard on her, but she was basically a nice person who kept to herself," one resident recalled. "She was a neighbor that if you needed her, she was there."

Divorced for the past few years, the victim's ex-husband was a guard at a federal prison in another state.

One son already returned to St. Vincent, while her other two children were staying with relatives at the time of the slaying, another neighbor told an officer.

The county coroner removed Huggins's body from the small apartment, crammed with boxes destined for a tomorrow that would never come. A few hours later, Dr. Taff returned to Horton Memorial Hospital for the slain woman's postmortem. The pathologist gazed at the series of small wounds covering the body before he began the autopsy. The cause of death, the physician discerned, was a single stab wound to the neck that severed Huggins's carotid artery, the main blood vessel from the heart to the brain. The doctor also verified crime-scene officers' suspicions: Huggins had been sexually assaulted.

Detectives learned that Huggins had been an excellent employee at a local medical insurance company. With no known boyfriends, and her ex-husband cleared, detectives began developing a list of male friends to question. Another detective rushed fingerprints found on the doorway of the building and other evidence to the FBI laboratory in Washington, D.C., for analysis.

This time—unlike in the Frank case—police had a crime scene. It was obvious to officers, from the scattered debris in the apartment, that Huggins had fought with her assailant before he inflicted the fatal wound.

Sergeant David Green, a spokesman for the Middletown Police Department, knew the victim personally. He met her once in the mid-1980s, he recalled, when they had a conversation about one of her children.

"She was very pleasant," he said.

Within four days of Huggins's death, police pumped more than 300 hours of overtime into cracking the case. Friends, relatives, acquaintances, and coworkers were interviewed over and over. But no suspect, weapon, or motive for the slaying surfaced. Using every investigative tool, technique, and trick available, pairs of detectives worked around the clock. The teams questioned store owners and patrons. They stopped traffic on the street in front of the victim's apartment. They searched for that one witness who might have seen something suspicious.

"Nobody's been ruled out," Green said. "[The killer] could be a complete stranger."

Two weeks later, while Middletown detectives were still searching for a killer, two women, 20-year-old Brenda L. Whiteside and 23-year-old Angelina Hopkins, were reported missing in the Poughkeepsie area, about 40 miles away. The pair were last seen on July 20, a relative told city police. Whiteside went to visit her cousin, Hopkins, about a month before. Hopkins lived with her 7-month-old son, the relative said. One evening the women went out for dinner and then to a club. That was the last time anyone saw them.

Back in Middletown, a woman told police that she remembered two men standing outside Huggins's apartment on the morning of her murder. Police jumped at their first possible break in the case. With nothing to lose, the sleuths asked the witness to be hypnotized by a retired police officer. If it worked, they wanted to extract every detail her subconscious mind preserved.

The hypnosis session took place on July 27 at police headquarters. In a bland room containing nothing more than a table, a lamp, and a few chairs, the hypnotist asked the woman to take four deep breaths and relax. A detective sat beside her, ready to take notes, as the hypnotist instructed the woman to lean her head back and stare at a spot on the wall.

A minute later, the woman, gazing into the hypnotist's eyes as he guided her into a deep sleep, slowly began answering questions about what she saw in front of Huggins's apartment.

"I was aware, but it was so wild, because I couldn't move and didn't want to," she recalled after the intense session. The woman vividly recalled one man walking from Huggins's apartment and another man leaning on a car in front of the building. After a few moments, the images became crystal clear. She was even able to go into detail on one of the men.

"I couldn't recall his shoes, but I could see the color of his pants, his frame, his skin color. . . . He had keys in his hands, something small. His fist was closed."

After the trance, she identified the man from a photo lineup. Officers scrambled to find the potential suspect and interrogate him. However, the lead fizzled a few days later when the suspect was cleared of any suspicion by police.

Middletown detectives were sifting through reports when a New York state trooper called to inform them about the discovery of another nude female body in Goshen. According to the trooper, a man walking his dog along the road discovered the body in a wooded area around 10 A.M. on Thursday, July 29, 1992. While the corpse hadn't been identified, it was that of an adult—eliminating the missing Goshen teenager, Christine Klebbe, he added.

At the Goshen crime scene, Orange County coroner Donald Parker assisted a contingent of troopers and Goshen police officers as a state police helicopter whirred overhead. Police dogs sniffed the ground for evidence. The nude figure appeared to have been placed gently on the ground of a former restaurant. The corpse was found about 15 feet from the roadway, just off a secluded dead end adjacent to a hospital.

After a preliminary investigation of the crime scene, the coroner removed the unidentified corpse for transport to Horton Memorial Hospital. Dr. Taff, the Long Island pathologist, returned to Middletown for a third autopsy.

Meanwhile, troopers set up a roadblock to question passing motorists.

Later that day, a relative of 27-year-old Adriane M. Hunter, of Middletown, called the state police barracks to report the woman missing. A few hours later, sobbing relatives positively identified the body found in the field as Hunter.

That evening, Dr. Taff huddled over the woman's corpse as detectives looked on. The body, judging by the early state of decomposition, had not been in the woods for more than a couple of days. Dr. Taff pointed out the pattern of small stab wounds over the entire body. The fatal motif was similar to the wounds he found on the other two victims. Again, as in the Frank and Huggins homicides, the killer mutilated Hunter's body, especially her head and face.

Unfortunately for detectives, whoever was responsible for the three slayings wasn't leaving any clues behind. The only solid bit of evidence was the killer's deadly signature of mutilation and multiple stab wounds.

At the state police barracks, detectives reviewed the manner of Hunter's death. Then they contacted Middletown police about their series of unsolved homicides. The wounds on all three bodies were strikingly similar; most likely, they were inflicted by the same person. While there was no hard evidence, the frequency of killings prompted detectives to theorize that Orange County might have a serial killer in its midst.

Unsolved serial killings present special problems for detectives. If they use the term "serial killer" in any press statement, they run the risk of scaring the perpetrator away; if they say nothing, they can only hope for a break before the killer strikes again. It's always a tough call.

In the Orange County probe, law-enforcement officials chose to remain silent.

At a news conference on Friday, July 30, New York State Police captain Michael Cahill released the latest victim's identity. He revealed that the bodies of all three women were found nude and had been repeatedly stabbed. No weapon was found at any of the scenes, nor were there any suspects, he lamented.

"We've contacted the city of Middletown Police Department to inquire into some of their unsolved homicides," the trooper added, referring to the Frank and Huggins cases.

Cahill stressed the dozens of phone calls state police received from people offering information. In one instance, investigators were checking out a tip about a woman who was seen getting into a cable-television van driven by a man with blond hair. Unfortunately, the company had about 80 vans, he added, so troopers were still checking out the lead.

Throughout the entire news conference, Cahill never mentioned the serial killer theory. The next day, a story appeared in the Middletown newspaper mentioning the stark similarities among all three homicides, but it, too, never used the terrifying phrase "serial killer."

State troopers and city detectives shared information about the three unsolved cases. They reviewed each case in minute detail. But the bottom line was a zero. There just weren't any clues to even hint at a direction sleuths should take. With three dead women and three other females missing, police needed a break soon—before the killer struck again.

What the investigators didn't know was that their break was about to come from some unconventional detective work.

A few of Angelina Hopkins's relatives drove from Middletown to Poughkeepsie in search of the two missing women.

The family members theorized that possible witnesses might be reluctant to speak with law-enforcement officials. But maybe someone would talk to a civilian.

On August 2, after scouring streets, bars, and nightclubs for hours, a relative entered a Poughkeepsie night spot frequented by one of the women. Inside, she was told that shortly before their disappearance, the pair were last seen with a frequent customer of the club known as Nate White.

The relative left the club, called the Poughkeepsie Police Department, and told an officer of her discovery. She said the family was going to stake out the parking lot and wait for White's arrival.

Hours later, Poughkeepsie patrolman Robert Perrotta drove past the club and noticed White in the parking lot. With the distraught relative behind him, Perrotta approached the man.

"I'd like to speak with you," Perrotta said to White.

"I don't like speaking with cops," the surprised man replied.

"Well, this lady would like to talk with you," the officer shot back, adding that the woman was searching for her missing relatives. The patrolman informed White that the relative found out he'd been seen with the women at a local nightclub shortly before their disappearance. The officer asked White if he knew anything about it, or about their possible whereabouts.

White admitted being with the women. He said he gave them a ride back to Middletown but hadn't seen them since. Not volunteering any more information, White ended the conversation and walked away.

The officer left, too, suspicious of White's cool attitude about the missing women.

When Perrotta returned to the police station, his hunch about White's possible involvement in the women's disappearance was fortified by police reports from the Middletown area. The memorandum highlighted Hunter's homicide in Goshen a few days earlier. It also listed the missing teenager Christine Klebbe. The officer relayed the information to his superior, who advised the patrolman to contact state police detectives.

Meanwhile, in another Poughkeepsie office, a parole officer stared at a file of one of his charges. The man, originally arrested for the kidnapping and assault of a 16-year-old girl, was on parole after serving a prison term on a reduced charge of unlawful imprisonment.

The officer, whose last contact with the parolee was on July 23, was now suspicious because the parolee failed to meet with him on July 28. The ex-convict has been arrested on kidnapping and assault charges on April 17, 1991—less than a month after Julianna Frank was found stabbed to death by the railroad tracks. In prison on the charges, he finally pleaded guilty to a reduced charge on September 16, and was sentenced to nine months in jail, along with 12 months for a parole violation. He was released on April 23, a couple of months before the rash of homicides and disappearances in the Middletown area began, the report disclosed.

Once a "model parolee," the man suddenly missed a scheduled meeting. The parole officer picked up his phone and dialed the state police barracks outside Middletown. He thought they should know about this ex-con—Nathaniel White.

Back in Middletown, state troopers and city detectives questioned men who knew Laurette Huggins. While they had assembled a list of male friends and acquaintances of the dead woman's, White's name wasn't on it. The two phone calls from the suspicious Poughkeepsie patrolman and the parole officer gave investigators the first set of solid leads that meshed.

On August 3, detectives staked out the parolee's home in a suburb of Middletown. Sooner or later, White would show up, and detectives were anxious to talk to him.

Waiting in an unmarked patrol car, detectives noticed stolen plates attached to a Renault sedan that White was known to have driven. Eventually a man emerged and walked toward the blue sedan. Detectives surrounded him before he made it to the vehicle. Caught off guard, he identified himself as Nathaniel White. Composed and showing no outward signs of suspicion, police told the 32-year-old unemployed parolee that he was under arrest for driving a car with stolen plates. After reading White his rights, one officer said they also wanted to question him about a few homicides.

Detectives began interrogating White at the state police barracks around 12:45 P.M. When asked about Adriane Hunter's death, White casually recalled playing basketball with a friend at Smith Clove Park, in nearby Monroe, on the night she disappeared. Moving from homicide to homicide, White supplied one alibi after another.

Questioned about Laurette Huggins's slaying, White recollected that he and a few friends were hanging around the woman's apartment one day. He said he had helped her move a few boxes inside. To the best of his memory, he was in her apartment a few days before the homicide occurred.

Unknown to the suspect, officers in another room checked out every minute detail of his keen recollection.

A few hours later, sleuths confronted White with two critical inconsistencies. First, they said, he couldn't have been playing basketball on the evening Hunter was killed, since weather reports indicated that it had been raining and, detectives knew, the lights at the park hadn't even been turned on. Second, none of his friends recalled him being at the apartment. Each friend had been contacted separately, the officer added.

As the hours passed, more inconsistencies surfaced. While White wasn't breaking down, his stories weren't holding up. The investigators changed gears and asked him to detail his whereabouts during the past few days. Cracks in his story prompted senior investigator Michael Long to ask the suspect to submit to a lie-detector test.

Long promised White that police would "leave him alone" if he passed the test.

White agreed.

In another room, a detective fitted White with a blood-pressure cuff on his arm, electrodes on his skin, and a set of tubes across his chest. State police investigator James

McKoy initiated the session by asking White a series of questions about his background and childhood.

"What's your ambition in life?" the trooper asked White.

"To get a good job and get married."

The officer then asked the suspect the best thing that ever happened to him, his favorite pastime, and his favorite organization. The machine calibrated, and McKoy embarked on a series of questions about the recent homicides and disappearances.

After three tests, McKoy leaned over and told White that the tests showed he was lying.

Under New York state law, the results of the failed polygraph tests couldn't be used against White in a court of law. From his 11 years of experience, McKoy knew the team of officers was in for a long night of playing cat-and-mouse with the suspect. The detectives conferred outside the interrogation room. They had a strong hunch that White had killed the five women and one teenager, but they still lacked three bodies. They needed a confession.

McKoy and another detective went back into the room, prepared to stay until White cracked.

It took a few hours of psychological prodding, but the ex-con finally began breaking down. As the minutes turned into hours, McKoy threw the weakening suspect a curve ball. He told White that his fingerprint had been found in a victim's apartment. The fingerprint story—in fact, the print had not yet been identified as White's—broke the suspect. Nathaniel White, going emotionlessly from one story to another, suddenly admitted that he had killed Adriane Hunter.

Every time White stopped talking, McKoy coaxed him to continue. The trooper reminded White that New York State does not have a death penalty. Even if he killed 20 people, White would never face execution.

"This is a perfect time to get everything off your chest," McKoy said. "Everyone deserves a decent burial," the detective said, adding that White should do "the right thing" and tell where the missing women were. Apparently, the trooper's psychological persuasion worked. One by one, White ultimately confessed to killing five women—Frank, Huggins, Hopkins, Whiteside, and Hunter.

Between bites on two slices of pizza, White detailed his crimes.

"I didn't know why I killed these people," White told detectives. "It's just when I get in these moods, I feel like picking up girls and doing anything I want with them."

The murder weapons ranged from a knife to a pair of scissors, White said. White recalled using part of a car axle to smash the skulls of Hopkins and Whiteside. He also admitted to sexually assaulting each of his victims before killing them.

But what really shocked the detectives was that the suspect personally knew each victim. And the victims all knew each other. Yet White's name never appeared on any list of male acquaintances police compiled. His preference for acquaintances was unusual in the extreme. Serial killers almost always prey on total strangers.

With five homicides cleared, McKoy zeroed in on the missing 14-year-old girl, Christine Klebbe. Hard as it might be, the detective said, White needed to talk about what happened to her, too.

White did admit knowing the girl. He met the teenager through a friend of his girlfriend he said. In his slow, methodical manner, White recalled how he picked Klebbe up one day and drove to a deserted spot. There, the couple parked for a while. Then, as with the others, he killed the teenager, then he dumped her body in a secluded area near Goshen.

Investigators couldn't help but notice that the only time White cried was during the Klebbe confession.

After more than 20 hours of continuous questioning, White signed an eight-page confession. He then agreed to take detectives to the sites where he dumped the bodies of Hopkins, Whiteside, and Klebbe.

The following morning, troopers ushered Nathaniel White,

in handcuffs, into a state police cruiser. From the backseat, White directed the driver to a wooded area on Echo Lake Road in Goshen.

A group of police officers entered the woods where White indicated. Moments later, they came upon the skeleton of the teenager, still clad in her weather-beaten clothes.

Back in the police car, White directed detectives to a field off Harriman Drive, not far from where Hunter's body had been found a few days earlier. A small contingent of searchers was already at the scene when White and the detectives arrived. Outside the patrol car, White pointed to an area, and not long afterward, the search party found the decomposed remains of Hopkins and Whiteside.

In the meantime, a dozen pizzas were delivered for the men who were searching the desolate spot. When offered, White eagerly accepted a slice. He even managed to strike up a conversation with a few officers.

Later, White led troopers to another Middletown location where he had stashed a box containing a pair of scissors which he used to kill Huggins and the dress she wore the day of her murder. The three-hour trek to locate the bodies and evidence ended back at the state police barracks.

After White's arraignment, Major James O'Donnell of New York State Police Troop F, in Wallkill, called a news conference. Newspaper reporters, television commentators, and cameramen crammed the room as O'Donnell announced White's arrest.

"This guy's just an out-and-out vicious killer," O'Donnell said. "If he wasn't in jail tonight, we'd be looking for more bodies."

When sleuths looked into the suspect's criminal history, they learned that White was arrested in 1986 for three robberies, one of which was an armed robbery of a convenience store. A plea bargain reduced the charges to one count of second-degree robbery, sending White to prison for three to nine years. Three years later, after correctional officials issued him a certificate of eligibility for early parole, White was released.

A year later, police charged White with misdemeanor assault and resisting arrest. On this charge, he used the name "Nathan White." He pleaded guilty to disorderly conduct and was fined $142, along with a conditional discharge. Ironically, because he used a variation on his name, the New York State Division of Parole had no account of this arrest in its records.

In April 1991, state police charged White with two felony counts in the kidnapping and assault of a 16-year-old girl. But when he faced a judge in September of that year, a plea bargain reduced the charges to unlawful imprisonment, a misdemeanor. White was sentenced to nine months in jail. The judged ordered the sentence to run concurrently with another 12-month sentence for parole violation in his original robbery conviction.

Less than seven months later, in April 1992, White walked out of the Franklin Correctional Facility in Malone, New York, a free man. The institution credited White with the five months he spent in the Orange County Jail while awaiting his court action.

White, according to police, was born on July 28, 1960, in Albany, New York. The third oldest of five children, he told an officer "he had it hard" and encountered more problems than friends while in school. He graduated from Poughkeepsie High School in 1979, where he'd been a C-student. Eventually he enlisted in the Army, where he became a fire directional specialist. A year after his honorable discharge in 1983, White moved back to Poughkeepsie with his family.

Even his landlord, who claimed White owed him about $2,300 in back rent since he was laid off, spoke well of the accused serial killer.

"I've never seen him in a rage or high," the landlord said. "He always appeared to be a very constant kind of individual. There were no weird things [about him] that were abnormal."

After Major O'Donnell outlined White's involvement in the six murders, a media blitz overtook Middletown and the surrounding county. Headlines and radio reports announced that Orange County's most notorious serial killer had been arrested.

Shortly after being booked into the Orange County Jail, White unexpectedly agreed to be interviewed by two reporters—one from WNBC-TV in New York City; the other from the *Times Herald-Record* in Middletown.

White told the television reporter that he would spend hours driving his victims around and talking to them before he had any inkling that he would kill them. Then they would drive to a remote area. Something would snap. He'd hear voices telling him, "She deserves to die. You should hit her. Why don't you beat her up?"

"I don't know where it came from," White said of the voice. "I fought with myself. Part of me didn't want to do it, part of me did. . . . Eventually I would lose it."

With the news crew taping, White confessed to killing the six females. He blamed it on drinking, saying the more he drank, the worse the violent emotions inside his head became. In addition to his drinking, White admitted smoking marijuana, but he denied doing heavier drugs. Another factor in his downfall, the self-confessed killer said, was violent videos.

"If a voice in my head said do it, I would do it. The more I thought about it, the more I would lose control."

Asked why he carried a knife in his car, White claimed it was for protection. He denied the weapon in his auto indicated he premeditated the slayings. After all, he said, he was just an ordinary guy before he killed his first victim. White said he came from a loving family and was not an abused child.

In the TV interview, White also went into some detail about the Klebbe murder. He said he drove around with Christine Klebbe on that fatal night drinking beer. Eventually the couple parked and began kissing.

"That's when the voice came again," he said. " 'You should kill her. You shouldn't let her live.' "

White grabbed his head, and Klebbe asked him what was wrong. White finally asked the girl to go for a walk. Without his knife that evening, the suspect said, he grabbed a screwdriver from a toolbox in the vehicle.

"That's what I used to kill her."

The Middletown newspaper reporter never got a chance to ask any questions. Jail administrator Theodore Catletti rushed into the room and stopped the incriminating interview. The official said the press conference was being cut short so White could consult his newly appointed attorney. If his attorney agreed, the interview would continue, he assured the two journalists.

Predictably, his defense attorney Bernard Brady advised against it. But it was too late. WNBC executives refused to permit New York State troopers to review the videotape at the barracks. A few hours later Nathaniel White, self-confessed serial killer, became the lead story on the station's evening news broadcast.

At the Orange County Courthouse in Goshen, District Attorney Francis D. Phillips II prepared to present evidence to the grand jury against White. For legal reasons, the district attorney said his office, for the time being, would seek an indictment only in the Klebbe murder. Declining to elaborate to reporters, Phillips said the slaying of the 14-year-old girl was selected because it was simplest in terms of legal evidence. The five other homicides would be presented to the official panel in the next few weeks, after detectives had concluded their investigation.

While the district attorney prepared his case, the public became outraged at news reports of how the judicial system failed to keep Nathaniel White behind bars. The Orange County Family Court issued a temporary order of protection to the daughters of White's girlfriend, but parole officials were never informed of it, a report revealed. The order, issued against White, accused him of abusing his girlfriend's child in April, shortly after he was released from state prison.

"If we had only known," one parole official lamented. "We would have investigated right away, and within hours we could have issued a warrant."

District Attorney Phillips was not aware of the court's protection order against the accused killer, either. Under New York State law, no procedure exists to notify parole officers about abuse complaints from the family court, Phillips added.

Had a procedure been in place, one official noted, the senseless slayings of five women could have been prevented.

Behind bars in the county jail, White wasn't talking to anyone except his lawyer. Brady, White's court-appointed attorney, and a Fordham Law School graduate, had convinced an Orange County jury in 1979 that a 19-year-old was not guilty of shooting his mother and father to death by reason of insanity.

Outside the county jail, Brady told newsmen that the voices that made White kill indicated a classic case of insanity. Admitting that White's interview with reporters probably wouldn't help his case, the attorney said prison officials were only following state regulations that permitted such interviews.

While Brady maneuvered for his client's best legal position, investigators tracked down more evidence to secure five more convictions against the self-admitted serial killer. However, one difficulty the team encountered was being able to identify the bodies of Angelina Hopkins and her cousin, Brenda Whiteside. The deteriorated remains of both women, housed at a nearby hospital, forced police to revert to dental or X-ray records. Investigators said the victims' families were having trouble tracking down records, which could force police to conduct DNA tests. The test results, if needed, could take months to obtain from a laboratory.

"The families have been very understanding, in light of everything they're going through," said one trooper close to the investigation.

A week after telling a TV news crew that he killed five women and a teen girl, White strolled into a courtroom and, through his attorney, entered a not-guilty plea in the murder of Christine Klebbe. Silent during the courtroom proceeding, the accused killer stood before a judge wearing a red jail-issued jumpsuit over a bulletproof vest. Orange County sheriff James F. Garvey explained that White wore the vest because jail officials had received about six telephone death threats on the prisoner's life within the past few days.

In a reverse move, White refused to allow journalists to videotape or record the arraignment.

"He says he's been in front of the cameras enough," Defense Attorney Brady quipped.

During the legal proceeding, the district attorney requested blood and hair samples from White for forensic analysis. He also revealed that about 26 police officers would probably testify about White's confession.

On the other side of the legal aisle, Brady asked for a private investigator and a psychiatrist to examine White. White wanted to help prove he was not guilty by reason of insanity, the defense attorney said. While White may have been insane at the time of the murder, he was now capable of assisting in his own defense, Brady told the judge. The attorney assured the court that he would not argue whether White was incapable of standing trial.

The judge, holding the indictment, remanded White to the county jail without bail.

The next few months were a rollercoaster ride for Orange County officials and residents. While detectives interviewed people who knew White and accumulated more evidence, the suspect's attorney took advantage of every legal loophole at his disposal.

After a lengthy investigation into the other five homicides, state police detectives concluded that White acted alone in all six slayings.

"We ran out all those leads," Major O'Donnell said. "We don't think there're any accomplices."

O'Donnell even offered an explanation of how White managed to kill two victims, Hopkins and Whiteside, at the same time without help. Police deduced from evidence and White's confession that the slayings were not simultaneous.

"They were five to ten minutes apart, by [White's] testimony," O'Donnell explained.

Prosecutor Phillips and Defense Attorney Brady both agreed with police, saying they had no knowledge of any accomplices, either. But that's where any agreement between the prosecution and defense ended. In the courtroom, Brady charged that state police strapped White to a lie detector, forcing him into confessing. Although the results were indeterminate, Brady asserted, police had made it seem as though White was clearly lying in order to coerce a confession from him.

After the judge granted Brady permission to hire an independent polygraph examiner to review the test results, the attorney revealed that he would move to have White's confession thrown out as evidence. The attorney also claimed that police handcuffed White to a chair, denying him food and use of a toilet for at least 12 hours during the marathon 27-hour interrogation session.

Prosecutor Phillips painted a difference picture of the interrogation. While a handful of detectives heard White confess, he said, 26 officers would probably be called to testify.

"Every time he asked someone for pizza, a ham sandwich, or soda, we listed the name of the person who took the order," the district attorney explained. And rules bound him to reveal to the defense anyone who may have overheard a defendant's confession, he added.

"We chose to err on the side of caution," Phillips emphasized.

In an ironic twist of legal fate, White was in family court on October 30 to testify about his relationship with Christine Klebbe, the teenager he was charged with killing. The girl was to have testified that White molested her. At the hearing he denied it.

"She would jump on my back, want me to spin her around," he said.

However, White took the Fifth Amendment when asked if he ever had sex with the youngster. The court's decision was not made public. It would be moot anyway if White were convicted of Klebbe's murder.

As the new year began, a series of legal motions kept White in the courtroom—and newspapers—in preparation for his insanity plea. In the end the motions were in vain. In February, Brady announced that he was dropping the insanity defense. The defense would instead try to prove that police illegally forced a confession from White.

On Wednesday, March 4, White's trial on all six counts of homicide began. Outside, two armed deputies patrolled the courthouse parking lot, while security was beefed up inside the judicial complex. In order to get to Judge Jeffrey G. Berry's courtroom, potential jurors had to walk through a metal detector. By the end of the day, deputies confiscated more than a dozen knives and razors. In one instance, a potential juror surrendered a canister of pepper spray. All the items, none illegal, were returned to their owners as they left the courthouse at the end of the day.

Judge Berry, who served on the Orange County bench for two years, had acquired a reputation for running a no-nonsense court. Jury selection was over in a day and a half. Twelve jurors took their seats to hear the now nationally prominent case.

"We will prove that the one thing [the victims] all had in common was that the last person they ever saw on this earth was that man, Nathaniel White," D.A. Phillips told the jury. The confessions White gave would be the best evidence in the cases, the district attorney explained, since there were no eyewitnesses to the slayings.

As Phillips paced the courtroom, White, dressed in black suit, black shirt, and no tie, calmly sat next to his lawyer.

One by one, the prosecuting attorney marched witnesses to the stand, unveiling his case against White in chronological order. The woman who discovered Julianna Frank's body told the jury she wasn't sure at first if the corpse was real. She said that Frank's torso had been cut down the center. Another witness said the victim's body was so mutilated, the only way she could be identified was from a homemade tattoo on her arm.

On the second day, a Middletown police officer recalled that Laurette Huggins's apartment was littered with debris when police discovered her body. Broken furniture and clothing were scattered around the body, along with blood and strands of hair. A bloody fingerprint found on a coat hanger incriminated White, the officer said.

As the trial progressed, the prosecution detailed White's involvement in each slaying.

But everyone in the courtroom was in for a shock the day White took the stand in his own defense.

"On or about the twenty-ninth day of June 1992, with intent to kill, did you cause the death of Christine Klebbe?" Brady asked his client.

"I did not," the defendant replied.

Gasps from the victims' relatives could be heard throughout the courtroom. The judge and jury were silent. White, looking directly at the jurors, repeated his denial five more times, saying he did not kill Frank, Huggins, Hunter, Hopkins, or Whiteside, either.

White told the jury that he confessed to the slayings because the police threatened to charge his live-in girlfriend with a homicide on the basis of her fingerprint being found in one victim's apartment. The confession, spawned out of love, was made only to keep her from going to prison, White said.

White claimed that investigators withheld food and bathroom facilities from him for hours. Without the aid of an attorney, he said, detectives handcuffed him to a chair in a cold, air-conditioned room. At one point, White noted, he shivered after police ordered him to strip so detectives could check his clothing.

White even offered the jury an explanation of why his fingerprints had been found in Huggins's apartment.

In a low monotone, White said he went inside her apartment

after seeing a strange man running away. Inside, he found her lifeless, bloody body.

"I panicked," White said. "I was on parole."

Outside the courtroom, the district attorney offered his theory on White's testimony.

"What's perjury when you're facing six counts of murder?" Phillips asked rhetorically.

The prosecutor expressed confidence in the two signed confessions to police, White's videotaped confession to reporters, and his bloody fingerprint.

The trial ended on Tuesday, April 13, when the jury reached their verdict. Deliberating for nine hours over two days, the jury found White guilty of six counts of second-degree murder.

The convicted murderer stood beside his attorney, showing no emotion, as the verdict on each count was read. The sixfold verdict meant White faced a maximum sentence of 150 years to life in prison. Ten deputy sheriffs stood in the courtroom as the verdict was read to ensure White's safety.

With the trial over, seven officers rushed White from the courtroom. One officer, armed with a videocamera, followed White and the circle of officers in the event of a scuffle. Officials didn't want the convicted killer to file a police-brutality charge.

Outside, the victims' family members lit six candles, one for each victim. A family member said the candles were a symbol for White "to burn in Hell." Nearby, deputies ushered White to a police car for his trip back to the Orange County Jail.

But just when everyone thought White had had his day in court, the convicted killer threw another curve at the legal system.

About three weeks before his sentencing, White agreed to appear on *The Maury Povich Show*. A glutton for publicity, the convicted killer—via satellite from the Orange County Jail—planned to discuss his conviction with the show's host and a few relatives of his victims.

On Wednesday, May 12, White donned a microphone and sat in front of an Orange County Sheriff's Office banner, while a television crew taped the show. In a Manhattan studio, relatives of three victims confronted White for the first time since his trial. The trio answered questions from Povich and the audience about their emotional ordeal, addressing White on occasion.

"You should be killed!" a sister of one victim shouted. "You are the lowest of the lowlifes I have ever known!"

Although the killer didn't have a monitor to see Povich, or his guests, it didn't stop him from agitating the panel. Shackled, and in prison garb, White ridiculed the relatives. He claimed they were appearing on the program to cash in on possible movie deals. When he wasn't talking, White either sneered or stared into the camera.

White, showing no signs of remorse, insisted police had coerced him into signing the confessions and then appearing on television with the reporter to detail crimes he never committed. His insistence of innocence evidently did nothing to sway Povich or his audience.

After the taping, White said he was disappointed because he didn't have an opportunity to address legal issues he wanted to publicize.

The following day, Orange County sheriff James Garvey disclosed that extra security was planned for White's sentencing. The sheriff said additional deputies would monitor security at the courtroom, along with implementing other security measures. Garvey stressed that no threats had recently been made against White's life. The frustration White displayed during the past few days, the sheriff reasoned, seemed to stem from his sudden realization that he'd probably be spending the rest of his natural life in prison.

"It's not one thing in particular," the sheriff noted, "but he's been kind of—appearing to be a little frisky, tense, and uptight lately."

The sheriff reminded reporters that White never gave deputies any trouble when being transported from the jail or courthouse, or during his several media appearances for that matter.

On Wednesday, May 27, eight Orange County deputies led

a handcuffed Nathaniel White into a Goshen courtroom. With the officers standing directly behind him, White sported a smirk on his boyish face as he sat next to his attorney. After a few minutes, the six-time convicted killer covered the grin with his hand. But the smile quickly faded as pain-filled family members of his six victims addressed the court one at a time.

"I wish I could do to you what you did to my sister and the others," one family member said.

Through it all, White listened virtually without emotion. After the verbal barrage by his victims' family members, it was White's turn to speak on his own behalf.

"I did not kill those people," he said. "Every right that the law said that I had was violated. The only right that was upheld was my right to a trial by jury."

When White remarked, "A poor black man has no legal rights," the spectator gallery, filled mostly with black people, erupted in hisses.

However, Judge Berry had the last word.

The judge imposed six consecutive life sentences on White—150 years minimum time to be served before being eligible for parole.

"I'm not sentencing you out of anger," Berry said. "Our society deserves to be free of a brutal killer."

In his order, the judge methodically mentioned each victim's name. But when he got to Christine Klebbe's name, the 14-year-old Goshen girl, the judge paused, swallowed, and then stared at White.

"Why the little kid?" he asked.

The question brought a deafening silence and searing chill over the courtroom.

"Is that a question?" White responded.

"You don't need to answer me," Berry replied, regaining his composure. "It's a rhetorical question."

Moments later, Nathaniel White left the courtroom without his freedom—or his smirk.

"THEY ROBBED, RAPED, AND SHOT PRETTY LOIS UNDER 'SUICIDE BRIDGE'!"

by Don Lasseter

Martial drumbeats. Piercing whistles. Thunderous cheering. These are the sounds you might hear if you could listen to the imagination of visitors who pause near the famous Rose Bowl stadium in Pasadena, California. Each New Year's Day, the "Granddaddy" of all college football bowl games is played there, and seven Super Bowls, including the 1993 edition, have been slugged out on the immortal gridiron. The thrill of the game has attracted millions to the class stadium for most of the 20th century.

The scene of so many pitched athletic battles became the site of a more elemental struggle on a cool autumn night in 1988. On October 18, a real-life drama, infinitely more violent than any sporting event, unfolded within a stone's throw of the Rose Bowl.

On that day, Lois Haro, 26, was at her Pasadena home, a few miles from the stadium, and had started preparing dinner for her husband when she suddenly remembered an important chore she'd left unfinished. Her coworkers in the sales department of a local seismographic-instrument firm had planned a baby shower for a friend the next day, and Lois had postponed buying a present until the last minute.

Setting aside dinner, the attractive young woman with sparkling brown eyes scribbled a note to her husband: "I went to the store, probably JC Penney's. I'll be back at 8 P.M. Lois. 7:15 P.M."

Lois brushed back her shoulder-length dark hair, changed into a beige, flower-print jumpsuit and high-heel shoes, then headed out the door. The fashionable clothing Lois wore enhanced her trim, 120-pound figure and made her look taller than her 5 feet 2 inches.

After parking her 1983 Toyota Tercel in the subterranean garage of the Plaza Pasadena Mall, Lois Haro rode the escalator up to the array of stores. The enclosed shopping center was bordered on one side by Colorado Boulevard, the street millions of people worldwide know as the address of the Tournament of Roses Parade.

The mall presents the image of being a sanctuary from violent crime. Security guards patrol the promenade to assure the safety of shoppers. A closed-circuit television camera monitors the parking garage, and radio-equipped guards patrol among the cars.

Lois browsed through several of the major department stores, but she still hadn't found the right present. Shortly after 7:45 P.M., she walked out of JC Penney's, near the escalator to the parking garage.

One hour and 18 minutes later, at 9:03 P.M., Officer Michael Villalobos of the Pasadena Police Department was on routine patrol along Arroyo Drive near the Rose Bowl stadium when he and his partner spotted something on the median strip in the middle of the block between Holly Street and Arroyo Boulevard. They stopped immediately and leaped from their black-and-white car to investigate.

About eight feet from the curb, a dark-haired Caucasian woman, clad in a beige, flower-patterned jumpsuit, lay crumpled in the dirt on her side. Blood dripped slowly from her nose and ears and from a wound in her head, which appeared to the officers to have been made by a bullet.

Officer Villalobos kneeled quickly to see if the still form exhibited any signs of life. He was surprised when he put his ear next to the victim's mouth and heard faint gasps. Realizing that the victim was struggling to breathe, the officer told his partner to radio for medical help.

Within minutes, a paramedic's ambulance screeched to a halt next to the patrol unit, and an emergency medical technician wasted no time starting life-saving procedures. He saw the pool of blood soaking into the ground and knew that the woman would need replacement fluids. Checking her respiration, he noted that it was agonal (symptomatic of agony), which often indicates that death is near. Loosening the victim's clothing—normal procedure during emergency treatment—the paramedic was startled to notice that the victim was wearing no underwear.

Moments after the victim was loaded into the ambulance, her breathing stopped, and the paramedic began administration of cardiopulmonary resuscitation, including intubation, or the insertion of a tube into her throat to facilitate breathing.

The heroic efforts of the officers and the paramedics continued, but the woman's tenuous hold on life slowly ebbed away. She was pronounced dead shortly after arrival at nearby Huntington Memorial Hospital.

Because of the circumstances of the death, it became necessary for an officer to observe the examination of the body at the hospital, to preserve a trail of any potential evidence. Michael Villalobos performed that unpleasant duty. He jotted in his notebook a confirmation of what the paramedics had noticed, that no underclothing had been found on the deceased victim.

The bloody head wound noted by the patrol officers clearly demanded the involvement of the homicide team.

Detective Brian Schirka drew the duty as lead investigator. Schirka's 12th year with the Pasadena Police Department had been on the homicide squad, and in that 12 months, he had investigated 10 brutal murders. A native of Utah, the slim six-footer joined the Ogden Police Department after graduating from Weber State College, spent five years there, then migrated to California. Lawbreakers who had faced Schirka would never forget his penetrating blue eyes, which could enhance his friendly smile or turn ice cold when he questioned a murder suspect.

Called out from his home at 10 P.M., Schirka went directly to the hospital where the body had been taken. Other members of his investigative team met him there. One handed Schirka some jewelry that the victim had been wearing: a ring, a bracelet, and a pair of earrings. When the detective looked at the victim herself, he was appalled at the damage the bullet had inflicted to her head and face. He knew that it would be difficult to identify her from the facial features, and no purse or documents had been discovered at the crime scene to reveal who she was. At that point, she was just another Jane Doe.

Near midnight, a police assistant contacted Detective Schirka at the hospital. In Pasadena, a police assistant is a khaki-uniformed, unsworn officer who takes crime reports, issues parking citations, helps at crime scenes, and performs other collateral duties not requiring contact with suspects. The police assistant, who had heard about the terrible discovery of the unidentified victim, told Schirka that he had a frantic woman on hold who was calling to report a missing family member. The details, the assistant said, seemed to match what he had heard about the Jane Doe.

Thanks to the attentive police assistant, Schirka identified the body within three hours of the discovery. Relatives were able to confirm that the jewelry and clothing belonged to Lois Haro.

The absence of underwear on the victim and the bruises on her body prompted Detective Schirka to summon Heidi Wolbart, criminalist for the Los Angeles County Coroner's Office, to examine the body for evidence of rape. The technician used the standard sexual-assault kit to take samples of fluid from body cavities and from the jumpsuit the woman had worn. Later, when criminalist Elizabeth Kornblum microscopically examined glass slides containing smears of the fluid samples, she found spermatozoa present in the victim's vagina and traces of seminal fluid on the jumpsuit.

The most difficult duty for homicide investigators is to interview relatives who have been waiting in vain for their missing loved ones to return home safely. Detective Schirka went to the Haro home to perform that painful duty. The shattered family members struggled through their grief to give the officer some information about Lois. "She was a friend to everybody, a friend to the world," one said. She was outgoing and tried to make the best of everything. "She really loved people," they said.

Lois's family had moved to Pasadena about seven years earlier from the Philippine Islands, where her American-born parents were involved in missionary work and where Lois graduated from high school. Lois herself had been born in Thailand. Recently Lois had been working on a degree in anthropology at Cal State, Los Angeles.

"She was planning to make a pie for the [baby shower]," a relative sobbed, "but she never got to do it."

Detective Schirka read the note that Lois had left, and learned that she owned a blue 1983 Toyota Tercel. The car was missing, so it was reasonable to assume that she had driven it when she left to go to the mall. The investigator ordered an immediate search of the entire parking structure at the shopping center. The car, Schirka realized, was the only tangible lead they had to the savage killer, or killers, of the young woman.

Working through the night, officers scoured the basement

parking area and all of the adjoining streets. The car was not located. Detective Schirka arranged for a description of the automobile, with the license number, and a BOLO (short for "be on the lookout") to be issued at morning roll call for all Pasadena Police Department patrol officers.

On the following morning, October 19, Dr. Sarah Reddy, of the L.A. County Coroner's Office, performed the autopsy on Lois Haro while Detective Schirka observed. The cause of death, Reddy found, was a gunshot wound that had traversed from the top of the head to the base of the skull, where the lethal bullet was found. The absence of "stippling" around the entrance wound indicated that the shot had been fired from at least 18 inches away. The pathologist also found "numerous small bruises" on the victim's thighs, knees, and both legs, along with "small scratches" on her right hand and bruising on her left hand. There was little doubt in the minds of investigators that the woman had been raped before she was savagely executed.

Another contact with Lois Haro's family became necessary. It was the exceptionally difficult task of the detectives to ask a sensitive and personal question. Had Lois Haro had sexual intercourse within the last few days? They found out that she had not. No, she did not have any bruises on her body. Yes, she certainly was in the habit of always wearing underclothes. That information underlined the probability that she had, indeed, been raped.

Detective Schirka also learned that Lois Haro had been carrying several credit cards, including one from Wells Fargo Bank. Her family had taken the precaution, hours after she was missing, of canceling the cards.

Homicide investigators often ponder the whims of fortune that influence a murder investigation and the little twists of fate, or more often the results of hard work, that cause the job to have speedy results or to stretch into weeks, months, or years. Such a twist accelerated the investigation into Lois Haro's death.

At 8:15 A.M. on October 19, at the same time the pathologist prepared to conduct a postmortem on the victim's body, Lawrence Zimmerman was still thinking about the BOLO description of a 1983 Toyota Tercel he had heard at morning roll call. Zimmerman, another Pasadena police assistant, was driving a marked white vehicle one mile east of the Rose Bowl when he spotted a car going in the other direction that seemed to match the Toyota's description. Quickly making a U-turn, he followed the vehicle.

The Toyota turned right on Pepper Street, sped to the end of the block, and pulled into a parking lot behind some apartments. Zimmerman halted a half block back, exited the car, and casually strolled to a point behind a concrete block wall, where, by cautiously looking over the wall, he could catch a glimpse of the Toyota.

A young black man emerged from the car, walked to the rear, looked around, and began to fumble at the locked trunk with a ring of several keys. After a few unsuccessful attempts, the youth found the right key, opened the trunk, and rummaged around inside it.

Zimmerman did not want to be conspicuous, so he alternately watched the suspicious scene, then concealed himself behind the wall. Just after he had dropped behind the wall again, he heard the trunk lid slam down. Peering over once more, he saw the youth disappear into one of the apartments. The rear license plate on the car, which Zimmerman had seen earlier, was now missing.

Back in his patrol unit, Zimmerman called in to report his observations and then waited for the arrival of Detective Sergeant Monty Yancey and another investigator.

When the lawmen arrived, the trio knocked on the door of the apartment. A youth opened it. He precisely fit the description that Zimmerman had given the officers.

Following a brief introduction, Sergeant Yancey announced that they were conducting an investigation and asked the young man for identification. "I'm Ronald Jones," came the frosty reply. He told the men he was 19 years old.

"We have a few questions, Mr. Jones," Yancey said. "Will you step out to the car with us?"

Jones sullenly complied. Outside, he didn't resist or object when Sergeant Yancey indicated he wanted to "pat him down" to check for any weapons.

A lump in Jones's right front pants pocket prompted Yancey to ask what it was. "Nothing," Ronald Jones snapped.

"Would you mind showing me?" Yancey requested.

Jones pulled a set of keys out of the pocket. "These are my house keys and the keys to my Audi." The lump, however, hadn't completely disappeared. Yancey wanted to know what else Jones had in his pocket. The youth insisted that he didn't have anything else, but he eventually pulled more keys from his jeans. The last set of keys had a metal tag inscribed with the word, "Toyota."

At Sergeant Yancey's request, Police Assistant Zimmerman tried the keys on the blue Toyota in the parking lot. They fit perfectly. Lying on the backseat of the car was a license plate that matched the numbers Lois Haro's family had given to the police.

Sergeant Yancey placed Ronald Anthony Jones under arrest on suspicion of murder.

Ronald Jones refused consent to a search of his apartment, but it didn't take Yancey long to obtain warrants authorizing investigators to examine the car and the interior of Jones's apartment. Sergeant Yancey found a wallet containing credit cards and other items with Lois Haro's name on them in a trash can.

Another member of the homicide team, Detective Donald L. Gallon, watched as Ronald Anthony Jones was booked on the morning of October 19. Gallon had to hold back a laugh when he saw Jones twisting into some odd positions while removing his clothing. The teen's gyrations didn't work as he apparently intended them to. A small plastic wallet insert fell from his crotch. It contained more credit cards in the name of Lois Haro.

In the back pocket of Jones's bloodstained jeans, the detectives found an automatic-teller-machine receipt for a transaction involving a Wells Fargo bankcard.

At ten o'clock that morning, Detectives Schirka and Gallon began questioning the suspect, Ronald Jones. After being read his Miranda rights, Jones announced, "I'll talk to y'all, but I—when I . . . if I have to go to court. . . . I'll talk to y'all . . .," and his voice trailed off.

"Well, Ronald, I'll be honest with you," Gallon said. "We have done some preliminary checking and some work with evidence we have. And all indications suggest that we are able to place you not only in the car where the victim of this crime was, but at a certain point in time, we are able to place you at another location . . .

"We're not going to b.s. you: We have some evidence that suggests that you were involved in a very serious crime."

Gallon was a skilled interviewer, a master of the bluff and the use of words that sound very specific, but are really just vague suggestions carefully designed to lull a suspect into spilling his guts. That technique usually takes reiteration and time. Just as Gallon expected, Ronald Jones started by denying any involvement or participation in the crime. He'd been with a girlfriend, he said, and later at the home of a relative. Then, he asserted, he went to the park to meet a friend of his named George Trone. He didn't know how the credit cards belonging to Haro got in the trash can or in his jeans.

"Were you at the Plaza Pasadena Mall last night?" Gallon asked.

"Yeah, man," Jones admitted. "Me and George Trone went there a little after eight. We went to a couple of stores, saw some people we knew, then left about nine. I went over to my [relative's] house till nearly ten. Then I went home on my bicycle and went to bed." His story conveniently put him and

Trone still at the mall during the time that Lois Haro was found.

"Do you think cops are stupid?" Gallon snapped. "We have witnesses who saw you driving the victim's car."

Jones had a ready answer for that. He had received the car on that same morning, he said, from another friend of his, and had just taken it for a short drive. Then the police showed up and arrested him. Maybe he had picked up the credit cards inside the car.

"Look, Ronald," the detective said. "I've been conducting interviews like this for eighteen years, almost as long as you've been living. I've been looking at your eyes and I've been watching your motions and listening to you talk, and everything you've told me is a basic lie."

Now, the sleuth thought to himself, it was time to escalate the bluff. Keeping a straight face, Gallon explained to the young suspect, "We've got something that you may not have heard about. It's called a mass spectrometer. It's a scientific instrument we can use to place people at certain locations."

Detective Schirka turned away, struggling to keep from laughing out loud. Gallon paused to watch the effect on the suspect.

Squirming in his seat, looking confused, Jones began to deny that he ever had a gun. Gallon shook his head and countered, "I didn't say anything about a gun." The trap was starting to work.

The detective pursued the subject of guns. "Do you know what a gun-residue test is?" He explained to Jones that such a test would show whether someone had fired a gun in the last three days. "Just how do you explain the fact that the test [on you] would come back positive?" he demanded.

Jones lamely replied that he had fired a BB gun.

While Gallon and Schirka were interviewing Jones, Sergeant Yancey and his partner were following the trail of the friend Jones had named, George Marvin Trone. They located a woman who knew the young man quite well and told the officers that she had seen him at about 9:30 on the evening of the killing. Trone, who was 18, had shown her a watch and ring and told her that he had bought them "from a girl up the street."

"Do you know any of his friends?" the investigators asked. The woman readily gave them names of people who would be able to tell them about Trone. One acquaintance was particularly helpful.

"I've known George for years," the friend admitted. The two pals had talked on the morning of the 19th Trone had told him, "We killed somebody last night," and described how "they" had taken her from the mall and killed her at the Rose Bowl. "Anthony was with me," Trone had told his buddy.

The friend added more. "George handed me a gun, one that he had all the time. And he had two rings."

Detective Yancey suspected that the youth had more to say and prompted him to do so.

"Yeah, okay," the friend went on. "I saw George just a little while ago. He came and got the gun. Said he was going to get rid of it up in the mountains."

With the help of the informant, the detectives located Trone's girlfriend. They learned from her that Trone had brought two rings to her house the night of the Haro murder and had tried them on the girlfriend's fingers. The rings were too small, so she gave them back to Trone. She confided that Trone had seemed "kind of distracted" and "mean" that evening.

Meanwhile, in the interview room at police headquarters, Detective Gallon continued to work on gaining the confidence of Ronald Jones. "You're in a real complicated situation," he told the suspect, "and the only way you get out of situations like this is to be completely truthful. And you're looking at me now like, 'Why should I trust you?'. . . . What I'm saying to you is, we have evidence that's going to link you directly with this crime and that's why I want to give you the opportunity to help us."

Jones was perspiring and squirming, but he still insisted that he was innocent. "How can I be on my bike and in a car at the same time?" he asked.

Trying another tack, Gallon asked Jones about some rolled-up wet underwear found in his apartment. He pointed out that the crime lab could still do "blood work" on underwear, even if it had been washed. Jones claimed he knew nothing about the wet underwear.

"Have you had sex in the last two days?" Gallon wanted to know. "We can tell if you have."

"I guess y'all are capable of doing anything," Jones whined.

Without making any promises, Gallon cajoled, persuaded, talked, suggested, and pleaded with the suspect to come clean with the truth.

Finally, after a short rest period, Ronald Jones began to cave in. He gradually revealed how he and George Trone had seen the victim at the mall, followed her down the escalator, and forced her to let them in her car. He was driving, he said, when Trone pulled out a gun, which "surprised" Jones. On the 210 Freeway, he continued, Trone made him pull over to a side street, then forced the woman to get in the backseat and take her clothes off.

"I saw George had his pants pulled down and was pushing her head down. I couldn't actually see what they were doing, but I heard her choke. I told George to cut that out." Trone then ordered the woman to "lay down" and had sexual intercourse with her, Jones claimed.

After that, they drove to the Colorado Street Bridge, popularly known as "Suicide Bridge," near the Rose Bowl. There, Jones said, Trone had sex with the victim again. The victim was then allowed to get dressed, without her underwear, and get out of the car. She started to walk away.

According to Jones, Trone yelled, "Bitch, what are you doing?" The woman stopped. Trone stood outside, in the dirt alongside the car, and talked to her.

"I heard a shot," Jones muttered, "and saw her curled up on the ground. George came back and said, 'Cool man, let's go.' I asked him why he had killed her. He said, 'Why do I let her live when she could report both of us?' "

Complimented by the detectives for his "honesty," Ronald Jones finally admitted that he, too, had sex with the victim. He had "only touched her on the breast," he confessed. Detective Gallon adroitly coaxed some more, and slowly Jones admitted that he had sexually penetrated her, but "just a little bit." He denied that he had ever engaged in oral copulation.

A member of the investigative team was sent to Wells Fargo Bank with the ATM receipt recovered from Jones's pocket. The detective was disappointed to find out that it was not associated in any way with Lois Haro's account.

At 9:30 that same evening, Officer Alejandro Peinado went to Brenner Park, a few blocks east of the Rose Bowl, where he found and arrested George Marvin Trone.

Two hours later, having worked nonstop for 24 hours, Detectives Schirka and Gallon, the master interviewer, confronted George Trone in a police station cubicle. Just as Jones had done, Trone started with denials. Yes, he had been at the mall on the night of the killing. It wasn't with Jones, he claimed, but with another friend. They met Jones later, after the mall had closed, in a park, when he drove up in a Toyota. He'd "bought it from a woman for eight hundred dollars."

"Did you touch the car anywhere?" Gallon wanted to know. Yes, he had touched it in several places, he said.

"Do you know much about police work, I mean do you ever watch television, things like *Miami Vice?*"

Yes, he had.

"Do you know what a mass spectrometer is, or do you know anything about the scientific evidence that police can use?" Both detectives kept a straight face.

"I just know a little about it," Trone replied.

After laying some more groundwork, Gallon looked directly at the suspect. "We know that you were in the car with Ronald Jones and that you were with the lady."

Trone shot back, "Well, there wasn't no lady in the car when I was there, and the only female I was with was my girlfriend."

Gradually, though, just as they had with Ronald Jones, the detectives convinced George Trone to start admitting details. They told him that Jones had confessed, on tape, and named Trone as the shooter. That opened the floodgates, and Trone stated that it was Jones who had actually been the triggerman.

"Did he [Jones] shoot her?" Gallon asked.

"Yes," Trone answered.

The suspect pieced together his story, confessing that he and Jones had taken the victim down the escalator at the mall, and Jones had driven the car while he rode in the backseat. The plan was just to rob her. She gave them her money.

"How much money, do you remember?"

"It seems like twelve . . . eighteen dollars." The victim's life hadn't been worth much to these two. In addition, Trone said, they had found a Wells Fargo ATM card on the victim, and Jones had demanded that she given him the personal identification number necessary to use the card.

"She asked him to let her go," Trone mumbled, "and she said he could keep the car. Then he told her to get out of the car by a bridge. All I heard was the gunshot, and he just ran to the car and drove off."

Now, both men had blamed each other for the murder. And Trone, just as Jones had, denied complicity in the rape. "I didn't have sex with her, [Jones] did. He got in the backseat with her, and made her take off all her clothes. I just sat there and watched." Little by little, though, Trone admitted that he had "touched" the victim, then he acknowledged that he had sex with her, including oral copulation.

At last, Trone agreed to write a confession.

"Me and Ronald Jones was [sic] hanging out at the park, drinking and smoking pot," Trone's statement began. "He said, 'Let's go to the mall.' We were walking around the mall. Ronald never mentioned anything about robbing anybody. I didn't even know he had a gun with him.

"We seen [sic] this lady. . . . We started to go down the escalator with her [to] the parking lot. Ronald was ahead of me by about seven feet talking to the lady. He followed her to the car and they both got in and he told me to get in the backseat. I thought he knew her, so I got in.

"We drove off. That's when I heard him tell her to give him the money and when I seen [sic] the gun. He told her to give the money to me, so she handed it to me, and the rings and watch. I just stuck them in my pocket of my jacket.

"She was asking him to let her go and he could keep the [car]. That's when I cut in and told him to let her go. He act [sic] like he didn't hear me.

"We got off the freeway and went down to Brookside Park [which surrounds the Rose Bowl]. We stop, and I got out, and Ronald and she got out. He told her to get in the backseat, and he got in which her. He told her to take off her clothes. She did, and he pulled down his pants and had sex with her. He finished and told me to go back there and get me some. I thought about it . . . and went back there with her and had sex with her.

"She got dressed, and Ronald told her to get back in front, and we drove off. We went to this little field, and she got out and was walking in the field. He got out, and then I hear [sic] a shot."

Part of Trone's confession included information that some jewelry taken from the victim had been given to a mutual friend of the two suspects. Detective Schirka tracked down the man and learned that he had sold two rings to a local jeweler. At the jewelry store, the sleuth was able to recover both items, which were subsequently identified by Lois Haro's family as her wedding rings.

The rings were the ones Trone had tried to give his girl-friend, but they wouldn't fit her fingers. When Detective Schirka reinterviewed her, she divulged that Trone had, within the last few hours, called her from the jail and told her about the killing, saying that Ronald "pulled a gun and forced the lady to drive them around. Then, over at the Rose Bowl, Ronald ordered her out of the car, pulled a gun, and shot her in the head."

When Detective Schirka presented the evidence to the deputy district attorney Walt Lewis, of the Los Angeles County D.A.'s Office, Lewis was sure he could convict both Trone and Jones. But he was still curious about the Wells Fargo automatic-teller receipt found in Jones's back pocket. It had not matched Lois Haro's account number, so why did Jones have it? Schirka agreed to find out.

Tracing the owner of the account number, the detectives found out that the man had simply left the receipt at the Wells Fargo ATM after withdrawing some cash. The time of the transaction was printed on the form.

With a subpoena, Detective Schirka obtained a printout of all transactions related to Lois Haro's account after she disappeared. Even though the card had been canceled by the worried family, attempts to access the balance were still recorded. Sure enough, the computer record revealed no less than six attempts to access her funds, within minutes after the time listed on the receipt found in Jones's pocket. He had gone to the ATM, found the unrelated receipt, jammed it into his pocket, and started trying to use Lois Haro's card to steal the money in her account.

The evidence against both suspects was substantial. The murder weapon would have been a nice complement, but it was never found.

D.A. Walt Lewis prosecuted both defendants at separate trials. In May 1991, Jones testified in his own behalf. He told the jury that after the killing, he went home, fixed himself a hamburger, and laughed while watching *The Honeymooners* on television.

The jury found Ronald Anthony Jones guilty of first-degree murder, kidnapping, robbery, rape, and forced oral copulation. After a short penalty phase of the trial, they recommended that he be sentenced to death.

In December 1991, another jury found George Trone guilty of the same charges.

Superior Court Judge Charles C. Lee looked sternly at Ronald Jones on June 6, 1991, and ordered him to be taken to San Quentin Prison to be held pending execution. Eight months later, the same judge sentenced George Trone to serve the rest of his life in prison without the possibility of parole.

The California legislature passed a new law, effective at the beginning of 1993, to allow condemned inmates to choose between the gas chamber and lethal injection. Ronald Jones will have several years to ponder that choice.

On the grassy strip along Arroyo Drive, near the Rose Bowl, there is a circle of white stones, placed there by the family of Lois Haro to mark the spot where she was found, robbed of her possessions, her dignity, and her life. It is a small memorial, to express the hope that she will never be forgotten.

UPDATE:
Jones has appealed his death penalty conviction, putting his appointment with execution on hold while the legal machinations wearily play themselves out.

"DIXIE'S PERVERT GARROTED TWO GRANDMAS!"

by John Griggs

The church lady walked into Hell at about 6 P.M. on Wednesday, April 5, 1989, in Greensboro, North Carolina.

She was worried about fellow church member Cara Lee Cross Bennett, a usually punctual woman of 86, who hadn't made her date to baby-sit kids during choir practice.

Bennett lived on West Friendly Avenue in an apartment near the First Baptist Church. Bennett's friend tried to reach her on the phone but couldn't get an answer. The friend left the church and entered Bennett's two-story, red-brick apartment building.

After knocking repeatedly, the friend tried Bennett's door and found it open. There, on the living-room floor, lay the body of Cara Bennett, her red-white-and-blue dress partially pulled off and her wrists bound to her knees with her stockings. A full cup of coffee, now cold, sat on a nearby table.

The friend felt the body, but couldn't find a pulse. The shocked friend stood there for a few seconds, trying to decide what to do. Finally, she walked back to the church to collect herself. From the church, the woman called the Greensboro Police Department.

Dispatchers got the call at 6:07 P.M. and sent an officer to the scene, telling him that he had a "possible homicide" on his hands. The dispatcher also sent emergency workers.

Upon arriving at the scene, emergency workers pronounced Cara Bennett dead. The officer who had been dispatched radioed for help. He knew this was going to be a tough case.

Supervisors and additional officers quickly arrived. They cordoned off the crime scene, began dusting for prints, bagging and tagging evidence, and shooting videotape and photographs. Other officers began a door-to-door canvass in search of clues.

At an apartment just upstairs from the crime scene, an officer found a door slightly ajar. Pushing the door open, he found a nightmare—yet another elderly woman's body. She was lying on her back, partially clothed. Stab wounds bloodied her chest and stomach, and a clear plastic raincoat was wrapped around her throat.

Neighbors who were huddled outside the door quickly identified the woman as the resident of the apartment, 86-year-old Mary Adelle Alexander Strickland. Emergency workers pronounced her dead, as well. Detectives would soon learn that the victims were longtime friends.

Greensboro police had one sordid mess on their hands. One law-enforcement official would later say he hadn't seen a more horrendous crime in the city's past 30 years.

By now, K.W. "Ken" Brady, a veteran Greensboro homicide sleuth, was at the crime scene. Strickland's wounds were the most severe. Brady studied those injuries. The killer had apparently made a long incision on the victim's chest. Her left nipple had been cut off, and she'd apparently been stabbed in the stomach and vagina, as well.

The apparent weapon, a broken-bladed knife, had been left nearby. Tests would later confirm that it had in fact been used to stab Strickland, and forensic scientists would speculate that the blade had broken during the stabbing. The knife had apparently belonged to Strickland, the sleuths would later find out.

Obviously, Detective Brady had strong reason to believe that Strickland had been raped. The autopsy would later show that Strickland had died from a combination of choking and stabbing, and had in fact been sexually assaulted. She was alive when she was stabbed, the pathologists would later say, but it was unclear whether she was conscious. They estimated that she probably lost consciousness within 15 to 30 seconds after the choking began, and died within minutes. But the pathologists would be unable to say whether Bennett was alive when she was raped.

Sleuths were almost sure that the murders were the work of one perverted killer, given the proximity of the crimes in time and space, the similarities in the killer's M.O., and the similarities between the victims. God help them, more than one detective thought, if they were dealing with *two* separate killers this sick.

Officers noted from the condition of the victims' apartments that some items may have been taken: jewelry boxes appeared rifled, and drawers were left open. Strickland had apparently just returned from shopping; a bag of groceries was spilled in her apartment.

From neighbors, sleuths soon learned that Strickland had in fact been shopping, and Bennett had returned from baby-sitting at church earlier that day. The women had last been seen about 12:30 that afternoon. Judging from the relatively low temperatures of the bodies, they must have been killed soon after they were last seen.

Officers found that telephone lines in the apartment building's basement had been cut, apparently by the killer. Building residents said their phones had gone out about lunchtime. Officers gathered samples of the snipped wires.

Neither victim's apartment showed signs of forced entry. The killer had either talked his way in, or had known his victims. Detectives quickly learned that the victims had much in common: they were the same age, they were both grandmothers and widows, and they were both longtime members and volunteers at First Baptist Church.

In fact, Strickland was the church's oldest member, having joined in 1914. Strickland, the quieter of the two, was a native of the Tarheel mountains and had earned a college degree in piano.

Bennett, more outgoing, was a well-known sight around her neighborhood, tooling around in the 1955 Pontiac she'd bought new. She was a native of Lexington, a nearby small town, and had retired years earlier from a woman's clothing factory.

The women were of a simpler, more peaceful age.

The Madison Apartments where the women lived is in a middle-class area of Greensboro, a progressive, cosmopolitan city of about 160,000 in the state's Piedmont area. The city is a manufacturing hub, as well as headquarters for several national businesses.

By 1989, Greensboro police, like officers across the nation, were already battle-weary from fighting a frustrating war with the drugs that had drastically increased their city's violent crime and murder rate. Cleaning up bloody turf disputes was one thing, but the brutal slayings of two kindly ladies in an apparently unprovoked attack was enough to outrage even the most cynical officer.

The door-to-door canvass was producing little of value. No one had heard or seen anything suspicious. If there were any pieces of the puzzle to be found in the physical evidence, that would come later, after forensic scientists had a chance to work their magic.

As the minutes ticked away that Wednesday night, the sleuths knew that a strong bet lay in finding someone who had the victims' stolen property. Lawmen got relatives and friends of each victim to help them compose a tentative list of things that might be missing. And they alerted their fellow officers in other departments to be on the lookout for those items: some jewelry from both victims, an AM radio of Strickland's, and groceries that may have been taken from Strickland's apartment.

Soon after the lookout was issued, some officers contacted the sleuths with some interesting information. At about 3:30 that very afternoon, they recovered an AM radio, some jewelry, and groceries fitting the descriptions all in the possession of a man they caught breaking into the rear window of a house on Cedar Street. And it turned out, the house was less than a block away from the crime scene!

At the time of his arrest, the officers had taken a handgun, knife, cable-cutting pliers, mace, and gloves from the man.

The best thing about this development was that the burglary suspect, 39-year-old Horace Benjamin "Ben" Beach Jr., was now in the Greensboro jail. Of course, Beach had been arrested about two-and-a-half hours before the victims' bodies were discovered, so police hadn't mentioned anything about the killings to him.

Detectives got a hard copy of Beach's record. A long list of charges against him, including breaking into cars, theft, possession of stolen goods, and assault. What was more interesting was that Beach, a drifter, had spent several years in California prisons for sex crimes and assaults.

Jailers hadn't known about the California record when Beach, a lumbering, unemployed housepainter, had been arrested the previous month on charges of disorderly conduct and assaulting a child under 12. According to the incident report an officer filed in connection with that incident, Beach was at a Greensboro Kmart when he grabbed and kissed two girls, 9 and 10, and tried to follow one into a rest room.

Jailers couldn't have known about Beach's California record when he was arrested because he'd told them his name was Benjamin Howard Taylor. Under that name, he'd spent most of the previous March in the Greensboro jail awaiting trial on the Kmart charges. Jailers had released him the previous Friday on a $1,500 bond. Now, he was back in jail on the burglary charge from that afternoon.

Brady and Detective L.H. Scott had Beach brought from the jail to Greensboro Police Department headquarters. At 8:55 P.M., they went in to talk with him. They told him they were just interested in the Cedar Street burglary where he had been caught breaking into the house, and they told him that the items officers had found on him connected him to thefts from two elderly ladies. Wisely, the sleuths didn't mention anything about murder; they said they just wanted to crack the burglaries and thefts.

They asked Beach where he lived. He said he'd lived on Greensboro's Cranbrook Street until he'd been evicted recently.

Where had he put all his belongings? the sleuths asked the burly, blond man. Beach replied that he'd left some items at Cranbrook Street and had stored others at a local self-storage business. Beach gave the investigators permission to search those places. He rode with them as they headed toward the addresses with warrant in hand.

At the small one-story frame house Beach had rented on Cranbrook Street, Detective Brady and others found a box of condoms, a homemade wooden dildo with a condom taped to it, the pornographic magazines *Unite, Mama-to-be,* and *Missy,* 12 survivalist magazines, and several mystery paperbacks. At the Wendover Avenue self-storage unit, sleuths found 27 condoms and more magazines: *New Combat, Guns & Ammo,* and *Soldier of Fortune.*

While the search had produced little hard evidence, it had yielded intriguing material that offered clues to Horace Beach's character.

Back at headquarters, the detectives asked Beach how he'd come to possess those items belonging to the victims.

He denied taking them but didn't say how else he'd gotten them. Officers had found jewelry worth $1,500 on Beach that had been taken from both victims. Strickland had been robbed of some groceries she'd just brought home, and officers had found on Beach cans of soda that may well have come from those groceries.

Detectives Brady and Scott bore down on Beach, telling him about the two murders and trying to get him to implicate himself. Beach said he was not guilty of the slayings.

Meanwhile, outside the interview room, other officers were putting their heads together on the case. One officer came forward to say he'd cited Beach for littering near the murder scene at about 12:30 that afternoon. That would have been about the time the victims got home. And, judging from the coolness of their bodies, they had probably been killed right around that time, as well. So the officer could place Horace Beach very near the murder scene about the time the crimes occurred.

But in the interview room, as Wednesday night surrendered to early Thursday, Beach wasn't talking. Outside the room, Detective Brady's coworkers brought him up to speed, telling him about the officer who could place Beach near the crime scene and about Beach's having been arrested for a break-in less than a block from the double murder.

Brady would later send the knife found on Beach off for analysis, although he doubted it was the murder weapon. The cable cutters found on Beach could possibly have been used to cut the phone wire that the killer strangled Cara Bennett with. Mary Strickland had apparently been choked with her coat. While officers had found cut wire in the basement, they hadn't found any in the apartment. If Beach had choked Bennett with the wire, he could have carried the wire out with him and later disposed of it. If he had, however, he sure wasn't saying.

The wire question would bear further inquiry.

For now, Brady felt he had enough to charge Beach. He swore out warrants charging Beach with first-degree rape (of Bennett), first-degree sex offense (against Strickland), first-degree kidnapping (he'd apparently forcibly dragged Strickland into her apartment), two counts of larceny, two counts of possession of stolen goods, and two counts of first-degree murder. With a warrant, Brady had blood, saliva, and hair samples taken from Beach. He also obtained the clothes the suspect had been wearing at the time of his arrest for testing.

Beach, now dressed in a county-issue orange jumpsuit, was placed in the Greensboro jail without bond.

Before lunch on Thursday, Lieutenant Jim Hightower was telling the press about Beach's arrest.

"He's not exactly Mr. Clean," Hightower said, speaking of Horace Beach's long record.

Detective Brady didn't stop working just because Beach was in jail. He couldn't afford to. At best, it was only a strong circumstantial case. Brady sent samples of the cut phone wire found in the basement to FBI forensic scientists, who would compare it with the cutters found on Beach. The scientists would find those cutters had in fact been used to snip the wire. While the sleuths hadn't found the wire used to strangle the victims, the FBI test was at least strong evidence that Beach had cut the phone lines.

The physical evidence just kept looking better and better. Best of all, DNA tests showed that the genetic profile of Beach's blood matched semen found on Cara Bennett's body. The odds that the semen came from someone other than Horace Beach were one in 1.7 million, FBI forensic scientists said. It was pretty strong evidence, although DNA testing, controversial enough as evidence now, was still in its infancy in 1989. But forensic scientists had more conventional evidence to buttress the DNA tests. They found that Beach's hair matched hair found at the scene, and fibers from his clothes matched fibers taken from the scene.

As expected, forensic scientists found no evidence to prove that the knife found on Beach at the time of his arrest had been used to stab Mary Strickland. But blood tests showed that the broken-bladed knife found near Strickland's body—and taken from her kitchen—had been used to stab her.

As best he could, Detective Brady reconstructed Beach's movements on the day of the killings.

Ironically enough, Beach had apparently shown up at the

home of one of Brady's fellow detectives hours before his 3:30
P.M. arrest and shortly before the murders.

The detective told Brady that a man answering Beach's description was yanking on his storm door when the detective
suddenly appeared and startled him. The man told the detective
that he was looking for someone whose house he'd painted,
then he left. The detective thought the man appeared suspicious, but he decided he didn't have enough to hold him on.

The detective came forward with the story after he saw
Beach's photo plastered everywhere after his arrest and realized who the man at his door had been.

Horace Beach had led a charmed life up until the time of
his arrest: his release from jail half a week before the murders,
his citation for mere littering around the time of the slayings,
his uneventful brush with a detective hours before the slayings.
Now, his luck had run out.

Prosecutors had vowed to seek the death penalty against
Beach, and Brady was making sure every "i" was dotted and
every "t" crossed.

Through witness interviews, investigators speculated that
Beach had killed Bennett first, then Strickland.

Apparently, Beach had met Bennett when he unclogged her
drain a few weeks before the killing, investigators learned.

After the killings and before his arrests, the sleuths also
learned, Beach had called a counselor who was helping him
with his drinking problem to say he'd be running late.

Investigators learned other facts about their suspect.

Beach was a California native who'd moved to Greensboro
at an early age but later moved back to California. A 12th-
grade dropout, he had been divorced for years. He came back
to Greensboro in 1982. His Cranbrook Street neighbors described him as a quiet man with a fondness for cheap wine.
He got around on a bike. Two or three times a day, he'd pedal
out for a can of soup or a pint of wine.

He'd had problems with booze and sexual deviance since he

was a teen and suffered from various other mental problems, as well.

One of Beach's defense lawyers would later say, "He was a ticking time bomb waiting to explode."

Beach would later say that he'd confused his two elderly victims with a relative of his that a voice in his head had told him to kill.

Horace Beach's trial began in late September 1991 in the modern Guilford County Courthouse in Greensboro. Beach, looking eccentric behind a long beard he'd grown since his arrest, had entered a plea of not guilty by reason of insanity. Doctors had him sedated for the trial.

Doctors had found Beach competent to stand trial, but what was at issue was his mental state at the time of the offense. By North Carolina law, a jury can find a person not guilty by reason of insanity if they find that the defendant had a mental disease or defect when he committed the crime and, as a result, was incapable of distinguishing between right and wrong.

The trial promised to be a classic confrontation between the county's two top lawyers. Public Defender Wally Harrelson, a gravelly-voiced legal scholar, would be defending Beach. District Attorney Jim Kimel, prematurely gray and pugnacious, would be representing the state of North Carolina on behalf of the two elderly victims.

Lawyer David Lloyd would be assisting Harrelson, while Assistant District Attorney Howard Neumann would play backup for Kimel.

In opening statements on Monday, September 23, Harrelson and Lloyd didn't deny that Beach had committed the murders. They told jurors that a life of rejection, emotional and sexual abuse, and alcoholism had fueled the mental illness that led Beach to snap on the day of the killings. School records and psychiatric reports traced Beach's mental disturbance from the first grade, Lloyd said.

One female relative constantly berated Beach for not being

a girl, Lloyd said, and told him she wanted to have sex with him when he grew up.

As D.A. Kimel began his case, he shocked the jurors by showing them 8-by-10-inch color shots of the victims and a videotape of the crime scene. Defense attorneys had objected to Kimel's move, saying the "excessive" graphic film and footage would unduly prejudice the jury, but Superior Court Judge Joseph John overruled when Kimel argued that they were proof of the crimes.

The next day, Tuesday, Kimel began to counter the defense's insanity strategy. He presented the testimony of the detective whose house Beach had visited on the day of the crime, and the officer who had cited Beach for littering that day. Both told the jury that Beach made them suspicious, but he seemed alert and coherent.

Another witness for the state testified that Beach had told her in 1988—almost a year before the slayings—that "anybody could plead temporary insanity . . . then get out and do whatever you want."

Forensic scientists, testifying for the state on Wednesday, told the jury about the DNA, hair, and fiber evidence that tied Beach to the crime scene. The witnesses held up well under battering cross-examination, and the prosecutors rested their case.

The defense attorneys began their battle on Thursday with the testimony of a clinical forensic psychologist. She told jurors that a voice in Beach's head told him to kill the two victims and that Beach thought his victims were relatives who would hurt someone else if he didn't stop them.

The doctor said she believed Beach was schizophrenic and legally insane on the day of the murders. The doctor said Beach would have been unable to understand the quality and nature of the acts he committed.

After the killing, the doctor testified, Beach remembered "thinking that when he cut [Strickland], he had to fix it so she couldn't have any more babies."

She said the defendant had grown up with poverty, rejection, and instability. She also testified that Beach had told her that men had sexually abused him when he was a boy. He confused the victims with an abusive relative, the doctor testified.

In a heated, often sarcastic, cross-examination, D.A. Kimel tried to discredit the doctor's testimony, suggesting that Beach's behavior after the murders seemed rational—not psychotic. For instance, the prosecutor said, Beach had lied to police about stealing the jewelry and groceries from his victims.

For a long time, the doctor testified, Beach said he couldn't remember details about the murders. But gradually, she said, he remembered seeing his hands around his victims' throats.

"He said he was responsible for something quite terrible," the psychologist said. "He said, 'I've hurt someone else's [relative]—not mine.' "

On Friday, a forensic psychiatrist testifying for the defense agreed with the first doctor—that Beach was legally insane and schizophrenic when he killed the victims. The doctor said Beach also suffered from other personality disorders and a variety of sexual perversions—including sadism, masochism, and necrophilia. He agreed with the first doctor—that Beach had acted from a voice in his head, believing the victims were his relatives.

The doctor, who had spent about 25 hours interviewing Beach, said Beach remembered nothing at first. But after some months, Beach began seeing flashes of the murders in his mind. And after a year, the doctor said, Beach began remembering them in detail.

The following Monday, a forensic psychiatrist testifying for the state said that Beach had been sane on the day of the murders. Based on the testimony of both the detective and the uniformed officer who had seen him on the day of the crimes, the doctor said there was no suggestion of psychosis.

Attorneys made their closing arguments to the nine-man, three-woman jury on Tuesday. Lloyd argued, "All of these acts were of a man possessed by the demon of psychosis."

Defense Attorney Harrelson, in his booming voice, maintained, "The facts of this case cry out and say this man was insane."

In his closing, D.A. Kimel countered, "This is not a crime of insanity; it is a crime of inhumanity."

After the jury had deliberated the case for about three hours on Wednesday, they sent a note to the judge saying they were deadlocked 11 to 1, although they did not indicate which way they were leaning. Judge John encouraged them to try harder.

Finally, the jurors came back with a verdict on Thursday, October 3: Horace Beach was found guilty of the two first-degree murder counts, as well as the rape, kidnapping, sex offense, larceny, and possession of stolen goods charges.

On Monday, October 7, attorneys argued for and against the death penalty.

Lloyd and Harrelson asked jurors to show mercy and spare their client's life because he was mentally ill. They hoped the jury would give their client life in prison.

But Assistant D.A. Neumann told jurors that Beach had already signed a death warrant by his actions.

"You should never feel, 'I put Ben Beach to death,' " Neumann said. "Ben Beach is responsible for what happens to him."

District Attorney Kimel told jurors that a death sentence was "the only way that you, the jury, can protect yourself and your children from this man. It's the only way to assure he won't do it again."

On Thursday, October 11, 1991, the jury came out hopelessly deadlocked after a day and a half of deliberation. Ten jurors thought the defendant should die; two thought he shouldn't.

By North Carolina law, the trial judge is required to impose life sentences in such situations. Before he set sentence, Judge John asked the defendant if he had anything to say.

In a soft, high voice, Beach said, "Well, Mr. Judge . . . the court has seen a lot of things that went on. I just wish people could see all the things that I see."

Judge John gave Beach two life sentences for the murder convictions and two more life sentences plus 70 years for the related convictions of rape, kidnapping, sexual assault, larceny, and burglary.

Given the length of Beach's sentence, prosecutors later dismissed the misdemeanor charges that had been lodged the month before the slayings.

After bailiffs led Beach out of the courtroom, and the judge recessed court, D.A. Kimel said, "We feel like the jury showed him more mercy than he deserved." But Kimel added that he was glad that jurors had rejected Beach's claims of insanity and found him guilty.

Defense Attorney Harrelson said he felt like the life sentence was "a great victory for the cause of the mentally ill in North Carolina."

"DEFILED/STRANGLED NUN IN THE CONVENT"

by Bruce M. Stockdale

On Friday, March 19, 1993, at 1:33 A.M., Sister Mary Ann Glinka's sleep was interrupted. The burglar alarm was sounding in the motherhouse of the Order of Franciscan Sisters, located on Ellerslie Avenue, just two blocks from Memorial Stadium, in Northeast Baltimore. As the chief administrator of the 42-nun convent, it was the responsibility of the diminutive, 51-year-old woman to monitor the sprawling complex's alarm system, which covered the motherhouse, an auxiliary building, and a school the nuns ran for exceptional children.

Donning a red robe to cover her white nightgown, Sister Mary Ann called the alarm company to report what she assumed was just another false alarm—a damaged door to the convent library had caused several earlier false alarms.

After advising the alarm company dispatcher to disregard the alarm, Sister Mary Ann made her way downstairs from her room on the second floor of the motherhouse to the main hallway, where the defective door opened to the convent grounds. Towering above the entrance was a large statue of St. Elizabeth, the order's patron saint.

Suddenly, Sister Mary Ann felt a presence behind her; but

before she could react, a powerful arm enveloped her throat. Too late came the horrifying realization—it was not a false alarm after all!

At 5:30 A.M., Sister Catherine was passing through the main hallway on her way to morning devotions. As she approached the statue of St. Elizabeth, her eye was caught by something that at first glance appeared to be a mannequin. Checking more closely, she recognized the hairline on the side of the face. "It's Sister Mary Ann!" she exclaimed.

Without disturbing the body, Sister Catherine went upstairs and dialed 911 for the Baltimore City Police Department (BCPD).

The first police officer to respond to the scene was Northern District officer Roger Epps. He immediately recognized the dead nun as a murder victim. Ligatures bound the body's neck, wrists, and legs.

Officer Epps reached for his handheld radio and put in a call for homicide unit assistance.

Responding to the 10-31 DOA call were the three homicide unit investigators working the graveyard shift that night: Detectives Daniel Boone, Ed Wilson, and Robert McAllister. They would be assisted with crime-scene search by criminalistics technician Michael Bailey.

The lawmen arrived on the scene at 6:05 A.M. and were pleased to find that the crime scene had been secured by Officer Epps and Northern District backup officers. Frecklefaced Detective Boone, who, at 35, was the most experienced sleuth on the squad, would serve as primary investigator on the case. He assigned his colleagues to the various tasks that would consume their energies at the crime scene as they tried to find out what had happened to Sister Mary Ann Glinka the previous night.

Detective Boone scrutinized the pitiful sight before him: the slain nun was lying facedown on the floor, her wrists tied behind her back. The ligature that bound her wrists together was attached to another around her neck. Thus, any movement of the wrists would have resulted in increased pressure on the neck. The victim's nightgown had been ripped down from the top, exposing her breasts, while the bottom had been pulled up. A rain hat and a change purse had been stuffed inside the victim's mouth.

While Detective Boone examined the body, Detectives Wilson and McAllister were searching the area for clues. Technician Bailey dusted the scene for fingerprints. Well versed in their line of work, the lawmen knew that a killer usually leaves something of himself at a crime scene—the trick lay in finding it. As a result, the lawmen were still hard at work at 8:25 A.M. when they were joined at the crime scene by Detective-Sergeant Roger Nolan, who would supervise the investigation.

As an ex-Marine and a 27-year-veteran cop, Nolan thought he had seen it all, but the particulars of the Glinka homicide shocked even this case-hardened lawman. It seemed to him that whoever had murdered Sister Mary Ann Glinka had not only committed a heinous crime against a person but a monstrous desecration of a holy place, as well. It appeared to the veteran detective, a Catholic himself, that this killer had deliberately displayed his contempt for the victim and what she represented by leaving her hog-tied body under the gaze of the statue of St. Elizabeth.

Sergeant Nolan's expectations for solving the brutal crime were considerably heightened by the news that possibly significant physical evidence had turned up in the crime-scene search. Criminalistics technician Bailey had lifted a latent fingerprint from an unopened box of candy that Detective Wilson had found in the building. The print would be processed through the BCPD's Printrak machine, a state-of-the-art fingerprint computer. This machine can take an unknown fingerprint and in just a short while, compare it with the thousands on file with the BCPD's identification section. This is a task that, if done manually, could consume the energies of a squad of detectives for days or even weeks.

Sergeant Nolan was also encouraged by the news that Detective McAllister, during his search of the convent's sewing room in the auxiliary building, had found a matchbook with what looked to be a telephone number written in it. As a former longtime burglary detective, Nolan knew that many burglars like to use cigarette lighters or matches as they search darkened premises looking for something to steal.

It was afternoon by the time Nolan authorized the release of the body to the Medical Examiner's Office. Meanwhile, downtown at the homicide unit office on the sixth floor of police headquarters, detectives on the day watch were taking written statements from witnesses.

They learned that Sister Mary Ann Glinka had joined the order while still in her early teens. After taking Holy Orders, she had served as a teaching nun in various upstate New York convent schools before returning to Baltimore 10 years before. Besides monitoring the alarm system, it was her responsibility to take care of the older nuns in the convent. The picture sleuths got of the victim was that of a devout woman—without an enemy in the world—who had done only good throughout her life.

Since Sergeant Nolan needed to know whether or not a sexual assault had occurred, he asked for and received priority handling of the victim's autopsy by the office of the state medical examiner.

By 8 P.M., that same evening, the homicide unit had an answer. Yes, Sister Mary Ann had been raped; however, it appeared that penetration had not taken place until after death—a fact that made prosecution for rape problematical.

At 8:49 P.M., Nolan was sifting through what was rapidly becoming a voluminous file on the Glinka homicide investigation when his musings were interrupted by a telephone call from an excited Mike Bailey. "We have a hit on the Printrak, Sarge!" he yelled excitedly. "We have a hit!"

"I'll be right down," replied Sergeant Nolan. "We've got a hit on the Printrak, Dan," said the elated sleuth to Detective Boone. The two detectives, not wanting to wait for the elevators, elected to use the stairwell to get down the two flights to the BCPD Identification Section on the fourth floor.

They were met at the Printrak machine by a beaming Mike Bailey, who handed them a printout containing its verdict on the fingerprint lifted at the crime scene: Melvin Lorenzo Jones, DOB 1/1/59, of East 32nd Street.

The two detectives immediately began to cull the records of the Identification Section for information on Melvin L. Jones.

Interestingly, the suspect had been no stranger to the convent, having worked for a painting contractor on the premises four years earlier. But this was not all. During that time, a theft had taken place at the convent, and Jones had been picked up for it on a felony theft warrant. Jones had also been wanted by North Carolina authorities for a 1986 escape from a minimum-security prison, where he was serving a sentence for a 1979 voluntary manslaughter conviction. So instead of prosecuting Jones for the theft, the Maryland authorities decided to take advantage of the opportunity to say "good riddance to bad rubbish" and let Jones be extradited to North Carolina to serve out the remainder of his sentence there.

When Jones was released in February 1993, on expiration of his sentence, he promptly returned to Baltimore, where he had family ties.

So, Jones had killed before, Sergeant Nolan thought. Furthermore, Jones apparently knew the layout of the convent—including, possibly, where the nuns' money and valuables were kept.

Convinced that they had identified the perpetrator of the heinous crime, Sergeant Nolan had Detective Boone draw up an application for a statement of charges. It was duly signed by a Baltimore district court commissioner at 10:35 P.M. that same evening. The commissioner's signature made Melvin L. Jones a wanted man.

A hastily organized dragnet was thrown out, with detectives from the day and evening shifts participating in the hunt. For some strange reason, Jones was making himself scarce in the northeast Baltimore neighborhood where he shared a row house with family members only 1.1 miles away from the convent. But where was he now? After searching in vain the whole evening of Friday, March 19, and Saturday, March 20, Sergeant Nolan enlisted the aid of the local television stations in his effort to catch his killer. As a result, the evening news programs broadcast wanted bulletins for Jones along with the phone number of the homicide unit.

By this time, Sergeant Nolan had been working on the Glinka homicide case for over 30 consecutive hours, pausing only for occasional brief catnaps. Finally late that night, the exhausted lawmen got the break they needed—an anonymous party had phoned in to say that the wanted man could be found in a house on the 1900 block of Pelham Place in East Baltimore.

Thus, at 1:05 on Sunday morning, March 21, 1993, Detective-Sergeant Nolan, assisted by Detective Fred Ceruti and a squad of uniformed officers from the Eastern District, entered the designated house on Pelham Place. They located Jones cowering beside a bed in a second-floor bedroom.

After advising Jones of his Miranda rights, Nolan undertook a search of the suspect. Interestingly, a pants pocket yielded a woman's wristwatch of unique design.

What was the suspect doing with a woman's watch? Nolan asked himself, making a mental note to find out an answer to this question as soon as possible.

Jones was taken to Eastern District, booked, and brought that morning before a magistrate, who ordered him held without bail. Jones proclaimed his innocence at the hearing and accused reporters of trying to sensationalize the case.

"They're trying to turn me into some sort of animal," he said. "I'm not an animal. I'm innocent of all charges."

Hearing this, Sergeant Nolan knew that a hard-fought jury trial was probably in the offing. Jones was not the type of killer to confess.

The case was referred to the Baltimore State's Attorney's

Office for prosecution. The chief of the Violent Crimes Unit, Prosecutor Tim Doory, decided to personally try the high-profile case.

A review of all the evidence convinced Doory that the state, indeed, had a strong case against the suspect. But a case of this nature called for a perfect prosecution—not just a good one. Jones could not be allowed to escape justice, the prosecutor thought.

Accordingly, the homicide unit continued to investigate and look for more evidence to buttress the state's case against Melvin Jones.

A relative of the slain nun told Detective Boone that he was sure that the watch retrieved from the suspect's pocket when he was arrested was the very same watch that he had given Sister Mary Ann for her 51st birthday.

This piece of information prompted Sergeant Nolan and Detective Wilson to drive to the funeral home on York Road in North Baltimore late Sunday evening on a grim errand. After explaining the purpose of their call to the funeral director, the two detectives were ushered into the room containing the casket of Sister Mary Ann, who was laid out in her nun's habit. Nolan took the watch and put it around the dead woman's wrist. It fit perfectly.

Baltimore defense attorney Phillip M. Sutley was appointed by the court to represent Jones. Sutley was to prove a worthy adversary to Prosecutor Doory and his assistant, Emmanuel Brown. Sutley served notice to the prosecutors that he intended to introduce an alibi defense for his client. The defense would argue that the defendant was at home suffering an asthma attack at the time the crime had been committed.

Upon learning this, Prosecutor Doory redoubled his efforts to construct an airtight case against the defendant.

The homicide unit responded by scrutinizing all available medical records on Melvin Jones. Strangely, no reference to any history of asthma could be found. Knowing this, Prosecutor Doory was confident that he could demolish the defendant's alibi defense when the time came to do so.

Finally, after months of pretrial maneuvering, the trial commenced in the case of *Maryland v. Jones,* Judge John Themelis presiding.

"Ladies and gentlemen, murder most foul brings us together," Prosecutor Doory told the jury in his opening statement. He then outlined the state's case against Jones.

For his part, Defense Attorney Sutley asked in rejoinder: "I know you're saying, what was he doing there?" He went on to say that the evidence brought out during the trial would explain why it looked as if his client had been there, even though such was not the case.

He argued that the matchbook was not Jones's but belonged to a female employee at the convent who knew Jones's girlfriend and had written down her telephone number. He also argued that Jones had obtained the wristwatch secondhand from someone else, and not directly from Sister Mary Ann.

Finally in an assertion that astonished Sergeant Nolan and his men with its absurdity when they heard it, the defense attorney suggested that the investigating police officers had confused the fingerprint taken from the candy box with an old print left by Jones when he had worked at the convent four years previously. It would be physically impossible for this to happen, the lawmen knew.

As ludicrous as the sleuths found these arguments to be, they still realized that justice could be delayed or even denied by the presence of just one juror who believed them. They noted, however, that Jones, apparently afraid that his guilt might show, did not take the stand to testify in his own behalf. They felt that the jury would probably take this decision as showing his guilty conscience—if he had a conscience.

They were right. On Monday, November 15, 1993, it took the jury only a short time to find the defendant guilty of first-degree murder, robbery, and attempted rape. The trial judge had thrown out the rape charge at the conclusion of the state's case because the evidence showed that penetration had not taken place until after the victim was dead.

Under Maryland law, a defendant convicted of first-degree murder where the state has asked for the death penalty can elect to have either the trial judge or jury decide his fate. In Melvin Jones's case, the jury would decide. They had three options to choose from: conventional life imprisonment with the possibility of parole; life imprisonment without the possibility of parole; or death.

In his argument for the death penalty, Prosecutor Doory explained to the jury that the murder was committed in the course of the attempted rape and robbery, special circumstances that justify the death penalty. The prosecutor pointed out, moreover, that none of the mitigating factors outlined in the death-penalty law applied to Jones.

On Jones's behalf, Defense Attorney Sutley told the jurors, "I personally think the death penalty is destructive to society; I don't think it accomplishes anything."

It proved harder for the jury to decide on the appropriate punishment for Jones than it did to decide on his guilt or innocence. After two days of deliberations, the jury came back with their decision: life imprisonment without the possibility of parole.

With this, court bailiffs led the convicted and sentenced killer away in chains to the Maryland Penitentiary in Baltimore, where he is now serving his sentence.

Interviewed by *Master Detective* after the trial, Sergeant Nolan expressed his belief that the hand of God had truly been on the homicide unit in the Sister Mary Ann Glinka homicide case and that this helped to explain how it had been solved so quickly.

"After all, a criminal can't rob, rape, and murder a nun in a convent under the gaze of the patron saint of her order without receiving divine retribution," Nolan said.

"STRANGLED BODY IN THE BATHTUB"

by Barry Benedict

Over the years, San Diego's Douglas Hotel has been the keeper of many secrets. Built in 1924, the hotel was home to the Creole Palace, a posh hot spot where, in the age of segregation, the races mingled freely. During the '30s and '40s it was the place to go. Count Basic and his band stayed there. So did Duke Ellington, the Mills Brothers, and Paul Robeson.

And who could forget Mabel the flamboyant madam? This aging dowager with her bedroom eyes and kindness to strangers knew them all. She had been a silent witness to some of the city's most intimate secrets.

One of those secrets was from the hotel's twilight years—the identity of the person who killed a young college student named Tammy Williams. It was one secret that a couple of San Diego detectives were determined to learn.

The killing was long since over when the manager of the aging hotel contacted San Diego police on October 9, 1984, to say that he wanted to report a murder.

Patrol officers arrived, followed by a detective team headed by Sergeant Ted Armijo, with Detective Paul Olson as the lead investigator.

In Room 314, they found the badly decomposed body of a young woman who was bound, gagged, and lying in the bathtub.

The hotel manager, a short heavyset man named Johnnie, had been at the front desk looking through the want ads when a woman called to ask him to check on Tammy Williams in Room 314. The caller said she hadn't heard from Tammy in several days and was worried that something might have happened to her.

Johnnie promised he would look into it right away. Putting down the want ads, he punched up Room 314 on the switchboard. When nothing happened, he went to the room.

Johnnie told police he pounded on the door but was answered only by silence from the room and a few angry stares from guests who poked their heads outside their rooms, alarmed at the commotion. He took the passkey he kept on a brass ring and opened the door. "I took one look at the place and knew something was out of whack," he said.

The room was turned upside down. Mail was piled under the letter slot in the entry door, furniture was pushed back, and clothing was tossed around. Perhaps worse was the odor— a distinctive smell that told Johnnie he had a very big problem on his hands.

Johnnie said he called out, but no one answered. He peeked in a bedroom, but it was empty. He looked in the second bedroom but there was no one there, either. Then he tried the bathroom.

Tammy Williams was in the bathtub, but she wasn't taking a bath. For one thing, she was fully dressed. And for another, she was all tied up.

"I felt like someone hit me with a fist," Johnnie told detectives. "I knew her personally. I hope you find who did this, and I bet you everyone else here does, too. Tammy was good people."

The fully clothed corpse sat in the tub with the feet pointed toward the drain, the head lolled backward haloed by the victim's thick black hair.

The victim's hands and legs were tied with strips of a bedsheet pulled from the queen-size bed in the master bedroom. A rag stuffed into the drain and a darkened bathtub ring indicated that the bound and gagged woman had been put in the tub while it was full of water.

It was a shocking sight, even to the detectives working the case, and particularly to Detective Olson.

Olson, it turned out, knew the victim. Before switching to homicide, Olson had been a vice cop, and the downtown was his beat. He recognized Tammy Williams as a regular at Cindy's Bar and a few other hangouts.

A strikingly pretty woman, Tammy was a rarity downtown in that she had the reputation of a person who didn't use drugs or alcohol. She just went to places because she liked to go out.

"She was a sweet kid," Detective Olson said, reflecting on his vice-cop days.

After investigators finished with their initial examination, crime-scene technicians stepped in. They snapped photos, took measurements, and dusted for fingerprints.

Investigators questioned hotel residents, checked the registry, and called the victim's next of kin. Tammy grew up north of San Diego, mostly in the seaside communities of Carlsbad and Oceanside. Although she was remembered as a happy child, Tammy had been plagued by periodic epileptic seizures that had developed from a bout with measles, which she'd had as a toddler. Later it was discovered that Tammy also suffered from diabetes and required insulin shots.

In 1984, after two bad marriages, Tammy had a serious automobile wreck that left her on crutches. That summer, in an effort to straighten out her life, Tammy moved to downtown San Diego.

Tammy lived a frugal life. She couldn't work because of her epileptic seizures, but survived on a monthly disability check.

Although she had been thrown a few bad curves in life, Tammy refused to feel sorry for herself. Outgoing, she volunteered at several downtown service organizations, worked with the disabled, and enrolled in courses at San Diego City College.

Friends recalled that Tammy wanted to get a degree and perhaps get work as a nurse, or if she couldn't because of her disease, then in social services.

Everybody liked her, Johnnie said.

Residents of at the Douglas Hotel were stunned when they learned that Tammy Williams was dead. Tammy knew just about everyone at the hotel and had made it known that her door was always open.

The autopsy was performed late on October 10. The preliminary indication was that the victim had died as a result of strangulation or suffocation and had been dead one to two weeks before her body was found. The pathologist also found ink stains, suggesting that Tammy might have been stabbed with a pen, and other wounds which indicated she might have been beaten and possibly tortured before she was killed.

Investigators had a good idea how the much-liked resident had died. But the motive for her brutal death was unclear. Tammy was fully clothed when submerged in the tub, which seemed to indicated that she had not been sexually assaulted. More likely, robbery had played a part in her death.

The suite Tammy had occupied—the largest in the hotel—had been ransacked. Doors were ripped from cabinets, pillows tossed on the floor, and the victim's mail had been torn open and dumped on the floor. Even a stuffed animal had been cut open and the stuffing pulled out.

Someone, detectives agreed, had been keen on finding something. But what?

Searching the apartment, investigators discovered a thick leather-bound diary, a stack of letters secured with rubber bands, and a few bills. The items, however, put police no closer to solving the killing in Room 314.

According to relatives, Tammy had been married twice, both

times ending in divorce. Her most recent husband was a sailor Tammy met at a social mixer at the U.S. Naval Training Center in Point Loma. Detectives found him in Denver, where he was living with his mother and trying to get his life straightened out.

"She's dead!" the sailor said in disbelief when told the bad news. "This is the first I've heard about it!"

Although they had shared a May-to-December marriage, he said he still had good feelings for his ex-wife. He had no idea who would want to murder Tammy. "She was such a good person," he said.

Although Tammy lived frugally, she was not down to her last cent. In addition to the disability check she drew each month, the pretty divorcee picked up odd jobs working for community centers and the nightspots she visited. When she died, she had a balance of over $800 in her checking account. She also had an automatic-teller-machine card, a novelty in those days. Detectives reviewed videotapes of deposits and withdrawals, hoping that they might produce a lead in the killing. The film, however, produced only the last recorded picture of the victim taken when she withdrew $20 in cash from her account. The videotape pictured Tammy wearing sunglasses standing before the ATM on Market Street just a few blocks from her hotel. The tape showed no one standing behind her, or anything that suggested foul play.

The ATM machine had revealed no secrets. However, in the month before she died, police learned that Tammy had boasted that she was going "to come into a lot of money."

But from where?

Police learned that Tammy had filed several lawsuits against the city, claiming she had injured herself while stepping from a city bus. The case, however, had not come to trial, and as far as police could determine, the city had not offered Tammy any out-of-court settlement.

With the few leads, Detective Olson hit the downtown streets. One man Tammy mentioned in her diaries was a tall, thin pool player whom Tammy had occasionally dated. The man hung out at the pool hall on 5th and Market, and that is where the detective found him one sunny afternoon playing a game of nine ball.

The detective learned that the man was a heroin user, and, according to a witness, he had fought with Tammy over needles she was legally allowed to carry for her insulin shots.

The man's fingerprints very nearly matched those found on mail in Tammy's house. "If he's got a brother, we're in," joked one fingerprint technician.

The man didn't have a brother—at least one he talked about or one who could be identified by a birth certificate. Nor was he the one who had tied up the disabled divorcee and plunged her beneath the waterline in the claw-footed bathtub. At the time Tammy had been killed, the man had been an inmate at the county jail, behind bars and blocks away from the hotel.

Over the next month, police chased down leads and questioned more witnesses, but the identity of Tammy Williams's killer remained a mystery. By the end of summer, the case was consigned to a dusty black three-ring binder in the back of a metal file cabinet on the second floor of police headquarters.

Homicide detectives don't like unsolved cases, and no one took it harder than Paul Olson. He made a copy of the case and kept it in his desk. Over the years, between other cases, he submitted fingerprints to be compared with those that were lifted from Tammy's room. Nothing worked.

Over the years, witnesses moved around, dropped out of sight, or simply died. Johnnie, the manager who found the body, died of liver failure. His assistant took over but he, too, died a few years later.

In 1985, the Douglas Hotel was demolished. The onetime hot spot fell to the wrecking ball, replaced with little fanfare by an apartment complex whose occupants had never heard of the Douglas Hotel or the murder in Room 314.

Detective Olson rotated out of homicide. After he cleared out his desk and walked upstairs, he took his copy of the Williams file with him. Periodically, when the mood came over him, or he simply had nothing to do, he would crack open the file, read through the reports that were so familiar he had almost memorized them, and try to picture what happened that day so long ago. Occasionally Olson would also get a call from Tammy's mother, who the detective had come to know well over the years, wondering if any progress had been made on the case. There was nothing to report; but after a call or Christmas card, he went back to the file.

The detective also kept the fingerprint detail busy by submitting written requests with the 36 fingerprints lifted from tammy's hotel room.

Since Tammy Williams's death, San Diego police had new weapons against crime: Cal ID, a computerized system that makes it possible for police to scan thousands of prints in a fraction of the time it once took by hand.

When a suspect came up that looked good, Detective Olson would make out a request slip and send it off to the fingerprint detail. Many of those print checks were done by John Torres, who wondered if Olson was ever going to quit on the case, which was now almost eight years old.

Then in 1992, it all came together when San Diego police got a call from the Crime Solvers Program in Salt Lake City, Utah. A tipster called in to say he had overheard two guys talking about killing a woman in San Diego in 1983. He thought the woman's name was Tammy.

A homicide detective who took the call went through the unsolved file directory but didn't find anything. The call was switched to Criminal Intelligence.

Paul Olson was working in the C.I. detail, when by coincidence, he got the Utah call. He nearly hit the ceiling when he heard the victim's name. The reason homicide didn't have any record of her was because she had been murdered in 1984, not 1983.

In cold storage for almost eight years, the Williams murder case was back on the front burner. The case was assigned to

Homicide Team 3, which was headed by Sergeant Jim Munsterman. Munsterman assigned Detective Mark Sanders as the lead investigator. Although Olson was in Criminal Intelligence and no longer in homicide, he worked with Sanders on the case because he knew as much about it as anyone.

They contacted the Crime Solvers in Salt Lake City and later questioned an Oregon man, who placed the tip.

The witness said he had been in San Diego several years earlier and was eating dinner at a downtown service center when he spotted two men talking to each other in sign language. By coincidence, the witness said he had learned sign language to speak to an old girlfriend who was partially deaf. He said he was about to join in on the men's conversation when the two started talking about a murder that had taken place a few years earlier.

The witness said the two talked about killing a woman named Tammy and ransacking her apartment. One of the men mentioned how they tied her up and stuck her head underwater.

The witness said he didn't know if the two men were just joking, or if they had really killed someone. He put it out of his mind and decided to come forward because "if they did kill someone, then they should be caught."

The two men were Harold Hagood, 36, and Scott Stonebreaker, 30, both of San Diego.

The names of the two men did not appear anywhere in the thick case file. But there was a connection. Tammy Williams had been a volunteer at the Deaf Community Services, the nonprofit agency that services the hearing-impaired in San Diego.

Both Hagood and Stonebreaker were deaf and communicated in sign language, and often used the community service center.

Both men had criminal histories: Hagood's dated back to a 1979 robbery conviction, and Stonebreaker served time for a 1990 felony conviction for indecent exposure, among other crimes. Together, they had been convicted in the bizarre attack on another San Diego woman six years after Williams's death.

In that attack, which occurred in August 1990, the two entered the home of a San Diego woman on the pretense of studying the Bible. Once inside, they refused to let the woman leave and took turns raping her. The woman eventually escaped and contacted police.

Hagood and Stonebreaker were picked up. Through a sign language interpreter, they told police they hadn't raped anyone and claimed the woman was not telling the truth.

The woman identified the men in a lineup but then changed her mind and said she did not want to press charges, and refused to testify in court. The rape charges were dropped in a plea bargain that had both men pleading guilty to charges of false imprisonment. Both were sentenced to 16 months in jail.

Over the years, the two were in and out of trouble. But they were never fingered for murder until the call from Utah's Crime Solvers.

Detectives went to work. Pulling old mug shots, sleuths got their first look at the two men suspected in one of the city's oldest unsolved cases. Hagood was black, 36 years old, with a narrow face and a full beard and mustache. Stonebreaker was white, 30 years old, with a square flat face and a bulldog jaw that could snap your leg off. Of the two, it was Hagood, however, who had the more serious criminal record and who was the purported leader.

Since leaving San Diego, Hagood had for the moment dropped out of sight. Stonebreaker, however, was on parole and living in Indio, California.

Detective Sanders contacted Stonebreaker's probation officer, explained what they were working on, and said that they wanted to question Stonebreaker on the Williams murder.

Sanders and Olson headed for the desert. Three hours later, they got their first look at Stonebreaker. In person, he looked even bigger and meaner than his mug shot.

Olson and Sanders sat across the desk from the hulking

ex-con. With them was a volunteer from Deaf Community Services who did the translation.

Told why he was being questioned, Stonebreaker scowled and bit down on his back teeth. "I don't know what you are talking about," he said in sign language.

But Stonebreaker did know what they were talking about. And eventually he let detectives in on the secret.

Turning back the clock, Stonebreaker said that in October 1984—he didn't remember the exact date—he and Hagood were in San Diego, living by their wits, when they decided to visit Tammy Williams's apartment. Williams was a friend, but Stonebreaker said this wasn't a social visit. Word was out on the street that Tammy had come into a lot of money as part of a settlement from a lawsuit she'd filed against the city.

Stonebreaker and Hagood decided to help themselves to Tammy's loot. Both men were broke and could have used the money. But another motive soon surfaced.

Stonebreaker said he had never killed anyone before and that he wanted to kill Tammy to see what it was like. Hagood, Stonebreaker said, agreed to show him the ropes. With that, they headed to the Douglas Hotel.

Tammy was home when they arrived. The pretty divorcee with a soft spot for the handicapped was happy to see them. As they chatted, Hagood got behind Williams and slipped a rope around her neck, according to Stonebreaker. Hagood then ordered him to bind Williams's hands and feet and gag her with a bedsheet.

"I did what I was told," Stonebreaker said meekly through the interpreter.

When Williams kicked and jerked in an effort to get free, Stonebreaker stabbed her with a ballpoint pen.

Hagood then strangled the struggling woman. Stonebreaker said he was ready to go. But Hagood was all wound up from the killing and celebrated the event by having sex with the dead body. They then carried the victim into the bathroom and dumped her trussed body into a tub filled with scalding hot water.

Before leaving, they searched the mail and ransacked the apartment looking for the money that Tammy had purportedly come into. They didn't find it, however, so they left, as broke as when they arrived.

After Stonebreaker's confession, detectives went after Harold Hagood. Since leaving San Diego, Hagood had completed probation and simply disappeared. No one seemed to know where he was or might be. Detectives issued an arrest warrant charging the 36-year-old deaf drifter with murder.

The next day, they got word from Los Angeles police that Hagood had been arrested for jaywalking. "You better get him soon," a jail deputy advised. "He walks today."

A few hours later, Hagood was released from the Los Angeles County Jail—and was rearrested, this time for murder.

Hagood and Stonebreaker were returned to San Diego where they were charged with the 1984 murder of Tammy Williams. Both pleaded not guilty at their arraignments.

On Easter Sunday, a friend went to visit Hagood at the Vista Jail after receiving a letter from Hagood. During the visit, Hagood told the visitor, who was also deaf, "We did it. We killed that girl."

He said he tied up Tammy's hands, and Stonebreaker put the gag in her mouth. Then Hagood put her in the bathtub where she died. "She was alive when I pushed her in," he said. "Then she wasn't."

He said he and Stonebreaker took money and clothing from Williams's apartment after killing her.

When the friend asked why they had killed a woman who had been nothing but nice to them, Hagood replied, "I can't tell you. It's private."

On September 27, Hagood pleaded guilty to first-degree murder and a prison term of 30 years to life. In return, the District Attorney's Office agreed to drop allegations that could have meant a sentence of life in prison without parole.

In pleading guilty, Hagood told the court through an interpreter that it was Stonebreaker who wanted to learn what it was like to kill someone, and that he agreed to go with him.

"Scott said he really didn't know how to kill anybody, so I taught him," Hagood said.

Stonebreaker was scheduled to go on trial on October 22, but he also accepted the same plea bargain as Hagood and pleaded guilty to first-degree murder.

Both men are currently serving their terms in the California prison system.

Appendix

"DIARIES OF A HOMICIDAL SOCIOPATH" *Front Page Detective*, June 1995

"RAPE AND MURDER ALL NIGHT LONG!" *Official Detective*, February 1994

"MOM AND TWO DAUGHTERS DEFILED—AND DUMPED AT SEA!" *Inside Detective*, May 1995

"CATCH THE PERVERT WHO PREYS ON JOGGERS!" *Official Detective*, April 1994

"THE HUNT FOR POLLY KLAAS'S BRAZEN KILLER!" *Inside Detective*, July 1994

"FIVE RAPED/MURDERED BY THREE-TIME SEX OFFENDER!" *Inside Detective*, July 1994

"CRYSTAL'S KILLER WAS HER PALLBEARER!" *Inside Detective*, November 1993

"KILLED EIGHT FOR HIS EIGHT YEARS IN JAIL!" *Master Detective*, December 1994

"RAPED GIRL OF 11 DIES . . . BUT HOW?" *Master Detective*, February 1995

"TEXAS'S SAVAGE FATHER-SON MURDERING SEX FIENDS!" *Front Page Detective*, January 1994

"THE KILLER DEFILED, BLUDGEONED, THEN CALLED 911!" *Inside Detective,* April 1993

"BOUND SEX SLAVE HAD HER THROAT SLIT!" *Master Detective,* April 1993

"THE OKLAHOMA SEX FIEND RAPED AND 'DOUBLE-KILLED' THE VIRGIN COED!" *Front Page Detective,* September 1995

"SILVER-HAIRED SEX-STRANGLER!" *Front Page Detective,* June 1993

"FREED TO RAPE AGAIN . . . THIS TIME HE ADDS MURDER!" *Official Detective,* January 1995

"THE GOOD WIFE MURDER MYSTERY" *Official Detective,* January 1995

"NATIONWIDE APB: GET THE DEADLY DRIFTER WITH THE DIXIE DRAWL!" *Official Detective,* February 1995

" 'GOOD SAMARITAN' SEX KILLER" *Official Detective,* January 1994

"MURDER IN THE FOG" *Official Detective,* February 1994

" 'MODEL PAROLEE' LET LOOSE, RAPES/KILLS SIX!" *Official Detective,* October 1994

"THEY ROBBED, RAPED, AND SHOT LOIS UNDER 'SUICIDE BRIDGE'!" *Official Detective,* August 1993

"DIXIE'S PERVERT GARROTED TWO GRANDMAS!" *Official Detective,* August 1993

"DEFILED/STRANGLED NUN IN THE CONVENT" *Master Detective,* September 1994

"STRANGLED BODY IN THE BATHTUB" *Official Detective,* April 1994

Depraved murderers prowl the highways for their next . . .

ROAD KILL

Cross-country killers on a high-speed rampage, homicidal truckers, roadside hustlers turned psycho-sex criminals, lust-murderers protected by the anonymity of the open highway—these are just some of the nightmarish figures who turn our nation's roadways into horrendous crime scenes.

Now, *TRUE DETECTIVE'S* ace crime writers expose the chilling truth about the depraved killers who ply the roads. And they capture all the pity, fear, and horror of the innocent victims who took a nonstop ride straight to hell:

—BERNARDINE PARRISH & BOBBIE JEAN HARTWIG: these two pretty moms hitched a ride near a Grifton, North Carolina military base and were raped and slain by three mean marines!

—JESSICA GUZMAN: the 10-year-old schoolgirl unwittingly entered the cab of the taxi-driving "Beast of the Bronx" who'd committed five previous child-sex kills!

—TINA JO SUTTON: a teen hooker in Portland, Oregon, whose last roadside trick turned out to be her killer!

And over twenty more horrifying true stories!

ROAD KILL **with 16 pages of shocking photos!**
Coming from Pinnacle books in October, 2000

From the Files of
True Detective
Magazine